Physical, Sensory, and Health Disabilities

An Introduction

Frank G. Bowe

Hofstra University

Merrill

an imprint of Prentice Hall

Upper Saddle River, New Jersey • Columbus, Ohio

This one is for my mother.

Library of Congress Cataloging-in-Publication Data

Bowe, Frank.

    Physical, sensory, and health disabilities : an introduction /
Frank G. Bowe.

      p.   cm.

    Includes bibliographical references.

    ISBN 0-13-660903-1

    1. Handicapped—United States.   2. Handicapped—Government policy—
United States.   3. Handicapped—Services for—United States.
I. Title.

HV1553.B69   2000

362.4'048'0973—dc21

          99-28064

          CIP

Cover art: Billy Sweazy, Southeast School, Columbus,
   Ohio, Franklin County Board of Mental Retardation
   and Developmental Disabilities

Editor: Ann Castel Davis

Production Editor: Sheryl Glicker Langner

Design Coordinator: Diane C. Lorenzo

Text Designer: LightSource Images

Cover Designer: Curt Besser

Production Manager: Laura Messerly

Director of Marketing: Kevin Flanagan

Marketing Manager: Meghan McCauley

Marketing Coordinator: Krista Groshong

Production and Editing Coordination: Clarinda
   Publication Services

Photo Credits: pp. 2, 40, 168 by Barbara Schwartz/Merrill;
pp. 6, 29, 187, 303 Daniel W. Wong; pp. 22, 44, 46, 104, 294
by Tom Watson/Merrill; pp. 49, 136, 194, 306 by Anne
Vega/Merrill; p. 64, Todd Yarrington/Merrill; p. 74, Photo ©
Rifton Equipment. Used by permission; pp. 84, 264 by Scott
Cunningham/Merrill; p. 89, Courtesy of Sentient Systems, Inc.;
p. 98, Courtesy of newAbilities Systems, Inc. Palo Alto, CA; p.
106, Harold Yuker; p. 116, Max Starkloff; p. 128, Elysse Power;
p. 132, Reprinted/adapted with permission from *Infants and
Young Children*, "The Infant and Young Child with Spina Bifida:
Major Medical Concerns," Catherine Shaer, Vol. 7, No. 3,
p. 17. © 1997 Aspen Publishers; p. 139, Kerri McCarthy;
p. 151, Jim Barry; p. 159, President's Committee on Employment of People with Disabilities; p. 194, John Conti; p 255,
Eunice Fiorito; p. 270, Anthony Magnacca/Merrill; p. 280,
Courtesy of DeGeorge Home Alliance, Inc.

This book was set in Optima by The Clarinda Company
and was printed and bound by R. R. Donnelley & Sons
Company. The cover was printed by Phoenix Color
Corp.

©2000 by Prentice-Hall, Inc.
Pearson Education
Upper Saddle River, New Jersey 07458

Printed in the United States of America

10 9 8 7 6 5 4 3 2 1

ISBN: 0-13-660903-1

Prentice-Hall International (UK) Limited, *London*
Prentice-Hall of Australia Pty. Limited, *Sydney*
Prentice-Hall of Canada, Inc., *Toronto*
Prentice-Hall Hispanoamericana, S. A., *Mexico*
Prentice-Hall of India Private Limited, *New Delhi*
Prentice-Hall of Japan, Inc., *Tokyo*
Prentice-Hall (Singapore) Pte. Ltd., *Singapore*
Editora Prentice-Hall do Brasil, Ltda., *Rio de Janeiro*

Preface

The intent of this book is to equip current and future special-education and regular teachers, therapists, school and rehabilitation counselors, and other professionals and paraprofessionals with the knowledge they need to be effective in working with individuals who have physical disabilities or health impairments (e.g. Getch and Neuharth-Pritchett, 1999; Rosenthal-Malek and Greenspan, 1999). The text is appropriate for a one-semester undergraduate or graduate course on special education or rehabilitation. A theme of this book is that regular and special educators need to collaborate with one another and work hand in hand with therapists and counselors. Such teamwork is a hallmark of today's leading edge programs serving children, youth, and adults with physical disabilities or health impairments. Yet professional preparation programs, with few exceptions, have not taught these workers how to collaborate—nor how to respond to physical and health needs (Heller, Fredrick, Dykes, Best, and Cohen, 1999). One purpose of this text is to begin such training.

This book focuses upon children, youth, and adults who have physical disabilities or health impairments. It also discusses teaching, therapy, and counseling with individuals who have secondary conditions that often accompany physical or health disabilities, including hearing loss, vision loss, learning disabilities, and attention deficits.

The emphasis throughout is upon the people themselves—the children, youth, and adults—rather than upon their limitations. That is why the text opens with chapters on rights and services and why material on specific disabilities is deferred until Part Three. This structure reflects the ways I have taught teachers, therapists, and counselors at Hofstra University on New York's Long Island. I adopted this approach because I believe that professionals must first understand how adults with physical or health disabilities function in the real world so that they can appreciate what children, youth, and adults with these conditions need to learn.

I have been fortunate over the past 30 years to know and work with individuals who have many of the conditions discussed in this book. I have taught people with physical disabilities (such as spinal cord injury, traumatic brain injury, and cerebral palsy), sensory impairments, and learning disabilities. At private and public organizations that I have headed, professionals with spinal cord injuries, multiple sclerosis, cerebral palsy, and other disabilities reported to me. As their employer, I had to understand their needs and work with them to find appropriate accommodations. I have also advocated side by side for many years with thousands of people who are members of advocacy and self-help organizations throughout the country as well as in other nations.

This kind of day-to-day interaction with people as they confront and surmount barriers in order to make a living and live a life has been invaluable in helping me to understand the physical and health disabilities that are the subject matter of this book. As a professor preparing special educators and rehabilitation counselors, I have long struggled with the problem of how to help my graduate students to acquire at least some of the knowledge and skills that I have learned over the years so that they become both competent and sensitive in teaching people with physical or health conditions. These students are not likely to have had the opportunities I have enjoyed. How, then, can I convey to them the values and the priorities I have learned?

My students have found it very helpful to spend time with adults who have these kinds of disabilities so that they can appreciate what it takes for someone to succeed in work and in everyday life. That interaction may take the form of visiting people in their homes, joining them for recreational sports events, and serving with them in consumer organizations. My students tell me that these experiences convince them that what really matters is a person's strengths, creativity, and training, with which people can surmount the limitations that disabilities impose.

My students also find it helpful to walk a mile in their shoes by, for example, spending a weekend in a wheelchair to experience firsthand the architectural and other barriers people with physical disabilities confront and the condescending attitudes of many members of the general public. While short-term experiences such as a weekend in a wheelchair have some drawbacks, they also have some real advantages. Even after studying these matters in class, my students who spent a weekend in a wheelchair noticed community barriers they had never seen before, encountered negative attitudes much worse than they had expected, and discovered, months and even years later, that their experiences in a wheelchair were more memorable than virtually anything else in their graduate programs.

As supplements to these kinds of firsthand experiences, students tell me that they learn a lot by reading what adults with disabilities have written, including articles in such tabloids as *The Ragged Edge* (formerly, *The Disability Rag*), a periodical edited and written by adults with physical disabilities, and such books as *People With Disabilities Explain It All for You,* compiled by Mary Johnson and other *Rag* editors. They also appreciated Christopher Reeve's *Still Me,* a painfully honest memoir by the famous actor. I strongly recommend this book because it details the stark realities of life with a severe spinal cord injury and because my students respond very well to his story because they have all seen Reeve's movies and have a personal interest in his life story. In fact, I would not be surprised if more Americans became acquainted with disability by reading *Still Me* than through any other source. I also recommend John Hockenberry's *Moving Violations,* by the television correspondent; *Staring Back: The Disability Experience From the Inside Out,* a collection of stories by well-regarded writers who happen to have disabilities, edited by Kenny Fries; and *Nothing About Us Without Us: Disability Oppression and Empowerment* by James Charlton. All of these books are written by people who have disabilities (as do I). My students find the perspectives in these books to be enlightening. They can then turn to their tasks as educators, therapists, and counselors of children and youth, knowing what really matters to people with disabilities and what they themselves believe is possible.

Another way to help students to learn to think as I do is to put together a text like this one. That is why this book takes a "life span" approach. It is also why the book includes chapters on housing, transportation, and other areas of everyday life. These are topics about which teachers and counselors need to instruct students so that they can prepare to lead productive and independent lives. Because significant barriers remain in most American communities, they are also areas in which professionals need to work with consumers as advocates for community change.

The text adopts "people first" language. Thus, constructions such as "children who have cerebral palsy" and "professors who are deaf" appear throughout this book. Similarly, the term *disability* is used to refer to the conditions people with disabilities have, while the word *handicap* is reserved for those instances in which what is being discussed is the attitudinal, architectural, transportation, or other barriers that obstruct individuals with disabilities. To anticipate a theme of the book, when societal barriers are removed *and* when individuals with physical and health disabilities have been given the education and training they need, we have done our job: We have freed our students and clients to achieve to the limits of their abilities. That is all they could ask of us.

Readers should note that the emphasis in this text is upon educating, treating, and counseling individuals whose disabilities do not prevent participation in most mainstream academic or work environments. That is to say that with the necessary accommodations, technology, and training, the people about whom this book is written can take at least some academic courses and can perform paying jobs. Sadly, not all people with disabilities can do so; this is something we will take up in Part One.

There is a growing population of individuals who not only have the physical and health conditions described in this book but also have significant cognitive limitations, notably mental retardation. Typically, people who have significant intellectual limitations in addition to physical or health impairments pursue a curriculum in school that is very different from that of students who have less profound limitations. Similarly, adults with severe, multiple disabilities often spend their weekdays in day activity centers rather than in the mainstream jobs that are held by many people who have less profound disabilities. There are, of course, exceptions; some people who have very severe, multiple limitations nonetheless manage to take "regular" courses and to work in "regular" jobs.

If you work or are preparing to work with this population, *Physical, Sensory, and Health Disabilities: An Introduction* will offer you much needed information. However, you will need to supplement this text with at least one other that specializes in services for individuals with multiple or profound limitations. I recommend three such books: June Bigge (Ed.), *Teaching Individuals With Physical and Multiple Disabilities,* Merrill/Prentice Hall; Paul Wehman & John Kregel (Eds.), *Functional Curriculum for Elementary, Middle, and Secondary Students With Special Needs* (PRO-ED); and Jennifer Leigh Hill, *Meeting the Needs of Students with Special Physical and Health Care Needs* (Merrill/Prentice Hall).

Outline of the Text

This book opens, in Part One, with two chapters that set the stage for our examination of the needs of people with physical or health disabilities. Chapter 1 defines key terms and provides estimates about the size of the population of interest to us in this book. Chapter 2 describes a paradigm shift that is of central importance to all of us who work with this population. Briefly stated, our focus is changing from a narrow or "medical" orientation to an interactive one in which we recognize that we—as well as the children, youth, and adults we serve—need to work as much on the built environment as we do on education, therapy, and rehabilitation. That is because "handicaps" (following Bowe, 1978) arise from *combinations* of disabilities and environmental barriers. The chapter then outlines the major American laws dealing with disabilities and barriers.

Part Two focuses upon the delivery of services to children, youth, and adults with physical or health disabilities. It opens with an introductory chapter that identifies the roles of the key professionals who work with this population and explores the parts they play in education, therapy, and rehabilitation. Chapter 4 then examines intervention techniques, particularly teaching strategies. Chapter 5 describes the exciting new technologies that are opening so many doors for people with physical or health disabilities and offers a forward-looking view at emerging and future technologies.

Part Three provides factual information about the many disabilities of interest to us in this book. Chapters 6 and 7 explore neurologically based physical disabilities, that is, conditions in which the underlying causes have to do with the central or peripheral nervous systems. Some examples of these impairments are cerebral palsy, spinal cord injury, and multiple sclerosis. Chapter 8 looks at physical disabilities that are rooted in the skeleton and the bones, such as muscular dystrophy and amputation. Chapter 9 focuses upon health impairments such as acquired immune deficiency syndrome (AIDS) and cancer. Finally, chapter 10 explores secondary conditions (e.g., disabilities that are not physical or health related in nature), such as learning disabilities and sensory impairments.

Part Four provides material on barriers to a full and rewarding life that we still find in the built environment. Once again, an introductory chapter explains the fundamental concepts. Chapter 12 then looks at housing, chapter 13 at transportation, and chapter 14 at employment. The intent in Part Four is to equip teachers, therapists, and counselors with the knowledge they need to understand the everyday lives of people with physical or health disabilities and to work on removing barriers in the community.

The text concludes with a resources section offering contact information for key organizations, a glossary of important terms, references, and an index.

Acknowledgments

It was a genuine pleasure for me to work with an editor as knowledgeable about disability and special education as Ann Castel Davis, senior editor, and her team, Heather Doyle Fraser and Pat Grogg. I would like to thank the following reviewers for their invaluable feedback: Janis Chadsey-Rusch, University of Illinois; Ann L. Lee, Bloomsburg University of Pennsylvania; Peter R. Matthews, Lock Haven University; Charolette Myles-Nixon, University of Central Oklahoma; and Ann Riall, University of Wisconsin-Whitewater. I also wish to express my appreciation to Amy Rumelt, principal of Carman Road School, Massapequa Park, New York; Linda Levy, at the time the assistant principal, United Cerebral Palsy Association of Nassau County, Roosevelt, New York; Dr. Christine Pawelski, director of Smeal Learning Center, National Center for Disability Services, Albertson, New York; and Sandra Englesher, head of occupational and physical therapy, Board of Cooperative Educational Services in Nassau County, New York. These people graciously allowed me to visit their programs, talk with their staff members, and examine materials they use in their curricula. At Hofstra University, where I am special-education coordinator, my assistant, Mrs. Kathleen Pelligrini helped me find people, photographs, and documents. I also thank my then undergraduate student assistant, Joshua Liebman, who painstakingly checked the text references.

Frank Bowe
Hofstra University

Contents

Acronyms

ABA	applied behavior analysis	dB	decibel
ADA	Americans with Disabilities Act	DNR	do not resuscitate
ADAAG	Americans with Disabilities Act Accessibility Guidelines	DoJ	U.S. Department of Justice
ADD	attention deficit disorder	ECU	environmental control unit
ADHD	attention deficit hyperactivity disorder	EFA	Epilepsy Foundation of America
AFP	alpha-fetoprotein	EPA	Environmental Protection Agency
AIDS	Acquired Immune Deficiency Syndrome		
ALJ	administrative law judge	FAE	fetal alcohol effect
AOTA	American Occupational Therapy Association	FAS	fetal alcohol syndrome
		FDA	Food and Drug Administration
APTA	American Physical Therapy Association	FHAA	Fair Housing Amendments Act
ASHA	American Speech Language and Hearing Association		
		GPS	Global positioning system
ASL	American Sign Language		
ATBCB	Architectural and Transportation Barriers Compliance Board	HCFA	Health Care Financing Administration
		HHS	U.S. Department of Health and Human Services
BEA	better ear average	HIV	human immunodeficiency virus
		HUD	U.S. Department of Housing and Urban Development
CARF	Commission on Accreditation of Rehabilitation Facilities		
CDC	Centers for Disease Control and Prevention	ICU	intensive care unit (also: NICU—neonatal intensive care unit)
CEC	Council for Exceptional Children	IDEA	Individuals with Disabilities Education Act
CMV	congenital cytomegalovirus	IEP	Individualized Educational Program
CNS	central nervous system	IFSP	Individualized Family Services Plan
COBRA	Consolidated Omnibus Budget Resolution Act	IPE	Individualized Plan for Employment
CPS	child protection services		
CP	cerebral palsy		

JAWS	Job Access with Speech	PL	public law
JDF	Juvenile Diabetes Foundation	PVA	Paralyzed Veterans of America
LED	light-emitting diode (in computer screens)	RAM	random access memory (in computers)
LD	learning disability	RSA	Rehabilitation Services Administration
LPA	Little People of America	RSI	repetitive strain injury
MD	muscular dystrophy	SBAA	Spina Bifida Association of America
MR	mental retardation	SCI	spinal cord injury
MS	multiple sclerosis	SIPP	Survey of Income and Program Participation
NCI	National Cancer Institute	SSA	Social Security Administration
NESS	National Easter Seals Society	SSDI	Social Security Disability Insurance
NIH	National Institutes of Health	SSI	Supplementary Security Income
NINCDS	National Institute of Neurological Disorders and Stroke	TBI	traumatic brain injury
NMSS	National Multiple Sclerosis Society	TTK	tongue-touch keypad (newAbility Systems Inc.)
NOD	National Organization on Disability		
NTD	neural tube defect (e.g., spina bifida)	UCPA	United Cerebral Palsy Associations
OASDI	Old Age and Survivors Disability Insurance	WWW	world wide web
P&A	Protection and Advocacy		
PCA	personal care attendant		

Part One

The two chapters of Part One provide theoretical and conceptual foundations for our study of physical and health conditions. Taken together, they introduce a way of thinking and a way of working with individuals who have such disabilities.

Chapter 1 outlines the ideas that characterize our approaches in education, therapy, and counseling with individuals who have physical or health conditions. Among these are the fundamental idea that many of the problems these people encounter in their daily lives are due not to their conditions as such but rather to their environments. This way of looking at matters—differentiating "disabilities" from "handicaps"—helps us to understand our responsibilities as educators, therapists, and counselors. Later in the chapter, important words are introduced and defined. Every field of study or discipline has its own special terms; services for people with physical or health conditions are no exception.

Chapter 1 also contains demographic information about the population. This information demonstrates that the vast majority of physical and health conditions occur during adulthood and the retirement years; such conditions are relatively uncommon among children and youth. However, these conditions are not as uncommon as one might conclude after reviewing reports from the public schools. That is because large numbers of children and youth with physical or health conditions do not require special education (specially designed instruction) and thus are not served as "children with disabilities" under the federal Individuals with Disabilities Education Act (IDEA). Rather, as chapter 2 explains, these young people take part in general education for all or most of the day; if they need related services such as occupational or physical therapy, they may receive them under the Rehabilitation Act's Section 504.

Chapter 2 outlines a paradigm shift that characterized work with individuals having physical and health impairments in the late 1990s and likely will shape our work in the 21st century. This shift looks to individuals with disabilities, even very severe ones, to acquire the skills needed to lead a fulfilling life. Making that shift possible is a set of landmark federal laws that, taken together, have removed or are removing environmental barriers that in years past made such a life an unreachable dream. Also discussed in chapter 2 are welfarelike laws that protect people who cannot lead such lives even when no major environmental barriers remain.

1

INTRODUCTION

It's about ability, not disability: Joe Hayward, 51, is athletic director and physical education teacher at St. Augustine School, a Catholic elementary school in Oakland, California. Before an episode of chicken pox put him in a coma and eventually led to quadriplegia at age 31, Joe had been a baseball coach and football official. After the illness, he returned to his childhood love of organized sports. Joe figured that his abilities had not changed, so why should his activities? It may seem obvious, but he's exactly right: "You can coach football from a wheelchair . . . It's just that you go about it a different way," he says (Levy, 1996).

Physical disabilities are conditions that primarily affect mobility (gross- or fine-motor control), including some conditions that are often associated with wheelchairs (muscular dystrophy, spina bifida, and spinal cord injury) and some that usually are not (arthritis, multiple sclerosis, and traumatic brain injury). Health impairments are conditions that limit other important human functions, notably endurance (cancer, asthma), or that are life threatening (cystic fibrosis, sickle-cell disease, and AIDS).

Many of the disabilities discussed in this book have severe, even devastating, effects on people. Some lead in virtually every instance to an early death. Others are not terminal but do have traumatic effects upon daily life. Nonetheless, the focus in this book is more upon what people with physical, health, or sensory disabilities can do rather than upon what they cannot do. This way of looking at people with disabilities is something I developed from a career spanning several decades, during which I got to know many thousands of individuals with such limitations. These individuals have taught me a great deal about their abilities. I have been deeply impressed by the potential these people have for living rewarding and productive lives. The knowledge that an individual who is blind, for example, can perform a very demanding job raises my level of expectation for other people who are blind. Similarly, after knowing thousands of people who use wheelchairs because of spinal cord injury or spina bifida or some other condition and seeing them lead fulfilling lives, I naturally look to others in wheelchairs not as people who can't but as people who can.

The issue is one of national importance. Programs that offer benefits to individuals with disabilities on the assumption that they are incapable of supporting themselves include Supplemental Security Income (SSI), Social Security Disability Insurance (SSDI), Medicaid, and Medicare. These programs, which are described in detail in chapter 2, are projected to cost the federal government some $150 billion per year as of 2000 (Daniels, 1998). By contrast, programs that provide instruction and other assistance to people with disabilities on the assumption that they can learn to support themselves include the Individuals with Disabilities Education Act (IDEA) and the Rehabilitation Act. These two programs are funded by the federal government at a combined level projected to be about $6 billion by 2000. Even if one adds the federal outlays for implementing and enforcing the Americans with Disabilities Act, the Fair Housing Amendments Act, and other civil rights laws benefiting people with disabilities, the proportion of federal outlays on "inability" of people with disabilities exceeds 95% of all federal spending on disability.

These sums may be better appreciated in graphic form than in numbers. As Figure 1.1 illustrates, the great bulk of federal spending on disability goes to mandatory or entitlement programs such as SSI, SSDI, Medicaid, and Medicare. A much smaller proportion is available for discretionary programs, such as special education and rehabilitation. If, as Woodward and Bernstein suggested in *All the President's Men* (1974), the way to the truth is to "follow the money," it is clear that American policy is far more weighted in favor of charity toward people perceived as being "unable" than

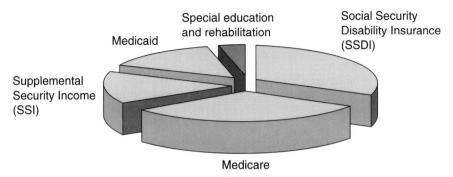

Federal spending estimates

Special education and rehabilitation

Medicaid

Social Security Disability Insurance (SSDI)

Supplemental Security Income (SSI)

Medicare

Figure 1.1
Estimated Fiscal Year 2000 Spending on Disability

Source: Personal communication, February 25, 1998, from Susan Daniels, deputy commissioner, Social Security Administration

than it is in favor of "ability"—and it needs to be changed. If change is to happen, the first steps must be taken by the readers of this book—special educators, therapists, counselors, and other professionals and paraprofessionals.

Fundamental Ideas

Traditionally, professional journal articles and textbooks have provided students and practitioners with the knowledge they need to address and rehabilitate physical and health impairments. As critical as that information is, the articles and books conveying it tend to overlook two equally essential areas of study: the abilities of the person and the characteristics of the environment.

A great deal is now known about the physical and health impairments discussed in this text. The chapters in Part Three that describe the major conditions are filled with details. As comprehensive as this body of knowledge may appear to be, more is constantly being added to our storehouse of knowledge. New medications are put on the market each year. New strategies and techniques for enhancing range of motion, strength, and motor efficiency for people with mobility limitations are introduced almost as frequently. Thus, an already formidable corpus of data continuously expands, requiring much time and effort to master. (For suggestions on keeping up, see "Resources" at the end of the book.)

As we attempt to learn about conditions and to keep abreast of new knowledge about them, we run a very great risk of overlooking the *abilities* of people who have these conditions. Physical therapy is undoubtedly important for someone who has cerebral palsy; otherwise, muscles may atrophy and become all but useless. Similarly, occupational therapy is crucial for this person; without it, he or she may not be able to perform everyday tasks and thus will be much more dependent upon other people than is necessary.

Much the same may be said about speech and language pathology. Yet an inescapable fact remains: Even after doing all that the state of the art allows in physical and occupational therapy and in speech and language pathology, we are left, at best, with a student, client, or patient who can do most of what people with no disabilities can do. This begs the question, So what? For people to be successful in today's economy, they need to be able to add value for employers. Stated differently, they need abilities. It is our job as teachers, counselors, and therapists to help them to develop those capabilities so they may use them in getting and keeping well-paying jobs and using the jobs, in turn, to finance a truly independent life.

Also overlooked is the environment. When I was a young boy in the 1950s, my father held out little hope that the world around me would change so as to accommodate my needs in any significant way. I was the one with a problem, he said, and it was up to me to find personal solutions. I was in my mid-20s before I realized that there was another side to this equation: Society, too, had to find some answers to the problems I experienced. This was true because there were many hundreds of thousands of other people in the United States with the same kinds of problems I had.

In the years since I made this discovery, America has indeed changed. Tremendous progress has been made in lowering barriers of all kinds. Nonetheless, more remains to be done. As teachers, counselors and therapists, we need to look anew at our environments, asking, about each new student, client, or patient with whom we work, "What environmental barriers stand between this person and his or her goals?" We need to focus upon eliminating those barriers, just as we do upon helping the person to adjust to and overcome physical limitations. In a word, the job descriptions of physical and occupational therapists, speech and language pathologists, school

People with disabilities are able to do things today that previous generations could only dream of—because architectural and transportation barriers are being removed. To reach this beach, this man needed curb cuts on sidewalks, lift-equipped buses, and ramps leading from boardwalks to the sand. Helping, too, are today's sporty wheelchairs that offer balance and stability.

and vocational counselors, and others who work with people who have disabilities must include one other role: that of an advocate.

We cannot be satisfied just to work on the weaknesses of our students, clients, and patients. We must work on their strengths as well. And we must strive alongside them to remove environmental barriers that otherwise would constrain them or even prevent them from reaching their goals. About 20 years ago, Howard A. Rusk, M.D., one of the world pioneers of rehabilitation medicine, told me what some of his patients had told him: "You have kept me alive. For what?" Dr. Rusk's patients were telling him his work was not yet done. Neither, today, is ours. That is why this text concludes in Part Four with three chapters on removing barriers in the community.

Terminology

Understanding the meaning of key terms will facilitate your study of physical disabilities and health conditions. These words are defined as they are introduced in the chapters that follow. Notice, too, that a glossary appears at the end of the text. Nonetheless, many readers may find it helpful to "meet" some of the most important words early in the book.

Disabilities and other conditions may be **congenital,** or they may be **acquired.** A congenital condition is present at birth. It may be genetic, or it may actually have been acquired—prenatally (before birth), perinatally (during birth), or postnatally (immediately following birth). We refer to a condition as "congenital" if it is present at or about the time of birth, regardless of its origin. Set against "congenital" conditions are "acquired" ones, which occur during childhood, adolescence, or adulthood or in the later years of life.

A related idea is **age at onset.** It is often very helpful for teachers, counselors, therapists, and others to know how old someone was when the condition first appeared. That is because any given disability or other condition can have very different effects upon a person's education, employment, and lifestyle, depending on age at onset. An example is deafness. If it occurs at birth or during the early-childhood years, deafness can have dramatic effects on language acquisition. The same level of hearing loss, however, that occurs during adulthood or the retirement years will have little or no effect on language development.

As we will see in chapter 3, age at onset has another effect. When people first become disabled during adolescence or adulthood, they must redefine themselves from a "self" that has no disability to a "self" that does. This can be very difficult to do and can produce a great deal of anger and frustration. Particularly common as disabilities that first occur during the teen years are spinal cord injuries (SCI) and traumatic brain injuries (TBI). Notice that the term is "age *at* onset." Our interest is not in "age *of* onset" (i.e., how old is the onset, in this case, the disability). Rather, we want to know how old the individual was at the time the disability occurred.

Physical disabilities generally are either **neurological** or **musculoskeletal** in nature. A neurological condition involves the central nervous system (CNS). A good example is multiple sclerosis (MS). Virtually every symptom or effect of MS is traceable to the fact that the condition interferes with the transmission of nerve impulses in the CNS. This includes the early pins-and-needles sensations as well as the blurred-vision effects characteristic of MS. If we did not recognize these as symptoms of a neurological problem, they would baffle us as seeming to be completely unrelated. By contrast, musculoskeletal conditions involve the muscles themselves or the skeleton. One example is muscular dystrophy (MD). In this condition, the muscles themselves are affected. Similarly, little people (dwarfs) have conditions affecting their bones and muscles.

Neurological conditions affect messages going to and from the brain. Nerves that carry messages to the brain are called **afferent** nerves; those that transmit messages from the brain are known as **efferent** nerves. It helps in remembering the difference to recall your Latin: "ad" (to) is the first part of "afferent" and "ex" (from) is the first part of "efferent."

When we talk about the number of people having different disabilities or health conditions, we use the words **prevalence** and **incidence.** The term *prevalence* refers to how many people have a particular condition at any one time. That is, it is a word referring to the total population of individuals with that condition. The term *incidence,* by contrast, relates to the number of *new* instances of that condition each year. When we talk about incidence, we are asking how many people acquire a given disability or condition annually. It is a measure of how rapidly the total population of persons with that condition is growing on a year-over-year basis. In this book, prevalence and incidence refer, unless otherwise noted, to numbers of people in the United States.

Disabilities and other conditions may be mild, moderate, or severe. This book focuses primarily upon severe disabilities and health conditions, but in a particular sense. In our use, the word *severe* suggests that the condition has real, measurable effects upon the daily lives of individuals. That is, the disabilities interfere with or actually prevent someone from performing important everyday activities. Deafness, for example, is severe; an ear infection, by contrast, produces only mild levels of hearing impairment. In this book, we are not concerned with conditions that have only minor consequences. Rather, our interest is in disabilities or health conditions that interfere with or prevent performance of such activities as working or going to school. Having said that, however, the emphasis of this text is *not* upon multiple or profound disabilities that obviate the feasibility of academic study or gainful employment; as indicated in the preface, a better source on that population is Bigge (1991).

We will be making a distinction between **disability** and **handicap,** following Bowe (1978). A *disability* is a condition that markedly affects important functions or activities. People have disabilities. By contrast, the environment may handicap someone by putting barriers in his or her path. People do not have handicaps. Thus, the term *handicap* (or *handicapped*) will be reserved for very particular meanings when we are discussing interactions between people and their environments. We will avoid using the word *handicap* to refer to people. That is because the term is a pejorative one—its origins are "hand in cap," or the charity people once showed individuals with disabilities by putting coins into their caps. One way of handicapping people with disabilities is to deprive them of opportunities. When children are "protected" from learning experiences, we say they are victims of **experiential deprivation.**

When we talk about environments, we will use terms such as **accessible** and **barrier free.** An accessible environment is one that has at least one entrance that people using wheelchairs or other mobility aids can use, at least one rest room they can use, and so forth. The term *accessible* usually is applied when we talk about retrofitting or changing an existing building or vehicle to make it useable by people with disabilities. It refers to a relatively low standard of access. *Barrier free,* by contrast, refers to an environment in which there are no architectural or other barriers. Thus, every entrance into the building, every rest room, etc., may be used by someone in a wheelchair. The barrier-free standard is a high one and is applied in most instances to new construction or to renovated portions of existing facilities.

A relatively new term is **universal design.** It refers to buildings, objects, and other things (including school curricula and materials) that are designed from the beginning to be useable by almost everyone. Universally designed facilities or products are barrier free. However, they are marketed—using the term *universal design*—to the mass market, not just to individuals with disabilities. The idea is to give accessibility a broad, or universal, appeal. Thus, universal design is a marketing tool.

Many people with physical disabilities use **orthoses** and **prostheses.** An orthosis is something that enhances a body part; for example, a splint on a finger helps someone make better use of that finger by stabilizing it. A prosthesis replaces a body part; an example is the Utah arm, which is an artificial arm.

Technology plays a large part in the lives of many persons with physical disabilities. **Assistive technology devices** are products (including software as well as hardware) that help people to accomplish important tasks despite disabilities. Today, there are hundreds of thousands of such products, including devices that help someone to reach, grasp, and manipulate objects; wheelchairs of various kinds; computer software programs, such as speech recognition software; and aids that assist in hearing and in seeing. **Assistive technology services** are steps taken to screen, select, acquire, program, install, maintain, and repair assistive technology devices.

Population Estimates

This book discusses physical and health impairments as well as common secondary conditions. Two important questions suggest themselves: How many Americans have such disabilities? and What do we know about these people? This section answers those questions.

First, it is necessary to dispel a common misconception. Many professionals, including so-called experts, believe that the number of school-age children and youth who have the disabilities discussed in this book is relatively small. This is because widely disseminated reports offer data *only* on children and youth served under the federal Individuals with Disabilities Education Act (IDEA) while ignoring hundreds of thousands of K–12 students with physical or health disabilities who are served, instead, under Section 504 of the Rehabilitation Act of 1973. (Chapter 2 explains Section 504.)

Our understanding of the population about which this book is concerned has grown dramatically over the past 25 years, in large part because far more and much better statistics have been gathered by the U.S. government and by private researchers. What all of these surveys have in common is that they do not include the estimated 2.1 million Americans with disabilities who reside in institutional settings. Rather, these are studies of the "noninstitutionalized population" in America. Readers who are interested in disability demographics are urged to consult the primary sources identified in this section because the original reports include the technical details necessary for full interpretation of the statistics presented here.

SIZE OF THE POPULATION

Conditions, Disabilities, and Severe Disabilities.   The U.S. Census Bureau's 1994–1995 Survey of Income and Program Participation (SIPP) estimated that 53.9 million Americans of all ages have disabilities. These persons represent about 20.6% of all Americans, or about 1 in every 5. The SIPP defined *disability* as a limitation in a functional activity (e.g., seeing, walking) or in a socially defined role or task (e.g., working, going to school). In addition, individuals who receive government assistance because of disability were included. According to the 1994–1995 SIPP (McNeil, 1997, Table 1), nearly 26 million individuals have severe disabilities or limitations that make them unable to perform everyday activities. They represent about 9.9% of all Americans, or about 1 in every 10. Figure 1.2 compares the sizes of the "severe" and "not severe" populations of persons with disabilities.

A very large number of Americans who have any kind of limitation have one or more of the disabilities discussed in this book. The 1994–1995 SIPP (McNeil, 1997) reported that some 9.3 million American adults need the daily assistance of another person to perform important activities. A similar study, done 3 years earlier, offered some additional details. Looking at people aged 15 and over who reported any kind of functional limitation, John M. McNeil, the U.S. Census Bureau's top expert on disability, found in the 1991–1992 SIPP that

- 17 million had difficulty walking as much as a city block and 9 million could not do this task at all.
- of the 16 million who had difficulty lifting and carrying a weight of 10 pounds or more, 8 million could not do this at all.
- of the 11 million who had difficulty understanding conversations, 900,000 could not hear them at all.
- 10 million had difficulty reading the words and letters in ordinary newsprint and 1.6 million could not read them at all. (McNeil, 1993, Table B, p. 6)

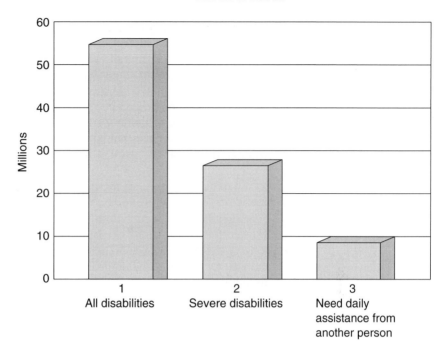

Levels of needs

Figure 1.2
Self-Reported Severities of Disability

Source: McNeil (1997)

Physical, Health, and Sensory Disabilities. The subject of this book is people who have physical, health, or sensory limitations. The number of such individuals increases as ages rise. Stated differently, these kinds of disabilities usually are acquired rather than congenital (present at birth). According to the U.S. Department of Education (1998) in its Twentieth Annual Report to Congress on Implementation of the Individuals with Disabilities Education Act, about 430,000 of the more than 5 million children between the ages of 6 and 21 who were served under the IDEA during the 1996–1997 school year had physical, health, or sensory disabilities. That was a direct-count study. To place the figure into context, we need a population-estimate study for comparison. The 1991–1992 SIPP is such a survey (McNeil, 1993). This study estimated that 700,000 children under the age of 15 were limited in their ability to "walk, run, or use stairs" (McNeil, 1993, Tables 1 and 34). That is about 1.5% of all children in that age range and some 26% of children under age 15 who had any kind of functional limitation. Comparing those proportions to the figures published by the U.S. Department of Education, we can see immediately that not all children who had physical limitations required special-education and related services under the IDEA. Many—about 300,000—were served under Section 504, which is described in chapter 2.

The number and proportion of Americans who have disabilities rise sharply in the subsequent age ranges. Consider, as a frame of reference, the

1994–1995 SIPP finding that 20.6% of all Americans had a disability. That is about 1 in every 5. The proportion among children under 3 years of age, however, was just 2.6%, or about 1 in every 40. Among 3- to 5-year-olds, the rate was 5.2%, or about 1 in every 20. By contrast, among people aged 55 to 64, 36.6%, or more than 1 out of every 3, had a disability, as did 47.3% of individuals aged 65 to 79, or almost half (McNeil, 1997, Table 1, p. 6). These numbers, which are illustrated in Figure 1.3, show that disability is a normal part of life. Indeed, most Americans become disabled at some point during their lives.

Driving this point home were important 1994 and 1998 studies by the Louis Harris & Associates, Inc., polling firm on behalf of the National Organization on Disability (NOD). These studies screened 20,000 American households to generate samples of 1,000 adults with disabilities. In the 1994 poll, a remarkable 88% of these adults reported having one or more of the disabilities discussed in this book: 54% said they had physical disabilities, 26% identified health conditions (heart, respiratory, kidney disease, etc.), and 8% said they had hearing or vision limitations. Just 1 in every 8 (12%) had none of these kinds of conditions but rather had mental or emotional disabilities. Of course, some people who reported physical, health, or sensory disabilities also had mental or emotional conditions. Figure 1.4 displays these proportions.

In both studies, the overwhelming majority (78% in 1998, 80% in 1994) of respondents with disabilities said that their conditions had begun *after* the age of 20. In fact, half (50% in 1998, 53% in 1994) said they had first become disabled after reaching 40 years of age (NOD, 1994; NOD/Harris,

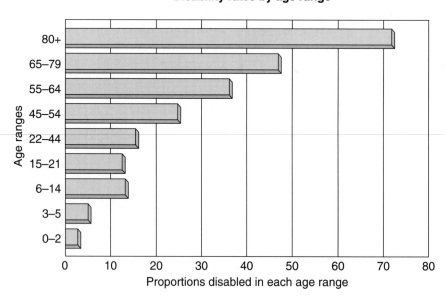

Figure 1.3
Disability Rates at Different Ages

Source: McNeil (1997)

Types of disabilities

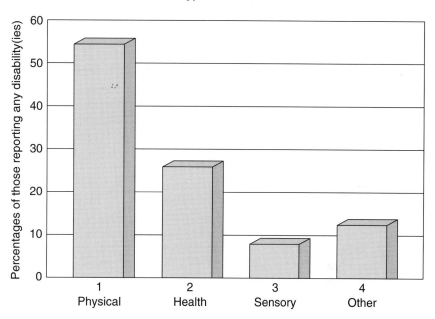

Figure 1.4
Self-Reported Types of Disabilities

Source: National Organization on Disability (1994)

1998). These numbers highlight something significant about physical, health, and sensory impairments: Such impairments usually occur in adulthood, not in childhood. In this they differ from developmental conditions such as mental retardation.

Important Age Ranges.   This book will consider programs that serve individuals with disabilities of different ages. The most important age ranges are birth to 2 inclusive (i.e., the first 36 months of life), 3 to 5 inclusive (i.e., the second 36 months of life), 6 to 18 or 21 (school age), 16 to 64 (the "working age years"), and 65 and over (the "retirement years"). In the United States, eligibility for services often depends on a person's age. For example, being under 3 years of age is a necessary condition (along with having a disability or a developmental delay) for eligibility under Part C (Infants and Toddlers) of the IDEA. Young children aged 3 to 5 inclusive may qualify for services under Section 619, Part B, of the IDEA. School-age children (6 to 18 or 21 years of age) may be served under Part B of the IDEA. Persons of working age may receive services under the Rehabilitation Act. Individuals over 64 years of age may receive benefits under the Social Security Act.

Our focus shifts now from the number of people with disabilities to the number of people who have which kinds of primary limitations. That is because educators, therapists, counselors, and others deliver educational and other services to children and adults in response to the most pressing needs these people have.

Under Six Years of Age.   The youngest age range is that of children called "infants and toddlers with disabilities" who are served under Part C of the IDEA. These very young children are entitled to early intervention services. The most recent report on these young children shows that such services were provided to 177,000 infants and toddlers as of the 1995–1996 school year (U.S. Department of Education, *Twentieth Annual Report to Congress on Implementation of the Individuals with Disabilities Education Act,* 1998, p. II-2). This figure represents 1.65% of the 11.5 million young children in that age range in America at the time (U.S. Department of Education, 1998, Table AF2, p. II-3).

The next important age range is that of "young children with disabilities" who are served under the IDEA's Part B, Section 619. These young children are entitled to preschool special education and related services. Children aged 3 to 5 inclusive numbered 559,000 as of December 1, 1996 (U.S. Department of Education, 1998, p. II-5). That figure represented 4.6% of the just over 12 million children in this age range in America at the time (U.S. Department of Education, 1998, p. II-6).

We do not know much about these young children. The 50 states, the District of Columbia, and other jurisdictions that carry out the IDEA are required only to report the number of children served. Thus, the data do not tell us about the children's disabilities (see, for example, U.S. Department of Education, 1997, Table AA14, p. A-43).

To learn what kinds of limitations children under 6 years of age have, we need to look elsewhere. An excellent source is the 1991–1992 SIPP (McNeil, 1993). Unlike the U.S. Department of Education's data-collection processes for its *Twentieth Annual Report,* the 1991–1992 SIPP asked questions about type of disability. (As noted earlier, the 1994–1995 SIPP lacks such data.) Parents were requested to identify the cause(s) of their children's disabilities. Of all birth–5 inclusive children who had any limitations, 25% were said by their parents to have two conditions; another 15% were reported to have three or more conditions. Asked to identify their children's primary limitation, parents named several conditions that are the purview of this book. Table 1.1, adapted from Bowe (1995c), presents the data on physical, health, and sensory conditions. In all, some 35% of children with *any* kind of limitation had a physical or health condition as their primary disability.

Among children under 6 years of age, physical, health, and sensory disabilities tend to be more quickly identified by parent and professional alike than are many other disabilities. Cerebral palsy, for example, is readily noticed in young children. Such limitations as emotional disturbance or learning disability, by contrast, are more likely to escape notice in the early childhood years or to be dismissed as something the child "will grow out of" (Bowe, 1995b). This is probably why larger proportions of young children than school-age children with any limitation are identified as having physical, health, or sensory conditions.

School-Age Children.   According to the *Twentieth Annual Report* (1997), a total of 432,000 children between the ages of 6 and 21 received special-education and related services because they have one of the disabilities that

Table 1.1 First (Primary) Condition of Children Under Age 6 With Any Limitation

Condition	Number (in Thousands)	Percentage
All Conditions	851	100.0
Physical, Health, or Sensory Conditions	299	35.1
Asthma	82	9.6
Cerebral palsy	52	6.1
Back/side/foot/ leg/arm/hand disability	49	5.8
Missing legs/feet/toes/ fingers	38	4.5
Epilepsy, other seizure disorder	25	2.9
Deafness, serious hearing loss	19	2.2
Blindness, vision problem	19	2.2
TBI, SCI, other paralysis[a]	14	1.6

Adapted from Table 2 in Bowe (1995c), p. 467.

[a]TBI = traumatic brain injury; SCI = spinal cord injury

is within this book's domain. Table 1.2, adapted from Table AA14 in the *Twentieth Annual Report,* offers the details.

Conditions such as learning disabilities or emotional disturbances, which are uncommon among children under 6 years of age, loom large in the school-age population. That is why the *proportion* of children reported as having physical, health, or sensory limitations is smaller in the 6–21 age range than in the under-6 age range. The absolute number of such children, however, is, of course, higher, although it is not as much larger as one might expect. Most likely, many of the "missing" children and youth were served under Section 504. Again, this issue will be discussed in chapter 2.

The term *other health impairments,* as used by the U.S. Department of Education, includes such conditions as epilepsy, AIDS, and cancer—all of which are within the purview of this book—but it also includes attention deficit disorder (ADD) and attention deficit hyperactivity disorder (ADHD), which are addressed only peripherally in this book as secondary conditions that children with physical, health, or sensory limitations may also have. The term *orthopedic impairments* includes conditions such as cerebral palsy and spinal cord injury.

Again, the SIPP offers additional information, especially about children and youth who may receive services under programs other than the IDEA.

Table 1.2 First (Primary) Condition of Children Aged 6–21 Who Were Served Under IDEA in the 1995–1996 School Year

Condition	Number (in Thousands)	Percentage
All Conditions	5,236	100.0
Physical, Health, or Sensory Conditions	432	8.2
Other health impairments	161	3.1
Multiple disabilities	100	1.9
Hearing impairments	69	1.3
Orthopedic impairments	66	1.2
Visual impairments	26	0.5
Traumatic brain injury	10	0.2

Adapted from Table AA14 in the *Twentieth Annual Report* (1997), by the U.S. Department of Education, p. A-45.

Table 7 in the SIPP report (McNeil, 1993) shows that over 5.5 million Americans between the ages of 6 and 24 have a disability. This age range is somewhat broader than that used by the U.S. Department of Education (it concludes at age 24 rather than at age 21). This is one reason the number of children, youth, and young adults identified as having disabilities is higher in the SIPP than it is in the *Twentieth Annual Report*.

Making our task somewhat easier is the fact that the SIPP report (McNeil, 1993) also uses the ages 15 and 17 as cutoff ages for some tables. One of these, Table 36, identifies a number of conditions reported by parents of children 0 to 17 years of age; note that this age range overlaps that discussed earlier (0–5 inclusive). Table 1.3, which is adapted from that SIPP table, contains estimates based on the number of children and youth aged 0–17 who were identified by their parents as having physical, health, or sensory limitations. Some parents reported that their children had two or more limitations; those parents were asked to identify the most important limitation.

The 28% prevalence rate of physical, health, and sensory limitations reported in Table 1.3 is much higher than the 7.7% of school-age children with disabilities identified in Table 1.2 as having received special-education and related services for such limitations under the IDEA. The most likely explanation for this apparent discrepancy is that some physical, health, and sensory limitations do not limit or otherwise affect children's ability to benefit from regular (i.e., nonspecial) educational services. For example, some children and youth with asthma or epilepsy may control their conditions with medication to the extent that they are minimally, or not at all, limited in edu-

Table 1.3   First (Primary) Condition of Children Aged 0–17 With Any Limitation

Condition	Number (in Thousands)	Percentage
All Conditions	3,357	100.0
Physical, Health, or Sensory Conditions	952	28.3
Asthma	281	8.4
Cerebral palsy	110	3.3
Epilepsy, seizure disorder	103	3.1
Blindness/vision problems	95	2.8
Back/side/foot/leg impairment	89	2.7
Deafness/hearing loss	74	2.2
Missing legs/feet/toes or arms/hands/fingers	66	2.0
Paralysis of any kind	41	1.2
Head or spinal cord injury	31	0.9
Heart condition	22	0.7
Cancer	16	0.5
Diabetes	14	0.4
Finger/hand/arm impairment	10	0.3

Adapted from Table 36 in McNeil (1993), p. 78.

cation. Because they have disabilities, however, they may be eligible for services provided under Section 504 (see chapter 2).

The Post-High School Years.   The 1991–1992 SIPP report in Table 30 identifies first (or primary) conditions among persons 15 to 64 years of age who had functional limitations. This age range includes a slight overlap (15–17) with the age range just discussed (refer to Table 1.3). Table 1.4, adapted from the 1991–1992 SIPP Table 30, is based upon self-report data. People who had more than one limitation were asked to identify their most important condition. Notice that the proportion of persons with any limitation who reported some physical, health, or sensory limitations as their first (primary) limitation has jumped significantly from that in the earlier tables.

It is among persons 65 years of age or older that physical, health, and sensory impairments really dominate. Table 1.5, adapted from Table 31 in the SIPP report (McNeil, 1993), offers the data. Many of these people have multiple limitations. We are looking, as we did in Tables 1.1 to 1.4, at conditions people describe as being their most pressing limitations, that is, the ones they most need assistance with.

Table 1.4 First (Primary) Condition of Persons Aged 15–64 With Any Limitation

Condition	Number (in Thousands)	Percentage
All Conditions	14,151	100.0
Physical, Health, or Sensory Conditions	10,603	74.8
Back or spine problem	3,189	22.5
Arthritis or rheumatism	2,299	16.2
Heart condition	1,031	7.3
Asthma or lung problems	999	7.1
Stiffness or deformity of foot/leg/arm/hand	745	5.3
Diabetes	341	2.4
Blindness or vision problems	311	2.2
Paralysis of any kind	288	2.0
Deafness or hearing loss	255	1.8
Head or spinal cord injury	254	1.8
Cancer	229	1.6
Stroke	216	1.5
Missing legs/feet/arms/hands/fingers	132	0.9
Cerebral palsy	126	0.9
Epilepsy	113	0.8
AIDS or AIDS-related condition	75	0.5

Adapted from Table 30 in McNeil (1993), p. 72.

PREVALENCE AND INCIDENCE

The most common conditions discussed in this book are very prevalent indeed. An estimated 40 million Americans, or fully 15% of the population, have arthritis. As many as 17 million have diabetes. Some 15 million have asthma. Other conditions are far less common in America today. About one-half million people are deaf or severely hearing impaired; approximately the same number are blind or have low vision. The prevalence of spinal cord injuries is about one-quarter million in America today. A very general rule suggests itself: The more common a condition is, the less severe it tends to be. To illustrate, comparatively speaking, asthma has less devastating effects on everyday life than does deafness.

Something else emerges from the flood of statistics in this chapter. If you add up the estimated prevalences for all the conditions discussed in this book, you get a total of some 80 million Americans. That number is substantially higher than the U.S. Bureau of the Census (McNeil, 1997) has

Table 1.5 First (Primary) Condition of Persons Age 65 and Over With Any Limitation

Condition	Number (in Thousands)	Percentage
All Conditions	13,138	100.0
Physical, Health, or Sensory Conditions	10,172	77.4
Back or spine problem	3,665	27.9
Heart condition	1,880	14.3
Asthma or lung problems	905	6.9
Blindness or vision problems	524	4.0
Stroke	464	3.5
Stiffness or deformity of foot/leg/arm/hand	444	3.4
Deafness or hearing loss	416	3.2
Diabetes	416	3.2
Cerebral palsy	358	2.7
Epilepsy	344	2.7
Cancer	284	2.2
Paralysis of any kind	203	1.5
AIDS or AIDS-related condition	121	0.9
Head or spinal cord injury	114	0.9
Arthritis or rheumatism	18	0.1
Missing legs/feet/arms/hands/fingers	16	0.1

Adapted from Table 31 in McNeil (1993), p. 73.

estimated—54 million. There are two reasons for the disparity in the figures: (1) Prevalence estimates for different conditions are just that—estimates; they can be, and at times are, wrong. (2) Many individuals have more than one condition. A traumatic brain injury, for example, frequently is accompanied by seizures, that is, by a form of epilepsy. Diabetes very often occurs alongside heart conditions and also blindness or low vision, simply because diabetes is a major cause of these latter conditions.

The number of Americans with disabilities is very large. That this population is one of the largest minorities in the United States still comes as a surprise to many people. To illustrate how sizeable the group is, consider that almost half of all Americans report that they encounter someone with a disability on a daily or other regular basis—a neighbor, a coworker, a friend, or even a member of the household. Only a very small minority of Americans say they never, or almost never, encounter people with disabilities (Coalition for Consumer Rights, 1997; NOD/Louis Harris & Associates, 1991).

Reflecting these realities, individuals with disabilities are becoming more and more visible as members of our society. As one example of this, President Clinton signed into law on July 24, 1997, legislation requiring that the Franklin Delano Roosevelt memorial in Washington, D.C., depict FDR in a wheelchair. Here's another: Corporations increasingly recognize the population as one they wish to reach. That is why the number of television commercials that are captioned increases every year. That is also why advertising-supported magazines targeted at people with disabilities are becoming more common. Launched within the past few years are *WE* Magazine (495 Broadway, New York, NY 10012; 1-800-WEMAG26; www.wemagazine.com), a glossy, full-color periodical; and *Enable* Magazine (3657 Cortez Road West, Suite 120, Bradenton, FL 34210), another advertiser-supported periodical. Both are targeted at Americans with disabilities. National Public Radio produced a series of four 1-hour programs, "Beyond Affliction: The Disability History Project," featuring interviews with leaders of the American disability rights movement. The weekly syndicated radio program "On a Roll" focuses on people with physical disabilities; its host is Greg Smith, who has muscular dystrophy. Heard on several dozen radio stations, the program is also available on the internet (www.audionet.com/shows/onaroll). "Living Without Limits," another disability-related radio program, is heard on 25 radio stations nationwide.

As large as it already is, the number of Americans with disabilities is rising, inexorably, year after year. The incidence estimates for the disabilities discussed in this chapter imply that the U.S. population of individuals with disabilities is growing by about one-half million individuals every year. Notice that fully 75% of adults aged 15 to 64 and 77% of persons older than 64 who have *any* functional limitation are restricted in activity because of conditions discussed in this book, while just 28% of school-age children and youth are. This dramatically illustrates the fact that physical, health, and sensory disabilities tend to be conditions that people acquire throughout their life span rather than conditions with which they are born. Stated differently, physical, health, and sensory impairments are a normal part of a long life.

Questions for Reflection and Discussion

1. Why should teachers, therapists, and counselors advocate for barrier removal in their communities and not just concentrate upon direct services to individuals?

2. The percentage of Americans having physical/health/sensory limitations rises steadily from age range to age range, *except* for which age range? How do you explain the divergence?

3. What is *experiential deprivation,* and why might it be important in understanding development among children and youth with physical or health disabilities?

4. Distinguish *incidence* from *prevalence.*

5. Give an example of a musculoskeletal physical disability.

6. Where is the underlying pathology in neurological physical disabilities?

7. Why is it important to know not only someone's condition(s) but also the age at onset?

8. Nerves carrying messages to the brain from the muscles are called _____ nerves.

9. Give an example of an orthopedic impairment.

10. How does a focus upon someone's ability rather than that person's disability alter goal setting by educators, therapists, and counselors?

Resources

National Organization on Disability
910 16th Street NW
Washington, DC 20006
1-202-293-5968
www.nod.org

U.S. Bureau of the Census
Room 2312
Washington, DC 20233
1-301-763-8300

U.S. Department of Education
Office of Special Education Programs
400 Maryland Avenue SW
Washington, DC 20202
1-202-205-5465
www.ed.gov

2

A PARADIGM SHIFT

Perhaps no event of recent years more closely captured the essence of the paradigm shift that has occurred in America—the change in focus from disabilities as personal problems to barriers as societal issues—than the February 1998 decision by a federal judge that professional golfer Casey Martin may compete on the Professional Golfers Association tour using a motorized cart. Casey, then 25 years old, was born with Klippel-Trenaunay-Weber syndrome, a rare circulatory disorder that makes walking painful. The Casey Martin v. PGA Tour (1998) decision is one that places the primary responsibility for making accommodations for people with disabilities upon society, in this case the PGA Tour. The publicity attending the decision made many Americans aware for the first time of the Americans with Disabilities Act and other civil rights legislation, and of the duty we all face as citizens of this country to remove barriers impeding people with disabilities (Heath, 1998).

For Americans with physical, health, or sensory disabilities, the United States at the turn of the century offers unprecedented opportunities. The change from just 30 years ago is nothing short of breathtaking, especially for people who were "present at the creation" and can vividly recall how things used to be. When I wrote *Handicapping America* for what is now HarperCollins in 1978, I drew a rather dark portrait of a largely inaccessible country. I am nothing short of stunned as I reflect upon just how complete the transformation of the past 20 years has been. To take just one of many examples of revolutionary change, consider subways. In *Handicapping,* I described an inaccessible subway system in Washington, D.C., and transit officials' recalcitrance about making it useable by people with physical, health, or sensory disabilities. Today, the entire subway system, called "Metro," is accessible. The only issue facing transit officials is *how* to make it even more accessible (see, for example, Reid, 1997). Similarly, in *Handicapping,* I expressed despair over the prospect that New York City subway stations and trains ever would be accessible. By 1994, amazingly enough, several stations and trains were in fact accessible, even by users of motorized wheelchairs. Robert Samuels, for example, commented in a story for *New Mobility* magazine about "10 Great Vacations":

> In the last decade, The Big Apple has made itself much more accessible. Once it was surprising to find corners with curb cuts; now it's surprising not to. Today, all city buses have wheelchair lifts. Many key subway stations are accessible too, but stick to the buses on a first visit (Samuels, 1994, 22).

Four revolutions of the late 20th century have raised, often dramatically, the potential of Americans with physical, health, or sensory disabilities to live lives defined much less by their disabilities than by their abilities, interests, and imaginations. The profiles of people with disabilities scattered throughout this book illustrate how people now can make career and lifestyle decisions on these bases and how they no longer are as limited by constraints imposed by their impairments as they and others with disabilities once were. Similar changes are sweeping through Europe, Asia, and other parts of the world, albeit more slowly than in the United States.

The first of these revolutions is giving individuals with disabilities and their families much greater control over the key events of their lives, especially in their interactions with professionals. The second has transformed the ability of these individuals to secure the education necessary to qualify for good jobs and to participate fully in the social, political, and economic activities of today's society. The third has opened American society—from transportation systems to shopping malls and stores to public buildings and facilities—so that people with physical, health, or sensory limitations can travel virtually at will throughout most American communities. The fourth and final revolution has made available assistive technologies that literally eliminate restrictions: There are devices that "move" for people with mobility limitations, that "see" for blind persons, and that "hear" for individuals who are deaf.

Three Models of Consumer-Professional Interactions

In a landmark 1962 publication, historian Thomas Kuhn proposed that scientific, political, and many other revolutions are characterized by a paradigm shift (Kuhn, 1962, p. 85). A paradigm, he suggested, is a way of looking at the world. It gives us a rationale for explaining things we see. At times, however, the paradigm fails us. Ptolemy, for example, thought the sun orbited the earth. His theory was limited, perhaps no more glaringly than in its inability to explain the seasons of the year. Copernicus's view of the earth orbiting the sun solved that problem. The move from Ptolemy's to Copernicus's view constituted a paradigm shift.

Something similar has now happened in the area of disability services. It is a political more than a scientific shift. In Kuhn's words: "Political revolutions are inaugurated by a growing sense . . . that existing institutions have ceased adequately to meet the problems posed by an environment that they have in part created" (p. 91). That is what is happening here.

We can trace approaches, or models, of serving people with disabilities back to ancient times (Bowe, 1978; Lenihan, 1976/1977). The first, dating from the beginnings of recorded history, we now call "the moral model." It derives from the seemingly mysterious ways in which people acquire disabilities. Lacking other explanations, ancient peoples ascribed them to the gods, reasoning that the gods must be punishing the person who has a disability. Alan Toy, a professional actor who has a physical disability, insisted that this supposedly old-world view continues to inform the opinions of many Americans. He summarized this world view of people with disabilities by saying, "[T]here is a really terrible reason you are like you are—too terrible to fathom" (Toy, 1994, p. 11).

When the first hospitals and residential schools appeared in America in the early and mid 19th century, professionals routinely advised people with physical, health, or sensory disabilities and their families to accept the inevitability of a starkly limited future and to accede to the professionals' judgment lest an even worse fate befall them. This approach says that the real problems are within the individuals who have disabilities. Solutions, therefore, may be found by experts who help these individuals to accept and adjust to their limitations. Today, we call this "the medical model," following John Gliedman and William Roth, who in 1980 wrote a devastating critique of the approach. Toy, concurring with Gliedman and Roth, characterized this model as declaring that people with disabilities can be helped, but only if they accept the "sick role" and defer to the wisdom of highly trained and certified professionals. The medical model, Toy observed, holds that there is a rational and fathomable reason for what has happened to you: "But you owe it to the godlike doctors of the world to allow them free rein—or reign—with your body in the name of Science. They can poke, prick, probe, slice, slash, stitch all day long if they want to. You must therefore be sick, an invalid, a victim. . . ." (p. 11).

The third approach, now known as "the social model" or "the civil rights model," dates from the early 20th century, especially to Helen Keller, who was decades ahead of her time in defining her problems as a deaf-blind person not in medical terms but rather in social and political terms (Keller, 1903). The idea, as I expressed it in *Handicapping,* is that the fundamental problem is not within the individual but rather within society: "America handicaps disabled people. And because that is true, we are handicapping America itself" (Bowe, 1978, p. vii). Political scientist Harlan Hahn (1985) of the University of Southern California insisted that this is the only human services approach that is consistent with the civil rights of Americans with disabilities. Whether it is called a "social" model or a "civil rights" model, the thinking is that individuals with disabilities can do as much and go as far as society will allow. That is, if society removes architectural, transportation, communication, and other barriers so that individuals can get into buildings, move around communities, and understand information despite hearing or vision impairments, disabilities matter far less than they otherwise would. The real problems, then, are not within people who have disabilities but rather are in the environment. Accordingly, the focus of both individuals with disabilities and professionals is not so much in "fixing" a disability as it is in "fixing" a societal barrier.

The civil rights (social) model identifies individuals with disabilities (or, in the case of children, their families) as the primary decision makers. This is consumer control, also called **empowerment.** The central concept is that individuals or families can take far more responsibility when they themselves make the basic decisions in matters regarding their everyday lives. The issue is not so much whether the person with a disability or the family members do everything or all important things by themselves but rather that they decide who does what and at what time (Bochel & Bochel, 1994; Hahn, 1985). As Frost (1996) put it: "Independence for people with chronic disabilities may not be about doing things for themselves, but about choosing how and when tasks are done and by whom" (p. 89).

Consumer control stands in sharp contrast to medical-model thinking that features, in the words of occupational therapy educator Jane Rourk (1996) of the University of North Carolina at Chapel Hill, "a medical orientation of curing or fixing the student's deficit (the work performance component)" (p. 698). Peloquin (1990) characterized this approach as authoritarian or parental in nature, because the professional makes all important decisions.

Occupational therapy educator Maureen Neistadt (1995) of the University of New Hampshire emphasized consumer-therapist collaboration. Her studies, including participants who had traumatic brain injury, spinal cord injury, multiple sclerosis, cerebral palsy, and spina bifida, convinced her that goals that are jointly set by consumers and therapists are more likely to be attained. Neistadt cited studies by others illustrating that jointly established goals are associated with shorter treatment cycles and correspondingly faster program discharges. In a survey of more than 260 occupational therapists, Neistadt found that virtually all (99%) reported "identifying referred clients' priorities" and nearly as many (95%) reported using informal interviews to elicit client goals. Neistadt's major concern was that occupational therapists dig deeply enough to ascertain the nature of those goals rather than just accept broad-brush goals such as "to take care of myself again" or "to go home":

> Occupational therapists should not be content with client goals like "I want to walk" or "I want to move my arm" or "I want to take care of myself." For an occupational therapist, the issue is not whether or not clients want to walk, but where they want to go when they can walk and what they want to do when they get there. (Neistadt, 1995, p. 435)

Bochel and Bochel (1994), who adopted the civil rights approach for a survey they did on housing and other care needs of persons with disabilities, reported that a social model changes the role of professionals: "Perhaps one of the most striking findings . . . was the overwhelming desire among respondents to both postal and interview stages for more (and more accessible) information across a whole range of services" (p. 84). When people are empowered, they seek information upon which they can base decisions. Armed with knowledge, they can decide upon their own course of action. This self-determination, in turn, motivates them more than any externally applied motivator can (Martin, Marshall, & Maxson, 1993; Wehrmeyer, 1995; Yancey, 1993).

This does not detract from the decisions of teachers, therapists, rehabilitation counselors, and other professionals. Rather, this approach of placing the consumer at the center sharpens the roles of personnel who work in the "helping" professions. Thus, while an individual with a disability may make the fundamental decision to have physical therapy be an important part of his or her program or daily life, the therapist nonetheless retains the decision-making roles of selecting assessment instruments, deciding between alternative treatment protocols, and deciding when and how to adjust therapy depending on the individual's progress toward goals.

To say that we have moved in a linear progression from the moral model to the medical model to the civil rights model is overly simplistic. Toy (1994), for example, suggested that most Americans still fear disability: "[A]blebodied people, as a group, are highly overrated and most of them require a lot of patience" (p. 12). For this reason, he concludes, "[t]he moral model still rules—that nasty and judgmental little credo best summed up by the old saw, 'There but for the grace of God go I'" (p. 12).

Four American Revolutions

Four revolutionary developments of the past 20 years have transformed disability services, the attitudes of professionals who work with people having disabilities, and the goals and expectations of Americans with disabilities and their family members. The first is the rise of empowerment among people with disabilities that was just discussed. The other three are the right to a free, appropriate public education; the ongoing removal of physical and other barriers in society; and the appearance of technologies that extend the capabilities of persons with disabilities.

A quarter century ago, many children and youth with physical, health, and sensory disabilities were denied an education in local public schools; those who were allowed to attend schools seldom received the services they needed. Many were passed from grade to grade without being expected to perform. Since 1977, however, people with physical, health, and sensory disabilities have enjoyed both equal access to elementary and secondary education and nondiscriminatory access to postsecondary education. The Individuals with Disabilities Education Act (IDEA) assures a free appropriate public education for all children and youth with disabilities in PreK–12 programs. Illustrative of the court cases (case histories) involving children with physical disabilities is the landmark *Timothy W. v. Rochester, N.H., School District* case. Educators in Rochester argued that because Timothy had multiple and severe disabilities, he was uneducable. They requested permission to exclude him from the public schools on the grounds that his multiple physical, sensory, and mental limitations rendered pointless any efforts to teach him. The first circuit Court of Appeals rejected their petition. Pointing to the word *all* in the law's original name (Education for All Handicapped Children Act), the court told the local school officials to find ways to teach Timothy (875 F.2nd 954, 1st Cir. 1989).

Section 504 of the Rehabilitation Act of 1973 (described later in this chapter) forbids discrimination in education as well as in other programs and activities that receive or benefit from federal financial assistance. Section 504 has proven to be very valuable for children and youth who have disabilities but who do not require special-education services. In addition, Section 504 offers equal access to colleges and universities as well as to vocational and trade schools. Although Section 504 does not pay for postsecondary education, it does provide for free accommodations to meet the special needs many students with physical, health, and sensory disabilities have as college students. Today, equal educational opportunity is an established idea in America. Parents and teachers alike assume, as a given, that children will complete at least some high school and that many will attend college or other postsecondary programs as well.

The next major revolution of recent years is the massive barrier removal instigated first by the 1973 Rehabilitation Act's Title V and later by the 1990 Americans with Disabilities Act (ADA). These laws require the leveling of barriers everywhere throughout America: social service agencies, stores, shopping malls, libraries, transportation facilities, and vehicles, even telecommunications. As a result, the barriers that once handicapped people with disabilities are gone or are rapidly disappearing. Parents, teachers, and therapists today can take for granted that most community programs and facilities will feature physical accessibility, accept referrals on a nondiscriminatory basis, and offer needed auxiliary services such as sign-language interpreting or media in appropriate formats (including cassette, Braille, and large type). Other barriers, too, are falling: Not only are employment offices physically accessible, but questions about disability are not asked on application forms.

Barrier removal this fast, on a scale this large, is, by necessity, limited in some ways. Many programs and facilities have become **program accessible—**

Inaccessible buildings, vehicles, and programs are "white elephants"—today we know better! The lives of all of us are enriched when activities, facilities, and transportation services are designed for full accessibility.

people with disabilities can receive services, but often only after a class or activity is moved from one (inaccessible) site to another. Some have reached a higher standard, that of **physical accessibility**—individuals with disabilities can get into each building, although often by only one door or entrance, and they can use rest rooms, albeit often just one per building. Only new buildings and facilities must comply with the highest standard, that of barrier-free—people with disabilities can enter through any door and can use any rest room or other room on any floor. These standards are discussed in depth in chapter 11.

The final revolutionary development was the emergence of technology that literally can do what disabilities once prevented. Computer software costing as little as $50 can "hear" words individuals who are deaf cannot. Similarly, people who are blind can take advantage of machines that "read" print and "speak" text aloud. Children and adults who cannot write or type may use computer speech recognition to "voice-type," that is, to dictate notes, letters, or even entire manuals simply by speaking to a machine. As will be discussed in greater detail in chapter 5, the impact of such programs and devices can be enormous because they enable individuals with disabilities to do virtually anything they could have done had they not been disabled.

These revolutions have, in turn, led to the consumer control, or empowerment, approach discussed earlier in this chapter. Thanks to higher education attainment levels, elimination of community barriers, and the emergence of new technologies, it is now possible for individuals with disabilities and their family members to interact with professionals on an equals-to-equals basis, a far cry from the sick-role approach required by the medical model. Legislation supports consumer control approaches in special education, rehabilitation, and such related services as occupational and physical therapy.

The IDEA requires that parents play an active role in their children's education, including the opportunity to serve on the multidisciplinary teams that create the child's educational plans (IDEA, Sections 614 and 636). Students with disabilities are to participate in this planning "as appropriate," which generally means once they attain the age of 14. The Rehabilitation Act requires that clients (usually adolescents and adults) not only take part in planning services but also give informed consent for such services to be provided (Section 102). In addition, the Commission for Accreditation of Rehabilitation Facilities (CARF), an accreditation body used by many programs and facilities, requires that therapists document consumer goals and show how consumer-therapist collaboration is occurring (CARF, 1994).

Taken together, these four transformations give people with disabilities a vastly brighter future. Such individuals may secure, free of charge, an appropriate education through the secondary level (and, if they continue to college, similarly appropriate education there, albeit not free). With this education, they can qualify for well-paying jobs. The ADA assures that they will have an equal opportunity at such jobs and that employers will provide whatever technology is needed to perform the work, as long as they qualify for employment. This is all most people with physical, health, or sensory disabilities have asked for—a chance.

The Landmark Laws Leading to Independence

These revolutions have been instigated by important federal laws, the most influential of which are introduced in the following subsections and will be examined in greater detail later in the text.

INDIVIDUALS WITH DISABILITIES EDUCATION ACT (IDEA) (20 USC 1400 ET SEQ.)

First enacted in 1975, what is now the IDEA guarantees a free education to the high-school diploma level for students with disabilities. The education must be appropriate in that it must meet each of an individual student's unique needs. This, in turn, requires that the education be custom designed, or individualized. The IDEA requires that this education be outlined in an Individualized Education Program (IEP). For students who have physical disabilities or health conditions, the IDEA assures an elementary and secondary education. Students who use wheelchairs or other mobility devices may not for that reason be denied access to an education.

The IDEA also provides for early-intervention services on behalf of infants and toddlers under the age of 3. These services may be offered in the child's home, at an early-intervention center, at a local clinic, or, if necessary, at a local hospital. They are to be outlined in an Individualized Family Service Plan (IFSP). Part C (formerly Part H) of the IDEA calls for services to be made available not only to infants and toddlers but also to other members of their families, notably to their parents. Early-intervention services include a wide range of services for children and for families such as speech and language pathology, physical and occupational therapy, orientation and mobility, special instruction, and family counseling.

The IDEA provides partial financing for these services. In 1998, some $3 billion in federal funds were offered to the states to carry out Parts B and C of the Act. The 50 states, the District of Columbia (Washington, D.C.), and American jurisdictions such as Puerto Rico, the Virgin Islands, and Guam added more than 10 times this amount, or in excess of $30 billion.

Children qualify for services under the IDEA if they meet the statutory definitions. With respect to elementary and secondary education, they must be "children with disabilities." That term covers children between the ages of 3 and 18 or 21 who have one or more of a statutory list of disabilities and for that reason need special education and related services. With respect to the subject matter of this book, that list includes orthopedic impairments (such conditions as cerebral palsy, spinal cord injury, spina bifida), other health impairments (including epilepsy, AIDS, etc.), hearing impairments (including deafness), visual impairments (including blindness), and traumatic brain injury. There is no similar list under Part C. Rather, "infants and toddlers with disabilities" are defined as young children under the age of 3 who need early-intervention services because they have a state-defined developmental delay or a state-listed condition.

REHABILITATION ACT (29 USC 706–794)

First enacted in 1918, what is now the Rehabilitation Act (so named in 1973) is a comprehensive piece of legislation. Title I authorizes vocational counseling and other services designed to prepare individuals with disabilities for gainful employment. Title VI of the Act authorizes what is called "supported employment"—services in which a trained professional accompanies a person with a disability to the jobsite and offers on-the-job training. Individuals with conditions that significantly limit their ability to work may be eligible for Title I or Title VI services. None of these services are entitlement in nature; that is, they are not guaranteed. In fact, budgetary constraints have meant, in recent years, that eligible individuals may receive fewer services than needed, may get services later than desired, or may not be served at all.

The Act also includes Title V, the first set of civil rights provisions ever enacted in federal law. All were part of the Rehabilitation Act of 1973. Section 501 prohibits discrimination in employment by federal agencies such as the Department of Defense or the Environmental Protection Agency. Section

502 authorizes the creation of a small watchdog agency, the U.S. Architectural and Transportation Barriers Compliance Board (ATBCB), which enforces the 1968 Architectural Barriers Act and other provisions relating to accessibility, particularly in federal buildings. More recently, the Access Board, as it is popularly known, has been given responsibilities to develop guidelines for accessibility to telecommunications pursuant to the Telecommunications Act of 1996 (see subsequent discussion). Section 503 calls for affirmative action in employment by private companies that receive federal contracts. IBM, for example, gets such contracts to provide computing equipment and services, as does Bell Atlantic to offer telecommunications services. Finally, there is **Section 504,** the most far-reaching of the four parts of Title V. Rules explaining its meaning appeared in 1977.

Section 504 prohibits discrimination on the basis of disability by federal agencies and by any organization or entity, including public schools, that receives or benefits from federal financial assistance. Virtually every school district in the United States gets such financial aid. Section 504 is very important to readers of this book. It is a very brief section (see Figure 2.1). In particular, readers need to understand that Section 504 is a nondiscrimination statute and emphatically is *not* a funding source. When children and youth are served by public schools under Section 504, no federal funds become available to the schools to support their efforts. In this way, Section 504 is very different from the IDEA, which does offer public monies to support school programs serving children and youth with disabilities.

Section 504 differs from the IDEA in two other important ways. First, Section 504 refers to a "free appropriate public education" as ". . . the provision of *regular* or special education and *related aids* and services" (34 CFR 1044.33, emphasis added). Those aids and services must ensure that an individual who has a disability receives benefits that meet his or her needs "as adequately as the needs of a non-disabled person are met" (34 CFR 1044.33). The point is that Section 504 applies to regular education even if the student does not require special services. Thus, even if they do not qualify for services under the IDEA because they do not need special education, children with epilepsy, asthma, or other conditions nonetheless must receive a free public education that meets their special needs. In addition, Section 504 protects jobseekers and employees who have disabilities against unjust discrimination on the basis of disability.

Section 504 uses a "civil rights definition" for disability. That definition has three prongs: (1) The individual has a medical condition that substantially limits him or her in major life activities; (2) the person once had such a condition, and a record of it was created or still exists, that may be used in discriminatory ways; (3) the individual is falsely thought to be disabled and is discriminated against on that basis. Note that *no list* of qualifying disabilities exists in the Section 504 definition. For this rea-

Section 504

No otherwise qualified individual with a disability in the United States . . . shall, solely by reason of disability, be excluded from participation in, be denied the benefits of, or be subjected to discrimination under any program or activity receiving Federal financial assistance or under any program or activity conducted by any Executive agency or by the United States Postal Service. [29 U.S.C. 794]

Figure 2.1
Section 504

son, children and youth who have conditions that are not listed in the IDEA, and therefore are not eligible for IDEA-funded services, may qualify, instead, under Section 504. Substantial numbers of children and youth who have physical or health conditions receive services under Section 504 rather than under the IDEA.

AMERICANS WITH DISABILITIES ACT (ADA)
(42 USC 12101 ET SEQ.)

Enacted in 1990, the ADA is a civil rights statute. As with Section 504, the ADA offers no authorization for services, nor does it provide funding for any activities. Title I of the Act prohibits discrimination in employment by any business having 15 or more workers and engaging in commerce. At least 2 million such companies must obey Title I. (The Rehabilitation Act bars discrimination only by federal agencies, not-for-profit organizations with federal grants, and companies with federal contracts; together, these provisions cover several thousands of employers. Accordingly, the ADA's Title I greatly broadened protection for jobseekers and workers who have disabilities.)

Title II (and part of Title III) of the Act prohibits discrimination in transportation. These provisions will be discussed in greater detail in chapter 13. The other part of Title III requires "readily achievable" steps by stores, hotels, restaurants, and other places of public accommodation so that individuals with disabilities can gain access and receive services on a nondiscriminatory basis. Readily achievable changes are those that may be made quickly and at low cost.

Finally, Title IV requires that telephone companies contribute to state-based dual-party relay services that enable people who are deaf or have severe speech impairments to make and receive voice telephone calls.

The ADA has had a tremendous impact in the United States in the years since its enactment. (It has also served as the model for similar statutes in many other countries throughout the world.) Particularly significant has been Title III, which opened up community stores, shopping centers, sports facilities, and other places of public accommodation such as hotels and restaurants. The net effect of all of these changes has been to make thousands of communities coast to coast accessible to and useable by Americans with disabilities. The employment provisions of Title I have helped many thousands of individuals with disabilities to get or to retain jobs for which they qualify by reason of training, experience, etc. To date, Title I has done far more for persons who already had jobs before becoming disabled than it has for people who were disabled at the time they first sought employment. That may change. As will be explained in detail in chapter 13, Title II has made commuter bus and rail services accessible in thousands of communities coast to coast. Title IV has made it possible for people who are deaf or speech-impaired to call and be called by others, both for important conversations (e.g., those related to work or family care) and for informal chats (e.g., calls to friends or family just to keep in touch).

FAIR HOUSING AMENDMENTS ACT (FHAA)
(42 USC 3601 ET SEQ.)

This Act prohibits discrimination on the basis of disability by real estate agents and by building owners and managers. The FHAA will be outlined in some detail in chapter 12. For our purposes now, it is enough to observe that the FHAA requires that new multifamily housing developments having four or more units (apartments, etc.) be designed so as to be accessible to and adaptable for use by individuals with disabilities.

The FHAA has had only a very limited impact to date for three primary reasons. First, the Act exempts all single- and two-family homes in the United States. Such residential houses are the predominant form of housing stock in this country. Second, housing developments tend to last for many decades. The stock of available apartments, condominiums, and cooperative apartments that were built prior to the March 13, 1991, effective date for "new" construction under the FHAA is extremely large; every one of those buildings is exempt from the Act's requirements on accessibility and adaptability. By contrast, the supply of "new" units is relatively small. Third and finally, the FHAA's impact has been constrained by the fact that it offered no funding for rental assistance or construction. The problem of housing for Americans with physical and health conditions is as much a problem of affordability as it is one of accessibility. These issues will be explored in greater detail in chapter 12.

TELECOMMUNICATIONS ACT OF 1996 (47 USC 157)

PL 104-104 is a massive piece of legislation. Among many other things, it offers some important provisions for Americans with disabilities. One such provision is Section 255, which calls for new telecommunications products (devices used to send information to or from other locations) and telecommunications services (regular phone service and special services such as last-call return) to be accessible to and useable by people with disabilities if it is "readily achievable" to do so. Another is Section 713, which requires captioning of video programming, including cable and broadcast television programs as well as movie videos. These sections potentially will make information age technologies more accessible to Americans with physical disabilities.

Other Important Laws

The preceding landmark laws are premised generally on the idea that people with disabilities are persons with abilities. Thus, these laws support individuals with disabilities who strive for independence and maximization of their potential. The goal is that people will take advantage of special education, rehabilitation, and civil rights so as to get well-paying jobs that offer comprehensive health coverage and by so doing become truly independent.

The other important laws briefly discussed in the following subsections are generally based on the notion that people with disabilities are persons with severe limitations. These laws are actually older than the landmark laws previously described. They were first enacted at a time when America was filled with architectural, transportation, and other barriers; when K–12 education often was denied children with disabilities; and when nondiscrimination in employment on the basis of disabilities was nonexistent in America. Thus, these laws provide for keeping people alive, albeit in a dependent way.

This dichotomy between "independence" and "dependence" laws is one that every person with a physical or health disability eventually has to confront. Choices must be made. In general, if a child, adolescent, or adult has vocational potential, teachers, therapists, counselors, and others are well-advised to emphasize the liberating effects of America's civil rights laws and to encourage the individual to take full advantage of them. On the other hand, for people who have very limited or no potential for paid work, professionals should focus mostly on the life-saving and sustenance-providing nature of the older entitlement laws. The real difficulty arises with people who have some vocational potential but who also have severe needs. In such cases, professionals should work with the individual and his or her family, outlining the various choices and explaining the trade-offs involved. The next chapter's discussion of counseling explores in greater detail the dependence-versus-independence dichotomy. Readers may find it helpful to read that section alongside this one so as to put together a comprehensive picture of the choices available to Americans with disabilities.

SUPPLEMENTAL SECURITY INCOME (SSI)
(42 USC 1381–1383f [1997])

Supplemental Security Income (SSI), as the name implies, is a federal-state entitlement program designed to supplement the income of eligible individuals so that their earned income and their SSI check would total about an amount equal to the poverty level. (To illustrate, in 1998, individuals with disabilities were eligible for SSI if their monthly income was below $570. The SSI check closes the gap between their earned income and the $570 level.) In 1974, Congress created this program in Title XIX of the Social Security Act, bringing together many diverse state programs. The timing is significant: SSI was created before the IDEA first required a free appropriate public education for children with disabilities and before Title V of the Rehabilitation Act took effect. Thus, SSI is a program dating from a pre-civil rights era. It is a welfarelike program. That SSI often stands in direct conflict with such laws as the ADA and the IDEA is not surprising, given this time frame. That conflict—whether to take advantage of civil rights laws or the older entitlement programs—is one that faces young people with physical and health disabilities. Every year, 15,000 more 18-year-olds enroll in SSI as adults qualifying under the "family of one" rule (Daniels, 1998). (That rule calls for the Social Security Administration to consider the young adult to be a "family of one" and thus not to count the parents' income in determining eligibility.)

Funded from general revenue (e.g., federal and state income taxes), SSI is made available to individuals who have severe disabilities, are over 65 years of age, or both. For children under age 18, the disability must be marked and severe. For persons aged 18 and over, the disability must be permanent (lasting 6 months or longer or expected to result in death) and must prevent the individual from performing virtually any job in the national economy. These are tough tests to meet. The intent of Congress was that SSI would be a safety net for individuals who truly need it. Enrollment in SSI usually also brings with it eligibility for Medicaid (see subsequent discussion). This coverage is very important for many people who have physical or health conditions. Indeed, the Medicaid eligibility often is the primary motivating factor why people with these kinds of disabilities seek to become enrolled in SSI.

SSI offers monthly checks (plus, in most states, eligibility for Medicaid, food stamps, and other benefits) for individuals who are both "poor" and "disabled" or "elderly." The term *poor* refers *both* to the person's earned income *and* to the person's assets, such as money in a savings account. What is called **substantial gainful activity,** or SGA, is in essence minimum wage. An individual is "poor" if he or she is unable to make that level of earnings because of disability and has no more than $2,000 in savings. The monthly checks vary in amount depending upon the state in which the individual resides (some states offer greater supplements to the federal SSI amount than do others) and upon the individual's earned income (the more one earns, the less SSI adds as a supplement).

In mid-1998, SSA Deputy Commissioner Susan M. Daniels projected federal spending on cash benefits for SSI recipients who have disabilities to be about $23 billion per year by 2000 (Daniels, 1998).

MEDICAID (42 USC 1396 ET SEQ. [1997])

Medicaid is the federal-state medical insurance program for people who are very poor. It is funded, as is SSI, from general revenues. Eligible are people who receive SSI because of poverty plus disability or old age. Under PL 104-193, the Personal Responsibility and Work Opportunity Reconciliation Act of 1996, as amended by PL 105-33, the Balanced Budget Act of 1997, children who lose SSI benefits because they do not meet the "marked and severe" test may continue to receive Medicaid from their state, provided that they meet state eligibility criteria.

Generally, Medicaid pays for in- and out-patient services at hospitals, physician services, and some home health-care services. In some states, physician services are included only if they are provided at a hospital emergency room.

In mid-1998, the SSA's Daniels projected that in 2000, the federal government would spend $25 billion annually to provide Medicaid coverage for people who are on the SSI rolls because of disability (Daniels, 1998).

SOCIAL SECURITY DISABILITY INSURANCE (SSDI)
(42 USC 401, 420–425)

SSDI is a federal program funded out of payroll deductions (OASDI—Old Age and Survivors Disability Insurance). Thus, benefits are contingent upon an individual's having worked a minimum amount of time (generally, for half the years since the person turned 21 years of age). In this sense, SSDI is very different from SSI because the latter does not require people to have contributed into the program from their own incomes. The SSDI program was created in 1956 as title II of the Social Security Act, long before any disability rights laws.

To qualify for SSDI, individuals must have disabilities that are so severe that they are prevented from working in any job in the national economy or from making on a job more than substantial gainful activity (SGA) amounts. Thus, anyone who earns more than about $570 per month for 9 months (those 9 months need not be consecutive) may be terminated from the rolls as no longer disabled. However, there is no limitation in SSDI on the amount of savings a person may have. Monthly checks from SSDI are much larger than are those from SSI. As of mid-1998, about 5 million American adults received SSDI checks averaging about $700 per month. Some individuals who qualify for SSDI are poor enough that they also qualify for and receive checks from SSI.

In mid-1998, the SSA's Daniels projected that in 2000, the federal government would spend about $51 billion on cash benefits for SSDI recipients (Daniels, 1998).

MEDICARE (42 USC 1395 ET SEQ.)

Medicare is the federal program providing medical insurance for senior citizens under Title XVII of the Social Security Act. Funded via payroll deductions, beneficiary premiums, and general tax revenues, Medicare is made available to people under the age of 65 who have disabilities that qualify them for SSDI benefits. Medicare Part A offers hospitalization coverage, some home health-care services, and related services. Part B, partly financed through premiums paid by beneficiaries, covers physician charges and some other costs, including medication. About 5 million Americans under the age of 65 receive Medicare coverage because they are on SSDI. However, with 33 million Social Security beneficiaries over the age of 65 receiving Medicare coverage, the program serves mostly seniors.

Medicare coverage is accepted by most private physicians. Thus, unlike with Medicaid, people who have Medicare may choose and patronize personal physicians. On the other hand, Medicare is also a program primarily geared toward meeting the needs of elderly persons rather than younger ones. This orientation becomes particularly apparent when Medicare beneficiaries seek reimbursement for assistive technology devices. As will be discussed in chapter 5, Medicare will pay for durable medical equipment but not for products that make people more productive in work or in education.

In mid-1998, the SSA's Daniels projected that in 2000, the federal government would spend some $50 billion on Medicare coverage for SSDI recipients (Daniels, 1998).

Questions for Reflection and Discussion

1. How does "the moral model" differ from "the medical model"?

2. How would educators, therapists, and counselors behave differently if they followed "the social/civil rights model" rather than "the medical model"?

3. What are the key provisions of the Individuals with Disabilities Education Act (IDEA)?

4. Why is *Timothy* such an important case in the history of special education in the United States?

5. Why were the employment provisions of the Americans with Disabilities Act (ADA) a significant step forward from those of Title V of the Rehabilitation Act?

6. What is the 3-part definition of "individuals with a disability" that is found in Section 504 and in the ADA?

7. Why is the Telecommunications Act of 1996 potentially important in our current information age?

8. How does the independence-versus-dependence dichotomy shape our understanding of U.S. social policy of the 1990s?

9. Why do many Americans with disabilities find Supplemental Security Income (SSI) to be attractive?

10. What are the more significant limitations of the Fair Housing Amendments Act (FHAA)?

Resources

Social Security Administration
Office of Disability
6401 Security Boulevard
Baltimore, MD 21235
1-410-965-1414
www.ssa.gov/odhome

U.S. Department of Education
Office of Special Education Programs
400 Maryland Avenue SW
Washington, DC 20202
1-202-205-5465
www.ed.gov

U.S. Department of Justice
Office on the Americans with Disabilities Act
P.O. Box 66738
Constitution Avenue NW
Washington, DC 20035-6738
1-800-514-0301 (toll-free ADA information number)
1-202-514-0381
www.usdoj.gov

(for ADA information: www.usdoj.gov/crt/ada/adahom1.html)

Part Two

The three chapters of Part Two present interventions that are used by educators, therapists, and counselors who work with children, youth, and adults having physical or health disabilities. The intent is to offer overviews of the major educational and therapeutic techniques that are used with these populations.

Chapter 3 presents an overview of these services. The chapter explores special education (specially designed instruction) and related services (noninstructional services that are needed for people to benefit from special education) and early intervention (instruction and related services provided to children under the age of 3). Included are occupational and physical therapy, speech and language pathology, art therapy, counseling, and advocacy.

Chapter 4 takes on more of a practical orientation. It examines the ways in which educators, therapists, and counselors work together and describes a widely used strategy, applied behavior analysis (ABA), in enough detail to explain the tactics employed. The focus then shifts to ways in which related services and other support services may be offered while children and youth take part in a school's general curriculum and to means of meeting the unique needs of the students through a parallel curriculum that provides important knowledge and skills such as self-care, use of devices, and transition from high school to life beyond high school. Chapter 4 also discusses universal design in education and conductive education.

Part Two concludes with an in-depth look at technology. The potential impact of today's devices, whether low-tech (nonelectronic and having no or few moving parts) or high-tech (electronic) in nature, is nothing short of amazing. Chapter 5 explores speech recognition, speech synthesis, global positioning systems, and the many varieties of wheelchairs.

3

THE SERVICES

Ronald Gordon, 1977 Nassau County (New York) poster boy for Duchenne muscular dystrophy and Phi Beta Kappa graduate of Hofstra University in Hempstead, New York, received special education and related services at what is now the Henry Viscardi School in Albertson, New York. The school specializes in serving K–12 students who have physical disabilities. After graduating as the school's valedictorian, Ron became a journalism major at Hofstra. At Hofstra, he lived in the dorms despite the fact that he needed assistance every day with such basic matters as dressing and bathing. The university provided paid personal care attendants who performed those duties. Ron played intramural wheelchair hockey and ran for homecoming king (he placed second).

   While a student, Ron did journalism internships at Newsday, the Long Island newspaper, and at News12, Long Island's all-news *television channel. After graduation, he worked at Hofstra, commuting daily on Long Island Bus vehicles (he convinced the company to schedule one of its first lift-equipped buses to accommodate his schedule). Later, he became a freelance writer for local newspapers. One story came from a 15-minute interview he held with Hank Aaron, the all-time home run record holder. In 1993, after nearly dying from MD, Ron had a tracheotomy and required a respirator. When MetraHealth, his medical insurance carrier, tried to terminate coverage, Ron sued the company; as a result, the State Supreme Court ordered MetraHealth to provide nursing care for 16 hours a day. That continued until Ron died at age 32 on May 18, 1998 (Goldhaber, 1998).*

Instruction, therapy, and counseling for persons with physical or health disabilities are our topics in this and the next chapter. Our task in this chapter is to lay the groundwork by introducing the various services that children, youth, and adults with physical or health impairments may require. Chapter 4 will then show how these services can be brought together to enhance development in individuals with physical or health disabilities.

Special Education

What many school-age children who have physical or health limitations most need in education is what the IDEA calls **related services**—special transportation, physical and occupational therapy, speech and language pathology, and assistive technology devices and services. (Part C of the Individuals with Disabilities Education Act—IDEA—calls these early-intervention services, while the Rehabilitation Act calls them rehabilitation services.)

Individuals who receive appropriate support services on a timely basis may in fact not even need special-education services. This is a remarkable idea. Let me explain it further. Many children with asthma or other conditions discussed in this book primarily have needs that emerge from the physical limitations imposed by the disabilities. If these needs are met, the children may be educated in the same ways, at the same pace, and in the same places as students with no disabilities. Other examples of disabilities that probably do not require special-education services include amputation, arthritis, cancer, cardiac conditions, cystic fibrosis, diabetes, spina bifida, and spinal cord injury. In addition, many little people (dwarfs) can learn in the same ways and at the same pace as others.

The IDEA defines **special education** as "specially designed instruction, at no cost to parents, to meet the unique needs of a child with a disability" (§602[25]). The U.S. Department of Education's regulations further explain that specially designed instruction is to be understood broadly. The rules in §300.24(b)(3) say that specially designed instruction

> means adapting . . . content, methodology or delivery of instruction—
> (i) To address the unique needs of the child that result from the child's disability; and (ii) To ensure access of the child to the general curriculum, so that he or she can meet the educational standards within the jurisdiction of the public agency that apply to all children. (U.S. Department of Education, 1999)

The regulations go on to say that specially designed instruction may include such related services as speech and language pathology and assistive technology under state laws and rules if those services are considered to be special education under state standards (§300.26[a][2][i]).

WHO MIGHT NOT REQUIRE SPECIAL EDUCATION?

Some children and youth with physical or health disabilities may need only very minor adjustments in instructional services. Those adjustments probably do not rise to the level of being special-education services. To illustrate: Children with asthma may require occasional absences from school, particularly if an attack occurred during the previous night that deprived the child of sleep. Students having asthma may be excused from some physical education activities if exercised-induced attacks are a reasonable expectation. Other than those instances, however, children with asthma can be expected to benefit from "regular" rather than from "special" education services. Much the same may be said for people who have diabetes. Such students may need one to three hours daily to take medication and perform self-monitoring of insulin levels. Scheduling flexibility that permits them to do so may be all they require in the way of special-education services.

The fact that some children with physical or health conditions might not require special education is a possible explanation as to why, as we saw in chapter 1, the number of children and youth of school age who are reported by various surveys to have disabilities is much smaller than one might expect. We are looking here at numbers that are a function of definition: Among school-age children and youth, the term *disability* in the IDEA refers to conditions that interfere with or even prevent one from benefiting from regular education services. Children with asthma, then, have a condition, but not necessarily one that is a disability with respect to the IDEA.

Similarly, children with epilepsy probably will not require special-education services. If the child is subject to tonic-clonic seizures (formerly called grand-mal seizures), teachers and other professionals should examine the room and remove from the child's immediate surroundings any sharp objects that might cause injury during a seizure. If, however, the child has absence seizures (formerly called petit-mal seizures), the teacher, counselor,

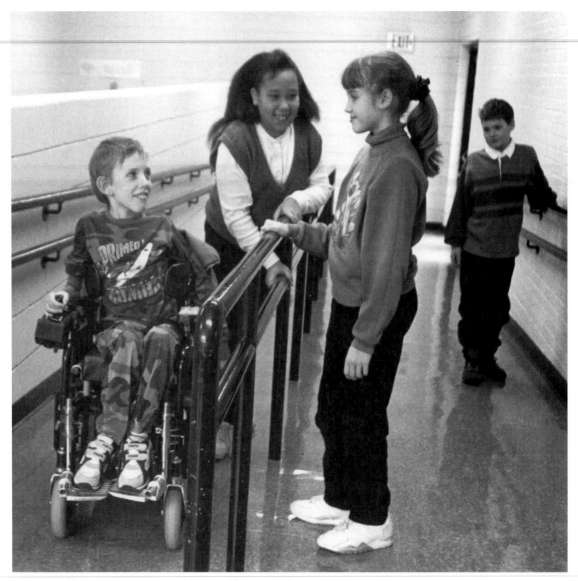

Students with physical disabilities may require related services (here, a wheelchair) but do not necessarily need special education (adapted instruction). Some school districts refer to students like these as "section 504 students." For them, integration into regular neighborhood public schools often is appropriate.

or therapist working with the child should be alert to these seconds-long "absences" and repeat the words or sentences the child missed during the episode. Teachers and other professionals should also be alert to any drowsiness caused by anticonvulsant medication. While essential to the child's education, such steps are so modest in nature that they probably do not qualify as special-education services.

For children with muscular dystrophy (MD) and other usually fatal conditions, special educators can develop intellectual interests to replace physical ones that no longer can be performed. Such interests can help enormously in deterring thoughts of morbidity and mortality, keeping morale up and motivation strong. Again, however, these steps may not constitute specially designed instruction.

Children and youth who require related services, but not special education, may be served under Section 504 of the 1973 Rehabilitation Act (29 U.S.C. 794). As discussed in chapter 2, Section 504 is a nondiscrimination provision that bars recipients of federal funds (meaning almost every public school in the nation) from excluding people who have disabilities from their programs and activities. The federal rules for Section 504 in K–12 education (U.S. Department of Education, 30 C.F.R. 104) indicate that one way of ensuring that services are nondiscriminatory is to offer needed support services through an individualized education program (IEP). Section 504 defines disability as a permanent health condition that significantly affects major life activities. Going to school is a major life activity for children and youth. However, Section 504 (unlike the IDEA) contains no list of eligible impairments. Nor does it contain any requirements, as the IDEA does, that the child "need special education and related services" to be eligible. Accordingly, many students with physical or health conditions are served under Section 504 rather than under the IDEA. Some educators call these children and youth "Section 504 students." The major downside of Section 504 is that it provides no federal funds to support services for children, youth, or adults.

To say that many children and youth with physical or health disabilities do not need special-education services is not to say that these individuals do not require related services (see discussion later in the chapter). Many do. Children and youth who have amputations, for example, need specially designed prostheses. People with severe arthritis may need adaptive devices such as alternatives to the keyboard or mechanical page turners. Individuals with spina bifida may require special or customized positioning and seating aids. Children who were victims of child abuse may need special counseling to help them to deal with their emotions and to learn to trust other people. Section 504 offers related services for these children.

WHO PROBABLY DOES REQUIRE SPECIAL EDUCATION?

Children who have, in addition to the physical and health disabilities previously mentioned, significant intellectual impairments do need specially designed instruction. Indeed, teaching these children typically involves using a radically different curriculum than is found in most public schools. To oversimplify the point, these students rarely take college prep courses. Rather, their education may be described, to use the words of Amy Rumelt, principal of Carman Road School in Massapequa, New York, as "a modified academic program." While the content includes traditional subjects such as math and science, the level of instruction is well below that found in mainstream public schools.

A growing number of children with physical or health conditions have such profound intellectual impairments that even this modified curriculum is too high for them to reach. For these students, a functional, or life skills, curriculum may be used. This approach focuses upon teaching the students to exercise independence in their everyday lives, by bathing and dressing themselves, feeding themselves, moving about on their own in the community, ordering items in stores, making change, and the like. This is, without a doubt, special education. It should go without saying, then, that a curriculum for students whose intellectual limitations are such that even a life skills curriculum is unreachable will require specially designed instruction. These students might be taught to help others to help them, thus reducing dependency; to recognize different sensory stimuli (sights, sounds, tactile sensations); to know when they need assistance and how to request that help.

In addition, many children and youth do *not* have significant intellectual limitations but nonetheless may need specially designed instruction. Some children with spina bifida also have learning disabilities that require special-education services. Similarly, children who have severe hearing losses as secondary conditions (as is the case with many people who have cerebral palsy)

A major responsibility of occupational therapists is to recommend, procure, adjust if necessary, and monitor a student's use of adaptive equipment. The augmentative communication device being used by the Chicago Bulls fan differs from the machine in use by his friend. Occupational therapists need to train students, their teachers, their parents, and often others as well (e.g., their siblings) on how to use and maintain the products.

will likely require special-education services in response to the hearing loss. Severe cerebral palsy itself is a condition that may call for special-education services. Some individuals with traumatic brain injury (TBI) may need to learn basic skills all over again. Even after mastering those skills, they may still need intensive instruction using applied behavior analysis (ABA) techniques so as to learn behaviors that are acceptable in the classroom or at their workplace (ABA is discussed in the next chapter).

People who have fetal alcohol syndrome (FAS) and many who have fetal alcohol effect (FAE) may need intensive training in recognizing and acting on cause-and-effect relationships. As illustrated in Michael Dorris's unforgettable *The Broken Cord* (1989), the seeming inability to learn cause and effect is one of the most remarkable effects of FAS. With training and with opportunities to generalize that training to other settings, however, many people with this condition can lead safer and more productive lives.

WHERE IS SPECIAL EDUCATION PROVIDED?

To say that most children with physical or health disabilities can benefit from regular education services is not to say that the IDEA calls for inclusion of these students. It does not. The law specifies that special education and related services be individually designed (customized) to respond to children's unique needs. Inclusion, by contrast, is an approach calling for identical (or nearly so) services for all children with disabilities. Congress heard extensive testimony in favor of inclusion prior to enacting the 1997 IDEA amendments. Despite that testimony, Congress elected to leave the law's least restrictive environment language unchanged. This decision shows again that Congress intended for special education to treat each child as an individual and to eschew one-size-fits-all approaches, even those as politically appealing as inclusion. (For a good summary of the law and case history about inclusion, see Murdick & Gartin, 1996.)

This raises the question, What placements are most common with students who have physical or health conditions? The U.S. Department of Education's *Nineteenth Annual Report on Implementation of the Individuals with Disabilities Education Act* (1997) helps us with this. The category "orthopedic" is one we may use as a proxy for the students we are most concerned about; this helps us to get around the fact that "other health conditions" is a category dominated by such conditions as attention deficit disorder that are of only secondary interest to us in this book. As shown in Figure 3.1 (based upon Table AB2 in the *Nineteenth Annual Report*), students aged 6–21 who have the "orthopedic impairments" label are educated in a variety of settings. About 2 out of every 5 (42%) are in regular classrooms, 29% are in self-contained classrooms, and 1 in every 5 (18%) is in a resource room. The "resource room" placement category is used if students spend 21% or more of their time outside the regular classroom. About 1 in every 12 (8%) is in a home or hospital setting. Very small proportions are placed in other settings. These placement patterns suggest that children with orthopedic impairments have a wide range of needs; some can function in regular

Placements: Orthopedic impairments

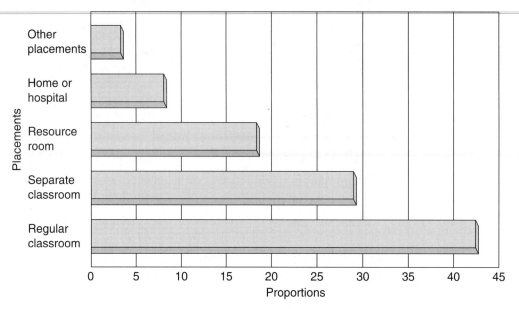

Figure 3.1
Placements of Students Aged 6–21 Who Have Orthopedic Impairments

Source: U.S. Department of Education (1997)

classes with little or no customized curricula, while others require considerable special-education instruction, and some are hospitalized.

Data on children with TBI are of somewhat dubious reliability, since reporting on this category has been required from the states for only a few years. Table AB2 tells us that 26% of children and youth aged 6–21 with the "TBI" label are in regular classrooms, 24% are in resource rooms, 30% are in separate classrooms, and 14% are in separate schools. Very small proportions are in other settings. TBI is one physical disability that often calls for special education services, which may include relearning basic intellectual skills and academic information. TBI may also encompass learning and studying skills, particularly organizing and carrying out multistep procedures.

Some children with physical or health conditions also have hearing or vision impairments. Table AB2 of the *Nineteenth Annual Report* does not clearly pull out these children with multiple disabilities. However, it does tell us where children with hearing or vision losses tend to be placed. Children and youth aged 6–21 who are deaf or hard-of-hearing tend to be in regular classrooms (35%), separate classrooms (29%), resource rooms (19%), and separate schools (12%), with very small percentages in other settings. As chapter 10 explains in more detail, hearing losses present significant problems in education because oral speech is so central to the way children are educated in most classrooms. Among children and youth aged 6–21 who

A major related service for students who are deaf is visual communication. Whether produced by the teacher or by an interpreter, sign language and fingerspelling offer clear, 100% visual access to the spoken word—if, and only if, the teacher or interpreter is competent in using signs. Here, a young man watches intently as a teacher signs, "seven weeks."

have vision impairments, a much higher 46% are in regular classrooms, 21% are in resource rooms, and 17% are in separate classrooms, while 11% are in separate schools. Very few children and youth who are blind or have low vision are in other settings.

Early Intervention

For people who are born with disabilities or acquire them during the early childhood years, the IDEA's Part C early-intervention services can be very helpful. Children with spina bifida, for example, may receive physical and occupational therapy services. For young children with spina bifida who also have learning disabilities, special instruction can help them to develop effective learning strategies. Similarly, parents and other family members may benefit from counseling and information services that help them both to cope with the child's disability(ies) and to take advantage of public services that will help the family and the child. Much the same may be said about muscular dystrophy (MD), which is almost always diagnosed in the early childhood years. Prompt intervention, particularly with physical and occupational therapy, can help to delay the all but inevitable declines in physical capacity that are characteristic of MD, while art therapy can help children to express and deal with their feelings about mortality.

Most early-intervention services are provided in the home, and some are offered in early-intervention centers. For families of children who are medically fragile/technology-dependent, in particular, an important early-intervention service is respite care. In this intervention, early-childhood workers assume responsibility for caring for the child for a day or a weekend, giving family members a much needed break.

Related Services

This section reviews what Part B of the IDEA calls related services and what Part C refers to as early-intervention services. Regardless of the name, these services can be the make-or-break elements in education of students with physical or health conditions. Major related services are physical and occupational therapy, speech and language pathology, counseling, art therapy and transition.

Physical therapists generally work on gross-motor control and on prevention of atrophy in muscles. They regard "movement science" as the core of their profession (Heriza & Sweeney, 1994). That is, physical therapy is concerned with motor behavior, not with possible underlying neurological causes (Heriza & Sweeney, 1995). Occupational therapists, by contrast, focus more on fine-motor control and on daily-life functioning. Their focus is upon helping people *do* physical tasks that are important to them. Some experts say that physical therapists focus on the lower limbs and the trunk while occupational therapists are concerned more with upper extremities, but that exaggerates the case. During the pre-K years, the differences between the two are minimal; occupational and physical therapists work hand in hand, and often interchangeably, with infants, toddlers, and preschool-age children.

Physical and occupational therapists are especially needed with children, youth, and adults who have cerebral palsy. Traditionally, therapy for these individuals has focused upon following developmental sequences; that is, children and youth with cerebral palsy were led through the same stages of mobility that children with no disabilities pass through: crawling, standing, walking, etc. Even if these capacities had not developed by the middle-school or high-school years, students were still trained on them. In

What Do Speech and Language Pathologists Do?

- Screen for articulation, breathing, feeding, and related problems
- Assess ability to express oneself in speech and in other ways (gestures, sign language, communication boards, etc.)
- Assess ability to use age-appropriate language (muteness, echolalia, language delays, etc.)
- Identify goals and interventions
- Monitor progress toward goals
- Identify, order, adjust, and train the individual to use adaptive devices such as communication boards
- Serve as a team member

many respects, this was movement for its own sake. Today, the focus has shifted to a more functional approach. Physical and occupational therapists ask, "Movement for what?" The intent now is to emphasize development of meaningful capabilities—skills these people need on a day-to-day basis. Therapy focuses upon the movements individuals use to read and write, speak, feed themselves, etc. This is movement *for a purpose*. As such, it is, of course, more motivating for the students.

Counselors are most needed once transition planning begins, usually at about age 14. They bring a firsthand knowledge of the world beyond the school, especially of the demands of the workplace, to the multidisciplinary team that is working with the youth who has a disability to plan and carry out transition services. Also helpful, especially with traumatic brain injury and spinal cord injury, are art therapists.

A very important aspect of education for some students with severe physical or health conditions is the extent to which the public schools are expected to deliver what may be seen as medical or health-care services. The controlling guidance on this issue was provided by the U.S. Supreme Court in its decision in the case of *Irving Independent School District v. Tatro* (1984). The court recently reaffirmed this guidance in its 1999 decision in the case of *Cedar Rapids Community School District v. Garrett F.* (No. 96–1793). Both cases involved school-aged students whose physical disabilities required the provision of nursing services during the school day. In *Tatro,* as in *Garrett F.*, the Court determined that the public schools are obligated to deliver health-care services if the services (a) are required for the student because of a disability, (b) are essential in order for the child to participate in education, and (c) could be delivered by a nurse or other qualified person but do not necessitate delivery by a physician. On this and other issues surrounding services for children with severe health-care needs, Rapport (1996) provides a very useful summary of what the law requires.

What Do Art Therapists Do?

- Assess physical and cognitive abilities, including perception of others and self-image, and problem-solving skills
- Set goals for treatment
- Identify appropriate individual and group therapy interventions, including not only artwork but also discussion of one's work
- Serve as a team member

PHYSICAL THERAPY

Physical therapists help people with physical disabilities and health conditions to adjust to their limitations, maintain proper posture, and prevent muscle atrophy (wasting away or weakening). Positioning is particularly important. Seating, for example, should be functional: If writing, talking, feeding, etc., is desired, people should be leaning *forward* rather than reclining slightly backwards. Physical therapists also work on walking, balance, and other gross-motor skills. Students, clients, or patients may throw or kick balls or walk along treadmills so as to build up muscle tone and endurance.

Physical therapy is particularly needed in cases of AIDS, asthma, arthritis, cardiac conditions, cystic fibrosis, diabetes, muscular dystrophy, spinal cord injury, and spina bifida, as well as with cerebral palsy (as mentioned earlier).

For individuals with AIDS, physical therapists may offer myofacial release and craniosacral therapy as pain-reducing interventions. Limited exercise may also help to enhance endurance. It is important not to overdo such activities, because fatigue will set in rapidly.

Proper use of inhalers and supervised exercise to build up lung capacity are areas in which physical therapists can help people who have asthma. Training to build up endurance is a principal focus with this disability.

People with arthritis (see chapter 8) frequently benefit from physical therapy, especially in the areas of strengthening muscles and preventing stiffness. Swimming is an excellent exercise for many people who have arthritis.

With persons who have cerebral palsy, the physical therapist is particularly concerned with muscle atrophy. Muscles that are not used gradually lose strength. For maintaining strength and muscle tone, physical therapists may lead children, youth, and adults through resistance exercises where the objective is to push against something, such as a wall or stationary object; sometimes weights are used to increase the burden on the muscles (Damiano, Kelly, & Vaughn, 1995).

Another key concern of the physical therapist with people who have cerebral palsy is positioning. Breathing, eating, and attending to work or school tasks are enhanced when the individual is seated properly (Mayall & Deshamais, 1995). In many instances, special seating or positioning devices are necessary. These may be custom-designed (e.g., with specially cut wood or other material), or they may be commercially acquired materials. (Many local United Cerebral Palsy Association programs have staff members who custom-design wheelchairs, standers, and related products.) The aim is to keep the person in the posture most appropriate for accomplishing the tasks at hand.

Individuals who have cystic fibrosis need physical therapy of a particular kind on virtually a daily basis. The approach is one of "pounding" the chest so as to loosen mucus build-ups in the lungs. Such pounding, if done correctly, is not painful.

Regular exercise, together with dietary measures, is essential in management of diabetes. Indeed, most people with Type 2 diabetes are seriously overweight. Physical therapists can design and monitor suitable activity programs to help these people to maintain good health.

Daily stretching exercises are recommended to alleviate muscle contractures in children, youth, and adults who have muscular dystrophy (Deering, 1996a). In addition, Deering wrote, playing a musical instrument can assist in maintaining the lung capacity needed for effective breathing. Physical therapists can also help people with MD with ambulation (until a wheelchair is needed), positioning, transfer, and other physical tasks.

Spinal cord injury (SCI) presents challenges to physical therapists in a number of ways. One is to prevent or at least ameliorate the danger of pressure sores (decubitus ulcers). Most people with SCI eventually will develop pressure sores, but techniques are available that can postpone them for many years. Primary among them is regular shifting of weight. This is much easier for people with paraplegia than for those with quadriplegia, but even the latter have strategies they can adopt. Physical therapists can also teach individuals who have SCI how to monitor their health so as to prevent and treat urinary tract infections and autonomic dysreflexia (discussed in detail in chapter 6).

With traumatic brain injury, physical therapists may need to help an individual to relearn such basic skills as walking, writing, and typing. There also may be a need for training in physical mobility, endurance, and hand-eye coordination.

OCCUPATIONAL THERAPY

An *occupation* is any goal directed activity that "has meaning for the individual and forms a part of her personal identity" (Creek, 1997, p. 33). Mocellin (1992) adds that the aim is occupational competence or skill at performing that activity. The American Occupational Therapy Association (AOTA) (Hopkins & Smith, 1993) breaks down skills into sensorimotor, cognitive, and psychosocial components. Examples of sensorimotor components include motor skills such as gross- and fine-motor coordination. Illustrations of cognitive components include attention, memory, sequencing, and problem solving. Examples of psychosocial components are self-control and self-expression.

Occupational therapists assist individuals to learn how to do everyday tasks such as dressing, eating, and keeping house. These professionals often focus upon new ways of accomplishing practical tasks, especially with arms, hands, and fingers. They may prescribe and teach the person how to use assistive technology devices, including low-tech products such as large-grip scissors or other kitchen utensils and elongated reachers and graspers, as well as high-tech devices such as environmental control units (ECUs) or personal computers. ECUs are control devices that operate anything electrical that is plugged into an X-10 transmitter which, in turn, is connected to the ECU control unit via house wiring.

Occupational therapy is especially important in cases of AIDS, amputation, cerebral palsy, muscular dystrophy, spina bifida, and spinal cord injury, as well as with little people (dwarfs) and people who are medically fragile/technology-dependent.

Individuals who have AIDS often are fatigued. Occupational therapists can assist them in learning less taxing ways of dressing and performing other everyday tasks. They can also teach the universal precautions necessary to prevent the spread of the HIV virus that causes AIDS. Even people with the condition may not know, or regularly follow, those guidelines.

With people who have had limb amputation(s), occupational therapists select, fit, modify, and adjust artificial limbs. Such devices may be replaced every few years as the child grows. In addition, exercises to strengthen the residual limb often help, even if an artificial limb is used. The growing interest by people with amputations in an active lifestyle has fostered the growth of an industry in sporty artificial limbs. These devices are lighter yet stronger and often are flexible enough to use in sports and other activities.

In working with people who have cerebral palsy, occupational therapists are particularly concerned with supporting motions that are necessary for accomplishing everyday tasks. As with physical therapy (see preceding discussion), the focus today is upon meaningful activities. Thus, if the student is using a personal computer, the occupational therapist may order or even custom-design a plastic keyguard. Keyguards offer surfaces on which a hand or arm may rest, plus holes over the keys into which a finger must be inserted to strike the key. The aim is both to prevent the wrong keys from being hit and to guide the fingers to the right keys. Occupational therapists may also prescribe and teach the person how to use other low-tech devices to assist with dressing, eating, and other everyday tasks. For example, there are hooks that assist with securing buttons on shirts or coats, large-grip eating utensils, and special dishes that have curved sides that make spooning corn or green beans much easier.

Orthoses (devices that assist in a limb function) may be recommended for people who have muscular dystrophy. In addition, occupational therapists can train individuals with MD on brushing, dressing, and other everyday tasks; this is especially a need because MD involves a gradual deterioration in physical capacity such that new ways of doing things may need to be taught every few years.

Little people (dwarfs) often require special seating and positioning devices that occupational therapists can prescribe, acquire, and customize as needed. Chapter 8 offers more details about these needs.

SPEECH AND LANGUAGE PATHOLOGY

Speech and language pathologists facilitate the efforts of people to communicate with others. This may include using a communication board, a pointing device, a personal computer, or even sign language. Speech and language pathologists also work with children, youth, and adults on proper breathing techniques and on feeding. In recent years, they have focused more upon working with language disorders, which is why the name of the profession was changed from "speech pathology" to "speech and language pathology."

Speech and language pathology is most often used with children who have cerebral palsy, some cancers (e.g., oral cancer), and traumatic brain injury, as well as with people who have such secondary conditions as deafness/hearing loss, learning disabilities, attention deficit disorder (ADD), or attention deficit hyperactivity disorder (ADHD).

With children, youth, and adults who have cerebral palsy, speech and language pathologists focus upon clear articulation. This is a demanding task for many people with cerebral palsy, because many hundreds of small muscles are involved in producing intelligible speech. Even after years of guided practice, people with severe cerebral palsy may still have difficulty making themselves understood. In such instances, speech and language pathologists may teach the individual how to use a communication board or an electronic device such as a Canon Communicator® or a Dynavox® machine. Another prominent goal of speech and language pathologists in working with people who have cerebral palsy is feeding. Many hours of guided practice often are required for the individual to train his or her muscles for proper chewing and swallowing in addition to placing food in the mouth with minimal spillage.

COUNSELING

Counseling professionals may be school or guidance counselors who focus mostly on helping children and youth to overcome emotional difficulties or other problems that interfere with academic success, or they may be rehabilitation counselors, working primarily to assist individuals to explore career options, learn job-related skills, and get and retain a paying job.

Counseling is a related service that is particularly helpful for many individuals with amputations, epilepsy, muscular dystrophy and other terminal conditions, spinal cord injury, and traumatic brain injury, as well as children and youth who are victims of child abuse and neglect. It is also helpful with persons who have a later age at onset. In general, when disability occurs prior to, at, or soon after birth, the person has no independent memory of being an able-bodied individual; however, when the age at onset is later, especially if it is in the teen years, there may be an internal struggle in which the "me" (able-bodied person) is at war with the "body" (the newly disabled person). This struggle often manifests itself as anger. Counseling, together with applied behavior analysis (see chapter 4), may be required to help the individual to control the anger and to channel it in more productive ways.

Amputation, involving as it does the loss of a limb, may call for counseling. People need to come to terms with the need for amputation and then to adjust to the artificial limb if one is used, as well as to deal with the loss itself.

With individuals who have epilepsy, one aim of counseling is to assist the individual in deciding how much to reveal about the condition, when, and to whom. The option of "passing" as an able-bodied person is open to many people with epilepsy, especially if the condition is well controlled by medication. However, fear of exposing themselves by having a seizure may lead these same people to withdraw from or even avoid social interactions. Counselors can help these people to weigh the pros and cons of disclosure and to determine the optimum timing of any such revelation.

Spinal cord injury (SCI) is one disability that often calls for counseling. SCI frequently is followed by depression; drug and other substance abuse is common; suicide rates are high. All of this makes counseling an urgent service for many individuals who sustain SCIs. At root is the fact that many people who have SCI were physically active individuals who sustained the injury during adolescence or early adulthood. As suggested earlier in this chapter, this may lead to an internal war in which the individual struggles to reconcile the self with the new reality of physical constraints. The person's self-concept must be radically reconstructed from an image of an individual for whom physical accomplishments are a major source of identity to one for whom physical achievements become of secondary importance. Counselors must first deal with the anger that this war produces. The aim is to show the person ways that important goals can still be reached or, failing that, to work with the individual to identify and find ways of reaching new goals. Peer counseling—where people who have lived for some time with SCI counsel newly injured individuals—is a particularly effective technique for accomplishing this task. Once the path toward important goals becomes clear, the anger often dissipates.

One strategy is to develop new interests and capabilities that can be pursued despite the injury. Another is to get and learn to use sporty wheelchairs so as to continue to participate in lifelong interests in physical activities. Finally, counseling is a large part of transition services. If the SCI occurred during the high-school years, the individual's career goals may need to be altered so as to comport with the realities of the injury. Alternatively, counseling can help the individual to realize that cherished goals are still attainable, but with new strategies and tactics for reaching them.

With traumatic brain injury (TBI), counseling often is a key component of an overall plan. TBI frequently leads to personality changes, which can be discomfiting for family members and friends, so much so, in fact, that one sad consequence of TBI often is that friends are lost. Counselors can help the individual to learn why this happens and to develop strategies for keeping old friends and for developing new ones. Counseling also is required for family members (and, if possible, for friends) so that they develop realistic expectations. Frequently, the fact that the individual looks the same misleads these significant others to expect that the "old" person will reemerge. Family and friends also may anticipate complete and rapid recovery, whereas reality may be that recovery is partial and occurs slowly over a period of time.

Children and youth who are victims of child abuse and neglect often are in need of counseling. They need to learn to trust others, learn to share their feelings, and acquire good study habits despite the problems caused by their emotions.

One issue that frequently surfaces in counseling with youth and adults is Supplemental Security Income (SSI). As was mentioned in chapter 2, teachers, counselors, therapists, and others working with individuals who have disabilities need to be aware of SSI as an option for people who have very limited vocational potential. The purpose of SSI is to keep people out of abject poverty. When looked at in that way, SSI has been a successful program.

There is another side to SSI, however. For people who have the ability to earn more than minimum wage at a job, SSI may actually present an obstacle to their success. The program contains significant work disincentives. First, by offering monthly checks to which people feel entitled and which they could lose if they worked, it discourages them from working to their potential. People, particularly adolescents, often feel that they have a right to SSI checks; accordingly, they deliberately set out to satisfy the Social Security Administration's requirements for eligibility in the program. Second, by constraining assets to some $2,000, SSI restricts people from embarking upon serious job searches. Finding a good job can take several months to a year and requires outlays for transportation, presentable clothing, and other search-related items. All of that is difficult to afford on a severely limited asset base. Finally, by tying Medicaid eligibility to SSI enrollment, Congress has all but forced people with severe disabilities who have and expect to continue to have high medical expenses, yet who fear they would not be able to get a job that offers commensurate health coverage, to seek to become and remain eligible for SSI. (As this was written, Congress was considering various proposals to separate Medicaid from SSI. For updates on this issue, call the SSA on 1-800-772-1213. This toll-free line is staffed from 7 a.m. to 7 p.m., Eastern time, M–F.)

Counselors should also tell individuals with physical or health conditions about the Health Insurance Portability and Accountability Act of 1996. This law forbids employers and their health insurers from excluding preexisting conditions (another term for disabilities) for more than one year. Thus, if an individual takes a job with a company that offers health coverage but whose insurer refuses to reimburse expenses related to a preexisting condition, the individual is assured of such coverage after waiting one calendar year. In addition, someone who worked for one company and had medical coverage for a condition for more than 12 months may leave that company and begin work at another company without jeopardizing medical coverage. The new employer and its insurance carrier must cover the disability (preexisting condition) immediately, with no exclusion period permitted.

The law also tightened the definition for *preexisting condition*. The condition must be one that was diagnosed by a physician *and* for which treatment was recommended, again by a physician, within the preceding 6 months. Thus, someone who is deaf and who has not sought treatment for the hearing loss in recent months cannot be denied reimbursement of expenses related to that hearing loss. In addition, genetic conditions—such as a predisposition for some disease—are *not* preexisting conditions under the law.

Other laws are also important in providing medical coverage for people with physical or health disabilities. One of the most important is known as COBRA (Consolidated Omnibus Budget Resolution Act), which requires employers to offer people who leave their employ continued participation in employer-sponsored health plans for up to 18 months after these people leave the employer. The individual pays the premiums. Coverage may be ended only when the individual secures participation in another health plan.

Dealing with Medicare is another story altogether. As was noted in chapter 2, Medicare's original purpose (and still its primary one) is to provide medical coverage for older Americans. People who are under 65 years of age and get Medicare through SSDI thus have to fight a system that is geared to meet the needs of a very different population. Braunstein (1997) offered a telling example in the story of Vicki O'Neal, a 32-year-old former schoolteacher. O'Neal has quadriplegia, for which reason she needs home health-care workers to assist her in getting out of bed, using the rest room, and dressing. She received those services until the home health agency realized that she often went out of her home for shopping, recreation, etc. At that point, Medicare ended her home health-care services on the grounds that she was not homebound. Medicare requires that people receiving home health-care services leave the home only at times that are "infrequent and for periods of relatively short duration" and that such excursions outside the home "require considerable and taxing effort."

O'Neal eventually got the services back by convincing a judge that her medical status remained unchanged. Still, she worries that the services could be cut off again at any time and that many other individuals face similar restrictions. The Medicare rules are clearly absurd—without home health-care services, O'Neal could not even get out of bed and dressed in the morning. With those services, she can use her motorized wheelchair to get around in the community and to live an enjoyable and active life. Interpreted strictly, as these rules were initially in O'Neal's case, O'Neal is entitled to home health-care services only if she remains in her home all day, nearly every day, very rarely making trips outside the house. O'Neal interpreted that to mean that she may exist but not truly live. This is an illustration of how the Medicare program often does not fit the needs of persons under 65 with disabilities.

ART THERAPY

Art therapy is a service that offers benefits similar to counseling (Wald, 1989). It is particularly helpful to individuals who are coping with strong emotions, as are some persons who have spinal cord injury (SCI) or traumatic brain injury (TBI) and many who have muscular dystrophy or other often fatal conditions. Art therapists assess the individual's physical and cognitive abilities, particularly the person's self-image, and then design ways for the person to "release rage against bodily assault" and to "ventilate fear" (Wald, 1989, p. 186). The aim is to help the individual to shape and accept a new self-image, restore self-esteem, and increase motivation.

The assignment to "draw a person" offers an opportunity to express one's sense of self, but at a distance, because one is drawing not oneself but rather some nameless "person." The task of "drawing the person sitting across from you" can yield insights into the individual's perceptive skills. Finally, the person may be asked to draw himself or herself. The art therapist notices whether the person minimizes or emphasizes the disability in this drawing, looking to see whether there is acceptance or rejection of the disabled body. Anger and confusion often can be seen in drawings and can be explored further in counseling sessions.

Especially with TBI, the art therapist assesses the individual's developing insight, problem-solving ability, and attention span. As we will see in chapter 7, many people with TBI have difficulty perceiving a logical sequence of problem-solving behavior, particularly with respect to identifying the precise nature of the problem and recognizing alternative possibilities for solving it. These problems may first surface in art therapy, in cognitive exercises such as drawing four-panel cartoons illustrating how a hypothetical individual solves a problem, and in group art therapy sessions where group members comment on each other's drawings.

TRANSITION

The IDEA requires that transition from high school to life after high school be part of the IEP of all students with disabilities aged 14 or over. It also calls for transition from early-intervention programs to preschool special-education programs when children turn 3 years of age. An excellent summary of these IDEA transition processes was offered by Repetto and Correa (1996). In the article, "Expanding Views of Transition," the authors outlined the steps that educators, students, and family members should follow to fashion successful transitions. (The Repetto and Correa article is somewhat dated because it was written prior to the 1997 IDEA amendments; however, the essential points in the article remain valid.)

Beakley and Yoder (1998) insisted that transition services should begin during the middle-school years (Grades 6 through 8). During those years, students can learn how to travel in the community, how to navigate architectural and other barriers, and how to buy things in community stores. The middle-school years are also optimal for students to begin initial career exploration—becoming aware of different job requirements so that when they prepare to enter 9th grade, they can make informed decisions about college-prep versus other course tracks.

With students who have physical or health conditions, the most important transition is the one from high school to life after high school. The key question in this transition is what the student aspires to do. The transition process is an excellent opportunity for 14-year-old and older students to begin asserting independence in setting career and life goals.

If postsecondary education is a goal, enrolling the student in precollege courses is an obvious step. Less obvious but equally important is preparing the student to face realities of transportation and housing, student support services, and other aspects of college life. In particular, accessible housing and daily transportation must be arranged. Both may be difficult to secure (see chapters 12 and 13). Federal laws, specifically the ADA and Section 504, require colleges and universities to provide *some* accessible dorm rooms and *some* accessible transportation on campus. However, the student may well have to work closely with college special-services staff to make sure that lift-equipped buses run on the routes the student needs and on the days and times the student needs to use them.

This introduces another key component of transition. While children and youth attending public schools enjoy rights whether or not they explicitly request them, this is not the case for college students, who must "self-identify" as requiring support services in order to receive them. The transition phase during high school is a good time to acquaint students with this and other differences between high school and college. An illustration is offered by the experiences of Brooke Ellison at Harvard, which the 18-year-old entered 6 years after sustaining a spinal cord injury in a car accident. Many buildings at Harvard do have elevators, though small ones; many doors in classroom buildings are barely wide enough to accommodate a wheelchair; many ramps are surprisingly steep. Brooke's motorized wheelchair occasionally stops working or becomes unpredictably jerky. Yet Brooke gets around. She does so because Harvard's special-services coordinator Louise Russell mounted a $10,000 renovation of the dorm room Brooke uses and made countless other access modifications throughout the campus. "We're relying on [Brooke] to tell us what still has to be done," Russell said (quoted in Abrams, 1996).

When the high-school student's goal is to work after school, different priorities arise. Again, transportation looms large as a problem. Accessible and affordable transportation is needed between the school and the sites of work-study, apprenticeship, or other work activities. Accommodations allowing the individual to perform tasks that he or she is qualified to do must be identified and made. The student needs to be taught about the importance of rules at the workplace, particularly about unwritten rules and about the nature of teamwork on the job. The change between rules in high school about what to wear and being on time and the much more rigid rules regarding the same things at work is one that many students find jarring. Later, near graduation time, if a job is found, the student needs to arrange both transportation and housing convenient to that job.

Some students will neither go to college nor begin work immediately following high school. For these students, transition to a life of relative independence requires much planning and work. These students may need to learn how to use public transportation, negotiate barely accessible features of the community (in particular, the "readily achievable" modifications that small businesses made to obey Title III of the ADA—changes that may bring them into compliance with the law but may not meet each individual's needs), and conduct transactions in stores and other community businesses with minimal need for assistance from other people.

Adaptive technology should be considered in all three kinds of transition. It is important to bear in mind that students need to become acquainted with and learn how to use adaptive devices and software programs *before* they have to use them in college, on the job, or in the community (see chapter 5). It is asking too much of most students to require them to deal with all the pressures inherent in new situations, such as a job, and at the same time begin to learn about technology. In these three types of transition, too, self-assertiveness by the student is a definite plus. Some ideas on fostering such active participation by students with disabilities are discussed in the following section.

Reporting on a longitudinal study of transition, Malian and Love (1998) highlighted the importance of training for students in the areas of handling money, exploring careers, and engaging in the job search. Students who successfully completed high school were contrasted with students who had dropped out of high school. Parents of both groups of students were interviewed. Malian and Love found that "completers" and their parents reported more services provided, especially in counseling and job-hunting skills, than was the case with dropouts and their parents. They also discovered that training in teamwork, or working cooperatively with others on the job, is an important component for successful transition to the world of work. Malian and Love urged educators to identify early those students who are at risk of dropping out (e.g., those who were kept back one or more years, those who have failed one or more courses) and provide those students with extra attention and additional training in coping strategies.

Advocacy

Teachers, counselors, therapists, and other professionals need to advocate on behalf of students, clients, and patients who have physical or health disabilities. While the laws discussed in this book are powerful, vigorous advocacy is necessary for the promises they offer to be translated into reality at the local level. Paradis (1998), for example, recounts example after example of instances in which people had rights but realized them only after litigation or other advocacy efforts forced entities subject to civil rights laws to honor those rights.

One essential step is to teach advocacy skills to students, clients, and patients. Battle, Dickens-Wright, and Murphy (1998) offered guidelines for this. They suggested that professionals begin by affirming the right of the individual to make his or her own decisions and to play an active role in meetings that are called to develop IEPs and Individualized Plans for Employment (IPEs). Such meetings allow students, clients, and patients with physical or health conditions to learn competencies in identification of problems and alternative solutions, as well as giving them opportunities to practice assertiveness skills. Students, clients, and patients learn how to negotiate with professionals and parents so that they can choose goals important to them as well as methods or approaches toward those goals that they feel comfortable using. Over time, individuals with physical or other disabilities will become effective self-advocates. The abilities to assume responsibility for one's own life and to identify and develop solutions to one's own problems are competencies that will help these individuals throughout their lifetime.

Other suggestions were offered by Van Reusen, Bos, Schumaker, and Deshler (1994) in their *The Self-Advocacy Strategy for Education and Transition Planning*. The manual features sections on motivating students for self-advocacy and on getting them to assume responsibility for their own actions in this area. The aim is to help students to set goals, identify resources they have available to help them to reach those goals, set forth a strategy, identify specific tactics to make progress toward the goals, and assess how they are doing over time. The manual is somewhat limited in utility with respect to people with physical or health conditions because of its emphasis upon reaching students with intellectual limitations.

An important resource is a book by Fred Pelka, *The ABC-CLIO Companion to the Disability Rights Movement* (1997). The book offers thumbnail sketches and inspiring life stories of the key leaders of America's disability rights movement. It also summarizes in easy-to-read ways the important laws that have transformed accessibility in the United States.

A resource provided by the American Bar Association (ABA) may help individuals with physical, health, or sensory limitations who need to consult a lawyer in order to secure removal of barriers or to protect their civil rights.

At www.abanet.org/disability, the ABA offers a nationwide directory of attorneys, many of whom are themselves persons with disabilities, who practice disability law. The directory is a project of the ABA Commission on Mental and Physical Disability Law, which also oversees publication of the highly respected journal *Mental and Physical Disability Law Reporter*. The commission's chair is a judge from Wisconsin who has a hearing loss, while another commission member is an attorney who is blind. The commission may be contacted via E-mail at empdl@abanet.org or by telephone on 1-202-662-1570 (voice) and 1-202-662-1012 (TTY). More than 3,000 lawyers are known to the ABA as practicing full- or part-time in the area of disability law.

Holicky (1996) cautioned individuals with disabilities to be careful about litigation. Although personal injury lawyers may claim to be able to win judgments in the millions of dollars, Holicky pointed out that such victories are few and far between. The typical damages lawsuit takes a minimum of 2 years, he wrote, and appeals might add another 2 years to the process. While many local, county, and state governments might seem to be tempting targets when they fail to comply with the ADA or other laws, Holicky noted that they can and frequently do place caps on their liabilities. Florida, for example, does not permit anyone to sue the state for more than $100,000. Even if someone were to win a case, Holicky observed, he or she may see few if any spoils of victory after paying the lawyer, expert witnesses, and other expenses. Finally, Holicky concluded, litigation can take over the individual's life. People may very well make far more constructive use of that time and energy. Gregg Trapp (1998) offered similar cautions.

It is much easier to file a complaint. Most of the ADA is enforced by the U.S. Department of Justice, which employs 30 attorneys specifically to carry out the ADA. The Disability Rights Section head John Wodatch reports that DoJ has "been inundated" by complaints under Titles II and III of the Act (which are handled by DoJ). To date, more than 3,500 complaints have been closed, most of them by means of settlements between the Department of Justice and the alleged offender. Justice has had to litigate only a handful of cases. Suggestions on filing complaints are provided in chapter 11.

Questions for Reflection and Discussion

1. What is special education, and why do many children and youth with physical or health disabilities not require it?

2. Give 2 examples of related services.

3. Why is "inclusion" a misinterpretation of the Individuals with Disabilities Education Act?

4. How do the roles of physical therapists and occupational therapists differ?

5. With which populations of interest in this book might art therapists make important contributions?

6. Why are counselors particularly important for adolescents aged 14 and over?

7. Use the "war" concept to differentiate how people might react differently to cerebral palsy than to spinal cord injury.

8. What is the standard of care that *Tatro* sets for public schools?

9. What are the most common placements for students with orthopedic impairments?

10. Name the 3 major directions for transition from high school.

Resources

American Occupational Therapy Association (AOTA)
4720 Montgomery Lane
P.O. Box 31220
Bethesda, MD 20824-1220
1-301-652-2682
www.etown.edu/home/ot/aota.html

American Physical Therapy Association (APTA)
1111 North Fairfax Street
Alexandria, VA 22314
1-800-999-2782
1-703-684-2782
E-mail: practice@apta.org
www.apta.org

American Speech-Language-Hearing Association (ASHA)
10801 Rockville Pike
Rockville, MD 20852
1-800-638-8255
1-301-897-5700
E-mail: webmaster@asha.org
www.asha.org

Council for Exceptional Children
1920 Association Drive
Reston, VA 20191-1589
1-703-620-3660
E-mail: cec@cec.sped.org
www.cec.sped.org/home.htm

4

TECHNIQUES

When he was 7 years old, "Bob" sustained a traumatic brain injury (TBI) when he hit a tree while riding on his bike. That was 2 years ago. Since then, Bob has done well in school. However, he has major problems in the areas of self-control, planning, and persevering at a task. Changes in routine especially seem to upset Bob, who has his teacher's permission to leave the classroom briefly when this happens. Bob benefits greatly from use of manipulatives that make information concrete. He often needs repeated directions and instructions. Bob's teachers, parents, and others (including substitute teachers) work together as a team to give Bob the structure he needs in order to learn (Witte, 1998).

Teamwork

Teamwork is the key word in today's leading-edge programs serving individuals with physical or health disabilities. Early-intervention program staff are accustomed to working as a team because Part C (Infants and Toddlers) of the Individuals with Disabilities Education Act (IDEA) has always required multidisciplinary approaches and because the services for families and their infants or toddlers usually are delivered in the home by a team of interventionists (Bowe, 2000). In K–12 education, however, occupational and physical therapists and speech pathologists usually have worked independently of the classroom teacher.

That is changing now. Closer cooperation between educators, therapists, and counselors is necessitated by several trends. One is the tremendous diversity of needs of children, youth, and adults who have physical or health conditions. Such diversity is the reason this chapter opens with a discussion of teamwork.

The chapter then looks at those individuals who can participate in regular academics and, later, in regular paid employment. These persons usually have average or above-average intelligence. Some have pressing health needs for which such related services as occupational and physical therapy are essential. Given such assistance, these individuals can take part in mainstream activities. Others need only minor adjustments (e.g., extended time to complete tasks, release time to take medication). Again, with these accommodations, this group can and should participate in regular activities. Working with this group is the topic of the following section, which includes a discussion of the concept of "universal design" as it applies to education.

A second group of individuals with physical or health disabilities can take part in some regular education activities but only when modifications are made in the curricula and when substantial assistance from specially trained personnel is made available. More often, individuals in this group are educated in resource rooms, separate classrooms, and even separate schools. In general, members of this group have normal or near-normal intelligence. They often have a secondary condition such as learning disability, a hearing impairment, or epilepsy. We will discuss this group in the section entitled "Modified Curricula."

Finally, members of a third group of individuals with physical or health disabilities have significantly limited intellectual capabilities, so much so that special curricula rather than regular education in schools as well as day activity programs rather than having students work after school are necessary. We will examine the needs of this population in the section entitled "Responding to Multiple Needs."

In the Mainstream

Success by students with physical or health disabilities in the regular classroom is most likely when schools practice **collaborative teaching** by general and special educators (Logan & Malone, 1998). The presence of special educators in the regular classroom allows for individualized attention to the special needs of students with severe physical disabilities. Logan and Malone

(1998), examining teaching patterns in integrated classrooms, found that when special educators collaborate with general educators, the result is far more individualized attention for special-education than for general-education students in the classroom. With respect to functional behavior goals (e.g., self-care, independent travel skills), which typically are not part of the general curriculum, special educators and therapists are particularly important. We will explore this kind of instruction later in this chapter in the section entitled "A Parallel Curriculum".

The medical model is particularly visible with respect to related services such as occupational or physical therapy (OT, PT) and speech and language pathology (SLP). The typical pattern in K–12 schools has been for the related-services personnel to pull out the child from the classroom and deliver services in some other location (Kerrin, 1996). Similarly, therapists commonly have set their own goals for children and used their own methods of reinforcement of desired behaviors. Therapy—whether OT, PT, or SLP—usually has been packaged as, say, twice-weekly sessions of 35 minutes each for the duration of the school year. Such "packages" rarely reflect differential needs of children, youth, and adults with varying severities of disabilities. Rather, the practice is convenient for clinic- or hospital-based practitioners (Hanf & Feinberg, 1997).

This medical-model approach has other important shortcomings. When therapists follow a medical-model approach, little or no continuity exists between the teacher's instructions and the therapists' interventions. That is, the therapists typically do not know what the educator is teaching or what types and schedules of reinforcement the educator is using. For these reasons, therapy sessions have seldom built upon and advanced the educator's goals for the child.

Similarly, the speech or motor activities the child engages in while in therapy frequently have borne little or no relation to educational goals. All too often, speech, fine-motor, and gross-motor activities have been pursued without regard to accomplishing educational objectives that are important for the child. When occupational or physical therapy or speech and language pathology activities are conducted for their own sake, the child may find them uninteresting or unmotivating because they seem to be pointless. By contrast, when speech, language, or movement activities are pursued as means to an educationally relevant goal, such activities take on meaning, and doing them becomes much more motivating for the child.

Meeting the needs of students requires that program staff maximize the productive use of time. The technique of pullout consumes considerable time as the child moves or is assisted to and from the therapy room. This usually is nonproductive time, both on the part of the therapist and on the part of the child. Some programs are trying "push-in" as a means of eliminating that dead time in the school day.

Another reason that cutting-edge programs are moving toward teamwork (to anticipate the topic of chapter 5) is that the availability of assistive technology radically alters the kinds of curricula teachers may pursue with these students. Take, for example, a student with cerebral palsy who cannot speak, write legibly, or turn pages independently. Were assistive technology devices and services not available, the curriculum this child pursues probably would need to be watered down to a significant degree. With such technology, however, the student likely can pursue the standard curriculum because software and hardware can be the student's "voice" while keyguards, mouthsticks, and other products make typing possible, and mechanical products can turn pages. Technology has similar and equally dramatic effects on the employment of adults with such disabilities. For these reasons, the knowledge and skills of occupational and physical therapists in the selection and use of technologies has become more critical than ever for the classroom teacher.

Finally, public school budgetary realities mean that, as one article's title put it, "School 'Nurse' Increasingly Is a Layman: Hiring Lag Gives Staff, Teachers, More Duties" (O'Hanlon, 1997). Educators must assume some responsibilities once left to staff members trained in other professions—in this case, nursing. Teamwork reduces duplication, thus saving money. With respect to adults, the expectation is that individuals with disabilities, helped by appropriate technologies, would perform most of the needed self-care tasks themselves.

Integration of students with and without disabilities is most easily accomplished when the curriculum and all the materials used in it are accessible to everyone. The term we use to describe this is *universal design,* a topic that was introduced in chapter 2 and will be discussed as it applies to buildings and other aspects of the built environment in chapter 11. This chapter focuses only on its applications in education.

Universal Design in Education

Universal design is a way of thinking that is recommended in buildings and consumer products. This same mode of thinking helps us, too, in developing curricula and course materials. Here, universal design is primarily a matter of attending to three issues. First, the amount of material that needs to be handled by students needs to be reduced. To illustrate, instead of requiring all students to read bound textbooks, the teacher might make at least some of the reading material available on floppy disk. This one small step—after all, most teaching materials (including, for that matter, this textbook) were first created on disk—can help many students with cerebral palsy, arthritis, quadriplegia, and other disabilities. Second, any videos shown to the class should be captioned. This helps some students who are hearing impaired or learning disabled. Finally, print materials should be made available in appropriate media (large type, Braille, and on audiocassette); any videos used should also be video-described, which helps people who are blind or have low vision, as well as some who are learning disabled.

A good resource is *Access to Multimedia Technology by People with Sensory Disabilities,* issued in 1998 by the National Council on Disability. The report's principal author, Paul Schroeder of the American Foundation for the Blind, is himself a person who is blind. He noted that most of these steps have been followed for years by materials developers who were working under a federal grant or contract. It is only in the past several years that the term *universally designed curriculum* has come into use to describe these efforts.

One important development in this area is the emergence of the World Wide Web (WWW) as, in effect, a huge library of "books" with no pages to turn. Insofar as the "pages" on Web sites are accessible—today, a tenuous assumption but something that is becoming more and more commonplace—the information one may find on the Web is a terrific way to extend the boundaries of knowledge for students and working adults alike. The main key to making Web pages accessible is "text" (unadorned words). Text is the graphics-free format that LYNX, a browser widely used by people who are blind or have dyslexia, presents. Competing browsers, such as Netscape's Navigator®, offer up both graphics and text.

As an example, consider the Web site for Plane Math (www.planemath. com). Created with assistance from scientists at the National Aeronautics and Space Administration (NASA), this site teaches mathematical concepts by asking students to consider problems they might encounter in dealing with airplanes. The site has been designed so that users immediately encounter a text version of the material (the accessible version), and only upon selecting a graphics-rich alternative would they see an inaccessible version. Another example is Chemtutor (www.chemtutor.com), which offers high-school and college-level chemistry material. Chemtutor has some graphics, but overall it is a text-friendly site.

And then there is **distance learning.** When people can enroll in and "attend" classes from remote locations, even from their living room, the technology required to connect distance-learning students and the professor/students on site can also enhance the accessibility of the course for all students. Such courses frequently make heavy use of electronic mail (E-mail); students send questions and professors reply with answers via E-mail systems. Students may also attach term papers to E-mail messages. By distributing course materials through E-mail rather than (or in addition to) on paper, professors give students options on how to "read" the information. If the student is blind or has dyslexia, it is a simple matter to listen to a speech synthesizer articulate the material aurally. Students may also research papers using the Web or other Internet resources, such as "gopher" (a text-based information retrieval system developed at the University of Minnesota that presents choices in list form, with each option accompanied by a number). Again, the information is offered electronically and may be listened to rather than read.

Distance learning can also be provided in a format that stresses independent study by students rather than the traditional lecture-and-note-taking format. Such approaches may appeal to older learners as well as to students with some kinds of learning disabilities (Schneider, Glass, Henke, & Overton, 1997). If universally designed, distance learning opens up opportunities for individuals with physical or health disabilities by obviating the need to physically travel to each class.

Rochester Institute of Technology supports a Web site known as "EASI" (Equal Access to Software Information) at www.rit.edu/~easi/. This site provides assistance on making educational materials accessible. It also offers details on distance-learning courses that the EASI project sponsors.

Modified Curricula

Many states are setting higher academic achievement standards for K–12 students, including those who have physical or health impairments as well as those who also have secondary conditions. Christine Pawelski, Ed.D., Director of Smeal Learning Center at the National Center for Disability Services on New York's Long Island, believes that team teaching can help students to reach state academic standards, in part by conserving valuable instructional time. The center's school, which specializes in educating students with physical disabilities, asks educators and therapists alike to find ways to collaborate so that students can master more material. Integration of educational and therapeutic interventions makes better use of available time. For students to achieve at the higher levels, therapists need to understand enough about the day-to-day curricula teachers are following to integrate those curricula into therapy sessions.

Integration works the other way, too. Physical and occupational therapy techniques, as well as speech and language skills, must be practiced not only in PT, OT, or SLP sessions but also throughout the day. This inevitably means that teachers and teacher aides must learn and use such PT/OT strategies and tactics as good positioning and such speech and language approaches as modeling. (Modeling is discussed later in this section and later in the chapter under "Applied Behavior Analysis.")

All of this requires that the educator inform the therapists about the educational objectives being pursued in the classroom; such communication gives the therapists opportunities to modify their own routines so as to work toward these same objectives. Similarly, the therapists must advise the educator about the child's needs with respect to and progress toward therapeutic objectives. Such information lets the teacher look for and reinforce classroom instances in which the child displays the desired speech, language, or physical capabilities.

One means of accomplishing teacher-therapist communication is being demonstrated at United Cerebral Palsy Association of Nassau County (UCPA-Nassau), in Roosevelt, New York. Teachers write a one-page synopsis of each child's goals for the day. As therapists enter the classroom, they can see at a glance what the child needs to work on; similarly, teachers can check the sheet to determine which scheduled activities have been completed by the therapists. It seems to be a simple enough idea, but the one-page synopsis greatly facilitates teacher-therapist collaboration.

Similarly, the belief that movement on the children's part should always be purposive motivated physical therapists at the UCPA-Nassau school to experiment with the use of **virtual reality (VR)** technologies. Wearing VR goggles permits students to "explore" far-flung geographical locations as they "walk" through imaginary settings (some of which, much to the point, they could not otherwise visit because of physical barriers). While still experimental at the school, VR promises to enliven physical therapy sessions by teaching and entertaining students while they engage in PT activities.

The following are some approaches being used in cutting-edge programs serving children and youth with physical or health disabilities who also have other limitations. These techniques respond primarily to those secondary conditions.

REPETITION

People with learning disabilities tend to have difficulty processing rapidly changing information. They may hear a sentence and then wonder, "Did I just hear 'bat'"? "Or was it 'pat'"? "Or maybe 'mat'"? While the student attempts to figure this out, the instructor's next sentence or sentences pass by without the student's being able to attend to them. This is why the first sentence should be repeated (Shaywitz, et al., 1998). Similarly, individuals with mild mental retardation may take longer to understand things, especially in the case of people with Down syndrome who may miss higher frequency sounds (Roizen, 1997). Educators, therapists, and counselors should repeat important things several times, using different words; they should also give examples.

MULTIPLE MODALITIES

Offering the same information via vision, hearing, and other senses (e.g., touching) often helps people who have different kinds of cognitive limitations as well as people with hearing or vision impairments. The personal computer can provide multiple-modality input while giving students opportunities to interact with the material, thus providing yet another vehicle for learning. (These uses of technology will be discussed in detail in chapter 5.) Using manipulatives also offers multiple modes of input.

MODELING

For individuals with cognitive limitations, showing the person what to do and how to do it has a great deal to recommend it. By demonstrating what is wanted, one provides very direct, very concrete instruction. Modeling avoids use of symbols, such as words, that may bear little obvious relation to their referents. (Modeling is discussed later in more detail under "Applied Behavior Analysis.")

SIGN LANGUAGE

For people who have difficulty speaking intelligibly, Signed English ("English on the hands") or even American Sign Language (a separate language with its own rules of grammar and syntax) may be used. Signs are particularly helpful for many children, youth, and adults whose cerebral palsy renders their voices indistinct. In addition, signs may be used as an *input* modality, especially for people with mild mental retardation. Unlike spoken words, many signs have direct relationships with the concepts they symbolize and for this reason are more easily learned and understood.

DESENSITIZATION

Individuals with recent traumatic brain injuries and some with learning disabilities are very easily distracted by various sights and sounds. One response of teachers, therapists, and counselors is to minimize such distractions in the classroom or therapy setting. Another is to make use of the brain's ability to habituate to distractions by placing students or clients into environments in which such distractions are gradually increased. In time, students and clients will become desensitized to these stimuli.

Responding to Multiple Needs

The third group we will discuss is sometimes referred to as students having multiple and profound impairments. Growing numbers of students and clients at programs serving people with physical or health disabilities have unusual genetic syndromes (e.g., "Joubert Syndrome," "Familial Dysautonomia," "−18Q Syndrome"); some are referred to as being "medically fragile, technology-dependent" individuals. In past decades, these syndromes often resulted in miscarriages (spontaneous abortions) or death at or shortly after birth. Today, medical technologies allow these people to live, albeit with multiple and severe conditions.

The syndromes have numerous effects. One is a sharp limitation of physical strength and mobility. Another is a severely reduced ability to express oneself through speech; many need to use communication boards or sign language. Some individuals have great difficulty in feeding themselves, even after years of training. Many have general health vulnerability such that they require one-on-one nursing care. In brief, these children and youth may not be able to stand alone or to walk, many cannot speak, some require tracheotomies for feeding, and others need constant supervision to keep them alive.

With many of these individuals, mental retardation accompanies physical or health disabilities. This is why we refer to their conditions as "multiple and profound." With such persons, major alterations are required in school curricula, in transition to life after high school, and in adult activities. This is because the cognitive limitations are primary in determining how these children and youth are educated.

The combined skills of team members often are required to meet these students' needs: special educators knowledgeable about modifying standard curricula and materials to accommodate for different learning styles or for learning disabilities, physical therapists trained in ways of preventing muscle atrophy, occupational therapists skilled in helping people to perform everyday tasks, and speech pathologists competent in training individuals in speech and language as well as in feeding.

Teaching, counseling, and providing therapy for such persons is qualitatively different from similar work with more cognitively capable individuals. The differences are so significant that I recommend that professionals, teachers-in-training, and others secure specialized texts focusing specifically upon this population. Although we will discuss here some approaches to working with this population, no attempt will be made in this book to duplicate the contributions of June Bigge's *Teaching Individuals with Physical and Multiple Disabilities* (New York: Merrill/Macmillan Publishing Company, 1991), Paul Wehman and John Kregel's *Functional Curriculum for Elementary, Middle, and Secondary Age Students with Special Needs* (Austin, TX: PRO-ED, 1997), and Jennifer Leigh Hill's *Meeting the Needs of Students with Special Physical and Health Care Needs* (Upper Saddle River, NJ: Merrill/Prentice Hall, 1999).

The Carman Road School in Massapequa Park, New York, like the UCPA-Nassau school, has specialized for many years in working with children and youth having multiple and profound limitations. Amy Rumelt, principal of the Carman Road School, explains that most of the school's students have severe or profound mental retardation in addition to their physical or health disabilities: "We have 20-year-olds functioning at the level of a 19-month-old, for example. Many of our students, even those in high school, read only at preprimer, primer, or third-grade reading levels." Linda Levy, assistant principal at the UCPA-Nassau school, concurs: "We need to focus upon functional goals, including self-help and daily living skills, with these children."

One approach used both at UCPA-Nassau and at the Carman Road School is known as MOVE (Mobility Opportunities Via Education). The approach was invented by Linda Bidabe in Bakersfield, California. The Kern County (Calif.) superintendent of schools and the Bruderhof Service Foundation in Rifton, New York, coordinate the program. The foundation of the program is its insistence that individuals with physical disabilities be given as many opportunities to move, especially to stand, as possible and that such movement should always be purposive. MOVE places great emphasis upon the use of adaptive technologies, specifically gait trainers and walkers. These products, as well as standing frames, potty chairs, activity chairs, and toddler chairs, are manufactured by Rifton Equipment.

The MOVE philosophy is one that asks educators, therapists, counselors, and others who work with individuals who have physical or health disabilities to perform an ecological analysis of what movements are needed for success in the current and in the postschool environments. Those movements should be taught first. The idea is to give the individual functionally useful capabilities. This thinking contrasts with approaches that hold that movements in the "normal" developmental sequence are the important ones to teach. Rather than teach children to crawl and then to walk, which of course is the usual developmental pattern, MOVE adherents believe that crawling be taught only if it is a necessary skill for the individual. According to MOVE, the most important movement skills probably will be sitting, standing, and walking. MOVE teaches that educators and therapists share responsibility for this instruction and should work as a team.

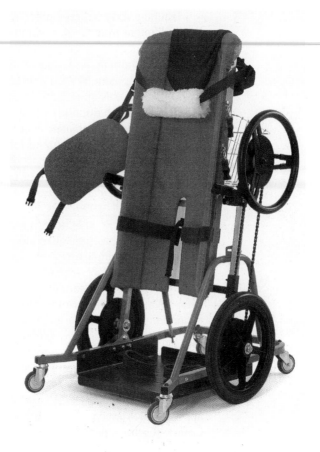

The MOVE (Mobility Opportunities Via Education) program
makes use of standers like this one, many of them
manufactured by Rifton Equipment.

MOVE teachers and therapists at UCPA-Nassau and at the Carman Road
School make frequent use of prone standers and supine standers that permit
children with severe physical limitations to stand up without assistance from
other people. (Prone standers let the child rest the chest against the unit,
while supine standers support the back. Both have firm straps, of course.)
This standing, which the children enjoy, seems to help them to breathe more
easily and to digest food more readily. Teachers and therapists have seen
beneficial effects. Reported UCPA-Nassau teacher Bill Goldstein: "They feel
better standing than sitting. Standing gives them a different 'look'—they
really do look more like 'regular kids' than they do when they are in the
chairs." Yet standing is done not for its own sake but rather as part of doing
something educationally relevant, for example, to wash their hands or to
paint pictures.

MOVE is similar to and different from conductive education (discussed
later in the chapter). The two approaches are similar in their insistence that
physical activity should always be meaningful. As Carman Road principal

Amy Rumelt observes, they differ in their use of technology: MOVE embraces it, and conductive education shuns it.

**A Parallel
Curriculum**

Even if they are served in general-education settings or other mainstream environments, many individuals with physical or health conditions still need extensive instruction in and therapy on ways of coping with their disabilities. For such students and clients, a **parallel curriculum** has much to recommend it. This approach provides the related services and special instructional services the students and clients need because of their disabilities (e.g., physical and occupational therapy, training in use of assistive technology devices) while the students and clients also receive academic instruction in traditional subject areas (e.g., English, history, math).

Logan and Malone (1998) studied such mixed curricula in general-education classrooms that had one or more students with quadriplegia and other severe physical disabilities. In these classrooms, the general educator tended to be the person who led the instruction in basic academic subjects. One would expect that. Special educators, in their roles as coteachers, offered one-on-one supplemental instruction and assistance to students with special needs but also provided instruction in functional areas such as personal care and transition training. Only rarely did special educators offer instruction or support to able-bodied students. Again, this is what one would expect. One of Logan and Malone's main conclusions from their observations was that separate classrooms are not necessarily required when students need individualized and functional instruction.

As suggested earlier, teachers, counselors, and therapists should strive to reach academic/vocational goals through these activities. That is, rather than follow a completely separate parallel curriculum, they should endeavor to integrate these abilities and skills into the larger curriculum. If the special educators have done their job right, the students already are motivated to achieve academic goals. By relating parallel curriculum activities to the same goal, teachers tap into this already existing motivation. Of course, for some students, especially those in our third group having multiple and profound disabilities, some of these activities *are* the curriculum because the students' intellectual limitations are so severe that academic instruction is minimal.

The following are specialized, or functional, areas of instruction and assistance that together constitute a parallel curriculum for students with physical or health disabilities.

USE OF ASSISTIVE TECHNOLOGIES

Children, youth, and adults who are blind make such heavy use of technologies today that learning how to use these devices comprises, for them, a major component of the parallel curriculum. Occupational therapists and speech pathologists have been trained in selecting appropriate devices, modifying them as needed to fit a given person's needs, training the person to use them, and assessing the individual's progress with them (Heriza & Sweeney, 1995).

It is not going too far to say that placement in a separate (e.g., specifically for preschoolers who are blind or have low vision) preschool precisely in order to focus upon mastering technologies is often an excellent way to prepare for integrated K–12 education. People who have cerebral palsy similarly need to take whatever time is needed to select, program, and learn to use augmentative communication devices, beginning with communication boards like the Dynavox® and progressing to regular personal computers. When speech-recognition technology matures, deaf students will need to learn how to use such devices to "hear" what others say.

Similarly, youth and adults need to understand important technologies well enough to appreciate what could go wrong with them and how to respond to such breakdowns. To illustrate, the temporary loss of speech synthesis is in many ways comparable to a temporary case of laryngitis. The individual needs to have a backup strategy ready for use.

SELF-DETERMINATION

Individuals with physical or health conditions should be encouraged to make as many decisions by themselves as possible. This is empowerment. Even children, youth, and adults who cannot achieve full independence can decide what will be done, when it will be done, and how it will be done. That is, they can direct the actions of teacher aides, personal care attendants, and others who help them. Beginning in elementary school years and accelerating as students enter middle school and high school, self-determination should be a major goal of the parallel curriculum.

SELF-CARE AND RESPONSIBILITY

One of the most striking differences between life in high school and life in college or in the workplace is the degree of self-care and personal responsibility that is expected. This includes not only getting up at the necessary time in the morning, selecting appropriate clothing, bathing and dressing, and using related "getting up" behaviors but also dealing with the unexpected. A child who misses a school bus home can expect adults, both at the school and at home, to take the steps needed to ensure that the child gets home safely. A college student or worker, being an adult and being regarded as such, cannot expect the same level of accommodations from others. Instruction needs to be offered that poses such problems for the student on a hypothetical level and engages the student in identifying appropriate solutions.

Self-care should be taught throughout the school years, and students should be expected to display ever more independent care. Take, for example, sitting. Individuals with spinal cord injuries need to reposition themselves every 20 minutes or so, usually by pushing down on armrests and lifting the body slightly so that the positioning changes. This serves to avoid pressure sores (or at least to postpone them; most wheelchair users will at some point develop pressure sores, even after responsibly changing position for years). While young children may be repositioned by a physical or occupational therapist, it is vital that the individual begin doing it himself or herself, without prompting, as soon as possible. Similarly, individuals with cerebral palsy need to position themselves properly. This means symmetrical seating, firm trunk support, and feet securely placed in footrests. Again, young children may be positioned by others, but middle-school and older children should position themselves.

Take also, for example, eating. While young children may be assisted in eating, older students should be expected to feed themselves (given that this is physically possible), making appropriate use of adapted equipment such as "scooped" dishes and large-handle utensils. Bigge (1991) and Dormans and Pellegrino (1998) have offered extensive descriptions of appropriate eating patterns for children and youth with cerebral palsy. Toileting skills also should be taught in the early elementary years, with gradual improvement in independence expected as the student moves into the middle-school years.

INDEPENDENT TRAVEL IN THE COMMUNITY

Students without disabilities routinely learn independent travel skills on their own after school, on weekends, and during vacations. For many individuals who have severe physical or health disabilities, however, this does not suffice. If, for example, a motorized wheelchair were to malfunction, the individual would need to know what to do and how to do it (e.g., to call a local center for independent living for assistance). Other travel skills include wayfinding, negotiating curbs that lack curbcuts, and opening doors to stores and restaurants. Think back to when you were 15 years old and first learning to drive; the fact that one does not learn wayfinding as a passenger becomes evident; most of us really learned where everything was in the community and how to get from one place to another *after* we began driving. If, as often happens, parents of individuals with severe limitations always or usually drive their children around in the community, it should be no surprise that development of wayfinding skills lags.

COMMUNICATION

Individuals with recent traumatic brain injury (TBI), severe cerebral palsy that makes speech barely intelligible to the layperson, early-onset deafness, and other disabilities that limit communication need to develop appropriate means of expressing themselves. Sometimes, this means use of a communication board or portable personal computer equipped with a speech synthesizer. At other times, it means using pen and pad. However the actual communication occurs, what is said and how it is phrased is important. Many individuals with cerebral palsy or deafness soon become resigned to the reality that laypersons in the community will vastly underestimate their intelligence. They need to anticipate and find nonconfrontational ways to respond to such condescension.

A related subject for such individuals is responding when people stare at them. It is a reality that when individuals with visible disabilities enter shopping malls, restaurants, hotels, and other public places, people stare. Others become very condescending, treating the person with a disability as if he or she were a child. Such behaviors are so common among members of the general public that preparation to deal with them is a key part of the parallel curriculum. Some individuals prefer to avoid eye contact with *any* stranger who comes into their field of vision. Others stare right back. Yet others use impolite staring as an opportunity to teach people about disability. Teachers, therapists, and counselors can help individuals with physical or health conditions by providing opportunities to discuss public staring and condescending behavior, to act out incidents, and to decide upon ways of responding.

TRANSITION

While schools strive to meet ever higher academic standards, it is urgent that transition services not be neglected. The transition from high school to college is a major one, and high-school students need preparation for it. Here is just one of many examples: Colleges do not provide accommodations unless the students request them (in the public schools, of course, the accommodations are offered if the IEP team decides they are needed—whether or not the student asks for them). The transition from school to work is, if anything, more abrupt and more demanding. The author's experience is that most cases of students being terminated from work are rooted more in the students' failure to be good team members and to follow the unwritten rules of the workplace than in their failure to perform the jobs themselves.

COOPERATION AND TEAMWORK

As just mentioned, much paid work requires people to function as members of a team, working effectively with other people toward shared goals. Schools seldom teach such skills, except in sports and some other extracurricular activities. Many children and youth with physical or health conditions do not participate in sports for reasons related to their limitations; similarly, they might not be chosen to take part in other team-oriented extracurricular activities by able-bodied classmates. Whatever the reasons, they may not acquire experience in and skill at teamwork. Thus, teachers, counselors, and therapists should provide those opportunities in other settings (e.g., the classroom).

Applied Behavior Analysis

Another technique teachers, therapists, counselors, and others can use to improve outcomes while saving time and money is what used to be known as behavior modification. This technique may be used with students on all three levels of instruction—mainstream, modified academic, and specialized. Some students and professionals are skilled at applying applied behavior analysis (ABA), but others are not. A brief overview of the technique may help.

Basic to the approach are techniques of reinforcing desired behaviors while ignoring undesired ones. This approach has been shown to be effective with students having attention deficit disorders (Lerner, Lowenthal, & Lerner, 1995), mental retardation, learning disabilities, and other conditions (Wolery, Bailey, & Sugai, 1988).

ABA teaches professionals to look for behavior they want to see more of and reinforce (reward) the individual for producing it. In **presentation reinforcement** (sometimes called "positive reinforcement"), something the person likes (will work for) is given after successful completion of assigned tasks; in **removal reinforcement** (often called, confusingly, "negative reinforcement"), something the person dislikes (will work to avoid) is removed.

To illustrate, suppose that John very much likes to play outdoors. He may earn 5 minutes of playtime for each successful completion of an occupational therapy training task; once he has accumulated 40 minutes' worth of privileges, he may spend one class period in the school's playground. This is an example of presentation reinforcement. The key to success with presentation reinforcement is to know John well enough to realize that he is highly motivated by outdoor activity. Suppose, now, that John very much dislikes doing homework. In removal reinforcement, for every 10 minutes of quiet, on-task, in-seat work in the classroom, John could earn a star; once he has accumulated 10 stars, he could exchange them for the privilege of being released from the burden of doing one night's homework.

Applied behavior analysis also teaches professionals to ignore behavior they want to see less of and to make only selective use of punishment. Punishment is any consequence that reduces the future likelihood of behavior it follows. Using John, again as an example, he might lose 5 minutes of outdoor play privileges each time he speaks in class without permission. That is a case of **removal punishment**—something John likes (will work for), in this case the opportunity to play outside, is taken away. We know this is punishment if John's unacceptable talking behavior decreases. In **presentation punishment,** something John dislikes (will work to avoid) is given. Each time John talks in class without being recognized by the teacher, he may be given a "frowning face" sticker; should he accumulate five such stickers, he has to clean up the classroom. Punishment works only if you understand John and know what he really dislikes.

It is important to recognize that punishment is defined by its results. If you "punish" John by making him sit quietly in the corner, only to find that the misbehaviors that occasioned that "punishment" increase rather than decrease, you have in fact not punished him. It may be, for example, that John finds quiet time restful. Once again, applied behavior analysis works only if the professionals know their students or clients as individuals and select reinforcements or punishments accordingly.

ABA theory tells us that behaviors are controlled by their consequences, as we have just seen, and also by their **antecedents.** That is, conditions or incidents that precede undesirable behavior by the student may set the behavior off. By removing the incentive for acting-out behavior, that is, the antecedent, the professional may prevent the behavior's occurrence.

Another technique of ABA is **modeling,** which was mentioned earlier in this chapter. In this approach, someone a child likes or respects performs the behavior we want the child to learn. The child watches as the "model" is reinforced for performing that behavior. Later, the child is given an opportunity to do the same thing under the same circumstances. If he or she does, learning has occurred. The keys to success with modeling are (1) careful selection of models (models must be people the children like or admire, and they must also be like the children in at least some ways, for example, about the same age); (2) appropriate selection of behaviors to be modeled and learned (these behaviors must be things the child can perform); and (3) reinforcement of the modeled behavior when the child produces it.

ABA may be particularly effective with children, youth, and adults who have traumatic brain injury (TBI). Research reviewed in chapter 7 shows that one common effect of a recent TBI is an inability to habituate to ambient sounds and sights. Individuals with TBI may display aggressive behavior because they feel overwhelmed by sensory stimulation. ABA teaches us to remove the antecedent, in this case by reducing environmental stimulation. For example, the therapist may see the individual in a quiet, padded room and may lower room lights. These approaches eliminate the antecedent that led to the acting-out behavior.

Conductive Education

This text emphasizes the importance of removing environmental barriers that otherwise would limit the mobility and the achievements of individuals with physical or health disabilities. This is why all of Part Four focuses upon barriers and their removal. The book also highlights the tremendous potential of today's technologies for enhancing the abilities of people with physical or health conditions. Chapter 5 is entirely devoted to this topic. This text also stresses the need for cooperation among professionals from different disciplines working together in teams. And this book promotes integration of children with disabilities into regular classes when an appropriate education is available there.

By all four measures, an approach known as **conductive education** contrasts with the themes of this book. The method deemphasizes both barrier removal and technology use. The philosophy of conductive education is one that discourages professionals and parents alike from removing environmental barriers, preferring, instead, to teach children how to cope with and surmount those barriers. Similarly, conductive education frowns upon the use of wheelchairs and electronic aids, looking instead for children to use only minimally assistive devices, if indeed they use any. Conductive education eschews multidisciplinary teams in favor of a single professional, known as a "conductor". The approach is designed to be implemented in separate (self-contained) environments (Rosenberg, 1993).

Conductive education has been practiced in Europe for more than 50 years and is attracting attention in the United States at the turn of the century. However, very little research has been performed; virtually no comparative studies exist in which children are randomly assigned to a conductive education or a traditional class and measures of progress are taken. In addition, very little descriptive material is available to interested readers. Those articles that do exist were written, almost without exception, by people who are supporters of the method. For these reasons, conductive education remains controversial in America. It is being tried and looked at by a substantial number of schools and programs for children and youth with physical disabilities, but (to the author's knowledge) no public school in the United States has adopted it.

The name, including as it does the word "education," is somewhat misleading. In the typical program, a small number of children, each led by a conductor, work in a group for 5 hours daily, 5 days a week. The focus is much more upon physical mobility than upon academic learning. The few programs in existence in the United States usually are early intervention and preschool programs for children under the age of 6, which makes some sense, given the mobility focus of the approach.

Some parents find conductive education's focus on "normal function" (Spivack, 1995, p. 75) to be appealing. However, claims that children and adults with cerebral palsy will learn to walk without braces or other assistance may overstate the potential. As previously mentioned, only a handful of journal articles about conductive education have been written, most by advocates or others directly involved in promoting the approach. Research, too, largely has been done by professionals already committed to the philosophy (see, for example, Hari & Akos, 1988). For these reasons, parents and professionals alike need to carefully evaluate claims, watching for exaggerations.

The conductor guides and facilitates but does not "do" for the child. The aim is to teach children and adults to be independent. Conductive education classes are very large by American special-education standards: 20 to 22 children, led by a conductor and a few assistants. The group is an integral component of the approach: Children watch and cheer as other children attempt movements. Thus, children serve both as models for other children and as cheerleaders.

Developed in Hungary by the late Andras Peto and promoted by his successor in Budapest, Maria Hari, conductive education is in use in some parts of Europe, the United Kingdom, and Hong Kong. In the United States, the approach has taken root only in the greater New York City metropolitan area and in a few other locations. The intended audience includes children who have cerebral palsy, spina bifida, or other neurological conditions. The approach is primarily used with preschool-age children. Few supporters advocate its use in elementary school, and none (to the writer's knowledge) suggest its use in middle and secondary schools. It is occasionally employed with adults.

Dr. Hari, speaking at the World Congress on Conductive Education in Budapest in 1990, emphasized that the approach is designed to guide children through problem solving. According to Andrew Sutton, head of the Foundation for Conductive Education in Birmingham, United Kingdom, "The fundamental conceptual leap of Conductive Education is to regard motor disorders as learning problems" (Sutton, 1993, p. 8). Children are taught to think about the movements they will make and to say what they will do (e.g., "We are standing tall"). These components of the method ostensibly help children to integrate cognitive with physical activities. The children practice movements throughout the day, relying only upon simple wooden furniture and low-tech aids. The aim is to help children master small tasks (reaching, grasping, taking steps), thus gaining confidence; only later are these elements combined into larger-scale activities (standing, walking, etc.). In most instances, the intent is for movement to have meaning—the children walk, for example, not for the sake of walking but to get where they want to go. The children are not just exercising; rather they are solving problems that matter to them.

Whatever the merits of conductive education as an approach, practical considerations may limit its appeal in the United States and elsewhere. To illustrate, no state education agency (to the writer's knowledge) recognizes conductors as professionals qualified for state certification in special education and related services fields. Stated differently, American authorities certify occupational and physical therapists, special educators, speech pathologists, and others as personnel who may work with children, youth, and adults who have disabilities. Conductive education, on the other hand, at least as practiced in Europe, has not employed such individuals. The Budapest leaders, in particular, have insisted that only persons who have completed a 4-year course of study at the Peto Institute have the right to call themselves conductors. At the turn of the century, no resolution of this impasse was in sight.

Conductive education has some things going for it, notably the important tenet that children should not be forced to move for the sake of moving but rather should be offered opportunities to move as a means of accomplishing something else. (After all, ambulatory people engage in walking to do something, that is, for a purpose.) Fortunately for Americans with physical disabilities, one need not adopt conductive education as a whole to attain those benefits. We are already seeing that teamwork (discussed earlier) is leading physical and occupational therapists, speech and language pathologists, and other professionals to place much more emphasis upon educationally meaningful outcomes.

Questions for Reflection and Discussion

1. What are some of the shortcomings of the medical model with respect to education and therapy?

2. Why is *removal reinforcement* a better term to use than *negative reinforcement* (which means the same thing)?

3. What are some components of the parallel curriculum?

4. How can universal design be applied in the curriculum?

5. What advantages might distance learning offer to students with physical or health disabilities?

6. What role is played in applied behavior analysis by antecedents?

7. How does conductive education conflict with the main themes of this book?

8. Which features of conductive education might prevent it from being adopted widely in the United States?

9. What three conditions are required for modeling to work?

10. How might you use presentation punishment?

Resources

Conductive Education Center of Long Island
91 North Bayview Avenue
Freeport, NY 11520
1-516-377-0591
E-mail: samym@aol.com

MOVE International
1300 17th Street
City Centre
Bakersfield, CA 93301-4553
1-800-397-MOVE (663)
E-mail: move-international@kern.org
www.move-international.org

Peto Institute
1025 Budapest, Kuumltvolgyi uacutet 6
Hungary
36-1-2014533

Rifton Equipment
PO Box 901
Rifton, NY 12471
1-800-777-4244
www.frodo.bruderhof.com/rifton

Smeal Learning Center
National Center for Disability Services
201 I.U. Willets Road
Albertson, NY 11507
1-516-465-1431
www.ncds.org

5

ASSISTIVE
TECHNOLOGY

Eamon Doherty, 34, of Parsippany, New Jersey, became interested in computers when a friend of his dived into a shallow pool and sustained a spinal cord injury. About a year later, he heard about the work of Dr. Andrew Junker on Cyberlink™, a hands-free controller that uses three electrodes strapped around the head to pick up brain-wave patterns transmitted through breathing patterns or facial movements. "Believe it or not," Eamon says, "there are tiny amounts of electricity every time you think or do not think or look your eyes this way or that way." At Felician College in Lodi, New Jersey, Eamon teaches adults who have quadriplegia or cerebral palsy how to operate the Cyberlink system, which is still in development. He also sends Dr. Junker suggestions on how to improve the program. Brain Activated Technologies of Yellow Springs, Ohio, may be contacted for more information about the technology (Budoff, 1998; Nicholson, 1998).

Technology is revolutionizing the lives of Americans with physical, health, and sensory limitations—in school, at home, in the community, and in the workplace. The possibilities that today's technologies open up are remarkable: These products and services literally can make the difference between a disability that substantially limits major life activities and one that does not. Here is one example: With today's technologies, people with severe cerebral palsy can and often do take "regular" courses in elementary and secondary schools, performing the same assignments and taking the same tests as do children and youth with no disabilities. A generation ago, when such devices and services did not exist, most school-age individuals with severe cerebral palsy were educated in separate classrooms, using non-standard curricula, which left them ill-prepared for good jobs.

According to the National Council on Disability (1993), the major obstacle standing between people with disabilities and the technologies they need is money. The Council estimated that as many as 75% of special-education students could be educated in regular classrooms if the appropriate technologies were made available. With respect to adults with disabilities, the Council projected that some 58% could become less dependent on personal assistance (PCAs) and 37% could make more money on the job as a result of assistive technology devices and services.

Today, about 2,500 companies, most of them small or midsize firms, offer assistive technology devices and services. They hope to market their offerings to the estimated 16 million Americans who potentially could benefit from these products. The companies are listed in AbleData, a national database resource (http://www.abledata.com/index.htm) (Seelman, 1997). The market was estimated in mid-1997 to be a 27-billion-dollar industry.

Only 1 American out of every 20 who potentially could use assistive technology devices and services has done so (Brand, 1997), for several reasons. Many people don't know that the products are out there. This is understandable in many cases because the markets are so small that the manufacturers can do only occasional advertising. Others know, but they can't or think they can't afford the products. Again, this often is an understandable problem. Still others shy away from devices that might make them appear to be impaired; stigma remains a concern of many individuals, particularly of people who have "invisible" conditions.

Low-Tech Versus High-Tech

There are two basic kinds of technologies. **Low-tech** devices are products that have one or no moving parts, rarely have any electronic components, and usually are low in cost. Similarly, low-tech devices do one thing. They include products that make opening doors easier, dressing faster, and eating both easier and faster. In general, user training is both simple and brief (Mistreet & Lane, 1995). By contrast, **high-tech** products tend to have numerous moving parts, feature complex electronics, and cost several hundreds to several thousands of dollars. These devices generally can perform many functions. As a rule, user training is extensive (Parette, 1997). Americans with physical disabilities are much more likely to have and to use regularly devices that are low-tech rather than high-tech (LaPlante, Hendershot, & Moss, 1992). However, that is changing. Already we are seeing electronics built into products once thought to be low-tech. Examples are artificial arms and knees—today's prostheses may be much more precisely controlled, thanks to electronics, than could yesterday's mechanical aids.

Definitions

Federal law recognizes **assistive technology devices** and **assistive technology services.** These terms are now found in and defined the same ways by such laws as the Individuals with Disabilities Education Act (IDEA) (on special education), the Americans with Disabilities Act (ADA) (on civil rights), and the Rehabilitation Act (on employment services). Assistive technology devices are the products themselves—wheelchairs, walkers, communication boards, personal computers, etc. Assistive technology services are whatever services are required to identify, evaluate, install, and repair such devices.

To illustrate, the IDEA defines assistive technology devices in Section 602(1) as

> any item, piece of equipment, or product system, whether acquired commercially off the shelf, modified, or customized, that is used to increase, maintain, or improve functional capabilities of a child with a disability.

Similarly, Section 602(2) defines assistive technology services as

> any service that directly assists a child with a disability in the selection, acquisition, or use of an assistive technology device. Such term includes—(A) the evaluation of the needs of such child, including a functional evaluation of the child in the child's customary environment; (B) purchasing, leasing, or otherwise providing for the acquisition of assistive technology devices by such child; (C) selecting, designing, fitting, customizing, adapting, applying, maintaining, repairing, or replacing of assistive technology devices; (D) coordinating and using other therapies, interventions, or services with assistive technology devices, such as those associated with existing education and rehabilitation plans and programs; (E) training or technical assistance for such child, or, where appropriate, the family of such child; and (F) training or technical assistance for professionals (including individuals providing educational and rehabilitation services), employers, or other individuals who provide services to, employ, or are otherwise substantially involved in the major life functions of such child.

Choosing Technologies

With many thousands of products available, selecting the right ones is imperative. Occupational therapists are trained in evaluating the needs of children, youth, and adults who have physical, health, or sensory limitations and identifying appropriate technologies to meet those needs. Even with the help of a skilled occupational therapist, involvement of the family (Parette & Angelo, 1996) and the individual with a disability remains essential. Probably the best source of information is adults who have similar disabilities and who have themselves used adaptive products. (To locate such individuals, contact a local center for independent living; contact information is available from ILRU R&T Center, 2323 S. Shepherd, Suite 1000, Houston, TX 77019; 1-713-520-0232; www.bcm.tmc.edu/ilru.)

Assistive technology devices generally are used for very personal tasks—speaking, eating, doing homework, taking care of a house, performing paid work—and thus are items about which people tend to be sensitive. The guiding principle in assistive technology is that the devices and services be appropriate, that is, meet the unique needs of the individual. A key element is user choice. Whenever possible, the individual for whom the device or service is being considered should have substantial input, preferably after an opportunity for hands-on trials. "Technology abandonment" is an almost inevitable consequence when assistive technology devices are chosen that do not meet an individual's personal needs and expectations (Dillard, 1989).

Good questions to ask about any assistive technology device include, What specifically is it that the individual wants or needs to do but cannot do without assistance? Where will the device be used (only at home, at school and at home, at work, etc.)? Is portability (the ability to take the device with you wherever you go) important? How often will the device be needed? Is extensive training necessary before the device can be used? Is the device durable (e.g., resistant to damage, likely to last for several years)? Is this the simplest and easiest to use of the various products that meet this need? Is repair easily and quickly available? Michael Paciello (1993) added some other important criteria: How easy are the device's commands to remember? Does the device promote productivity? Does it reduce the likelihood of error? Does it satisfy the user? The National Center to Improve Practice in Newton, Massachusetts, offers a forum for discussing such issues. It also has a good library of resources about technology and education.

Money Issues

One important element in choosing technologies is cost. The costs associated with assistive technology devices and services vary widely. In general, devices that also appeal to and are marketed to able-bodied individuals are more widely available and cost less. By contrast, devices that are useful only for people with disabilities tend to be harder to locate and to cost comparatively more. This is a simple matter of supply and demand. To illustrate with products that are discussed later in this chapter, speech technologies have fallen dramatically in price over the past several years, despite the fact that they are ever more useful, simply because they have proven to be popular in the mass market (i.e., among able-bodied individuals). By contrast, augmentative communication devices have remained high in price because no such mass-market appeal exists for them.

Another aspect of cost is the overall cost of acquiring, programming, using, maintaining, and repairing a device. Although these other costs fre-

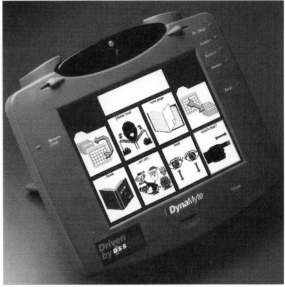

Portable communications devices, such as those made by Dynavox Systems, offer a "voice" for children with communication-related limitations.

quently are overlooked when a device is acquired, they can be substantial. To illustrate, the purchase price of a Dynavox® communication device does not include the preuse programming that is required to set up the machine so that it offers the user the options (words, phrases, commands, etc.) that this particular user wants. Similarly, the individual is not the only person who needs to be trained in the use of the device; teachers, counselors, and parents also need training.

Assistive technology devices and services are 100% paid for by education agencies only if they appear in the child's individual plan (Individualized Family Service Plan—IFSP—or Individualized Education Program—IEP). If a given device is approved as part of an IFSP/IEP, families often can negotiate to have the device used in the home and during vacations. In general, devices that have a purely personal use (e.g., are used at home rather than at school or are worn on the body, such as a hearing aid or glasses) rarely qualify. Family insurance plans often cover the costs of such devices. Low-income families that are on Medicaid will find that the federal Health Care Financing Administration (HCFA) in the U.S. Department of Health and Human Services (HHS) will pay for some assistive technology devices and services if evidence is presented that the devices/services reduce dependency. However, Medicaid will usually purchase the least expensive product on the market that performs the needed functions and may do so only after many months of delay. Families receiving Medicare benefits likely will fare even worse because HCFA will allow only "durable medical equipment" that is "medically necessary" (Bowe, 1995b).

The National Cristina Foundation (Greenwich, Connecticut) accepts donations of used personal computers and such peripherals as monitors and printers from individuals, organizations, and corporations and then makes them available, usually free of charge, to individuals with disabilities who need them.

Low-Tech Products

A wide variety of one-function products is now available, ranging from wide-handled spoons and other kitchen utensils (easier to grasp) to dishes with curved edges (that make picking up peas, etc., far easier) to gameboards and game pieces with Dycem on the bottoms (preventing them from slipping). There are grabbers that grasp and hold objects, reachers that extend one's reach, and combinations that both reach and grasp. Although the devices themselves are usually simple, the assistance of a trained occupational therapist frequently is needed to evaluate the individual's needs and to select appropriate products from the vast array of available options.

Many common-use products are accessible to people with physical limitations. Buttonhooks and zipper pulls are available in general stores such as Home Depot because they are convenient for many able-bodied persons. Toothpaste now comes in tubes equipped with pushbuttons that are easier for many people with arthritis, cerebral palsy, and other disabilities to use than traditional squeeze-function toothpaste tubes. Velcro or plastic can be used to wrap utensils or other objects, making them easier to grasp and manipulate. Alternatively, one may purchase wide-handled utensils, garden supplies, and other devices in general purpose household supply stores such as Williams Sonoma. Examples include Friendly Fit forks and spoons. A wide selection is offered in Sammons/Preston and AdaptAbility catalogs.

Other low-tech devices are special purpose products. A knee separator, as the name suggests, keeps the legs apart while someone sits in a wheelchair, thus increasing stability and decreasing perspiration. A car door opener (which also works to open refrigerator doors, cabinets, etc.) enables people to open doors with one open hand. A soda can cuff acts much like a pen cuff, allowing someone with quadriplegia to wrap the hand around the object and lift it effectively; similarly, a sandwich cuff allows these individuals to eat a sandwich independently. The list goes on, and on, and on.

The low-tech category includes a large number of switches. Mouthsticks, head wands or head sticks, foot-operated rocker switches, and many other switches make it possible for someone who can control one muscle (virtually any one anywhere in the body) to control devices as simple as light switches or as complex as personal computers. Although the switch itself is simple and low-tech, the computer program that allows multiple functions to be controlled with the switch is both high-tech and complex, for which reason it can be expensive. In general, hand switches are easier to learn and to use than are head switches, especially by young children (Glickman, Deitz, Anson, & Stewart, 1996).

Also in that no-man's-land between low- and high-tech products are single-purpose electronic systems. One example is Bell Atlantic's Voice-Dialing™ service in which computer software embedded in the telephone switching network recognizes the caller's voice and the names the caller speaks and dials the phone numbers corresponding to those names. The caller uses an ordinary, unmodified telephone. Bell Atlantic markets the service for about $4 per month. It can be very helpful for individuals with strokes, some traumatic brain injuries, and some learning disabilities because the service obviates the need to remember and dial phone numbers.

Wheelchairs

A new generation of wheelchairs is enhancing the ability of many people with physical or health conditions to get around outside the home. Individuals with physical disabilities have altered the wheelchair industry almost beyond recognition. Chairs that are customized for use in races are now commonplace, as are sports chairs that make tennis, basketball, and other participatory sports not only possible but also enjoyable. In fact, many users prefer sports chairs for everyday use because they look much less "medical" and weigh far less than standard wheelchairs. There are even chairs designed for use on the beach and chairs that support users in a standing position. Briefly stated, today's chairs offer access to environments once off-limits to people needing wheelchairs.

Much of this technology has been consumer driven. The late Evan Kemp, who had a muscle disease, was active in guiding Invacare, an Ohio-based medical devices firm, as one of its founders. He told me that he was motivated to respond to what wheelchair users wanted rather than to what medical doctors or insurers wanted. Marilyn Hamilton reached a similar conclusion after becoming a paraplegic as a result of a hang-glider accident. With her partners, she built Quickie wheelchairs with aluminum tubing and bright colors. Her company sold the "screaming neon chairs" as quickly as it could make them; the firm was later acquired by Sunrise Medical and is now known as Quickie Division of Sunrise Medical. Hamilton is a senior vice president of Sunrise Medical.

All of this represents a major change in the industry. From the end of World War II until the late 1970s, Everest & Jennings dominated the field. It produced bulky, heavy, hospital-style wheelchairs that it sold to medical care professionals. Then, in 1977, the U.S. Department of Justice brought an antitrust suit against the company. By the time the suit was settled 2 years later, Kemp and others had entered the business. Today, the market is vibrant. Manual wheelchairs cost half what they did in the mid-1980s. Electric chairs of a dazzling variety are now available, some of which cost more than most cars. The field now features three-wheeled scooters from Amigo; lightweight, colorful chairs from the likes of Quickie; sports chairs from Invacare; and standing chairs from American Medical Technologies. Even Everest & Jennings has responded to the consumer demands of the 1990s with Vortex chairs that are narrower than most other chairs and offer reclining capabilities useful in reducing the likelihood of pressure sores.

An important consideration in selecting wheelchairs for children is the basic fact that children grow. A new category of growth chairs allows adjustments to be made to accommodate this growth. That is good news, because purchasing a new chair every year is prohibitively expensive. Then, too, many insurance companies limit the number of chairs that may be acquired over a period of time. With power wheelchairs costing as much as $25,000 or even more, chair adjustability becomes a very desirable feature. Kuschall of America offers a "Munch'kin 3000" manual chair that features adjustable seat and footrest. Freedom Designs counters with adjustable "Spectrum" power chairs.

Despite the many varieties of wheelchairs now available, some children, youth, and adults need specially designed chairs. This is particularly true of children with cerebral palsy. Fortunately, many local chapters of United Cerebral Palsy Associations have shops that build chairs to specification. UCPA-Nassau is an example. Its shop makes all kinds of wheelchairs for the students at the program's children's learning center. An affiliated for-profit company designs chairs for others, including families. (Contact UCPA of Nassau County, 380 Washington Avenue, Roosevelt, NY 11575; 1-516-378-2000; 1-516-378-3791 fax.)

Today's wheelchairs can also be customized through the use of such add-ons as backpacks or cargo nets of all sorts, trailers for lugging groceries or computers, mountable drink holders and even fishing-rod holders, brightly colored wheel covers, canopies to protect from rain, and lapboards that feature pop-up mirrors. Cushions are very important because they help to prevent pressure sores. One study found that 50% of people with quadriplegia and 30% of those with paraplegia are hospitalized at some point in their lives as a result of pressure sores (Krousop, 1983). A long list of cushions is available, some in thermoplastic, some foam-filled, a few fluid-filled, and some rubber-and-air. Sources are listed in AbleWare and AdaptAbility catalogs, among others.

Wheelchairs generally are considered to be personal items. As such, they usually are not provided by local education agencies pursuant to IEPs. The major exception is where a special chair is used in school and a different one at home. This may be the case, for example, where a child uses a manual wheelchair at home but needs a power chair at school to get to classes on time. Government insurance programs, notably Medicaid and Medicare, generally will cover all or most of the cost only of the least expensive wheelchair that will meet an individual's basic needs. For these reasons, unless their condition was caused by an accident that generated sizeable insurance payments or their employer-provided insurance policy covers the kind of wheelchair they want, people desiring a lightweight, sporty, or special purpose chair usually need to pay for the chair themselves.

Paralyzed Veterans of America (PVA) Publications annually issues a survey of wheelchair users that features user evaluations. Appearing in *Sports 'n Spokes* magazine, the surveys include information about wheelchair weights, features, delivery times, and warranties. Miramar Publishing offers a similar annual report. And the federal Department of Veterans Affairs has a publication, "Choosing a Wheelchair System," that provides assessments from users, medical specialists, and researchers. Highly recommended in such publications is a series of questions that help to guide the user to the appropriate kind of chair. For example, will the chair be used indoors only or also out of doors? and is it important to be able to fold the chair and fit it behind a car seat?

Many states have so-called lemon laws that apply to wheelchairs. As illustrated by laws in New York and Massachusetts, these statutes provide recourse for someone whose chair has become inoperable four or more times within 1 year of delivery or if it is out of service for a total of 30 calendar days. Repairs are to be free during the first year of ownership. Dissatisfied customers may demand replacement from the manufacturer or, if that is not forthcoming, may sue for double damages (twice the financial loss).

Speech Recognition

Perhaps the most explosive area of high technology today is that of computer "hearing"—a computer's ability to understand the spoken voice. Today's Pentium-based personal computers can run software programs that respond to the spoken word. IBM's ViaVoice™ and Dragon Systems' NaturallySpeaking™ were tremendous breakthroughs. The Dragon product was introduced in June 1997, and the IBM program 3 months later. These speech-recognition capabilities can be trained to comprehend speech that is near conversational in speed—and to do so at truly amazing prices. The programs retail for about $60 to $160. The IBM system comes equipped with a 22,000-word vocabulary, expandable to 64,000 words; it lets the user dictate at a speed of up to 140 words per minute. In mid-1998, Lernout & Hauspie, a European firm specializing in voice products, introduced Kurzweil VoicePad™ a somewhat less complete system, for just $30; VoicePad can recognize 40 to 60 words per minute and comes with a 17,000-word vocabulary, expandable to 20,000 words. To place this price/performance into context, consider that just a few years ago, it required $5,000 to $10,000 to purchase a program that could understand words if the speech was slow . . . and . . . filled . . . with . . . pauses . . . like . . . these.

The IBM, Dragon, and Lernout & Hauspie offerings are standalone speech-recognition programs. The trend now is for computer voice-comprehension capabilities to be built into commercial software, such as Corel's WordPerfect Suite™ and Lotus's SmartSuite™. For example, Intellivoice Communications Inc. of Atlanta, Georgia, packages Lernout speech-recognition capabilities into a number of products marketed under the Persona™ brand name that are aimed at the general market but also are useable by people with disabilities. Examples include EasyDial™ (a system that lets drivers dial phone calls without taking their hands from the steering wheel), E-mail Reader™ (a system that reads E-mail to people calling in from any phone), and InfoDial™ (a system that automatically completes calls after directory assistance reads the number).

Speech recognition is also expected shortly to become the predominant way by which people surf the Net and operate computer devices in their cars. Such uses require three things: speech recognition (so that the device understands your voice), natural language processing (so that it comprehends what you mean), and speech synthesis (so that the unit can tell you what you want to know). For individuals who need speech recognition because of disability, the importance of these trends is that they are driving the capabilities of software much higher and much faster than otherwise would occur and are bringing prices down far more and, again, much faster than would otherwise be possible.

Speech recognition places heavy demands on personal computers. Users of these programs should expect to need a Pentium-class (Pentium, Pentium II, Merced) computer running at a clock speed of 266-megahertz (MHz) or faster, having at least 48 megabytes of random access memory (RAM), and featuring at least 60 to 125 MB of hard disk space. They also need a Sound-Blaster 16 compatible sound card. Fortunately, the costs of both clock speed and memory have been falling in recent years, making such machines quite affordable.

Another feature of these programs that potential users need to be aware of is that the programs handle business communication (e.g., the kinds of words that appear in correspondence and speeches by people in business) much better than they do other kinds of text. Thus, users will need extensive training before they can use these programs effectively to write a term paper on, say, chemistry or earth science. A good speech-recognition program will correctly understand some 90% to 95% of words drawn from subjects in which it has been trained; ask it to comprehend text from an unfamiliar topic and the rate drops to 70% or even lower. Accuracy will be even less in a noisy environment. IBM, Dragon, and Lernout & Hauspie offer specialized programs that are custom designed for specific fields such as law, journalism, or medicine.

For individuals who have quadriplegia and thus find typing both onerous and slow, computer speech recognition offers a dramatic improvement in productivity. Many people who have learning disabilities may find it far easier to speak than to type; thus, individuals with dyslexia and other reading disorders may be attracted to computer speech recognition. Similarly, some people with traumatic brain injury (TBI) will find that they can do much more with speech recognition because the technology eliminates the need to remember and correctly use the often arcane commands of word-processing or spreadsheet software. For example, it is much less intellectually demanding to say, "Bold this paragraph" than it is to recall and correctly implement, say, the Shift-F6 command of WordPerfect 5.1. For others with TBI, the cognitive demands of entering text, formatting it, and doing spell and grammar checking may prove overwhelming, even with speech recognition. People with dyslexia may need help to train the program; for example, a teacher may sit nearby and quietly (so that her voice is not picked up by the unit's microphone) read the material on the screen which the individual with dyslexia then repeats, this time into the microphone.

Speech-recognition software can even be trained to comprehend the speech of some individuals with severe cerebral palsy or who have been deaf from birth. That is, the program doesn't much care whether words are pronounced "correctly" or not—as long as they are pronounced consistently, that is, so long as the individual always says them in the same way. However, there are important limits. Many people with cerebral palsy and many who were born deaf have great difficulty pronouncing words consistently. For them, it may be better to rely upon more traditional means of text entry (e.g., keyboards, augmentative communication devices) or to turn to discrete speech-recognition programs that require pauses . . like . . these. Such programs (Dragon Dictate™ is an example) generally do better with inconsistent or "different" speech than do speaker-independent programs. For some users, a combination of discrete speech-recognition software and alternative input devices may be the most appropriate solution. Also possible is tweaking, or making adjustments to, the speech-recognition system, such as modifying the microphone's settings, reducing ambient noise, or having someone with better speech handle the timed-input training sessions that the programs require.

As a general rule, if the program understands less than 80% of the words you speak, you are probably better off entering text in other ways. At that rate, the program will make about 40 mistakes per double-spaced page of type, meaning that the individual will probably spend more time correcting those errors than he or she would need to enter text in more conventional ways. Some people with physical or sensory disabilities may also find that speech recognition is not particularly helpful for them; that is, they find that they can be more productive using other methods. Most people who are blind or have low vision can type far faster than they can enter text by speaking.

Speech Synthesis

Computers able to "talk" have also become commonplace over the past several years. Virtually every Apple Macintosh computer now in use has speech synthesis built in. The ability to talk is now embedded in a single chip that contains all the needed signal processing functions; all the computer needs is a "voice box" or hardware that does the actual speaking. Today's speech synthesis sounds surprisingly human, compared to yesterday's robotic voices that were unmistakably mechanical. Prices, too, have fallen. To illustrate, consider the famous Cambridge University theoretical physicist Stephen Hawking, author of *A Brief History of Time*. The speech-synthesis technology he used until recently when lecturing cost $4,500 twenty years ago; today, an even better capability is available for just $200.

Who needs speech synthesis? One obvious group includes people who are blind or have low vision; these people can listen to text that others read. Another clear candidate is individuals with dyslexia or other reading disabilities. Many people with severe cerebral palsy can benefit, too: They can have the computer "speak" for them because the computer's voice is much more understandable to laypeople than are their own voices. Many individuals who are deaf do not have intelligible voices; they, too, can use speech synthesis to talk for them.

<table>
<tr><td>

Augmentative Communication

</td><td>

The word *augmentative* means supplementing or expanding. The idea is to assist individuals in expressing themselves. Augmentative communication technologies date back to the 1970s when simple communication boards were introduced. These boards were particularly helpful for many individuals with severe cerebral palsy. The boards featured very large pressure-sensitive pads. By touching (or using an implement to touch) a particular section on the board, the person could communicate a simple message, for example, "I'm thirsty." Later, as speech synthesis capabilities improved and became less costly, boards that "talk" appeared.

</td></tr>
</table>

Initially, only very limited communication was possible. The first boards contained a small number of "boxes," each of which stood for one thought or idea (e.g., "I want my Mom"). Later, exchangeable board coverings were introduced that multiplied the number of messages one could send. By removing one membrane and installing another, the user added a whole phalanx of new messages. One major drawback was that even customizable boards could communicate only the ideas depicted on their "boxes." Another was that the user was not required to generate properly spelled words or construct correctly formed sentences. The best communication boards today require people to actually produce both words and grammar. This is far preferable to the limitations of earlier boards. First, the user can create unique messages, no longer being constrained by the preset messages of the board. And second, the user must produce correct spelling and grammar—two competencies that are very important in today's information society.

Perhaps the most popular of today's augmentative communication devices is the Dynavox line of machines made by Sentient Systems of Pittsburgh, Pennsylvania. The Dynavox 2 and 2c, at 6 pounds, and the DynaMyte, at just 4 pounds, are small, versatile, and portable machines. One-switch operation is used together with scanning to select words or phrases to be spoken aloud. Any of 10 "voices" (male/female, child/adult, etc.) may be selected; because the voice represents the person, this matters, especially to children. Accessories include a padded carrying case and a wheelchair mount. The machines are not inexpensive: Prices range from about $5,000 to some $8,000. Potential users should be aware that Dynavox machines require considerable computer programming. Someone needs to identify virtually all of the words and phrases a child or adult is likely to want to say and program the unit both to prompt the user to select it and to make the machine produce it. This is true even though the 2c, for example, comes with a 42,000-word vocabulary.

Another augmentative communication product that is popular with many individuals with physical limitations is the Liberator, from Prentke-Romich. It, too, requires considerable programming in advance of everyday use.

Augmentative communication is very different from facilitated communication. The whole purpose of augmentative communication is that the individual himself or herself is the only one communicating. These machines make it possible to express oneself even if only one muscle in the body (e.g., an eyebrow, a toe) can be controlled voluntarily. Facilitated communication, by contrast, has a "facilitator" or able-bodied adult touching or even holding the individual. Considerable research, which began appearing in 1993 (e.g., Wheeler, Jacobson, Paglieri, & Schwartz, 1993), has demonstrated that much of the alleged "communication" is actually produced by the facilitator, albeit usually unconsciously. For this reason, it remains a hotly controversial topic. Augmentative communication, because it is so clearly a process by which people with disabilities alone are doing the expressing, has never been anywhere nearly as controversial.

Personal Computers

Many individuals with physical, health, or sensory impairments can use personal computers without modification. For some, however, special peripherals (add-ons) or other aids are necessary. Fortunately, a wide variety of such devices is available.

A common add-on is a **keyguard,** a plastic sheet that fits over the computer keyboard. Holes punched in the sheet correspond with the keys on the keyboard. The value of keyguards is that they prevent the user from accidentally hitting the wrong keys. Prices range from about $80 to $120. Keyguards are made by IBM and by a variety of smaller companies.

People who have difficulty using a computer mouse because of a physical disability may find that such functions as MouseKeys and such devices as a trackball may help. MouseKeys is software allowing the arrow keys on the numeric keypad to be used in lieu of the mouse. All Apple Macintoshes come equipped with MouseKeys (in the control panel), and the software is provided as part of Windows for IBM-compatible machines. Users should be aware that it takes longer to position a cursor via MouseKeys than it usually does via a mouse. Trackballs are mouselike devices (the bottoms are similar) but are easier to use than a mouse for people with quadriplegia, cerebral palsy, or other muscle-related limitations. Madenta (Edmonton, Alberta, Canada) offers a hands-free "tracker" mouse substitute that monitors the user's head's movement; the tracker can also be used with an on-screen "keyboard" to give the user complete control of the computer.

StickyKeys (built into all Macs and available for IBM-compatible computers via Windows) assists when people cannot press and hold more than one key at a time. The software makes the computer "think" that a key remains depressed even after the user has released it. Thus, one may touch, sequentially, CTRL, ALT, and DEL. The computer thinks that CTRL and ALT remain depressed even though they do not. Another important function is "key-repeat-defeat." As the name suggests, it produces only one letter/number even if the key is pushed for a long period of time (without this function, touching and continuing to depress the letter *r* would result in "rrrrrrrrrrrrrrrrrrr" appearing on the screen). Similar capabilities are called SlowKeys (on Macintoshes) and FilterKeys (in Windows). They help computers to ignore keys that are struck accidentally or that are pressed for too long a time.

Some individuals require special keyboards for text or data entry. IntelliKeys is an example of an **alternative keyboard.** The units, sold by IntelliTools Inc., offer larger "keys" that may be "struck" by head wands, light beams, or other alternative entry tools. Another example is the Eyegaze Computer System, offered by LC Technologies of Fairfax, Virginia. A small camera located beneath the computer monitor tracks the user's eye movements as the user looks at an on-screen keyboard. If the eye is found to focus on a particular letter or number for about one-quarter second, the computer "thinks" the user has entered that character on the keyboard.

newAbilities Systems of Palo Alto, California, offers Tongue Touch Keypads™ (TTK), a remarkable technology that permits people to control computers, environmental control units (ECUs), power wheelchairs, and other devices by moving the tongue. Kymberly Bashaw (k.bashaw@aol.com), a sales manager for newAbilities, showed me how sensitive the tongue is and how easy it is to learn how to manipulate the tongue to press controls on the tiny TTK. For people with very limited fine-motor control, quadriplegia, or severe cerebral palsy, the sophisticated mouthpiece-based device may well be worth its $12,000 cost.

Also important is **prediction software** (also called expansion software). The program will search its dictionary of words and phrases after the user has typed one letter or a few letters. It will then present a dialog box in which its

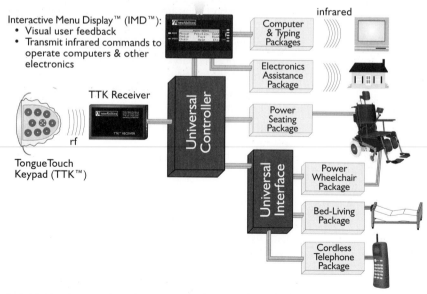

UCS 1000™ with TongueTouch Keypad™ System Diagram

Individuals who cannot move any muscles in a consistent fashion may benefit from the tongue-controlled newAbilities mouthpiece.

predictions of what you intend to type appear. Each prediction is accompanied by a number. By typing the number associated with the correct prediction, the user automatically expands the few letters actually typed into the complete word or phrase intended. This can save many thousands of keystrokes in a term paper or report. Because so many people with physical limitations type slowly, even with adaptive equipment, such savings are important. The most popular prediction programs are published by Aurora Systems of Vancouver, British Columbia, Canada.

For individuals who are blind or have low vision and for many who have learning disabilities, **screen readers** are very important. These technologies translate what appears on the screen into text (at least as much of it as can be transcribed into text) as words, numbers, punctuation marks, and labels. The speech synthesizer then takes over, reading that material out loud in a synthesized voice. Among the most popular screen readers is JAWS (Job Access With Speech), from Henter-Joyce. Also helpful are screen **magnification** programs, which enlarge selected screen items as many as 8, 16, or even more times normal size. Limited screen magnification capabilities are built into Macintoshes and come with today's Windows operating system software for IBM-compatibles. For greater magnification, users need to turn to companies that provide specialized services.

Notetakers

Some individuals with physical, health, or sensory disabilities can take notes in conventional ways, for example, with pen or pencil and paper. Others need laptop computers. Many individuals who are blind or have low vision enjoy the convenience of the Braille 'n Speak™ device, invented by Tim Cranmer, an inventor who is blind, and marketed by Blazie Engineering of Forest Hill, Maryland. Small and lightweight, the device looks much like a compact version of the machines that stenographers use. After entering notes in class, the individual can take the unit home and upload the material into a personal computer, where the information is instantly transcribed into English. The information can also be printed out as Braille, if desired, or spoken aloud via a speech synthesizer.

Where Am I?

Global positioning systems (GPS) are known to most Americans as options on cars they can buy or rent. These devices use signals from a dozen orbiting satellites to determine the location of the car. The technology has obvious implications for people who are blind. Arkenstone, a not-for-profit organization in Sunnyvale, California, offers an "Atlas Speaks" GPS-like system. The software, which uses CD-ROM drives in IBM-compatible PCs, provides detailed information about 23,000 cities in the United States. Users can take directions with them on tape, in hardcopy Braille, or in a Braille 'n Speak unit. It's not quite GPS, but at $300, it is an affordable alternative.

In late 1997, Magellan Systems of San Dimas, California, introduced a handheld GPS device for less than $100. The GPS Pioneer has obvious benefits for blind and low-vision individuals who wish to use it as a means of identifying where they are. The commercial unit itself offers a visual display that is difficult if not impossible for most such persons to use; however, by the time you read this, someone likely will have solved that problem. Already, researchers at the University of California—Santa Barbara are developing a GPS system that features a "virtual acoustic display" that blind people can listen to (Tyson, 1995).

Futuristic Products

Now in development is a technology that promises to be truly revolutionary for many individuals who have had strokes, have very severe cerebral palsy, or have other debilitating physical conditions. The chapter-opening story about Cyberlink illustrated this kind of product. Called "neural digital signal processing technologies," these devices tap neural signals produced by the brain or eye to control devices—no muscle movement is required. In effect, one thinks a thought, and the neural pattern generated in the brain is captured by the device, which then obeys the thought. Much of this work is being done by laboratories holding contracts with the U.S. Department of Defense. The military objective is to allow fighter pilots to control their planes without having to use their hands or voices. Nonetheless, the potential for people who *cannot* use hands or voices is obvious—and exciting (Jacobs, 1997).

Another promising category of futuristic products is the service robot—robots capable of providing assistive services in the home and at the workplace. Surveying the state of the art in 1995, Lees and LePage (1995) concluded that useful service robots are unlikely to appear before the turn of the century. They found only two prototype service robots that were able to perform important tasks, and even those robots provided assistance for just 4 hours a day. A great deal more research and development are needed, they concluded, before service robots become cost-effective replacements for human attendants.

Questions for Reflection and Discussion

1. Outline how students with physical disabilities could use the technologies described in this chapter to take part in general K–12 classrooms.

2. Define *low-tech* and give two examples.

3. Do the same with *high-tech.*

4. Why does technology abandonment occur, and what could you as an educator, therapist, or counselor do to forestall it?

5. What features of today's wheelchairs are particularly important to people with physical disabilities?

6. What characteristics of the market for speech-recognition software are especially promising for people who have physical disabilities?

7. People with what kinds of disabilities discussed in this book might benefit from speech synthesis (computer talk)?

8. Compare and contrast "augmentative communication" and "facilitated communication."

9. How might prediction software assist someone with a severe physical disability to write a report?

10. Comparing two markets—that for speech-recognition software and that for tongue-touch keypads—explain why the latter cost so much more than the former.

Resources

AbleData
Silver Spring, Md.
1-800-227-0216
www.abledata.com

AbleWare Catalog
Maddak, Inc.
Pequannock, N.J.
1-201-628-7600

AdaptAbility Catalogs
Colchester, Conn.
1-800-288-9941 or
1-800-266-8856

Alliance for Technology Access
2175 East Francisco Boulevard,
Suite L
San Rafael, Calif. 94901
(800) 455-7970
(415) 455-4575
E-mail: atainfo@ataccess.org
www.ataccess.org

American Medical
Technologies
Canton, Ga.
1-800-700-8009

Amigo Mobility International
Bridgeport, Mich.
1-800-MY-AMIGO

Apple Disability Solutions
Cupertino, Calif.
1-800-600-7808
www.speech.apple.com

Arkenstone
Sunnyvale, Calif.
1-800-444-4443
www.arkenstone.org

Aurora Systems Inc.
Vancouver, B.C., Canada
1-800-361-8255
www.djtech.com/aurora

Blazie Engineering
Forest Hill, Md.
1-410-893-9333
www.blazie.com

Closing the Gap
Henderson, Minn.
1-507-248-3294
www.closingthegap.com

Brain Activated Technologies
Yellow Springs, Ohio
www.brainfingers.com

Dragon Systems
Newton, Mass.
1-800-437-2466
www.naturalspeech.com
or, www.dragonsys.com

Enrichments Catalog
Sammons/Preston
Bolingbrook, Ill.
1-800-323-5547
www.sammonspreston.com

Everest & Jennings
Earth City, Mo.
1-800-235-4661

Freedom Designs
Simi Valley, Calif.
1-800-331-8551

Henter-Joyce
St. Petersburg, Fla.
1-800-336-5658
www.hj.com

IBM
Somers, N.Y.
1-800-825-5263
www.software.ibm.com

IntelliTools Inc.
Novato, Calif.
1-800-899-6687
www.intellitools.com

Invacare Corp.
Elyria, Ohio
1-800-333-6900

Kuschall of America
Camarillo, Calif.
1-800-654-4768

LC Technologies
Fairfax, Va.
1-800-733-5284

Lernout & Hauspie
c/o T-Soft Inc.
Urbandale, Ill.
1-888-242-9527

Madenta Communications
Edmonton, Alberta, Canada
1-800-661-8406

Magellan Systems
San Dimas, Calif.
1-909-394-5000
www.magellangps.com

Microsoft Corporation
Redmond, Wash.
1-800-426-9400
www.microsoft.com

Miramar Publishing
Culver City, Calif.
1-800-543-4116

National Center to Improve
Practice
Newton, Mass.
1-617-969-7100
www.edc.org/fsc/ncip/

National Cristina Foundation
Greenwich, Conn.
1-800-274-6000
E-mail: ncfnasd@gteens.com

newAbilities Systems
Palo Alto, Calif.
1-800-829-8889

Paralyzed Veterans of America
(PVA) Publications
Phoenix, Ariz.
1-602-224-0500

Prentke Romich
Wooster, Ohio
1-800-262-1984

Quickie Division of Sunrise
Medical
Carlsbad, Calif.
1-800-456-8165

Sentient Systems
Pittsburgh, Pa.
1-800-344-1778
www.sentient-sys.com

Trace R&D Center
Madison, Wis.
1-608-263-2309
www.trace.wisc.edu

U.S. Department of Veterans
Affairs
Veterans Health Services
Washington, DC 20420

Part Three

The five chapters of Part Three offer descriptions of many physical disabilities, health conditions, and common secondary impairments. The intent of this part is to provide educators, therapists, counselors, and others with enough information to appreciate the unique characteristics of the major disabilities. However, a large number of unusual conditions exist that produce physical or health limitations. An excellent source of information on these uncommon impairments is the National Organization for Rare Disorders (NORD). Based in Connecticut, NORD provides thumbnail sketches of genetic and other conditions. More information on many of the same impairments is available from NORD via U.S. mails: National Organization for Rare Disorders (NORD), 100 Route 37, P.O. Box 8923, New Fairfield, CT 06812-8923; (800) 999-6673 or (203) 746-6518; E-mail: orphan@nord-rdb.com; on the Web: www.nord-rdb.com/~orphan.

Chapters 6 and 7 describe neurological disorders. The common thread throughout these physical conditions is damage to or mutation in the central nervous system (CNS). The CNS links our brain to the rest of the body via afferent (to the brain) and efferent (from the brain) nerves. The underlying pathologies in these two chapters are thus not in the muscles or bones but rather in the messaging system connecting muscles to the brain. Perhaps the clearest illustration of neurological impairments is multiple sclerosis (MS); every one of the many symptoms of MS, from the pins-and-needles feeling to the visual impairments, emerges from the CNS.

Chapter 8 takes up musculoskeletal conditions in which the underlying pathologies are in fact found in the muscles or other body parts. Perhaps the most vivid example is muscular dystrophy (MD), in which the muscles themselves deteriorate, in many cases to the point of causing death.

Chapter 9 examines a wide range of health disabilities, some of them comparatively severe (e.g., AIDS) and some relatively minor (e.g., asthma). Child abuse and neglect are also considered in this chapter.

Part Three concludes with a review of three important secondary conditions: hearing loss (including deafness); vision impairment (including blindness); and attention deficits, learning disabilities, and mental retardation. These are significant disabilities in their own right. The use of "secondary" to describe them is specific to the nature of this book: These impairments are common corollaries of the physical and health disabilities that are the primary focus of this book.

6

CEREBRAL PALSY, SPINAL CORD INJURY, AND SPINA BIFIDA

This chapter opens our two-chapter consideration of physical disabilities of the neurological kind, that is, conditions in which the site of the lesion or the problem area resides in the central nervous system. The prototypical impairment of this type is cerebral palsy, with which we open the chapter. The other two conditions reviewed in this chapter, spinal cord injury and spina bifida, are remarkably similar to each other except for the age at onset, which, as it turns out, has important consequences. Chapter 7 will look at three other neurological impairments: traumatic brain injury, multiple sclerosis, and epilepsy.

A note on format: Chapters 6–10, which describe different disabilities, will each present, at the end of the chapter, questions for reflection and discussion and resources for additional information for all conditions discussed in the chapter.

Cerebral Palsy

My former colleague at Hofstra, psychology professor Harold E. Yuker (1924–1997), always regarded his cerebral palsy as a condition, not a handicap. Harold spent 5 decades at Hofstra, building an international reputation for his research on attitudes toward persons with disabilities. He also played a leading role in Hofstra's 30-year effort to make the campus accessible to people with disabilities. Harold's speech was labored, as is that of many people with cerebral palsy, but it was understandable. Harold walked slowly, with a cane. But those things mattered little to Harold. What he cared about, with a passion, were his teaching and his many research projects. He preferred to see the world, not himself, as "handicapped," and he devoted his life to changing that world. In a lot of ways, over 73 years, he succeeded.

The late Harold Yuker, Professor of Psychology and Provost of Hofstra University, was a world-renowned scholar on attitudes toward persons with disabilities. His attitude toward himself was revealing: Harold always regarded his cerebral palsy as a nuisance, not as a handicap.

WHAT IS IT?

Cerebral palsy (the two words mean, respectively, in or of the brain and muscle weakness or muscle-control problems) refers to a group of conditions that affect muscle movement and control or coordination. Perhaps the most critical fact to recognize about people with cerebral palsy is that each person is an individual: These people differ so much from person to person that generalizations are difficult. Nonetheless, there are several types of cerebral palsy. The most common are *spastic* cerebral palsy, in which muscles are stiff (hypertonia) and movement is awkward (Damiano, Kelly, & Vaughn, 1995); *athetoid* cerebral palsy, in which the child makes contortions or twisting motions as a result of sudden, involuntary, and uncontrolled muscle movements; *ataxic* cerebral palsy, in which balance and depth perception are disturbed and in which fluctuating muscle tone causes the child to overreach for things; and *mixed* cerebral palsy, in which several of the above characteristics are present. Spastic cerebral palsy is the most common type, occurring in about two thirds of all children with cerebral palsy (Albright, Cervi, & Singletary, 1991).

In addition, cerebral palsy may be congenital (present at birth) or acquired (occurring after birth but usually before 3 years of age). Congenital cerebral palsy is by far the more common of the two.

Our brains and spinal cords signal muscles to contract or to relax; normally, both kinds of signals are sent, resulting in a balance. Signals to contract, or tighten, muscles produce muscle tone; an overabundance of such signals can result in hypertonia, or too much muscle contraction. Signals to relax muscles, if not counterbalanced by contraction signals, may produce hypotonia, or too much muscle relaxation. Hypotonia often occurs in cases of Down syndrome. In cerebral palsy, by contrast, what frequently happens is that the signal system is damaged to the point that muscles are unable to relax. The term *spasticity* refers to tightness of muscles; that is, there is too much muscle tone because signals to suppress muscle contraction are either not sent or not received. Athetoid cerebral palsy, on the other hand, seems to result from sudden and irregular bursts of signals from the brain or spinal cord such that muscles abruptly contract and relax in unpredictable ways.

Cerebral palsy of whatever type is better understood to be a condition rather than a disease. Conditions are lifelong and, at least with respect to the cerebral lesion or physical damage in the brain, unchanging; diseases, on the other hand, usually are short-term in duration and subject to change.

The late William Cruickshank (1976) offered a three-prong description of cerebral palsy (CP) in which he detailed what it is *not:* Cerebral palsy is not inherited, with the exception of one very rare type (United Cerebral Palsy of Washington, 1997) (adults with cerebral palsy tend to have children who are able-bodied). It is not communicable (people around individuals with cerebral palsy cannot catch it). And it is not progressive (the condition itself does not worsen over time). Stated somewhat differently, CP is not remittent, coming and going (in contrast to, for example, multiple sclerosis).

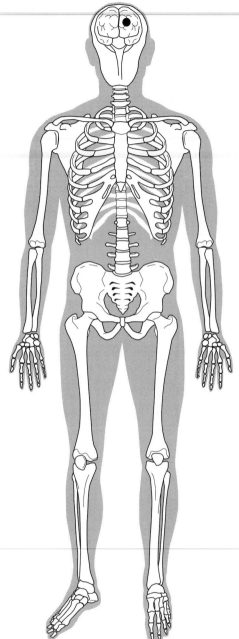

In this figure, and in subsequent figures depicting the human body, small dots are used to indicate the site of the lesion, that is, the point of origin of the condition.

Congenital cerebral palsy may be caused by oxygen deprivation in the brain prior to, during, or shortly after birth. Most often, this occurs because of elongated or too abrupt labor, perhaps because the fetus is in a position that makes birth awkward or because the umbilical cord tightens around the neck or head. In addition, premature separation of the placenta from the wall of the uterus may interrupt oxygen for the fetus. In the past, these kinds of oxygen deprivation were thought to be the most common causes of cerebral palsy. New evidence, however, suggests that most cases might *not* be due to interruptions of oxygen supply (United Cerebral Palsy of Washington, 1997; "When Your Child Has Cerebral Palsy," 1996). Certain infections (including rubella, or German measles), RH incompatibility between the mother and the fetus, premature birth or low birth weight, lack of proper nutrition during pregnancy, unnecessary exposure to X-rays, and microorganisms that attack the fetus account for many cases. In about one third of the instances, the cause or causes are unknown. Acquired cerebral palsy usually results from head trauma in motor vehicle accidents, falls, or child abuse.

Cerebral palsy is markedly more common in families who are of low socioeconomic status (poor, undereducated, and residing either in rural areas or in central cities) than among families in the middle and upper classes. This is usually because of inadequate nutrition during pregnancy and inconsistent or minimal prenatal care from physicians (Gerales & Ritter, 1991). In addition, cerebral palsy is more frequent in instances of multiple births (twins, triplets, etc.) than in singletons. In the 1990s, increasing numbers of women in their late 30s or early 40s have given birth, often with the assistance of fertility drugs, which frequently produce multiple births. Babies born in multiple births tend to be smaller, are more likely to be premature, and are at greater risk for health conditions than are singletons (United Cerebral Palsy Associations [UCPA], 1997).

Prematurity is a major contributing factor in cerebral palsy. According to Steven Bachrach, of the duPont Hospital for Children in Delaware, who has studied cerebral palsy for many years, cerebral palsy may be 50 times as likely among very premature babies as among full-term babies ("When Your Child Has Cerebral Palsy," 1996). Others estimate the likelihood as low as 25 to 30 times (Gerales & Ritter, 1991) or as high as 65 to 70 times (Nelson & Grether, 1995;

Schendel et al., 1996). Whatever the actual figure, it is clear that low-birth-weight, premature infants are at risk for cerebral palsy.

Prevention is advanced if women receive consistent, high-quality prenatal care, including immunizations prior to the onset of pregnancy. Women who have diabetes should consult a physician if they become pregnant. Prompt treatment of any infections in the mother is essential, as is treatment of any jaundice in the newborn. Pregnant women should also avoid unnecessary exposure to X-rays, drugs, and medications. Older women considering use of fertility drugs should be advised that cerebral palsy is one possible outcome of multiple births. With respect to RH incompatibility, the likelihood of cerebral palsy's occurring in the newborn may be minimized by exchange transfusions; the occurrence of CP in a subsequent birth may be prevented by immunizing the mother within 72 hours after the current pregnancy ends.

If at all possible, premature births should be avoided. In the event of prematurity, however, recent research suggests that administration of magnesium sulfate can dramatically lower the likelihood of cerebral palsy in newborns. Studies by Diana E. Schendel and her colleagues at the Centers for Disease Control and Prevention (CDC) and earlier studies by Karin Nelson of the National Institutes of Health (NIH) indicated that when magnesium sulfate was given to pregnant women who later gave birth to very low birth weight children (defined as less than 3.3 pounds), far fewer of those infants had cerebral palsy than otherwise would have been the case (Nelson & Grether, 1995; Schendel et al., 1996). Magnesium sulfate often is given to stop preterm labor.

Acquired cerebral palsy may be prevented by use of seat belts and other safety measures in motor vehicles, child-protection measures and equipment in and around the home to prevent falls, and similar steps in child-care and early-childhood programs. Not all accidents can be prevented, of course, but sensible safety precautions can limit their number and severity.

HOW PREVALENT IS IT? WHAT IS THE INCIDENCE?

About 500,000 Americans have one or more symptoms of cerebral palsy, according to UCPA; some estimates rise as high as 700,000 (National Information Center for Children and Youth with Disabilities, 1997). UCPA suggests that about 5,000 babies and infants are diagnosed with this condition annually; again, others have offered higher estimates. Bachrach, for example, estimated that 10,000 new cases of cerebral palsy occur each year. As these variations suggest, making the diagnosis in newborns who are otherwise healthy is often difficult. If the cerebral palsy is mild, definitive diagnosis may not be possible until after the child's first birthday ("When Your Child Has Cerebral Palsy," 1996).

In addition, there is a custom in the field to identify as cerebral palsy certain injuries to the brain that are sustained during the prenatal, natal, or postnatal period, up until about 3 years of age, but to use such terms as *traumatic*

CP v. all neurological

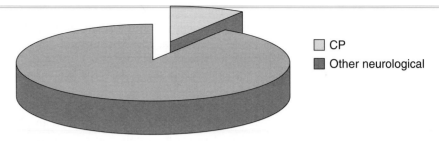

Figure 6.1
Population Estimates: Cerebral Palsy As Compared to All Neurological Physical Disabilities

brain injury (TBI) or *stroke* for cerebral injuries affecting motor control and coordination that occur after 5 years of age. Cerebral palsy is a developmental disability, while neither of the other terms (TBI and stroke) is limited to the developmental period. Some practitioners diagnose cerebral palsy until about 3 years of age, others as late as 5 years of age. Thus, it is not a surprise that UCPA is careful to preface its estimates of the population size with the phrase "have one or more symptoms of cerebral palsy."

WHAT EFFECTS CAN IT HAVE?

Although the brain lesion causing cerebral palsy neither progresses nor regresses, the effects of cerebral palsy can, and often do, change over time. In particular, muscles that are not used may atrophy. As children grow, their muscle strength may not keep pace; walking may become more and more difficult in adolescence and adulthood. As people with cerebral palsy age, muscle coordination and control may become increasingly problematic. Life expectancy approaches normal for people with mild cerebral palsy but is shorter than normal for individuals with severe conditions ("When Your Child Has Cerebral Palsy," 1996). Individuals with cerebral palsy appear to have the same kinds of problems that able-bodied people encounter as they age but tend to have them earlier in life (UCP Research & Educational Foundation, 1996).

Cerebral palsy may be mild, moderate, or severe. Moderate is most common, followed by severe; relatively few people have mild cerebral palsy. In mild cases, children need a little more time to do things and may need assistive technology devices to hold and manipulate objects (Gerales & Ritter, 1991). Children with moderate or severe cerebral palsy usually have a variety of needs, requiring services from a range of specialists, including occupational therapists, physical therapists, speech pathologists, and special educators (UCP Research & Educational Foundation, 1997). In severe cases, they literally cannot express themselves through speech, handwriting, or other conventional means and must use assistive technology devices, such as "talking" personal computers. Such technologies help children with severe CP to dramatically reduce their dependence on others. Before the advent of modern microprocessor-based assistive devices, such children depended on others for virtually every major activity of daily life.

The varied effects of cerebral palsy can be understood if you recognize the many hundreds of fine-motor control muscles people use in speaking, eating, swallowing, writing, or typing, and of the many gross-motor control muscles used in maintaining posture and in walking. In each instance, the root problem of the person with cerebral palsy is not in the muscles but rather in the brain's ability to control the body's muscles.

This way of thinking about cerebral palsy has several important implications. One is that CP is a condition affecting expressive communication. Many hundreds of small muscles are needed for speech and for writing or typing. To some extent, children, adolescents, and adults with cerebral palsy can learn to assert strong control over at least some of these muscles. To some extent, however, they cannot. A second important implication of this way of viewing CP is that the muscles themselves, not being manipulated on a regular basis, may atrophy or weaken over time.

WHAT SECONDARY CONDITIONS ARE COMMON?

Oxygen deprivation in the brain and infections bringing high fevers can also cause hearing and vision impairments as well as mental retardation, seizures, and learning disabilities. Thus, it should not be a surprise that many individuals with cerebral palsy also have these secondary conditions. It is important to recognize that cerebral palsy itself does not produce these other impairments. Rather, they coexist because the same cause or causes that led to cerebral palsy also produced these other conditions.

The muscle control and coordination problems that cerebral palsy causes may lead to additional limitations. In particular, malnutrition may occur among young children who have not yet learned how to chew and swallow food. Bladder and bowel control is performed by muscles; again, muscle control and coordination problems due to cerebral palsy may lead to limitations in bladder or bowel control. If good posture is not maintained, people with cerebral palsy may have problems breathing. If they use a wheelchair and do not practice pressure-sore prevention and amelioration techniques, they may have serious problems with decubitus ulcers (pressure sores).

WHAT NEEDS DO PEOPLE WITH IT HAVE?

Arguably the biggest need people with CP experience is to be recognized as people with abilities. The symptoms of cerebral palsy are often so visible that passersby, neighbors, and others (notably employers) underestimate the abilities of people with this condition. Equipped with the right assistive technology, many people with cerebral palsy function at a high level of independence.

Individuals with cerebral palsy usually have strong needs for physical and occupational therapy, for speech and language pathology, and for assistive technology devices and services. A key goal in each of these kinds of services is to enable the person to express himself or herself: Expressive communication is an urgent need for people with CP. According to UCPA, some 4 million Americans have temporary or permanent speech impediments as a result of cerebral palsy. Of this number, about 750,000 to 1.5 million have severe speech limitations such that they cannot make themselves understood to the person on the street (UCPA, 1998). Even individuals with mild cerebral palsy report having problems being understood; many say that people hang up on them when they phone, mistaking their labored speech for the slurring of a drunk.

Another important need is for accessible and affordable transportation. Although some people with CP do own their own cars and do drive, it is more common for these individuals to rely upon public transportation. Depending on the severity of the condition, accessible and affordable housing may be an equally urgent need.

Cerebral palsy is the single physical disability most likely to require multidisciplinary intervention. Children with CP frequently have problems related to learning, social-emotional growth, perception, vision, hearing, and intellectual functioning, as well as housing and transportation. They may require assistance from special educators, physical and occupational therapists, rehabilitation counselors, speech pathologists, and others.

WHAT SPECIAL-EDUCATION AND RELATED SERVICES MAY HELP?

Mild cerebral palsy is one of the physical disabilities that call for related services more than for special education. If children, youth, and adults with mild cerebral palsy receive the related services they need (e.g., special transportation, assistive technology devices and services, occupational and physical therapy, speech and language pathology), they may not require more than minimal special-education services. Children with severe forms of cerebral palsy, particularly if they also have other disabilities such as mental retardation, will have much more need of special education.

With people who have cerebral palsy, the primary role of the physical therapist is to maintain muscle strength and tone, preventing atrophy. Resistance exercise, in which children use ankle weights, wrist weights, etc., to build up muscle strength, remains somewhat controversial despite recent evidence of efficacy (Damiano, Kelly, & Vaughn, 1995). Physical therapists may also focus upon maintaining proper posture and seating position and upon strengthening muscles so that they can bear the load of the person with CP, whether standing or sitting. While most wheelchairs are designed to support the back at a slightly reclined position, physical and occupational therapists today recognize that a better position for speaking, eating, reading, writing, and some other activities is one in which the individual is leaning slightly *forward*. This is an example of how therapists help individuals with cerebral palsy to do the things they want to do.

In addition, the physical therapist may order appropriate assistive technology devices and provide assistive technology services such as installing the device, testing it, and teaching the individual how to use it. Some important devices and services were described in chapter 5.

The occupational therapist, on the other hand, focuses upon helping the individual with cerebral palsy to accomplish important tasks—eating, dressing, turning pages while reading or writing, and using assistive technology devices. He or she may also fine-tune assistive technology devices and teach people to make effective use of them. Such technologies literally may become the voices and the writing implements of people with CP. Physical and occupational therapists also assist the child with spastic or athetoid cerebral palsy to loosen muscles that have become tight. Maintaining good posture while standing or sitting is another goal of physical and occupational therapy, as severe atrophy may result from chronic, abnormal posture. Speech and language pathologists teach articulation and use of language and often assist in feeding individuals with cerebral palsy.

One cautionary note: Palisano, Kolobe, Haley, Lowes, and Jones (1995), writing in the journal *Physical Therapy,* warned against use of the popular Peabody Developmental Gross Motor Scale (PDMS-GM) as an outcome measure with very young children who have cerebral palsy. While the PDMS-GM may still be used to monitor *group* progress over time, these authors expressed doubt that it will detect individual gains over a 6-month period.

WHAT OTHER INTERVENTIONS CAN BE EFFECTIVE?

One controversial intervention is known as **conductive education.** Although it is just now gaining recognition in the United States, the approach is not a new one; it dates back to 1945, when Dr. Andras Peto developed it in Hungary (Kozma & Balogh, 1995). As mentioned in chapter 4, conductive education features one professional (called the "conductor") assuming responsibility for all of a child's needs. The conductor sets the child's goals, motivates the child to reach them, leads the child through the tasks that lead to those goals, and monitors and reports the child's progress.

WHAT ASSISTIVE TECHNOLOGY DEVICES AND SERVICES MAY HELP?

Many people with cerebral palsy need **positioning aids,** low-tech devices, often custom-made, that help people to maintain proper posture and seating position. Eating, writing, and attending to instruction are among the many activities that are facilitated when individuals maintain proper posture. In addition, good seating and standing positions are important for breathing.

Individuals with cerebral palsy often have fine-motor control problems such that **alternative means of input** often are needed. These range from the simple (a keyguard, or plastic covering for the keyboard) to the complex (still experimental systems that translate brain EEG patterns into words). Keyguards are especially helpful in assisting the individual to avoid hitting the wrong keys by mistake. Keys may be struck only after a finger has reached into the opening over the desired letter; involuntary movements will not result in key entry.

Some people with cerebral palsy, especially young children, need an alternative to the keyboard. Specialized communication boards are available. Many feature membrane pads with extra-large "keys" that feature letters/numbers or pictures. Touching a picture of a cup/glass, for example, might produce the message "I am thirsty." People with voluntary control over at least one muscle (even an eyebrow) can use these alternative input mechanisms. Some devices offer spoken output via computer speech synthesis, while others provide printed or displayed text output, and still others offer both spoken and printed output. Computer speech synthesis systems offer a choice of voices (male, female, child, etc.); this is important psychologically, because the synthesizer is the child's "voice."

As a general rule, children and youth with cerebral palsy should use picture-based communication boards only as much and only for as long as necessary. It is much better if the student must produce full written English—that is, to generate grammatical language—than if the student just touches a picture and the machine produces grammatical English. This is because humans learn language best when they create it. Teachers should insist upon full production of written work even if a student requires additional time to do that.

Other important assistive technology devices are orthoses and prostheses. An orthosis enhances the function of a body part; thus, a splint on a finger may stabilize the finger and make typing easier. Another example of an orthosis is a positioning aid. A prosthesis, by contrast, replaces a body part; thus, an artificial knee and lower leg may make ambulation possible. Children, youth, and adults with cerebral palsy sometimes need orthoses, such as braces, but seldom need prostheses.

Individuals with cerebral palsy have frequently told me how much difficulty they have using the telephone. Pay phones that accept only coins are a particular irritant, since many individuals with CP cannot effectively insert the coins. Even when using their home phones, many people having CP complain that people they call hang up on them, wrongly interpreting their voices to mean that they are drunk. Jenifer Simpson, then a policy analyst with UCPA, recently completed a survey of 100 Americans with CP. Most reported that they avoided use of the phone: 45% ask someone to make or receive calls for them, 29% write letters or otherwise use U.S. mails, and 11% send faxes (Simpson, 1997).

WHAT ARE THE PROSPECTS FOR POSTSECONDARY EDUCATION?

Today, they are quite bright. Young people with cerebral palsy who have completed an academic curriculum leading to a high school diploma will find that postsecondary programs, including colleges and universities, provide assistive technology devices and services as part of their obligation to offer "reasonable accommodations" to individuals with disabilities. In addition, time to complete tests may be extended in recognition of the very time-consuming nature of expressive communication for many people with cerebral palsy, even when they have access to assistive technologies. Two individuals with severe cerebral palsy, other than Dr. Yuker, have worked with me over the years; each received advanced training at universities, with one earning a Ph.D.

WHAT ARE THE EMPLOYMENT PROSPECTS?

These also are quite bright today. The same laws—including the Americans with Disabilities Act and the Rehabilitation Act—require employers with more than 15 workers to practice nondiscrimination in such aspects of employment as hiring, placement, assignment of duties, and fringe benefits. These employers must provide reasonable accommodations on the job to the extent that an individual with a disability is capable of doing that job with or without such devices.

The most promising jobs are those involving use of high technology, particularly personal computers and workstations, because these machines are readily fitted with the kinds of assistive technology devices that many people with cerebral palsy need in order to work effectively. A baccalaureate degree is a minimum requirement for many such jobs. Accommodations enabling high productivity in jobs requiring physical activity (especially manual labor jobs) are not yet widely available; accordingly, employment prospects in jobs requiring a high-school diploma or less education are not good. These factors reinforce the importance of education for people with cerebral palsy.

WHAT ARE THE PROSPECTS FOR INDEPENDENT LIVING?

Most individuals with cerebral palsy can learn to live in the community, whether in an apartment, a semi-independent apartment, or a group home. A semi-independent apartment setting is one in which one or more individuals reside with only occasional assistance from others (e.g., a few hours each day or each week from a housekeeper). A group home is a residential house in which up to a dozen individuals with disabilities and about half that many staff members reside.

Many people with cerebral palsy can establish and carry out a routine that makes independent living possible. They can hold full- or part-time jobs that provide enough financial resources to cover rent, utilities, food, and clothing. **Environmental control units** (ECUs)—which use a small personal computer to turn on or off and manipulate a wide range of electrical devices throughout the home—make independent living easier for people who have limited mobility or fine-motor control.

Spinal Cord Injury

My friend Max Starkloff (1937–) of St. Louis, Missouri, acquired a quadriplegic spinal cord injury (SCI) in 1959 when he was involved in an automobile accident while a college student. After living at home for a few years, he moved into a nursing home—the only option available to him at the time. He

Max Starkloff began Paraquad because of his own needs for housing, transportation, and personal care services in St. Louis.

hated it. After 12 years there, at age 38, he began what he called a life-or-death effort to create community support services so that he could escape from the institution. In time, his efforts led to Paraquad, the not-for-profit organization he still leads today. Paraquad coordinates transportation, housing, attendant care services, and other support services for people with disabilities in the St. Louis area. After living with SCI for more than 40 years, Max is still energized by the promise of independent living—the marshaling of community support services so as to enable people with severe physical disabilities to live as freely and as productively as others in the community. Today, he is the father of three teenagers.

WHAT IS IT?

A spinal cord injury (SCI) is a lesion, usually from flexing (extension) or bruising but occasionally from an actual break (severing) of the spinal cord that results in paralysis (partial or complete loss of function, especially with respect to motion and sensation in a body part). A lesion is a site or location where damage has occurred. Both motion and sensation are involved in spinal cord injury. The spinal cord is the principal mode through which efferent (from the brain) and afferent (to the brain) messages are transported.

Accordingly, when the cord is injured, both kinds of messages may stop. Children or adults with SCI are unable to "tell" the legs or other body parts what to do (efferent messages). They also may injure a toe, for example, and not feel any pain (afferent messages).

The spinal cord contains millions of nerve cells. Neurons (individual nerve cells) have receptive fibers (dendrites) and sending fibers (axons). Axons are covered by a protective myelin sheath, which helps the impulses to travel efficiently. (The myelin sheath is important; one possible cause of SCI is loss of the myelin sheath rather than damage to the nerve cell itself.) Impulses from one neuron's axons are picked up by another neuron's dendrites through a connection known as a synapse. The impulse "jumps" across the synapse to stimulate a second neuron, which subsequently sends a signal through its axons to yet another neuron's dendrites. The process continues until the signal reaches its intended target. In spinal cord injury, the neurons below the site of the lesion are no longer under voluntary control (they may, however, cause uncontrolled movements, known as spasms).

An SCI differs from a back injury such as a ruptured disk. Someone who broke his or her back or broke his or her neck would not have an SCI unless the incident damaged the spinal cord. Most back injuries damage the bones around the cord (the vertebrae) but not the cord itself. Paralysis seldom occurs once the bones have been stabilized.

The vast majority of SCIs are externally caused in a sudden accident. A few people sustain disease-induced SCIs; causes include tumors and polio. These cases have attracted relatively little scientific interest. What we know about SCI relates almost entirely to acute, accident-caused injuries.

In most such injuries, the higher (closer to the head) the cord is traumatized, the more pervasive the effects. High-level SCI produces paralysis not only in the legs but also in the arms, hands, and fingers. This is called **quadriplegia** (on occasion, tetraplegia, from *tetra,* for four). Lower-level SCI, by contrast, principally affects the legs in what is called **paraplegia.** Today, according to the National Spinal Cord Injury Statistical Center (NSCISC) at the University of Alabama at Birmingham (1997), half of all SCIs produce paraplegia and the other half lead to quadriplegia (NSCISC, 1997).

The spinal cord is surrounded by rings of bone called vertebrae, which are named pursuant to their location. The eight vertebrae in the neck are called the cervical vertebrae: C1, C2, . . . C8. Chest-level vertebrae are called thoracic vertebrae (T1–T12). Vertebrae from the lower back to the pelvis are called lumbar vertebrae (L1–L5). Finally, vertebrae from the pelvis to the end of the spinal column are called sacral vertebrae (S1–S5). According to the NSCISC (1997), the most common injury level is C5, followed in order of descending frequency by C4, C6, T12, and L1. In general, cervical or C-level (high-level) injuries lead to quadriplegia and lumbar or L-level (low-level) injuries to paraplegia.

In a *complete SCI,* no sensation or motor function remains below the site of the injury (e.g., in the legs in the case of paraplegia). It is not necessary that the spinal cord be severed for an injury to be considered to be complete, although it is necessary that no meaningful feeling or control

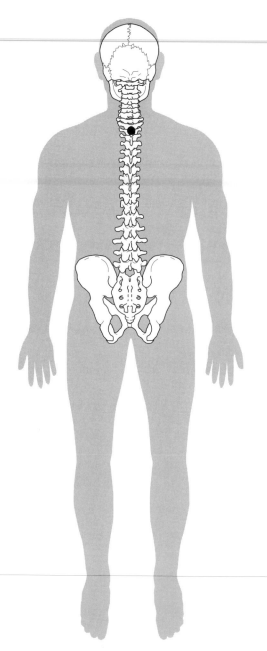

Spinal cord injuries originate, as the name suggests, on the spinal cord. If the bruising, or even bifurcation, occurs near the "tail," the injury affects volitional control of the legs (paraplegia). If it happens near the "neck" of the spinal cord, it affects control of the arms and hands as well as the legs (quadriplegia).

exist below the level of the injury. An *incomplete SCI,* by contrast, leaves *some* sensation or motor function at the lowest level of the spinal cord, that is, in the last sacral segment (S4–S5). In some instances, people with incomplete SCIs can move limbs on one side of the body better than on the other side. Both complete and incomplete injuries can lead to paraplegia and to quadriplegia. Dr. Wei Young, of New York University, a nationally recognized expert on SCI, has noted that the term *complete* is a controversial one, because saying an SCI is complete has unfortunate connotations of finality and hopelessness. It also overlooks the fact that people who receive prompt treatment may recover some sensation or function or both (Young, 1996). According to the NSCISC (1997), about 45% of all injuries documented since 1988 have been complete, and the balance have been incomplete. The number of incomplete injuries is rising as acute treatment techniques improve.

WHAT CAUSES IT? CAN IT BE PREVENTED? IF SO, HOW?

The NSCISC has reported that many of the accidents that cause TBI can also cause SCI. The difference is that with SCI, the spine rather than the brain itself is traumatized. As with TBI, accidents, in particular, automobile, bicycle, and sports accidents, are the most common cause of SCI. Diving accounts for some two thirds of all sports accidents. Falls are also a common cause. Since 1995, acts of violence have emerged as a prominent cause of SCI, overtaking falls for second place behind motor vehicle accidents. Meanwhile, the proportion due to motor vehicle and sports accidents has been declining (NSCISC, 1997; Young, 1996). The NSCISC estimates that 37% of SCIs are due to motor vehicle accidents, 26% to acts of violence, 24% to falls, 7% to sports, and 6% to all other causes. The National Spinal Cord Injury Association (1997) offers slightly different estimates: 42% for motor vehicle accidents, 24% acts of violence, and 22% falls.

Between 1995 and 1997, acts of violence, particularly with firearms, increased dramatically. These acts occur most often in urban areas, and the victims most frequently are members of ethnic or racial minority groups. Victims also are, as a group, younger than individuals who sustain SCIs in other ways. Stab wounds are another cause of violence-related SCI. Whereas gunshot wounds tend to produce complete injuries, stab wounds more often lead to incomplete ones (Walters, Cressy, & Adkins, 1996).

Acts of violence most frequently lead to paraplegia because gun or knife wounds generally are to the chest or abdomen. Sports accidents, on the other hand, more often lead to quadriplegia because the injury is usually at the neck level (Stover, 1996).

Prevention measures appear obvious considering the causes. Use of supplemental restraint systems (air bags) and seat belts in motor vehicles, safety helmets for motorcycles and bicycles, and safety equipment in sporting events reduces the number and severity of injuries; the evidence is that such equipment has in fact resulted in fewer SCIs. Similarly, use of protective equipment, strict enforcement of rules against unsportsmanlike conduct, and other measures have reduced the frequency of injury in sports. In fact, the proportion of all SCIs due to sports injuries has fallen by more than half since 1979 (Stover, 1996). Warning signs about shallow pools and ponds or lakes could help to reduce the number of diving accidents.

Research by Dr. Young's team at NYU and the National Acute Spinal Cord Injury Study II (NASCIS II) revealed in 1990 that administration of high-dose methylprednisolone (MP) within 8 hours of the time of the accident substantially improves recovery (Bracken et al., 1992). However, methylprednisolone is a steroid and as such has undesirable side effects in humans. This is why research is now being conducted in an attempt to isolate from methylprednisolone the active agent(s) that help in SCI. Another experimental drug is GM-1, or Sygen. This is the treatment that enabled former New York Jet football player Dennis Byrd to walk (with crutches) after a career-ending spinal cord injury. This drug, too, must be administered shortly after the incident, usually within 72 hours.

The brain and the spinal cord taken together make up the **central nervous system** (CNS). In humans, the CNS does not regenerate. By contrast, motor and sensory nerves in the **peripheral nervous system** (PNS) may regenerate. (A third system of nerves controls such involuntary functions as blood pressure.) A major thrust of research is to identify exactly how PNS nerves regenerate and then to see whether this can be made to happen in the CNS. Recent research suggests that some cells in the adult CNS may be stimulated to divide and to develop into new neurons.

HOW PREVALENT IS IT? WHAT IS THE INCIDENCE?

Spinal cord injuries occur each year to about 8,000 to 10,000 Americans, of whom the vast majority (82%) are male. This is an incidence rate of about 40 cases per million population. According to the NSCISC, between 183,000 and 230,000 Americans with SCI are alive today. The National Spinal Cord Injury Association (1997), however, has estimated that 450,000 Americans have SCIs. Spinal cord injuries occur most frequently to people in the 16–30 age range. Injuries peak at age 19; about 10% involve children under the age of 15. Most individuals who sustain SCIs are single at the time of injury.

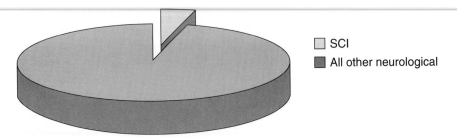

SCI v. all neurological

SCI

All other neurological

Figure 6.2
Population Estimates: Spinal Cord Injury As Compared to All Neurological Physical Disabilities

WHAT EFFECTS CAN IT HAVE?

The extent of the effects of SCI vary according to (1) the type of injury (e.g., complete vs. incomplete) and (2) the level of the injury (e.g., C5 vs. T9). For example, someone with a complete injury at the C5 level could achieve some control over the shoulders and biceps but not usually over the wrists, hands, or fingers. An individual with an incomplete T9 injury, on the other hand, could control the abdominal muscles well and achieve good seating posture; the arms, wrists, hands, and fingers would not be affected by the injury.

To appreciate the impact of these kinds of effects, consider that most individuals who sustain SCIs are younger males. Many led a physically active lifestyle prior to the injury. For example, Marini, Rogers, Slate, and Vines (1995) found that about 33% of Arkansas residents who were working at the time of injury held physically demanding jobs (e.g., machinery operators, day laborers). Thus, the transition to a sedentary lifestyle that features dependence upon other people may be a jarring one. Marini et al. found that self-esteem among individuals was lowest in the second year after injury because by that time, the family and social support that sustained them during the first year had largely dissipated and because the injured individuals no longer could assume a "sick role" that excused them from having to take responsibility for their own lives. The sick role (see Gliedman & Roth, 1980, for an excellent discussion) protects the individual from self-doubt because it offers a temporary reprieve from most adult roles. "Two years postinjury, however, most people with SCI have returned home, made maximum physical strength gains, are unemployed, and experience a markedly lower level of social support than during hospitalization" (Marini et al., 1995, p. 204).

WHAT SECONDARY CONDITIONS ARE COMMON?

Secondary conditions directly caused by SCI are quite common. Examining data from one regional spinal cord injury center, Anson and Shepherd (1996) reported that only 4% of participants were free of *any* secondary conditions at the time of their regular physical examination. An obvious such condition is **pressure sores** (decubitus ulcers), which occur when the individual does not shift weight on a wheelchair cushion or bed. Frequent weight shifting (e.g., pushing down on the wheelchair arm rests, lifting the trunk and legs and repositioning them) is necessary, and special cushions may be helpful for preventing pressure sores. Pressure sores may also appear on the foot or heel (Anson & Shepherd, 1996).

Pressure sores occur deep in the tissue, close to bone, and so are well developed before visible damage is apparent. This makes monitoring by the individual and professionals urgent. Garber, Rintala, Rossi, Hart, and Fuhrer (1996) added that education programs designed to teach SCI patients how to detect and treat pressure sores have been shortened greatly in recent years, a victim of managed-care-related pressures for early discharge: "Thus, individuals with SCI are now returning to the community with less information about self-care. . . .Persons with SCI and their families must take even more responsibility for the prevention and appropriate management of pressure ulcers" (p. 748).

Other common secondary concerns are bowel and bladder control, spasticity, pain, and obesity. Anson and Shepherd noted that spasticity can be related to bladder function, and bladder function in turn with spasticity. People with SCI may also have low blood pressure, inability to sweat below the level of the lesion, and chronic pain (National Spinal Cord Injury Association, 1997). Urinary tract infections may occur; the lack of afferent messages to the brain means that the individual may not complain about urinary pain. People with SCI learn that they must check for infections on a regular basis; family members, friends, and professionals should also be alert to signs of infection. About one third to one half of all individuals with SCI are rehospitalized in any given year, usually because of secondary conditions.

Max Starkloff has called attention to **autonomic dysreflexia** as an important secondary condition with SCI. Here, a stimulus such as bladder distension (which may be caused by intestine or colon obstructions) leads to high blood pressure, sweating, and headaches. If left untreated, it could become life threatening. This is one example—urinary tract infections are another—of why people with SCI need readily available medical facilities in order to maintain health even years or decades after the initial accident (Starkloff, 1997).

Although pain below the site of the lesion may not be felt, other kinds of pain are very definitely felt. Anson and Shepherd reported that 45% of patients at one spinal-cord center complained of pain, with 13% feeling pain even after taking prescribed medication. They commented that pain was reported by individuals who were injured as long as 5 years previously. This was particularly true of patients who also complained of muscle spasticity.

Fertility usually is not affected by SCI in women; men, however, may have reduced fertility. Women with SCI can become pregnant and deliver healthy babies, while many men with SCI can become fathers.

About half of all accidents producing SCI lead to other injuries in addition to the direct effects of spinal cord injury, according to the NSCISC (1997). A frequent one is a head injury (traumatic brain injury).

WHAT NEEDS DO PEOPLE WITH IT HAVE?

Aside from removal of architectural, transportation, and other barriers in the community, individuals with SCI often need help with self-esteem because their postinjury lives leave them more dependent upon others (Marini et al., 1995). In extreme cases, depression may develop. In a sweeping review of the literature on depression and SCI, Elliott and Frank (1996) noted that preinjury histories of social maladjustment, drug abuse, and use of alcohol frequently accompany depression in individuals with SCI: "These data imply that individuals who have exhibited difficulties coping with the general demands of life will have greater difficulty coping with SCI" (p. 819).

Research has shown that positive self-esteem is related, not surprisingly, to good overall health, a positive outlook both about the disability and in general, economic security, activity (people who are active socially, recreationally, and in other ways such as employment tend to have better self-esteem), and accessible living environments (Boschen, 1996). The fact that many individuals with SCI have problems in one or more of these areas may be related to their lowered self-esteem as much as, if not more than, the injury itself. Indeed, Boschen (1996) found no significant correlations between life satisfaction and the injury itself. Rather, life satisfaction varied as a function of perceived control, choice, and independence in daily living:

> Because none of the variables that were significant predictors of life satisfaction were disability related, there is no inherent reason for individuals with SCI to experience a lower level of life satisfaction than their nondisabled peers experience, other than those relating to societal and attitudinal barriers, many of which affect choice and control over their living circumstances. (p. 240)

WHAT SPECIAL-EDUCATION AND RELATED SERVICES MAY HELP?

Individuals with SCI who have not yet graduated from high school and who are under 22 years of age generally qualify for the free, appropriate public education offered by the IDEA. Schools usually classify SCI students as "orthopedic impaired" or "other health impaired" because the IDEA does not provide a separate category for spinal cord injury. The IDEA guarantees both special-education (specially designed instruction) and related services (noninstructional services a child needs in order to benefit from special education).

Students with SCI usually can do the same academic work at the same pace as can students with no disabilities. The major needs of children and adolescents with SCI are for physical and occupational therapy and for assistive technology devices and services. Also essential are **transition** services. The student may need to change post-high-school plans. Even if career or postsecondary education plans remain unchanged, ways to reach goals may have to be altered. That is why transition services (which the IDEA requires as part of the Individualized Education Program for all students aged 14 or older) are so critical. In transition services, goals are established in one or more of three general areas: employment, postsecondary education, and independent living in the community. Services then are scheduled to assist the student to meet those goals.

Some individuals, especially those whose injuries are new, will benefit from personal counseling. **Peer counseling,** in which an individual with a long-standing SCI counsels the student with new SCI, can be very effective, particularly in offering real-world, practical solutions to everyday problems. My former student Dennis Mooney, who is a quadriplegic, offers such counseling to newly injured adolescents and adults. He observes that nondirective counseling, in which he answers questions by talking about his own experiences and those of other people with SCI but does not tell the individual what to do, seems to be most effective (Mooney, 1998).

An implant designed by NeuroControl Corporation was approved by the Food and Drug Administration (FDA) in mid-1997 for certain people who have quadriplegia. The "Freehand" prosthetic is a microprocessor about the size of a pacemaker. Implanted in the chest and connected by wires running under the skin to electrodes in hand and forearm muscles, the device helps people to grasp, manipulate, and release objects such as pens, forks, and books. It does this by signaling the thumb and fingers to pinch together or to separate. The device retails for about $60,000, which includes the surgery to implant it and follow-up training, usually of 5 months' duration, in its use (Ingersoll, 1997).

In a study of 53 children and adolescents who sustained SCI prior to age 18, Massagli, Dudgeon, and Ross (1996) found that physical and occupational therapy and an aide to assist in the classroom were the most common related services provided to the students in their elementary or secondary schools or in college. Related services are support services such as transportation, counseling, physical and occupational therapy, and speech pathology that are necessary for a child to benefit from special education. The most frequent special-education services were extra time to complete in-class work, relocation of the class to another classroom, and alternate assignments in academic courses. The students generally did well in school (e.g., secondary school students with SCI most often ranked in the top quartile of their classes, and a strong 82% eventually went on to receive at least some postsecondary education).

WHAT OTHER INTERVENTIONS CAN BE EFFECTIVE?

Because the need for accessible and affordable housing and public transportation is so great among persons with SCI, and because choice and control in other areas of life also are highly correlated with life satisfaction for individuals with SCI (Boschen 1996), professionals and family members alike should place high priority on these areas. Often, this means becoming an active advocate for barrier removal in the community—for curbcuts in walkways, for lifts on buses, for wide doors and ramps in places of public accommodation. But it also means leaving the decision about what to do, when to do it, how to do it, etc., to the individual with SCI whenever feasible.

With alcohol and other drug abuse being relatively common prior to or at the time of the injury, with pain being a common secondary condition in SCI, and with addiction to pain killers always being a possibility, other alcohol and drug counseling and treatment programs may be very helpful. To be effective, these programs should be paired with family and professional advocacy for accessible and affordable housing and transportation and with family and professional measures to grant the individual with SCI maximum control and choice. This is because counseling itself helps little unless the world around the individual is accommodating. Max Starkloff's life story illustrates this. Max needed to fashion in his St. Louis neighborhood the support services he needed before he could take charge of his life.

WHAT ASSISTIVE TECHNOLOGIES AND SERVICES CAN HELP?

Most people with SCI use wheelchairs. Some individuals, with help from physical and occupational therapy, can avoid need of a wheelchair except for distance mobility. There are even "walking quads" who have learned to walk independently with a cane or other means of support. However, most individuals with quadriplegia use power (motorized) wheelchairs. People with paraplegia usually do well with manual wheelchairs.

An important point is that wheelchair users are not confined to a wheelchair. They can, and do, get out of the chair. People can transfer from a manual wheelchair onto an automobile seat or a boat. They can also transfer to toilet seats or beds. Some individuals make a point of using braces and other mobility aides several times daily for purposes of exercise and health maintenance.

Sports wheelchairs for recreation and sports uses are now readily available. Such wheelchairs may be particularly attractive to people with SCI because so many of these persons were very active physically prior to the accident and sports are a major part of their lives and of their identities. Sports chairs are very different from everyday chairs: They are much lighter and more streamlined and have fewer parts. Some come with wheels that are angled outward for greater stability at high speed and for more maneuverability in wheelchair basketball, soccer, and other sports. Unfortunately, most insurance plans (including Medicaid and Medicare) reimburse costs for only one, primary wheelchair.

WHAT ARE THE PROSPECTS FOR POSTSECONDARY EDUCATION?

These prospects are excellent. Today, virtually all of America's 3,000+ colleges and universities have achieved program accessibility. This means that all academic courses and most extracurricular activities are held in accessible locations. If, for example, a class is scheduled in a nonaccessible room, it would be moved to another, accessible classroom. Recall that the Massagli et al. (1996) study found relocation of classes to be a common accommodation. In addition, most colleges and universities have special-services coordinators who are familiar with the needs of individuals with SCI and experienced in meeting those needs.

According to the National Spinal Cord Injury Model Systems Data Base, 49% of persons who were 17 years of age or younger at the time of the injury continued their education after the injury. The proportion is much smaller for individuals who were 18 or older at injury. In general, the data show, individuals with more severe injuries (those with complete injuries and those who sustained quadriplegia) get more education following the injury than do those with less serious injuries. This may reflect their understanding that they need more education to become more employable (Dijikers, 1996). Krause (1996), reporting on an 11-year longitudinal study, found exactly such a relation: Persons with SCI who were college educated were much more likely to work (95%) for some time in the postinjury years than were those who lacked even a high-school diploma (38%).

WHAT ARE THE PROSPECTS FOR INDEPENDENT LIVING?

The major independent-living problems for people with SCI are securing accessible residences and accessible transportation and meeting personal care needs. Homes or apartments often must be altered so as to be accessible. In most instances, the cost for these changes is borne by the individual because little in the way of government or private third-party support is available. The major exceptions are (1) when the SCI is a service-connected disability sustained while on active duty, in which case the federal Department of Veterans Affairs often will pick up the costs of residential alterations, and (2) when the SCI results from an insurance-covered accident, in which case the insurance company may pay all or most of the costs. Veterans also may secure accessible cars, vans, or trucks from the Department; private insurance policies may pay for alterations to a motor vehicle. An example of such an alteration is hand controls in a car or van.

Accessible and affordable housing and transportation remain two of the most vexing needs of many individuals with SCI. Only a very small proportion (1% to 2%) of private homes and apartments in the United States meet barrier-free code standards. The number meeting accessibility standards is just a few percentage points higher. Thus, although most individuals who sustain SCIs are discharged from the hospital or rehabilitation facility to a private home (Dijikers, 1996), alterations usually are required in those homes to make them liveable. Such changes are important for the individual's self-esteem: Living in a private home or apartment gives people with SCI far greater control over their daily lives than does living in an institutional environment. In addition, it fulfills lifelong expectations that they, like others, will live in such a setting (Boschen, 1996).

Personal care attendants (PCAs) help many individuals with spinal cord injuries, especially quadriplegics, in daily life activities. They may assist in dressing, cooking, and transferring from bed to chair or chair to toilet and may perform household chores such as cleaning. The best model is one in which the individual with an SCI personally selects, hires, supervises, and pays the PCA. That way, the person with the disability is in control and makes the key decisions, not some impersonal third-party nursing organization. A continuing problem is turnover among PCAs, largely because their pay seldom rises much above minimum wage.

WHAT ARE THE EMPLOYMENT PROSPECTS?

They are excellent as well. Once the individual's health status has stabilized and the individual has learned to cope with the injury, little stands between a person with SCI and employment. The Americans with Disabilities Act, the Rehabilitation Act, and many state laws require employers with 15 or more workers to practice nondiscrimination in such aspects of employment as hiring, placement, assignment of duties, and fringe benefits. These employers must provide reasonable accommodations on the job, including accessibility at the work site in common areas such as lobbies and cafeterias and in rooms used for interviews and testing. In addition, employers may not discriminate in any aspect of employment, from job descriptions to testing to hiring to compensation to benefits to termination.

One of the favorable aspects of SCI as compared to many of the other disabilities discussed in this book is that SCI is a stable injury. The needs of the individual with the injury do not change over time much more than do those of able-bodied people. In addition, most accommodations that people with SCI need are one-time, capital outlays such as wider doors or ramps.

For all of these reasons, one would anticipate that the rates of gainful employment among people with SCI would be rather high. The reality is quite different. Whereas 60% of people of working age (16–64) who sustain SCI were employed at the time of the injury, just 16% return to work within 1 year. It is only by the 10th anniversary of the injury that as many as 30% have jobs (34% among paraplegics and 24% among quadriplegics). By contrast, 49% of those who were homemakers at the time of the injury and 71% of those who were students at the time return to those roles within a year (Dijikers, 1996).

Krause (1996) suggested that employment is highly correlated with education: Individuals with a college degree were much more frequently working than were individuals with lower levels of education attainment. Krause also found that continued education is most likely to occur when people are young at the time of the injury. Of persons in Krause's sample who were aged 17 or younger at the time of injury, 60% were employed at the time of the study and 89% had worked at some point following the injury. Both proportions were much higher than those for people aged 18 or over at the time of injury. However, many who reenter employment later discontinue work, most often when they reach their 50s. Krause speculated that they, in effect, take early retirement. His 11-year longitudinal study of individuals with SCI indicated that employment has a "spread effect" (p. 253), such that it tends to enhance other aspects of life. Discontinuance of employment, on the other hand, is associated with declines in other areas of life. Krause commented that the data do not clearly show whether stopping work led to those other declines or whether the opposite occurred: People stopped working because their overall quality of life had begun to decline. One apparent reason for early retirement is that life expectancy for people with SCI is about 10 years shorter than that for able-bodied persons. It might just be that simple: Many people with SCI may feel the need to retire from gainful employment several years before others their age do.

Spina Bifida

My former graduate student Elysse Power (1973–), of Rockville Centre, New York, likes to say: "I don't look at myself as being disabled. I feel that I am able to do everything that anyone else can do. I just do things sitting down and sometimes differently" (Power, 1997). Elysse has had surgery 30 times; that is a high number, even for someone with spina bifida. A graduate student in special education, she was chosen Ms. Wheelchair New York 1997. She also lent her considerable energies and effervescent personality to the Games for the Physically Challenged held near Hofstra in mid-1997.

WHAT IS IT?

Spina bifida (the name refers to the spine's being divided into two or open spine or cleft spine) is a condition in which the spinal cord does not completely close during the first month (28 days) of fetal development during pregnancy. It is an incomplete closure in the spinal column. The condition is a **neural tube defect** (NTD), and spina bifida is the most common NTD.

There are three distinct kinds of spina bifida but only one that routinely leads to serious health, education, and other problems. That form is **myelomeningocele,** the most severe kind of spina bifida (*myelo* means 'marrow' in Greek, *meningo* refers to 'meninges', the covering that protects the brain and spinal cord, and *cele* means 'swelling' or 'tumor'). In myelomeningocele, nerves of the spinal cord protrude through the back. Although surgery can and usually does help, the condition leads to significant, permanent limitations. Myelomeningocele can be thought of as a condition-caused spinal cord injury (refer to previous discussion of spinal cord injury in which SCIs caused by traumatic accidents were contrasted to disease- or condition-caused SCIs).

A second form is **meningocele.** Here, the covering (meninges) around the spinal cord pushes through an opening, but the spinal cord itself remains intact. Meningocele usually can be resolved surgically, with few or no lasting effects. Myelomeningocele and meningocele together are sometimes referred to as "spina bifida manifesta." According to the National Information Center for Children and Youth with Disabilities (1997), 96% of all instances of spina bifida manifesta are of myelomeningocele, with just 4% being of meningocele.

Ms. Wheelchair New York 1997's smile endures despite two dozen surgeries in her young life. Elysse Power says she does everything anyone else does. She just does some of them differently.

The third form is **spina bifida occulta.** In this variation, there is an opening in one or more of the vertebrae of the spinal cord, but it is not visible and it causes no noticeable effects. Because meningocele is so readily repaired and spina bifida occulta leads to no disability, the first form (myelomeningocele) is considered, for all practical purposes, to be spina bifida. In fact, in the professional literature the words *spina bifida* and *myelomeningocele* are used interchangeably. The discussion of spina bifida that follows focuses on myelomeningocele.

As with all kinds of spinal cord injuries, the site of the lesion is a critical factor in spina bifida. Functions that are controlled by neurons below the cleft or incomplete closure are affected. Spina bifida interferes with afferent

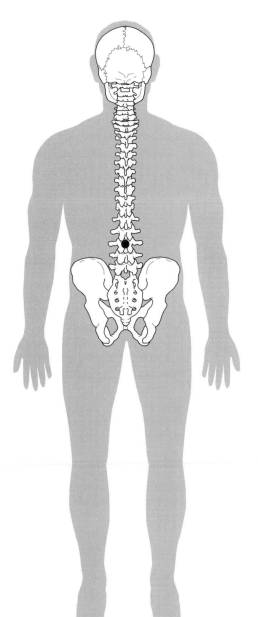

(to the brain) and efferent (from the brain) messages, limiting the child's ability to monitor bodily functions, pain, etc. (afferent) and to control voluntary muscle and other brain-directed patterns (efferent). For these reasons, some paralysis is common with spina bifida. As is the case with spinal cord injury, the basic problem is not that the muscles do not work but rather that the brain messages telling them what to do never reach those muscles.

WHAT CAUSES IT? CAN IT BE PREVENTED? IF SO, HOW?

Some cases of spina bifida may be traced to a gene that acts in concert with environmental factors. Research sponsored by the National Institute of Child Health and Development (NICHD), one of the National Institutes of Health (NIH), in 1995 identified an error in the gene that makes an enzyme that plays a key role in the body's use of folate. This error, taken together with folic acid insufficiencies in the mother's diet, appears to cause at least some instances of spina bifida.

One intervention that appears to prevent at least some occurrences of spina bifida is diet supplementation. If the mother-to-be has been taking 0.4 milligram of folic acid daily during the month prior to conception and continues to take that amount throughout the first three months of pregnancy, the likelihood that spina bifida will occur is dramatically lowered. This dosage is the Recommended Daily Allowance of folic acid. Since 1992, the U.S. Public Health Service has urged that all women aged 16–44 (the so-called childbearing age range) who might become pregnant should take this amount of folic acid daily. In 1996, the U.S. Food and Drug Administration (FDA) ordered that all "enriched" foods be fortified with folic acid as of January 1, 1998 (enriched foods include certain flours, cornmeal, pasta, rice, and other grains that have had vitamins and other nutrients added to them). Women who are pregnant might also eat foods rich in folic acid (a B vitamin), including orange juice, broccoli, beans, peanut butter, spinach, and peas. However, because it is difficult to consume the recommended amount through diet alone, multivitamins containing folic acid may be helpful (Centers for Disease Control and Prevention, 1992; Lary & Edmonds, 1996).

The Spina Bifida Association of America (SBAA) (1997) estimated that the incidence of spina bifida could fall by as much as 75% if all women of childbearing age regularly took appropriate amounts of folic acid. The association stressed that folic acid-rich diets should be followed or sup-

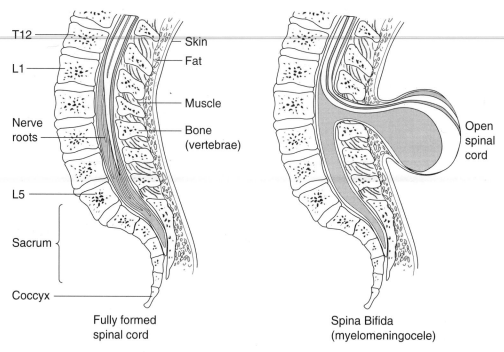

T12

L1

Nerve
roots

L5

Sacrum

Coccyx

Skin

Fat

Muscle

Bone
(vertebrae)

Open
spinal
cord

Fully formed
spinal cord

Spina Bifida
(myelomeningocele)

Adapted with permission from *Infants and Young Children*, "The Infant and Young Child with Spina Bifida: Major Medical Concerns," Catherine Shaer, Vol. 9, No. 3, p. 17. Copyright 1997 Aspen Publishers, Inc.

plements taken by all women in the 16–44 age range, because waiting until such women decide to become pregnant might not work: More than half of all pregnancies are unplanned.

Some occurrences of spina bifida can be identified during pregnancy. One such test is the alpha-fetoprotein (AFP) blood-screening test. If elevated levels of maternal serum AFP are detected, a second test, the ultrasound examination of the fetal spine, and a third, amniocentesis, where amniotic fluid is withdrawn with a needle so that amniotic levels of AFP can be measured, may be performed (Shaer, 1997). A few cases of prenatal surgery following such tests have been reported, some as early as 23 weeks into the pregnancy. About 20% of instances of spina bifida feature skin or thick tissue covering on the cleft; these "closed" cases of spina bifida usually will not be detected by AFP tests. Occasionally, women elect to abort rather than carry the fetus to term; in other instances, the expectant parents can be counseled, and delivery in a specially equipped medical center can be planned.

HOW PREVALENT IS IT? WHAT IS THE INCIDENCE?

The March of Dimes has estimated that spina bifida occurs about once in every 2,000 live births, or about 1,500 times each year in the United States. The condition is most common among Hispanics and non-Hispanic whites of European origin, but less often among African Americans and Asian Ameri-

Spina Bifida v. all neurological

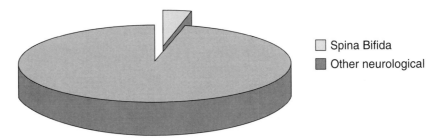

Spina Bifida

Other neurological

Figure 6.3
Population Estimates: Spina Bifida As Compared to All Neurological Physical Disabilities

cans. Neural tube defects of all kinds are about twice as common (about 1 per 1,000 live births) as spina bifida, the most common NTD. The National Easter Seals Society has offered estimates that are 4 times those of the March of Dimes (2 per 1,000 live births), or some 6,000 newborns annually (National Easter Seals Society, 1997). Shaer (1997) halved the above differences, estimating the incidence at 1 per 1,000 pregnancies. That is also the estimate of the Spina Bifida Association of America (SBBA) (1997), which notes that more children have spina bifida than have muscular dystrophy, multiple sclerosis, and cystic fibrosis combined. Given that 4 million infants are born in the United States annually (including at least 4,000 with spina bifida) and that most individuals with spina bifida live well into adulthood, the prevalence may be in excess of 200,000.

WHAT EFFECTS CAN IT HAVE?

As many as 70% to 90% of persons born with myelomeningocele develop **hydrocephalus,** a buildup of cerebrospinal fluid in the brain. This fluid cushions and protects the brain and spinal cord. However, if it cannot drain normally because of the spinal cleft, it collects in and around the brain, enlarging the head and leading to mental retardation or other neurological damage. A **shunt,** or straw-shaped drain, must be used to relieve this fluid buildup (Shaer, 1997). The shunt tubing snakes through the body to the abdominal cavity, where it empties the fluid. As is the case with any other mechanical device used in the body, problems may emerge; for example, the shunt may become infected at either or both ends. Shaer (1997) has offered an excellent summary of indicators of shunt infection or failure.

The concept of functions being lost below the level of the lesion in the spinal cord was introduced earlier (refer to the discussion of spinal cord injury). Virtually all children with myelomeningocele have paralysis of functions below the incomplete closure or cleft (Shaer, 1997). Most such lesions are in the lumbosacral region (the lower levels of the spinal cord). Because bladder and bowel control are governed by connections near the bottom of

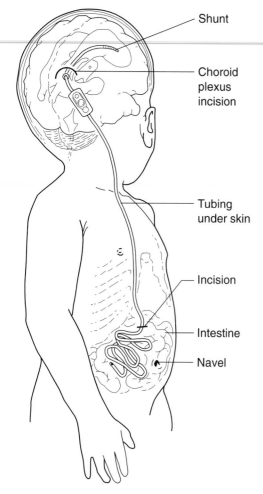

Shunt

Choroid plexus incision

Tubing under skin

Incision

Intestine

Navel

A shunt collects fluid from the brain and drains it into the abdominal cavity. This prevents build-up of excess fluid in the brain.

the spinal cord, these functions almost always are affected in spina bifida (Lutkenhoff & Oppenheimer, 1996; Rowley-Kelly & Reigel, 1993). Mid-lumbar sites may lead to constant urinary dribbling. The less common thoracic or higher sites may be associated with loss of control over and sensation of pain from the lower limbs, the upper limbs, or both.

WHAT SECONDARY CONDITIONS ARE COMMON?

Some children with severe conditions are at increased risk of developing meningitis, which often proves fatal with these children. In severe cases, retardation may occur, often because of hydrocephalus. In some instances, tendinitis, obesity, learning disability, and depression may occur.

Latex (natural rubber) allergies are common with spina bifida. While individuals with other impairments may also have latex allergies, especially if they are often exposed to surgery, the problem is most common in those with spina bifida. This is a very serious matter. Some children with latex sensitivity must be educated at home, because just one exposure to latex (e.g., in a party balloon) could trigger a fatal reaction.

Latex-free substitutes should be used whenever feasible. Latex is commonly found in many products, including catheters, diapers, elastic bandages, rubber bands, balloons, and pacifiers. Particularly worrisome are catheters, because many individuals with spina bifida must use catheters for urine elimination, and surgical gloves, because many people with spina bifida, such as my student Elysse Power, have frequent surgery (Landwehr & Boguniewicz, 1996). Fortunately, virtually all products made with latex have latex-free alternatives; for example, erasers come in tubing, much like pens or mechanical pencils, and gloves are also manufactured from vinyl. SBAA maintains a lengthy list of such substitutes at its website (www.sbaa.org).

WHAT NEEDS DO PEOPLE WITH SPINA BIFIDA HAVE?

Surgery immediately after birth is common; the protruding sac is pushed in, and the infant's back is closed. The objective is to prevent further deterioration. Further surgery often occurs, sometimes to control the condition itself, at other times, to insert or repair a shunt. Still other times, surgery takes place to make standing and walking possible. It is important that parents not subject their child to excessive surgeries out of a misguided hope that the child will someday walk. People who have spina bifida can lead very fulfilling and exciting lives without the ability to walk. Repeated surgery also is one reason lifetime costs associated with spina bifida are very high.

Frequent exposure to surgery, including to latex surgical gloves, may be a factor in the development of latex allergies. Because individuals with spina bifida often report difficulty with bladder and bowel functions, they usually need to catheterize themselves (which again raises the issue of latex allergies).

WHAT SPECIAL-EDUCATION AND RELATED SERVICES MAY HELP?

Because spina bifida virtually always occurs prior to or at birth, early-intervention services for young children birth to 36 months of age should be considered. Authorized under Part C of the IDEA, early intervention includes a wide variety of family counseling, child therapy, and other services that can help. Such services usually are free; if not, they are priced according to the family's ability to pay according to a sliding fee scale.

With respect to children aged 3 to 18 or 21 (depending on whether they are high school graduates or have "aged out" of IDEA eligibility), physical and occupational therapy are obvious related services. Physical therapy can help to enhance range of motion and to support normal motor development, while occupational therapy can assist children, youth, and adults to learn to perform important tasks.

Most children with spina bifida do not require specially designed instruction (which the IDEA calls "special education"), because their learning needs are not affected by the condition. A few, however, have learning disabilities such that they need help with paying attention and organizing tasks. Special-education and related services are guaranteed by the IDEA to be free to the family and the child.

WHAT OTHER INTERVENTIONS CAN BE EFFECTIVE?

Accessible transportation and housing are important. Grimby et al. (1996), for example, found that the 20 young adults with spina bifida they studied in Sweden reported having most difficulty with public transportation, followed by cleaning around the home, shopping, and negotiating stairs. Each of these problems is traceable to environmental barriers rather than to the condition itself.

WHAT ASSISTIVE TECHNOLOGIES AND SERVICES CAN HELP?

Assistive technology devices and services frequently are very helpful. Some children with spina bifida can learn to walk after surgery, using canes, crutches, or leg braces. Shaer (1997) points out that new orthotic devices can assist even people with thoracic-level lesions to stand and ambulate. Other individuals use manual or motorized wheelchairs.

WHAT ARE THE PROSPECTS FOR POSTSECONDARY EDUCATION?

As Elysse Power's story shows, they are excellent. Students with spina bifida benefit from today's accessible college campuses. Because spina bifida usually does not limit the ability to learn, few barriers stand between individuals with spina bifida and a college education.

WHAT ARE THE EMPLOYMENT PROSPECTS?

They are quite good. The major issues are accessibility of transportation to and from work, accessible housing near the place of employment, and reasonable accommodations on the job. Grimby et al. (1996), for example, found that half of the young adults with spina bifida that they studied in Sweden were employed full-time, with another 25% working part-time.

WHAT ARE THE PROSPECTS FOR INDEPENDENT LIVING?

Given affordable and accessible housing, they are very good. On New York's Long Island, which is dominated by one-family homes, none of which are required by any federal or state statute to be accessible for people with disabilities, and where the cost of living is high, that can be a challenge. Yet Elysse Power quickly found an accessible and affordable apartment just minutes from her university. Apartment dwellers and homeowners with spina bifida sometimes have to be creative in finding solutions to everyday problems, such as finding alternatives to today's prevalent top-loading washing machines.

Questions for Reflection and Discussion

1. Now that you have read about three neurological physical disabilities, explain in your own words what *neurological* means.

2. How could signals from the brain help to account for the movements common in spastic and athetoid cerebral palsy?

3. What secondary conditions often occur with cerebral palsy? How could common causes help to explain these?

4. Why is cerebral palsy the physical disability most likely to require multidisciplinary services?

5. Explain how afferent and efferent messages not being transmitted to and from the brain help us to understand the different symptoms of spinal cord injury.

6. Why are spinal cord injuries caused by sporting accidents usually more severe than SCIs caused by violence (e.g., gunshot wounds)?

7. Why do people with SCI tend to be more vulnerable to depression during the second year following the injury than during the first year?

8. What is a possible reason that so many people with spina bifida are susceptible to latex allergies?

9. What is the single most significant difference between spinal cord injuries and spina bifida? Of what relevance is this difference?

10. What diet supplement might help to prevent spina bifida?

Where is more information available?

Miami Project to Cure Paralysis
University of Miami School of Medicine
1600 Northwest 10th Avenue #R-48
Miami, FL 33136
1-800-STAND-UP
1-305-243-6001
www.cureparalaysis.org

National Easter Seals Society
230 West Monroe Street #1800
Chicago, IL 60606
1-800-221-6827
1-312-726-6200
www.seals.com

National Spinal Cord Injury Association
8300 Colesville Road, #551
Silver Spring, MD 20910
1-800-962-9629
1-301-588-6959
www.spinalcord.org

National Spinal Cord Injury Statistical Center
544 Spain Rehabilitation Center
University of Alabama at Birmingham
1717 Sixth Avenue South
Birmingham, AL 35233-7330
1-800-962-9629
1-205-934-3320
www.spinalcord.org

Spina Bifida Association of America
4590 MacArthur Blvd #250
Washington, DC 20007-4226
1-800-621-3141
1-800-394-5387 (Hotline)
1-202-944-3285
www.sbaa.org

United Cerebral Palsy Associations, Inc.
1660 "L" Street NW, #700
Washington, DC 20036-5602
1-800-USA-5UCP
1-202-776-0406
www.ucpa.org

7

TRAUMATIC BRAIN INJURY, MULTIPLE SCLEROSIS, AND EPILEPSY

This chapter concludes our examination of neurological physical disabilities. We look first at traumatic brain injury (TBI), one of the fastest growing categories of physical conditions in the United States today. We then explore multiple sclerosis (MS), a disability that remains widely misunderstood despite being one of the most common physical conditions in this country. Finally, another high-prevalence condition, epilepsy, is considered, together with other seizure-related impairments. All three disabilities have lesions in the central nervous system (CNS).

Traumatic Brain Injury (TBI)

Gregg Silverman (1967–), a former graduate student of mine at Hofstra, had a mild traumatic brain injury in 1994. Fortunately, the injury has had few lasting effects on Gregg's cognition or personality. For months after the injury, however, Gregg felt overwhelmed by the demands of everyday life. He had memory problems, attention deficits, and difficulty in screening out auditory and visual stimuli. Most people quickly learn to ignore sights and sounds that are not relevant to what they are doing. Gregg had great difficulty doing that: "In a restaurant, I would literally hear 20 conversations at once, trays being put down, glasses being clanked, people coughing, and the sounds of the street outside. I could not tolerate any public place" (Silverman, 1996).

WHAT IS IT?

The National Head Injury Foundation Task Force defined traumatic brain injury (TBI) as "an insult to the brain, not of a degenerative or congenital nature, but caused by an external physical force that may produce a diminished or altered state of consciousness which results in impairment of cognitive abilities" (1988, p. 2). This definition makes clear that TBI is a sudden, externally caused injury and that it does not result from brain tumors or other illnesses. A TBI need not result in loss of consciousness. Segalowitz and Lawson (1995) provided insight into the injury when they defined TBI as "a blow to the head such that the subject was not able to continue whatever activities were engaged in at the time because of dizziness, pain, unconsciousness, and so forth" (p. 311). TBI corresponds to "skull fractures and intracranial injuries" in the *International Classification of Diseases* (ICD-9), where it is described in codes 800–804 and 850–854.

The U.S. Department of Education (1992) offered a definition of TBI in its regulations governing special education. This definition is similar to that of the Foundation's but has the advantage of calling attention to the many, varied effects that TBI may have on academic and social behavior:

> "Traumatic brain injury" means an acquired injury to the brain caused by an external physical force, resulting in total or partial functional disability or psychological impairment, or both, that adversely affects a child's educational performance. The term applies to open or closed head injuries resulting in impairments in one or more areas, such as cognition; language; memory; attention; reasoning; abstract thinking; judgment; problem-solving; sensory, perceptual and motor abilities; psychosocial behavior; physical functions; information processing; and speech. The term does not apply to brain injuries that are congenital or degenerative, or brain injuries induced by birth trauma. (Sec. 300.7[a] [12])

(An **open** head injury occurs when there is penetration of the skull; in **closed** head injuries, no penetration occurs.)

Most TBIs are mild, requiring little or no hospitalization (Koch, Merz, & Lynch, 1995). The skull is remarkably effective in protecting the brain from serious damage even in accidents or other incidents that produce serious injury to other parts of the body. A whole issue of the *Journal of Head Injury*

Gregg Silverman vividly recalls being overwhelmed by sensory stimuli in the months after his traumatic brain injury. Fortunately, as often occurs, these have abated considerably, to the point where he is able to function independently.

Rehabilitation (Barth & Macciocchi, 1993) recently was devoted to mild TBI. In that volume, the American Congress of Rehabilitation Medicine's Mild Traumatic Brain Injury Committee defined "mild" TBI as

> a traumatically induced physiological disruption of brain function, as manifested by at least one of the following:
> 1. any period of loss of consciousness;
> 2. any loss of memory for events immediately before or after the accident;
> 3. any alteration in mental state at the time of the accident (e.g., feeling dazed, disoriented, or confused); and
> 4. focal neurological deficit(s) that may or may not be transient, but where the severity of the injury does not exceed the following:
>   - post-traumatic amnesia (PTA) not greater than 24 hours
>   - after 30 minutes, an initial Glasgow Coma Scale (GCS) of 13–15; and
>   - loss of consciousness of approximately 30 minutes or less. (pp. 86–87)

Moderate and severe TBIs, by implication, *do* exceed the parameters in (4) of the preceding definition (e.g., feature posttraumatic amnesia for longer than 24 hours). The vast majority of reported instances of TBI are mild, with relatively few producing moderate or severe injuries. Kraus, Rock, and Hemyari (1990), examining TBI among children, adolescents, and young adults, estimated that 86% of TBI cases requiring hospitalization involved mild injuries, 8% moderate injuries, and 6% severe injuries.

WHAT CAUSES IT? CAN IT BE PREVENTED? IF SO, HOW?

Nine out of every 10 traumatic brain injuries are caused by falls and by bicycle, motor vehicle, and sporting injuries (DiScala, Osberg, & Savage, 1997), although gunshot wounds are becoming more prominent as a cause of severe TBI (Sosin, Sniezek, & Waxweiler, 1995). A major cause, especially among people aged 15–24, is motor vehicle accidents involving alcohol use (Waxweiler, Thurman, Sniezek, Sosin, & O'Neill, 1995). In fact, DiScala et al., who analyzed nearly 24,000 records of hospitalization following TBI, estimated that 80% of all instances of TBI among children and youth involve modes of transportation (cars, motorcycles, bicycles). TBI may also result from child abuse, which tends to be underreported; as a result, it is difficult to estimate the incidence and prevalence of TBI from child abuse. One source suggested that as many as one fourth of all hospital admissions of young children for TBI result from child abuse (Duhaine, Alario, Lewander, Schut, Sutton, Seidl, et al., 1992).

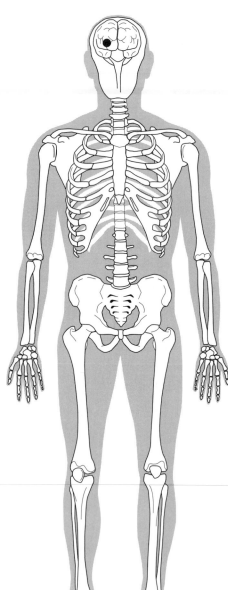

Incidents resulting in TBI most frequently occur on streets and highways (firearms and motor vehicle accidents), in private homes (household accidents and child abuse), and on sporting fields (athletic accidents). DiScala et al. (1997) reported that 50% of injuries occurred on the road and another 32% at home. They also noted that two thirds of the incidents causing TBIs in their large sample of children and adolescents occurred between noon and midnight. Much more rare are TBIs occurring at the workplace, probably because safety rules are both common and strictly enforced (Forkosch, Kaye, & LaPlante, 1996).

Prevention measures (use of safety equipment, reduction of driving while intoxicated, gun control measures, etc.) are obvious. Counseling and training for parents and other caregivers about alternative ways to respond to anger and frustration might help to prevent child abuse.

HOW PREVALENT IS IT? WHAT IS THE INCIDENCE?

According to the Disability Statistics Center at the University of California—San Francisco, nearly 2 million Americans sustain traumatic brain injuries each year. The incidence is 0.8% (i.e., 8 per 1,000 population) in any given year. Among children and adolescents under 18 years of age, the incidence rate is higher, at 1.1%. It is particularly high (1.6%) among adolescent and young adult males (Forkosch et al., 1996). However, these numbers greatly overstate the scope of the problem for educators, therapists, and counselors, because most such injuries are both minor and transient, and

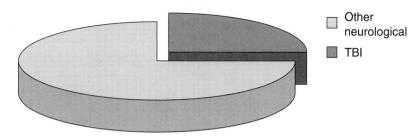

TBI v. all neurological

Other
neurological

TBI

Figure 7.1
Population Estimates: TBI As Compared to All Neurological Physical Disabilities

only half of such injuries produce any disability, even of short duration. If we use that rate, the incidence (number of new cases annually) of TBI leading to disability in the United States is about 125,000 annually, and the prevalence (total number of cases) would be about 2 million in this country.

The prevalence and incidence of TBI among children and youth are notoriously difficult to ascertain for a number of reasons. First, instances of child abuse and household accidents involving children may not be reported by parents, usually for fear of embarrassment. Second, accidents that *are* reported often lead to more visible physical symptoms; these accidents may be reported by medical personnel as producing physical rather than brain injuries. Indeed, DiScala et al. (1997) reported that most children (63.6%) sustained bodily injuries in addition to TBI. Third, young children typically do not perform certain mental tasks such as self-monitoring and metacognitive control. Injuries affecting such functions may therefore remain hidden until the child is older and fails to demonstrate what are then age-appropriate self-restraining behaviors. Fourth, children mature at different rates; this natural variation may mask effects of a TBI (Segalowitz & Lawson, 1995). For these and other reasons, realistic estimates of the size of the population are hard to find.

WHAT EFFECTS CAN IT HAVE?

Perhaps the most dramatic feature of TBI—and the one that most differentiates it from other disabilities that are discussed in this text—is that the effects vary. Particularly during the first year following injury, great change may occur in the individual's abilities, interests, and even personality (Jaffe, Polissar, Fay, & Liao, 1995). Levin (1995) reported that most improvement occurs during the first 6 months following the injury, with relatively little change in the subsequent 6 months.

TBI may have any of several types of effects. One of the more severe occurs when the injury is to the **frontal lobe (prefrontal cortex)** of the brain. This area specializes in self-monitoring (control of impulses; etc.) and planning or "executive function" activities. Damage here may lead to inability to

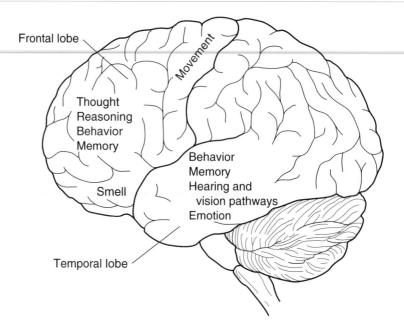

Frontal lobe

Thought
Reasoning
Behavior
Memory

Movement

Smell

Behavior
Memory
Hearing and
    vision pathways
Emotion

Temporal lobe

control behavior, especially to defer gratification. Also possible are problems in planning a course of action, such as saving money for the purpose of buying new clothes.

When the injury occurs to the **temporal lobe,** very different consequences are observed. Since the temporal lobe specializes in storing new information, a TBI to it may cause an individual to forget things learned just an hour earlier. This usually is a short-term phenomenon. With good nutrition, therapy, and (perhaps most important) time, the ability to retain new information returns. Sometimes, temporal lobe damage also can lead to frequent and violent aggression, both physical and verbal: Children, adolescents, and adults alike may swear or hit others.

Damage in motor-control functions is very common, leading to spasticity, ataxia, or both (see discussion on cerebral palsy) (Brink, Imbus, & Woo-sam, 1980). One study (Chaplin, Deitz, & Jaffe, 1993) reported that children with TBI are markedly slower than are other children of the same age in both gross- and fine-motor activities. Levin (1995), similarly, found slower motor speed in arm/hand functions and slower information-processing speed. He also reported that the spoken language of people with closed head injuries may be poorly organized, off the topic, and lacking in necessary information.

Recovery of function is rapid during the first year after the injury. However, individuals then seem to plateau, making little additional progress for long periods of time thereafter (Jaffe et al., 1995). Kenneth Jaffe of the University of Washington and his colleagues have shown that deficits remain in a wide variety of cognitive functions as late as 3 years following the injury. Most children with mild TBI eventually achieve within normal ranges on intelligence, problem solving, and academic performance. Children with moderate or severe TBI do recover but remain deficient in many such measures. Jaffe et al. (1995) concluded with these words of caution:

> Full recovery implies reestablishing academic, intellectual, and neurocognitive parity with peers. Achievement of such parity would require not only reacquisition of those skills that were impaired as a direct consequence of the injury, but also an accelerated acquisition of posttraumatic skills across all developmental and academic areas. Given the "plateauing" of recovery that we have found, extraordinary measures would indeed be needed to achieve parity with peers, if parity were possible. (p. 25)

Kendall, Shum, Halson, Bunning, and Teh (1997) offered some important insights into the nature of the difficulties many people with TBI experience in the area of problem-solving skills. They found that the adults with TBI they studied encountered most difficulty in (1) identifying and defining the problem and (2) generating alternative solutions. Later steps in problem solving (choosing a solution and carrying it out) presented relatively less difficulty. Kendall et al. pointed out, however, that most training programs on problem solving that are used with individuals with TBI concentrate on those latter steps. That many such programs are ineffective is thus not a surprise, they concluded. Kendall et al. studied only 15 persons, all adults, in Australia; replication studies are thus needed before their findings can be considered to be authoritative.

WHAT SECONDARY CONDITIONS ARE COMMON?

TBI involving the prefrontal cortex may affect impulse control and purposive-activity planning to such an extent that it leads to symptoms associated with **attention deficit disorder** (ADD), **attention deficit hyperactivity disorder** (ADHD), or both (Dinklage & Barkley, 1992). Such symptoms may include lethargy, difficulty maintaining attention, and fatigue. Seizures are also common following TBI; however, they are much less likely to occur in children than in adults (Annegers et al., 1980). Disturbances of visual and auditory processing are frequent with TBI but rarely to the extent of producing blindness or deafness. Rather, vision impairments involve diminished acuity (near and far) or reduced depth perception, while hearing disorders involve conductive losses, often because the TBI includes damage to the temporal lobe (McLean et al., 1995). The article by McLean and her colleagues offered a concise summary of many of the varied sequelae of TBI among children and youth. For a readable account of one child's TBI, see Witte (1998).

WHAT NEEDS DO PEOPLE WITH IT HAVE?

Needs vary, not only between people but also within each person, over a period of time. This necessitates frequent monitoring by educators, counselors, therapists, and others, including parents. Typically, an individual with TBI will have far greater needs for support and assistance during the first year following the injury than in subsequent years. During the first and often the second year, individuals generally will benefit from help in getting started with an activity, organizing the tasks in that activity, finishing the activity, and otherwise maintaining attention over increasingly long periods of time. They may also benefit from training and practice to increase speed, endurance, and hand-eye coordination in physical activity. With respect to social behavior, many need assistance in developing behaviors that can substitute for inappropriate, impulsive responses to frustration.

This characteristic of TBI—that change, including rapid progression as well as regression, is a fundamental consideration—suggests that individualized educational programs (IEPs) be reviewed and, if necessary, revised several times during each school year. The law requires that IEPs be developed for each school year and reviewed at least annually (U.S. Department of Education, 1992). With TBI, IEPs should be reviewed every 3 to 6 months, especially during the first year following the injury (Doelling & Bryde, 1995). These IEPs should specify what supports and other services the student will receive, what tasks the student will be expected to perform (and under what circumstances), and what year-end goals the student will pursue.

One need that surfaces again and again in the professional literature about TBI is for assistance in social behavior. Individuals with TBI often become isolated socially, as former friends desert them and as making new friends proves to be problematic. Blosser and Pearson (1997) offered a poignant case study illustrating this problem. "Max," a 7-year-old boy who was outgoing and athletic before his TBI, became quiet and reclusive in the months following the injury: "From the family's standpoint, their son had changed significantly in almost every aspect. His friends, one by one, had drifted away. Everyone missed the 'old Max,' and no one knew how to interact with the new one" (p. 22).

This is a pattern that repeats itself almost ad nauseam in the literature:

> Perhaps the most difficult and long-lasting effects of traumatic brain injury (TBI) for children and young adults are the loss of friends, decreased involvement in social activities, and absence of social support. (Glang, Todis, Cooley, Wells, & Voss, 1997, p. 32)

Glang et al. tried using a training program to assist young adults with TBI in overcoming these problems of social isolation and alienation. The "Building Friendships" program (Cooley, Glang, & Voss, 1997) stresses a team approach to building the student's social life. Although the process appeared to help some students, the effects sadly were not long-lasting. The investigators described the fragility (p. 44) of the changes, suggesting that long-term follow-up may be required to maintain the gains achieved by the program.

DiScala et al. (1997), studying 24,000 hospital and rehabilitation facility records of TBI, found that physical therapy, occupational therapy, and speech pathology services were among the most recommended post-discharge services. A major concern reported by many individuals with TBI is counseling and education for family members so that their expectations will become more appropriate (Springer, Farmer, & Bouman, 1997). Gervasio and Kreutzer

(1997) concurred, reporting that many family members experience high stress, anxiety, and depression. Springer et al. (1997) suggested that much of this may be due to misconceptions about the nature of TBI. Family members tend to believe that recovery will be rapid and complete, that restoration of physical capacity is most important, and that the speed and effectiveness of recovery is largely a function of personal will. Springer et al. report the facts as being quite different: that recovery from TBI usually is sporadic, lengthy, and seldom "total"; that regaining cognitive functions is likely to be much more helpful than restoration of physical capacity to individuals with TBI; and that the speed and completeness of recovery are mostly a function of the severity of the injury. *Understanding Brain Injury: Acute Hospitalization, a Guide for Families and Friends* (Mitiguy, Thompson, & Wasco, 1993) is an example of a resource that might help family members.

What people with TBI need depends a great deal upon what they are expected to do. College students, for example, are expected to demonstrate far more self-discipline than are young children. Employed persons are required to attend to tasks despite distractions much more than are people who do not work. Educators, therapists, counselors, and other professionals can offer considerable help to individuals with TBI by identifying in advance the physical, cognitive, social, and other demands of situations before the individual is placed into those situations. Is the person ready for such demands? If not, it may be well to delay such placements and to provide training in the required skills and competencies before the placements are made. These decisions should influence the IEP.

WHAT SPECIAL-EDUCATION AND RELATED SERVICES MAY HELP?

The Individuals with Disabilities Education Act added TBI to the list of conditions included in "children with disabilities" in 1990 (PL 101–476). The law authorizes a broad variety of special-education and related services to include, among others, specially designed instruction, assistive technology devices and services, physical and occupational therapy, speech pathology, and special transportation. All services are free to the families of children and youth with disabilities. All must be provided promptly, usually within 30 days of identification of the need. Transition services easing the move from school to postsecondary education, employment, and independent living are key elements of special education under this law.

All of this makes it especially puzzling that the most recent figures published by the federal government indicate that only 7,000 children and youth with TBI were being served in special-education programs during the 1994–1995 school year (U.S. Department of Education, 1996, p. 9). Even granted that TBI was added as a label in 1990, meaning that many schools were not yet using the label, and granted that many schools continued to use other labels (e.g., "other health impaired") for students with TBI, the number is surprisingly low.

DiScala et al. (1997) made a major contribution to the literature in helping us to understand this. They were very surprised to find that only 1.8% of school-age children with TBI in their 24,000-case sample were discharged from a hospital or rehabilitation facility to special-education programs (the vast majority were discharged to the home). All the physicians had to do to begin the process of referral to special education was to request that the family's school district, through its IEP committee, evaluate the child for special education. Why, then, DiScala et al. wondered, don't they do so? First, DiScala et al. observed, many hospitals and trauma centers lack close ties with local school districts. They neither understand nor communicate regularly with public schools. (Research facilities that are certified by the Commission on Accreditation of Rehabilitation Facilities, by contrast, must have in place nearly automatic referral processes that initiate the special-education evaluation.) Second, DiScala et al. commented, many rehabilitation facilities specializing in treatment for people with TBI are situated in cities that are geographically remote from the communities of residence of their patients; facilities that serve children are not as numerous as those serving adults with TBI. Third, many injuries occur during summer months. Most school districts offer summer instruction only for students identified well in advance as needing such services. Concluded DiScala et al.: "Since pediatric injuries are particularly frequent in the summer, it is possible that for a good portion of the children, the recommendation for special education is not made because the service is in fact not available at the time of discharge" (p. 9).

Occupational therapists may help the person with TBI to develop specific coping skills for use in school and at home. This is particularly important during the early years when the abilities of the individual are rapidly changing. Physical therapists may help individuals with TBI to increase endurance and motor speed. Speech pathologists may assist them to communicate more clearly and appropriately in different settings.

A well-established intervention technique with students having TBI is **applied behavior analysis** (ABA). Formerly called behavior modification, ABA features teacher/counselor alteration of antecedents (conditions or incidents that precede undesirable behavior by the student) and especially of consequences (events that follow the behavior). By removing the incentive for acting-out behavior, for example, the professional may prevent its occurrence. As an example, many individuals with TBI become frustrated when they feel overwhelmed by sensory stimulation; an answer here is to reduce such stimulation. A college student who cannot attend to his or her studies because of distracting behavior by a roommate might be assigned an individual dorm room. Alternatively, by changing consequences, the professional may remove the rewards previously associated with the behavior. To illustrate, an individual may be reinforced for *not* acting out, something that previously brought no rewards.

Closely related is training in **metacognition.** By increasing the individual's understanding of his or her own motivation and behavior pattern and by giving the individual more options to use in different situations, training in metacognition helps people to monitor themselves and to choose more effective strategies and tactics (Doelling & Bryde, 1995). If Kendall et al. (1997) are correct, the focus of such training should be on the early steps in problem solving (identifying the problem and generating a range of possible solutions) rather than (as now done in many instances) on the latter steps (selecting a strategy and carrying it out).

Peer counseling may be particularly helpful during the first few years following the injury. When someone else who has had a TBI describes his or her experiences, an individual may feel less frustration. Counseling may alleviate the depression that commonly occurs once the individual realizes that a rapid, complete recovery may not take place. In addition, persons experienced in coping with TBI can pass on very specific and concrete tricks of the trade, such as coping skills and mechanisms.

As noted earlier, counseling and education for family members so that they better understand TBI are urgent (Gervasio & Kreutzer, 1997; Springer et al., 1997). Family counseling and support are related services available under the IDEA.

WHAT OTHER INTERVENTIONS CAN BE EFFECTIVE?

TBI is much like cerebral palsy in that its management requires multidisciplinary interventions. Especially in the first year or two following the injury, educators, therapists, and counselors will benefit from consultation with the medical professionals who managed the individual's care during the recovery and rehabilitation phases. In fact, the first IEP meetings should be held prior to discharge from the rehabilitation facility so that educators, parents, and the individual with a TBI himself or herself can gain from medical professionals a clear understanding of the individual's present level of functioning as it relates to postdischarge services and settings. Physical, cognitive, social, and other goals need to be set at these initial meetings.

Savage and Mishkin (1994) urged that the transition between hospital or other rehabilitation facility and school not be rushed. The individual with TBI may not be ready to handle the sensory stimulation of a school setting, the memory demands of academic work, or the social expectations common to his or her age group. As much as 6 months to a year following hospital discharge may be needed before these competencies are sufficiently well developed as to make success in school likely.

In the early months, it is important that people with TBI avoid overstimulation; thus, quiet settings, low lights, etc., may help. This is another reason not to rush placement into formal educational or occupational settings, which typically are highly stimulating. Step-by-step directions are far easier to follow than complex instructions for people recovering from TBI. Such individuals may require more time to process and respond in conversation; teachers, counselors, and family members should allow them the necessary time.

Medical and rehabilitation interventions are suggested in *Guidelines for the Management of Severe Head Injury* (Bullock, Chestnut, Clifton, Ghajar, Marion, Narayan, Rosner, & Wilberger, 1995). The *Guidelines* have been well received in the medical community (e.g., Meythaler, 1996). However, educators and rehabilitation personnel may be disappointed by the publication's focus on early medical treatment at the expense of later, nonmedical interventions.

WHAT ASSISTIVE TECHNOLOGIES AND SERVICES CAN HELP?

Software that facilitates the learning and practice of appropriate behaviors in different situations can be very helpful for many individuals with TBI. Particularly important is learning, or relearning, pragmatics—what to say in which situation. Programs designed to assist people in organizing time and tasks, in problem solving, and in memory could also be helpful (Harris & DePompei, 1997). The great advantage of such software is that it can be infinitely patient in teaching skills and in forgiving errors. However, technologies that directly compensate for impulsivity or other behaviors associated with TBI are not as yet widely available. A review of assistive technology for children with TBI (Reid, Strong, Wright, Wood, Goldman, & Bogen, 1995) provided suggestions on selecting from among those technologies. A careful reading of the Reid et al. article reinforces the impression that relatively few devices currently on the market assist individuals with TBI as compared, for example, to cerebral palsy or quadriplegia.

More help can be offered if the TBI is accompanied or followed by disturbances in hearing, vision, or both. A wide variety of hardware and software peripherals is available. FM/AM listening systems, assistive listening systems and devices, hearing aids, and other products can help with hearing loss, while closed-circuit television, handheld enlargers, prescription glasses, and other products can help to accommodate for a visual impairment. Because TBI so often leads to limitations in mobility, gross- and fine-motor control, and other physical functions, assistive technology devices and services can help.

WHAT ARE THE PROSPECTS FOR POSTSECONDARY EDUCATION?

The challenge of college life for many individuals with TBI is that it provides so little structure. College students are expected to have good organizational skills, to use sound time management practices, and to display behavior that is appropriate to a wide variety of settings. TBI, by its very nature, may interfere with or sharply restrict such skills and behaviors. However, if the individual receives training in these areas and support as needed, success in college should be attainable (Cook, 1991; Harris & DePompei, 1997).

Support often is available from the "Special Services" or "Disabled Student Services" office. Because of their obligations under Section 504 of the 1973 Rehabilitation Act and under the 1990 Americans with Disabilities Act to make reasonable accommodations for applicants and students with disabilities, most colleges and universities have such offices on campus. Often staffed by counselors who themselves have disabilities, these offices can advocate for individuals with TBI. They may arrange for, to take a few examples, extended time to take tests, tutoring, notetaking, and similar services.

Support will be made available only if the individual is known to need it. College special-services offices depend heavily upon self-identification by the individual as someone with a disability. Applicants are given the opportunity to make such self-identification declarations as part of the admissions process. Matriculated students may identify themselves directly to the college's special-services office. Identifying oneself as a person with a disability, however, requires a certain amount of initiative and personal maturity. Harris and DePompei (1997), in their survey of Ohio college special-services personnel, reported that students with TBI comprised about 3% of college students in the state. The actual number may be higher, as many colleges reported that relatively few students with TBI self-identify. Stated differently, the special-services offices become aware of only those students with TBI who report problems.

WHAT ARE THE EMPLOYMENT PROSPECTS?

Working requires even more independence, initiative, self-monitoring, appropriate social behavior, etc., than does going to college. Meanwhile, employers generally offer much less than colleges in the way of support services. For these reasons, individuals with TBI should work closely with high-school or college transition staff members and other professionals in planning steps toward work well in advance of the anticipated date of employment. For students enrolled in K–12 special-education programs under the IDEA, transition services are guaranteed to be provided, to begin promptly, to be free of charge, and to be of at least minimal quality—all statements that cannot be made of many post-high-school services. Counselors, teachers, and others who advise individuals with TBI and their families accordingly should emphasize transition services during the school years, because post-high-school services may not be available, may require lengthy waits before services begin, may involve considerable costs for the individual or the family, and may not meet minimum standards for quality of service.

Thomas and Botterbusch (1997) reported finding a long list of neuropsychological, social-emotional, and physical problems among 149 individuals with TBI who were being served at 20 different facilities or programs. Most individuals had more than one kind of problem and encountered multiple difficulties attributable to each type of problem. Levin (1995) identified verbal memory performance as a factor closely associated with successful employment. Clearly, assisting individuals with TBI to get and keep good jobs often is a major undertaking requiring instruction, tutoring, support, and practice of a wide range of specific skills and competencies.

Even the best-trained individuals might do something wrong. It is the nature of employment that often just one or two such wrong moves might result in termination. **Supported employment,** authorized under Title VI of the Rehabilitation Act, is one mechanism for dealing with such problems. In supported work, a job coach (whose salary is paid by government or nonprofit organizations) works side by side with the individual over a period of time, usually at least a month. The job coach and the individual with a disability together are responsible for completing the job. That is in fact precisely why many employers are willing to take a chance on workers with disabilities—they are assured that the job will be done, even if the job coach has to do the whole thing. Supported employment is particularly well suited for many individuals with TBI because it offers an opportunity over a moderately long period of time for the individual to recover from initial mistakes without penalty and to learn to do the job appropriately before the job coach retreats from the scene (Kreutzer & Witol, 1996).

WHAT ARE THE PROSPECTS FOR INDEPENDENT LIVING?

Individuals with TBI face the same problems in daily life that they do in academics and in employment. In particular, their difficulties in problem solving, in making and keeping friends, and in being egocentric and impulsive may interfere with independent living. They may fall behind on the rent and not respond in a timely and appropriate manner to this. They may also have difficulty retaining a roommate.

On the positive side, relatively few people with TBI will find that architectural barriers prevent them from living independently. In this respect, their prospects are much brighter than those of persons with cerebral palsy or spinal cord injuries.

Multiple Sclerosis

James Barry (1947–), a staff director for adaptive communication technology at Bell Atlantic, the regional phone company serving 13 northeastern states, is a telecommuter, working out of his home most workdays as an accommodation for his multiple sclerosis (MS). Jim's condition makes walking difficult; although he can and usually does walk (rather unsteadily) with a walker, he finds a scooter more convenient for distance travel. Multiple sclerosis also limits his vision, such that he must use a magnifying glass to read printed materials and a speech synthesizer with his personal computer to listen to what is on the screen.

In all the years I have known and worked with him, Jim has resisted the limitations imposed upon him by MS. For example, he continued walking long distances for several years after he should have converted to use of a wheelchair or scooter. His persistence or stubbornness may trace to his 20+ years as a marathon runner, most prior to the diagnosis of MS when he was 31. Jim continues to be an enthusiastic booster of technology for people with disabilities and takes great pride in his work developing markets for special-needs customers of Bell Atlantic.

WHAT IS IT?

Multiple sclerosis—the name refers to the number (many) and to the nature of the problem (scarring of the demyelinated areas of the central nervous system)—is an autoimmune condition in which the sheath surrounding nerve

Jim Barry believes his background as a marathon runner contributes to the quality of his life by giving him a gutty determination to surmount all obstacles.

cell fibers in the brain, spinal cord, and optic nerve is damaged or even destroyed. This sheath, or covering, is known as myelin. It facilitates the transmission of electrochemical messages in the nerves. In MS, the body's immune system seems to regard the myelin sheathing as foreign ("non-self") and attacks it. Demyelination at numerous sites in the central nervous system

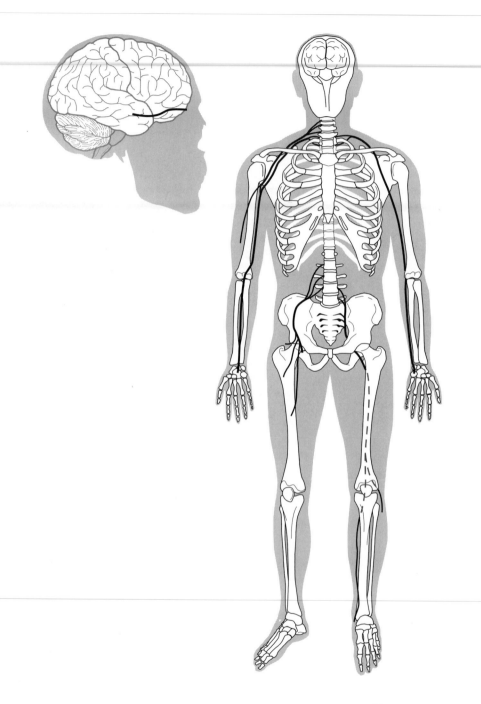

results, interfering with message transmission. The basic problem in MS is that nerve signals are interrupted, blocked, or garbled. Strong signals are more garbled than weak signals. What this means to an individual will vary from day to day, month to month, and year to year: MS is the single most unpredictable neurological disability.

WHAT CAUSES IT? CAN IT BE PREVENTED? IF SO, HOW?

No one knows what causes MS, other than that it is not inherited nor is it contagious. There is no shortage of theories, however. Most experts believe that environmental factors are involved. According to the National Institute of Neurological Disorders and Stroke (NINDS, 1997), a unit of the National Institutes of Health, it may be that people get a virus at or about the time of puberty. This virus appears to have a long latency period and may not express itself for many years. Some recent evidence suggests that childhood inoculations may actually cause autoimmune conditions such as MS.

A genetic predisposition may also be involved in MS. This is suggested by the fact that if one person in a family develops MS, other family members likely will as well. Such people would have a 1-in-3 chance of getting MS, which is far greater than the 1-in-1,000 probability that members of the general public have of acquiring MS (NINDS, 1997).

The NINDS has added that MS is 5 times more prevalent in temperate climates (the northern United States, Canada, and Northern Europe) than in tropical zones (Africa, the Middle East, etc.). Even holding geography constant, prevalence rates may vary widely. To illustrate, when the Mayo Clinic began tracking MS in Minnesota during the 1950s, the incidence was about 30 to 50 cases per 100,000 population; today, it is 170 per 100,000 (Talan, 1997). This suggests that something in the environment may be triggering the disease. Equally odd, MS is very uncommon among Asian people and among Native Americans. Why this should be so remains unknown. No method of prevention has been found, nor is one likely until the causes are better understood.

HOW PREVALENT IS IT? WHAT IS THE INCIDENCE?

According to the National Multiple Sclerosis Society (NMSS, 1997), about 300,000 Americans of all ages have MS. Some 10,000 new cases are diagnosed annually. MS is twice as common among women as among men, and it occurs twice as often among Caucasians as among other races. The youngest age at onset appears to be 15; most cases are diagnosed between the ages of 20 and 50; and the disability rarely appears for the first time after age 60. The NINDS (1997) has suggested that the age of 15 appears to be significant in MS, such that individuals living in temperate zones and younger than that age seem to have the risk of developing MS that is associated with cooler climates, whereas people moving to such a zone after age 15 maintain the risk associated with the area in which they grew up. Why all of this should be so remains a mystery.

WHAT EFFECTS CAN IT HAVE?

The initial symptoms of MS include blurred or double vision; fatigue; pain, especially pins-and-needles sensations in the limbs; problems with coordination and balance; and spasticity (increased muscle tone or stiffness). Speech impediments, tremors, and dizziness may also occur (NINDS, 1997). Control

MS v. all neurological

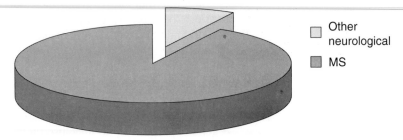

Figure 7.2
Population Estimates: MS As Compared to All Neurological Disabilities

of the bladder and the bowel may be compromised. In each of these instances, the basic problem is in disruption of afferent (to the brain) or efferent (from the brain) nerve signals. For example, signals from the bowel to the brain indicating the need for a bowel movement may be disrupted or even blocked, leading, in time, to constipation. As another example, dizziness seems to occur because of disruption of nerve signals carrying messages to the brain about the body's position. Sclerosis on the optic nerve may lead to vision impairment. (Jacquelin Gorman offers a moving story about MS and blindness in *The Seeing Glass,* 1997.) Finally, spasticity may arise because inhibitory (relaxing) signals from the brain may not be reaching the muscles.

Most people with MS have mild symptoms; only about 1 in every 4 will ever need a wheelchair. Indeed, some individuals show symptoms for a brief period but become and remain symptom-free for long periods of time. This relapsing-remitting (RR) pattern is very common in MS. People who have severe MS, on the other hand, may follow a primary-progressive (PP) pattern of continual worsening of symptoms, followed by a plateauing (NINDS, 1997). They may be unable to walk, feed themselves, or even speak intelligibly. This variability of MS symptoms, combined with the fact that many of the symptoms are also indicators of other conditions (e.g., fatigue could signal Guillaine-Barre syndrome), contributes to the experience common to many people with MS of having had to visit numerous specialists over a period of many months or even years before a definitive diagnosis was made.

MS is a chronic, lifelong condition. It is very seldom fatal; usually, people with MS have normal life expectancies. While MS cannot be cured, many of the symptoms can be treated successfully. This requires education about what is causing these symptoms and about what interventions may work.

WHAT SECONDARY CONDITIONS ARE COMMON?

Many individuals with MS become depressed at one point or another because the condition is so unpredictable that planning and carrying out normal life activities are severely compromised. MS seldom leads to major secondary conditions. This is good because there are so many primary ones tied to MS: Virtually every physical problem people with MS experience is a direct result of the disability.

WHAT NEEDS DO PEOPLE WITH IT HAVE?

The most important need of individuals with MS may be for understanding. The condition is notoriously variable. People with MS may have periods of extreme symptoms (fatigue, for example) during which they are not able to perform work or schoolwork, followed by periods of relief from those symptoms. They may have days, weeks, or even months when they are essentially incapacitated. It is thus not surprising that divorce rates among persons with MS are high, as the spouse resents the individual's dependency and unpredictability. Financial stresses, too, may contribute to marital discord. The high cost of medication, combined with the individual's frequent inability to engage in gainful employment, may lead to worries about money. MS may cause students to miss school for unpredictable lengths of time. Again, understanding is essential, as is a willingness to work with the individual to find mutually satisfactory solutions.

Stress does not cause MS. This is a common misconception, although stress might contribute to a temporary worsening of symptoms. Accordingly, common sense steps to prevent unnecessary stress, perhaps combined with a program of stress reduction, may prove to be helpful. Pregnancy, on the other hand, may temporarily alleviate symptoms. This appears to occur because in pregnancy a woman's body naturally adjusts to accept as "self" the cells of the fetus. At any rate, MS has no discernible adverse effects on a pregnant woman or on the fetus. However, women with MS who become pregnant should consult a physician, because medication they take for MS may have deleterious effects on the fetus. A good compilation of articles on these and other MS-related subjects is available at http://www.infosci.org/MS-Internet/.

WHAT SPECIAL-EDUCATION AND RELATED SERVICES MAY HELP?

Flexibility in services may be the most important step schools can take. Students with MS may need extended periods of at-home instruction. Flexibility in scheduling activities so that, for example, the student can spend an hour swimming or in a cooling garment (discussed later) can make the difference between being able to continue with education and dropping out.

WHAT OTHER INTERVENTIONS CAN BE EFFECTIVE?

Treatment of MS often features beta-interferon drugs (immune system regulators) and Copaxone, a new drug approved by the FDA in April 1997. Although all appear to reduce the severity of symptoms in many individuals who have MS, none really controls the condition. Experts now believe that treatment should begin at the first sign of symptoms rather than, as currently usually occurs, after symptoms have worsened to the point of debilitating the patient (Talan, 1997).

For about 60% of people with MS, symptoms worsen in heat and alleviate when temperatures drop (NINDS, 1997). According to the NMSS, nerve signals are stronger when temperatures are high than when they occur during lower temperatures. As noted earlier, in MS, strong signals are more distorted than are weak ones. Even if body temperature is reduced by as little as 1.5 degrees Fahrenheit, signals will be weakened enough that their transmission is improved. For these reasons, air conditioning can be an effective accommodation for MS. A cold bath may help. Swimming, too, is a good exercise choice because it helps to cool the body. One-hour sessions, perhaps while reading or watching TV, in a special cooling garment, such as those made by Life Enhancement Technologies (LET) (Redwood City, California), may be very helpful. The effect of cooling, whether with LET garments or otherwise, appears to be cumulative, such that three or four cooling sessions spaced throughout the day may be most effective.

Most people with MS can learn to treat their symptoms. For example, many individuals with MS experience bladder problems, which they mistakenly attempt to treat by limiting fluid intake. However, restricting fluids just makes constipation worse. People learn that it is far better to treat bladder concerns directly, with medication that alleviates the need to use the restroom.

One area of controversy is that of the role of diet in MS. In the 1950s, Dr. Roy Swank came up with an "MS Diet" that he vigorously promoted for the next 40 years. The diet is a low-fat, high-unsaturated regimen that aims to keep fat intake to less than 20 grams per day. The NMSS (1997) remains skeptical of this and other diets because independent scientific evidence for their efficacy is lacking (Scheck, 1997). David Saunders, who recently was calling himself "Q", has been an enthusiastic booster of low-fat diets as well as exercise. He has promoted some unconventional ideas, including the idea that stress is the no. 1 cause of MS and that symptoms may be exacerbated by mercury amalgam fillings in teeth (he has had his fillings replaced) and by fluorescent lights (Maddox, 1997). With the cause(s) of MS remaining a mystery and no intervention as yet proven to be effective, controversial approaches such as those of "Q" are certain to continue.

Research is being conducted by the Myelin Project and other organizations on remyelinating nerves. Ian Duncan and his colleagues at the University of Wisconsin School of Veterinary Medicine recently transplanted glial cells from fetuses into dogs that had been born with a genetic mutation that produces symptoms similar to those of MS. They speculated that human glial cell transplants may begin in the near future (Archer, Cuddon, Lipsitz, & Duncan, 1997). Other work includes attempting to limit the demyelination that occurs in MS by reducing inflammation and modifying the immune response, notably with interferon (Miller, 1997).

WHAT ASSISTIVE TECHNOLOGIES AND SERVICES CAN HELP?

Intermittent catheterization (IC), in which a thin tube is inserted into the bladder through the urinary opening, can assist when MS causes problems with the bladder. IC is a simple procedure with which people with MS quickly become comfortable. It requires only minimal instruction and practice. Women seem to take to the procedure more readily than do men, perhaps because women often have had experience with tampon insertion.

Assistive technology devices can also help with tremors, a common problem with MS. Jim Barry, for example, uses a cane to stabilize himself when standing or walking. Many individuals with MS find that computer-related assistive technology devices help a great deal. An example is an optical character reader-*cum*-speech synthesizer that enables the person to listen to printed words. Crutches and wheelchairs help with mobility. Occupational therapists and physical therapists are good sources of information about such products.

WHAT ARE THE PROSPECTS FOR POSTSECONDARY EDUCATION?

Other than the need for flexibility in scheduling and for some means of delivering instruction at home, MS should not restrict anyone's ability to complete college. Important will be a knowledgeable college counselor, such as a special-services coordinator, who can arrange for the necessary schedule or site changes. Most colleges and universities have such support personnel. The special-services staff can educate the student's professors, helping them to become more flexible and accommodating, especially about deadlines.

WHAT ARE THE EMPLOYMENT PROSPECTS?

The NMSS has reported that most individuals with MS worked prior to the onset of symptoms but that fewer than half remained employed after symptoms began appearing. One study (Kornblith, LaRocca, & Baum, 1986) found that 70% to 80% of adults with MS were not employed. A common reason for this is that neither the individual nor the employer could predict how much work the person would be able to do or even which days the person could come to work. Employers are most likely to find creative solutions to these problems if they value the individual. To illustrate, employers may develop with the worker a contract for performance of a certain amount of work over a 6-month period such that how much of this was accomplished in any given week or month would be disregarded. Such a plan is not likely to be favored by an employer unless the individual is a proven, valued worker. For this reason, people who acquire MS in adulthood likely will have much more success if they focus upon returning to the same employer than if they must try new employers.

Fatigue is another important reason for the low levels of employment among persons with MS. Because as many as 77% of persons with MS experience fatigue and because most report it as a daily occurrence (Schwartz, Coulthard-Morris, & Zeng, 1996), fatigue is a major factor in employment. Schwartz et al. commented that fatigue typically worsens as the day wears on but improves with rest, moderate exercise, and positive experiences during the day.

WHAT ARE THE PROSPECTS FOR INDEPENDENT LIVING?

Attendant care services are important for many individuals with severe MS. In one of a series of articles in the magazine *New Mobility* that profiled adults with MS, Kathleen Newroe (1997) of Santa Fe, New Mexico, expressed her appreciation for the assistants who have helped her. A total of 29 personal assistants worked with Newroe over the past 5 years. Newroe had someone with her 24 hours a day, 7 days a week, to cook, clean, and meet her personal sanitary needs. Most people with MS do not require that much help, but personal assistants nonetheless are an important element in independent living for many individuals with MS.

Assistive technology devices and services also help people with MS to achieve independence. One example is environmental control units (ECUs) that feature a small computer that controls a raft of electrical products throughout the house or apartment by signaling the X-10 controllers connected to each device. With an ECU, an individual can turn on lights anywhere in the house, manipulate the house temperature, turn on the TV and select a channel, and even start up a coffee machine or microwave oven—all from one location, using a handheld controller.

Epilepsy

While he was Majority Whip in the U.S. House of Representatives, Tony Coelho led the fight for the world's first comprehensive civil-rights law for people with disabilities. The Democrat from California's San Joaquin Valley spoke of his own experiences as an individual with a disability in making the case for what became the Americans with Disabilities Act (ADA). Again and again, Coelho told his fellow lawmakers how he had been turned down for jobs simply because he had epilepsy. Watching committee and floor debates in 1988, 1989, and 1990, I saw firsthand how effective his stories were. Republicans and Democrats alike were impressed that one of their leaders, a man they knew well and respected, was himself a member of the group the ADA was designed to protect. Coelho spoke with passion about how he had even been dissuaded from his initial career choice, that of a minister, by ostensibly well-meaning but woefully misinformed church leaders. Mr. Coelho is now Chairman of the President's Committee on Employment of People with Disabilities. He also holds a large number of volunteer positions, including Honorary Lifetime Director of the Epilepsy Foundation of America (EFA).

WHAT IS IT?

All of us have electrical activity in the brain that occurs when we think, when we see something, and when we hear something. In epilepsy, sudden, uncontrolled bursts of electrical discharges exceed a certain threshold and provoke a seizure. That threshold differs from person to person. People with epilepsy have lower than normal thresholds, such that they are more prone than other people to seize. Thus, epilepsies are conditions producing irregu-

While a United States Representative from California, the Honorable Tony Cuelho was a leader in the creation of the Americans with Disabilities Act. He pointed to his own success as Majority Whip of the House as evidence that disability (in his case, epilepsy) is no bar to employment.

lar electrical discharges in the brain such that an individual has recurrent, unprovoked seizures. The name *epilepsy* derives from a Greek word referring to seizures, which are a symptom of epilepsy. Epilepsy itself is the physical brain damage that makes the brain susceptible to seizures. Epilepsy is not a disease. Rather, it is an underlying neurological disorder that interferes with the ways brain cells communicate with each other (Epilepsy Foundation of America, 1997).

Important in the definition of epilepsy is that seizures occur frequently (ruling out people who have one or two seizures and never seize again) and that they not be caused by some external event or agent (ruling out, for

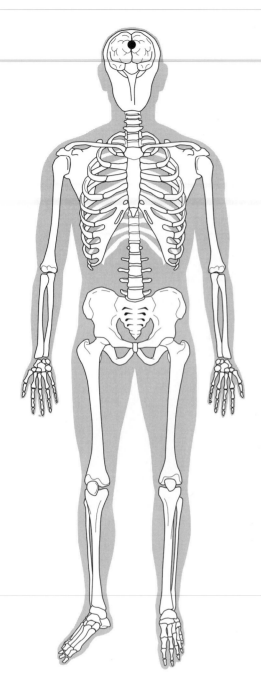

example, seizures caused by withdrawal from alcohol or other drugs). Nonepileptic seizures can be caused by low blood sugar, fainting, heart disease, strokes, narcolepsy, and extreme stress or anxiety. Such seizures do not repeat over time and are not characterized by unprovoked, abnormal electrical activity in the brain, thus failing to satisfy the two major criteria for diagnosis of epilepsy.

There are several epilepsies, which fall into two major categories: **partial** and **generalized.** If the electrical discharge is contained within one section of the brain, the seizure is partial; if, however, it originates in both hemispheres, it is generalized. Partial seizures are much more common than generalized ones, comprising about 60% of all cases of epilepsy.

Partial seizures are grouped into three categories. *Simple partial* seizures begin in one hemisphere of the brain and can produce involuntary twitching of muscles, altered sensations in some part of the body, and a turning of the head or eyes. No loss of consciousness occurs. *Complex partial* seizures often involve loss of consciousness. People may also change their behavior—they may engage in repetitive muscle movements such as rapid eye blinks or chewing in the mouth. A period of disorientation or confusion commonly follows the episode. *Partial seizures—secondarily generalized* are partial seizures that begin in one hemisphere but rapidly spread to the other. They may appear to be tonic-clonic seizures ("Understanding Epilepsy/Seizures," 1997).

The most widely recognized generalized seizure type is **tonic-clonic** (formerly called grand mal). In this form, there is a convulsion that has two phases: a tonic phase, in which the person loses consciousness and falls, and a clonic phase, in which the limbs jerk and twitch. That is, *tonic* refers to the stiffening that occurs in the body, which typically lasts for up to 1 minute, while *clonic* points to the 2- to 6-minute period of jerking that follows; in some cases, stiffening and jerking alternate. Tonic-clonic seizures are characterized by a loss of consciousness. The individual may appear dazed and may engage in apparently meaningless movements. Tonic-clonic seizures last between 1 and 7 minutes on an average; the individual may need rest, or even sleep, after recovering from the seizure. The seizures may be preceded by an aura, or warning, which the individual experiences as an odd smell, sound, or taste.

Also common are generalized **absence** seizures (formerly called petit mal). In this type, there may be 5 to 15 seconds of lapses in consciousness. Absence seizures are not preceded by an aura. They are characterized by staring into space, as if daydreaming, blinking, rhythmic movements of the facial muscles, and a "blank" feeling. People who have these seizures typically do not recall the episodes. Children may have as many as 100 absence seizures in a single day. In most cases, absence seizures disappear by adolescence; however, the underlying condition may continue well into adulthood and may express itself in other kinds of seizures.

Two other types of generalized seizures are recognized: myoclonic and atonic seizures. In myoclonic seizures, the arms or legs jerk, while in atonic seizures there is a sudden, brief loss of muscle tone or posture such that the head or upper body may drop or bend over.

Status epilepticus is a life-threatening condition in which seizures repeat without recovery. Lennox-Gastaut syndrome, which affects about 20,000 children in the United States, causes massive, repeated seizures, as many as 100 to 200 per hour. If not treated, these seizures may lead to mental retardation, as brain cells literally burn out. Similarly, if the brain cells specialized for speech or for motor control are affected, the individual may not be able to talk or walk. According to the Epilepsy Foundation of America (1997), some 22,000 to 42,000 deaths in the United States each year may be attributable to epilepsy, usually to status epilepticus.

WHAT CAUSES IT? CAN IT BE PREVENTED? IF SO, HOW?

In many instances (estimates run to 65% or 75%) of epilepsy, a discernible cause cannot be identified; these are referred to as cases of "idiopathic epilepsy." Of those that can be isolated, the most common causes are blows to the head (e.g., traumatic brain injuries in automobile accidents), high fever, and excessive shaking or rough handling of a baby (shaken-baby syndrome). Examples of illnesses producing high fevers that may in turn lead to epilepsy include meningitis and viral encephalitis. Other causes include poisoning (e.g., lead poisoning), brain tumors, and strokes. Those instances where a cause is isolated are called "symptomatic epilepsy." Only rarely is heredity involved, although a genetic predisposition to lower seizure thresholds (i.e., higher likelihoods of seizing) has been documented in some populations (NINDS, 1997).

Seizures may occur because of flashing or intermittently shining lights; this is known as photosensitive epilepsy. In some cases, loud or monotonous sounds may trigger seizures. Sleep deprivation and alcohol are known to lower seizure thresholds; people with epilepsy usually are advised by their physician to get adequate amounts of rest and to avoid alcohol. In addition, alcohol can interact with seizure-control medications in deleterious ways, providing yet another reason for abstinence.

HOW PREVALENT IS IT? WHAT IS THE INCIDENCE?

Some 25 million Americans will have a seizure of some kind at some point during their lifetime (Epilepsy Foundation of America, 1997). The vast majority of these people do not have epilepsy. In the United States, about 125,000

Epilepsy v. all neurological

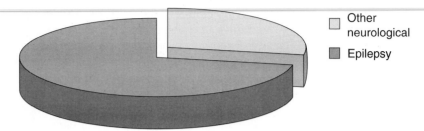

Other neurological
Epilepsy

Figure 7.3
Population Estimates: Epilepsy As Compared to All Neurological Physical Disabilities

individuals annually will develop epilepsy; that is the incidence. As for the prevalence, the Epilepsy Foundation of America (1997) has estimated that 2.5 million Americans of all ages have epilepsy. This means that epilepsy is more common than all of the other physical disabilities discussed in this chapter combined.

About 50% of cases appear before age 25; 1 in every 4 occurs before the age of 5. Some forms disappear after childhood or adolescence; a good example is absence seizures. However, as can be seen from the causes, such as head trauma or high fever, epilepsy can occur to anyone at any age.

WHAT EFFECTS CAN IT HAVE?

Epilepsy seizures range from the brief, transient absence seizures that are much like blinking and last for seconds to the debilitating tonic-clonic seizures, in which electrical storms in the brain trigger loss of consciousness, to the Lennox-Gastaut seizures, which persist to the point of threatening life itself. As should be evident from this range of symptoms, epilepsy is not one condition but rather a variety of disorders.

For Albert Jean (1982–), a teen from Reading, Massachusetts, epilepsy meant that he could not ride a bike or swim alone; he even had to be escorted from class to class by a teacher. Beginning with the 1997–1998 school year, however, those restrictions are history. Albert is participating in a field trial of a new implant, a pacemaker-like electrode that sends seizure-blocking signals to his brain. The Cyberonics (Webster, Texas) product has been hailed as "the advance of the century" by analysts excited about its value for people who cannot benefit from medication and are not candidates for surgery (Forest, 1997). An estimated 200,000 Americans are potential candidates for the device.

WHAT SECONDARY CONDITIONS ARE COMMON?

Frequent and severe seizures can lead to brain damage and even to mental retardation. Learning difficulties may also result from medications taken to control seizures. Individuals may find that keeping lists and writing reminders suffice to allow them to continue with normal school or work activity. Although epilepsy does not cause learning disabilities, the fact remains that learning disabilities are more common among children and youth with epilepsy than among the school-age population as a whole ("Understanding Epilepsy/Seizures," 1997). In addition, severe seizures (as with Lennox-Gastaut syndrome) may render an individual unable to walk or talk.

WHAT NEEDS DO PEOPLE WITH IT HAVE?

Epileptic seizures usually do not require medical attention. Educators, parents, and others near an individual who has a tonic-clonic seizure should remove sharp objects from the immediate surroundings and perhaps place a pillow or other soft cushion under the person's head. Nothing, however, should be placed into the person's mouth. After the seizure, the individual should be allowed to rest before resuming activity. In the case of absence seizures, immediate resumption of activity is normal. In neither instance is it necessary to call emergency medical personnel. Such specialized attention is required only in the event of status epilepticus or Lennox-Gastaut seizures.

About 85% of seizures can now be controlled with medication; in about 50% of instances, seizures disappear altogether, while in the remaining 35%, they are reduced in frequency and severity to the point that the individual can resume a normal lifestyle. However, many drugs have important side effects. Dilantin (phenytoin) can disrupt coordination and cause gum conditions; Tegretol (carbamazepine) can produce blurred vision; Depakene (valproic acid) can cause hair loss. Other drugs used include Mysoline (primidone), Frisium (clobazam), and Rivotril (clonazepam). About half of all Americans with epilepsy benefit from medications introduced before 1980, including Dilantin and Tegretol. The 1 million-plus Americans of all ages who could not be helped with those drugs may benefit from the newer Felbamate, Lamotrigine, and Gapapentin, which were approved for general use by the Food and Drug Administration (FDA) in late 1993. Felbamate (Felbatol) appears to help children with Lennox-Gastaut syndrome, the brutally severe form of epilepsy; it is not recommended at present for children under 14 with other kinds of epilepsy.

In some instances, persons who are seizure free for several years may begin, under a physician's guidance, slowly to withdraw from the medication. The Epilepsy Foundation of America (1997) has stated that the brain sometimes "learns not to seize."

WHAT SPECIAL-EDUCATION AND RELATED SERVICES MAY HELP?

The major interventions for persons with epilepsy are flexibility in scheduling, such that an individual who has a tonic-clonic seizure is permitted to make up the work at another time, and awareness/understanding. The person's usual surroundings (e.g., preferred seats in class, workstation) should be examined with care, and any sharp, protruding objects should be removed. Teachers in classrooms known to have children prone to absence seizures may watch for evidence of such seizures and simply repeat what was said in the seconds the child was temporarily "out." Depending on the student's wishes, an orientation session may be held for class members in which the disability is briefly explained, questions are answered, and reassurance is given that nothing dangerous is happening. These sessions are best held before any seizures occur; it is a mistake to wait until after a seizure has happened, because totally unexpected seizures can be very disconcerting to observers.

Spiegel, Cutler, and Yetter (1996), writing in *Intervention in School and Clinic* about "What Every Teacher Should Know About Epilepsy," suggested that teachers, counselors, and others should be alert to drowsiness caused by anticonvulsant medication. Some drugs can even produce hyperactivity and impulsivity. Professionals observing such side effects should bring them to the family's attention; it is possible that a change in medication is indicated. With complex partial seizures, which are characterized by post-seizure confusion, teachers and other professionals should time and observe the seizure and remain with the individual for several minutes after the seizure begins until it stops. The confusion may persist much longer than the seizure itself.

Aside from these possibilities, most students and workers with epilepsy do not require special accommodations. Indeed, some federal courts have ruled that epilepsy is not necessarily a "disability" under the Americans with Disabilities Act, because it does not routinely result in substantial limitations in everyday activities. That is particularly true today, when so many effective medications are available that frequently prevent seizures altogether or make them extremely rare. Even so, **withdrawal** may occur because the individual so much fears a seizure.

Paradoxically, today's medications are so effective that many people with epilepsy can "pass" as being able-bodied. The fear of being found out may cause people with epilepsy to avoid social occasions, especially activities that are associated with pressure. These individuals may be helped by counseling. In particular, they may, with guidance, understand that they will be much more relaxed if they openly admit to the condition and educate friends and colleagues about it. Counseling can also help children, youth, and adults who skip injections to control their weight. This is particularly a problem among teenage girls. Skipping injections makes people much more susceptible to blindness or other vision loss.

WHAT OTHER INTERVENTIONS CAN BE EFFECTIVE?

In a few instances, surgery can help. These are cases of "intractable epilepsy," that is, epilepsy that does not respond appropriately to drugs or other interventions. An expert panel convened by the National Institutes of Health (NIH) in 1990 recommended that surgery be considered only when (1) epilepsy is definitely present, (2) all appropriate medications have been tried without success, and (3) the electrochemical syndrome (the precise location of the lesion) has been identified. In addition, the NIH group recommended that surgery be considered only if the seizures are of a frequency, duration, or severity that would interfere markedly with the individual's daily life or threaten health, intelligence, or even survival ("Surgery for Epilepsy," 1990).

The NIH group recommended that complex partial seizures be considered for surgery more than tonic-clonic or other common forms of epilepsy. Children with Lennox-Gastaut syndrome may benefit from surgery that resects the corpus callosum. The idea is to prevent seizures from generalizing bilaterally to the entire brain. Such surgical procedures rarely stop the seizures altogether, but they can reduce them in number and severity ("Surgery for Epilepsy," 1990).

Individuals who do not get appreciable help from medication and who are not candidates for surgery may benefit from newly developed devices such as the vagus nerve stimulator of Cyberonics. Users like Albert Jean also have the option of activating the device if they feel a seizure coming on (e.g., if they get an aura). Cyberonics received FDA approval to market the $9,000 product on July 16, 1997. The FDA was impressed with research findings showing that the device significantly reduces both the number of seizures and their severity (Forest, 1997).

For some people, the *ketogenic diet* may help. The Epilepsy Foundation of America (1997) has cautioned that this is an approach that does not help all persons with epilepsy and that it should be considered only after medication fails to control the condition. Experts at the University of Florida's Brain Institute and College of Medicine have added that only persons who are not candidates for surgery should consider this diet (Ross, 1995). The ketogenic diet is rich in fats (lipids) and oils but low in proteins and carbohydrates. Patients begin the protocol by fasting for 2 to 3 days (fasting alone is known to reduce seizure frequency). A strict regimen of adherence to the diet is required for 2 to 3 years.

WHAT ASSISTIVE TECHNOLOGIES AND SERVICES CAN HELP?

Other than the vagus nerve stimulator (previously discussed), none are needed. People with epilepsy generally function normally, as long as seizures are controlled.

WHAT ARE THE PROSPECTS FOR POSTSECONDARY EDUCATION?

They are excellent. There is no inherent reason why anyone with epilepsy should be prevented by the disability from attending postsecondary programs or from participating fully in all activities, including sports.

WHAT ARE THE EMPLOYMENT PROSPECTS?

These are quite good. Federal law forbids employers from refusing to hire or from firing people on the basis of disability. The same laws require employers to make reasonable accommodations, in this case, removing sharp objects from the workstation. Some jobs may be inappropriate for an individual who has a recent history of seizures, including such jobs as machine operatives and pilots. However, for the vast majority of individuals with epilepsy whose seizures are effectively controlled by medication, no significant limitations in employment should be necessary.

According to the Epilepsy Foundation of America (EFA) (1997), some 20% to 30% of people with epilepsy who are physically able to work (i.e., have no other significant limitations that would prevent them from working) do not work. The EFA traces much of this to lingering attitudes about or fear of epilepsy.

WHAT ARE THE PROSPECTS FOR INDEPENDENT LIVING?

These are excellent. In most states, people with epilepsy can get a driver's license after providing certification from a physician that they have been seizure-free for at least 1 year (up to 5 years in some states).

It should be noted that anticonvulsant medications are costly. Some individuals take as many as 30 pills daily. Alternatives to medication (the vagus nerve stimulator device, surgery) similarly are expensive. While essential for living a seizure-free life, these outlays may limit an individual's ability to afford other products and services.

Women who use anticonvulsant medications must exercise great care if they plan to become pregnant. Some anticonvulsant drugs may cause oral birth control pills to fail. Some may harm the fetus; indeed, some may lead to birth defects. If the woman takes multiple drugs, the risks multiply dramatically. On the other hand, withdrawal from medication can greatly increase the likelihood of seizures, leading to falls or other accidents that could also hurt the fetus.

Questions for Reflection and Discussion

1. Why do most estimates of the size of the population with traumatic brain injury (TBI) greatly overstate the scope of the problem?

2. Explain how the effects of TBI vary over time and what implications that fact has for educators, therapists, and counselors.

3. What does research tell us about the problem-solving difficulties many people with TBI have?

4. How do family members' expectations about recovery from TBI often diverge from reality? What does this suggest about what counselors should do?

5. How does the site of the lesion in multiple sclerosis (MS) explain virtually all of the condition's typical symptoms? What are those symptoms?

6. Why are air conditioning, cold baths, and even special cooling garments so often recommended for people with MS?

7. Why are employment levels of adults with MS so low?

8. What conditions commonly occur with epilepsy?

9. Describe the ketogenic diet and explain why the Epilepsy Foundation of America cautions that it is not a cure.

10. What is the dilemma facing women with epilepsy who become pregnant?

Where is more information available?

Brain Injury Association, Inc.
(Formerly: National Head Injury Foundation)
1776 Massachusetts Avenue NW, #100
Washington, DC 20036-1904
1-202-296-6443
www.biausa.org

Epilepsy Foundation of America
Garden City Drive
Landover, MD 20785
1-800-332-1000
www.efa.org

Myelin Project
1747 Pennsylvania Avenue NW, #950
Washington, DC 20006
1-202-452-8994
E-mail: myelin@erols.com
www.myelin.org

National Multiple Sclerosis Society
733 Third Avenue
New York, NY 10017
1-212-986-3240
1-800-344-4867
www.nmss.org

Solutions Web Page
www.netvoyage.net/~daveq

8

MUSCULAR DYSTROPHY, ARTHRITIS, AMPUTATION, LITTLE PEOPLE

The focus of this chapter shifts to neuromuscular disabilities. In contrast to the conditions discussed in chapters 6 and 7 that have sites of the lesion in the central nervous system, the impairments reviewed in this chapter occur because of lesions or problems in the muscles themselves or in the skeleton. As an example, little people (dwarfs) are short in stature for reasons having to do with their bones and muscles, not with anything in their central nervous system.

Benjamin Cumbo (1987–), of Upper Marlboro, Maryland (near Washington, D.C.), served as National Goodwill Ambassador for the Muscular Dystrophy Association (MDA) in 1996 and again in 1997. His Duchenne MD has not yet prevented him from walking unaided, although statistics indicate that he may require a wheelchair within the next 2 to 3 years. Meanwhile, Benjamin is an honor student in his elementary school, and he hopes someday to become a jet pilot. With so much positive news on the research front, it may indeed be that gene therapies or other treatments might someday make such a career possible ("They Are the Inspiration," 1997).

WHAT IS IT?

Muscular dystrophy (MD) is a group of some 40 genetic disabilities that feature progressive weakness and degeneration of muscles. The most common types are **Duchenne MD,** the most frequently occurring and also the most severe form, and **Becker MD,** a less frequent and less severe form. (Other, less common types include facio-scapulo-humeral, Emery-Dreifyss, limb-girdle, and myotonic MD.) The focus here will be on the former two types. Duchenne and Becker MD are caused by a lack of or a deficiency in a protein called (after the disease) "dystrophin." The gene that codes for this protein is located on the X sex chromosome; for this reason, Duchenne and Becker MD are referred to as "sex-linked" conditions. The genetic factor is recessive.

Duchenne MD and, to a lesser extent, Becker MD express themselves primarily among males. Because females have two X chromosomes, the affected X chromosome is suppressed by the normal (dominant) X chromosome, making females carriers of the disease. Males, however, have one X and one Y sex chromosome, which is much smaller. With no normal X chromosome to counter the affected X chromosome, boys develop the disease. Thus, women who are carriers will pass on the condition to half of their sons; similarly, half of their daughters will become carriers.

Dystrophin is a very large protein usually found on the inner side of the membrane surrounding each muscle fiber. Paula Clemens, M.D., of the University of Pittsburgh, described it as "comprising 2.4 million base pairs of genomic DNA [where] each base pair is a 'letter' in the genetic 'alphabet'" (Clemens, 1997). Dystrophin was discovered by a professor of genetics at Harvard, Louis Kunkel, who named it after the disability it causes. The protein's functions appear to be to maintain the shape and structure of muscle fibers and to keep calcium stored in appropriate compartments called the "sarcoplasmic reticulum." During the regular cycles of muscle fiber degeneration (breakdown) and regeneration (rebuilding), the absence of (Duchenne MD) or alteration of (Becker MD) dystrophin gradually causes regeneration failure. Muscle fiber is then gradually replaced by fibrous and fatty connective tissue (Clemens, 1997).

The crucial feature of dystrophin with respect to muscular dystrophy is that without it muscle fibers cannot regenerate. Robert Prendergast, M.D., of Johns Hopkins University, who has studied MD extensively, commented: "In the absence of dystrophin, too much calcium builds up in the limb and heart muscle cells and activates enzymes inside the muscle that break down protein" ("Healthy Eye Muscles," 1996).

In Duchenne MD, dystrophin is lacking altogether or is seriously deficient; the condition is one of the few in which the *absence* of a protein causes disability. Duchenne MD affects boys exclusively. It generally

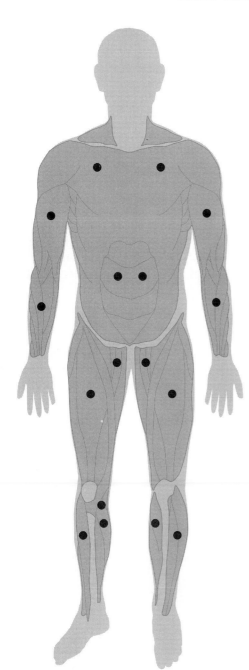

becomes evident in the toddler years, as the child is unable to walk or run as easily as before. Rarely does it first appear as late as age 7. The muscles that had been growing begin to atrophy; usually, the individual needs a wheelchair by about age 13. In the late teens or early 20s, muscle atrophy has weakened the lung and heart muscles, leading to death, usually in the 20s.

In Becker MD, dystrophin is present but is truncated (much shorter). Symptoms make their first appearance later than is the case with Duchenne MD (between the ages of 5 and 25 in most cases), are considerably milder, and progress less rapidly. In this condition, muscles weaken but not to the point of causing premature death. Individuals with Becker MD may continue walking well into adulthood. In these and other ways, Becker MD may be a variation on Duchenne MD, with both having the same underlying cause but each expressing a different mutation.

Facio-scapulo-humeral dystrophy may appear in infancy but is more common in adolescence and adulthood. It begins in muscles of the face, shoulder, and upper arms, hence its name. Limb-girdle dystrophy begins in the lower trunk and legs; it may begin in the shoulders, in which case progression is slower. Life expectancy usually is normal with limb-girdle dystrophy. Myotonic dystrophy, the most common adult-onset MD, starts with the fingers, hands, feet, and lower legs (Emery, 1994).

Principally affected in Duchenne and Becker MD are the skeletal or voluntary muscles that are used in movement; these striated muscles comprise about 40% of body weight. In Duchenne MD, the first symptoms are a clumsiness in walking, a tendency to fall, and the inability to run. Upper limb (arms) weakness often appears 5 years after lower limb (legs) weakness is detected. Boys typically can no longer walk independently by age 10, with a range from 7 to 11 years of age. The less prevalent visceral (smooth) muscles, including gastrointestinal muscles, may be affected as well, especially in individuals who have used mechanical ventilation to prolong their life (Bensen, Jaffe, & Tarr, 1996). The diaphragm, which aids breathing, is a sheet of smooth muscle that contracts during inhalation and relaxes during exhalation. Weakness in the diaphragm leading to respiratory distress often is the immediate cause of death in Duchenne MD.

WHAT CAUSES IT? CAN IT BE PREVENTED? IF SO, HOW?

Although absence or alteration of the protein dystrophin is known to cause Duchenne and Becker MD, we do not yet know what causes the underlying genetic problems. Accordingly, it is not yet known how to prevent the disorder. Two thirds of all instances are traceable to a mother who is a carrier; the remaining one third appear to be genetic mutations (e.g., the mother is not a carrier). That is a very high rate of mutation for an X-linked disorder. Virtually no cases occur because of the genetic makeup of the father. All of this suggests that the incidence of MD could be lowered somewhat through genetic counseling for women who are carriers.

Identification of the proximal cause (absence or truncation of dystrophin) has stimulated considerable research. In theory, it should be possible to insert dystrophin into the bodies of young boys, thus preventing or greatly alleviating the disability. The dystrophin could be transplanted via normal myoblasts into muscles or via the gene itself.

HOW PREVALENT IS IT? WHAT IS THE INCIDENCE?

Muscular dystrophy in all its forms occurs at a rate of about 1,000 new cases annually. The incidence of Duchenne MD is 1 per 3,500 boys; the less common Becker MD appears in about 1 out of 8,000 boys. According to the MDA, approximately 20,000 American males have Duchenne or Becker MD, of whom 15,000 are children (these are the prevalence figures).

WHAT EFFECTS CAN IT HAVE?

Among the first symptoms of MD is a tendency to fall more than most children of the same age. Difficulty climbing stairs is also an early sign. Duchenne MD produces much greater muscle weakness far more rapidly than does Becker MD. Duchenne MD itself can vary considerably in the severity of symptoms. Boys with Duchenne MD typically are harmed by

MD v. all musculoskeletal

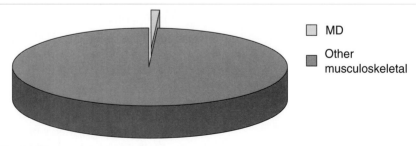

Figure 8.1
Population Estimates: Muscular Dystrophy As Compared to All Musculoskeletal Physical Disabilities

excessive rest. Even when the child has a severe cold or virus, he should not be kept in bed for more than one day at a time, except in the latest stages of MD when there are few other choices available (MDA, 1997).

WHAT SECONDARY CONDITIONS ARE COMMON?

Obesity is common in Duchenne MD, usually because of a combination of lack of physical exercise and overeating. Some reports have indicated that a number of individuals with Duchenne MD, perhaps 1 in every 3, have mild to moderate mental retardation. However, the MDA (1997) has insisted that mental retardation is no more common among persons with MD than it is in the general population. Because the heart is a muscle, cardiac conditions may occur in all forms of MD; they are especially common in Duchenne MD. Occasionally, individuals with Duchenne or Becker MD will be delayed in developing speech; this is not surprising—speech is a motor activity produced by many hundreds of muscles acting in concert. Some individuals with MD will have drooping eyelids and other indications of vision difficulties because of weakness in eye muscles.

WHAT NEEDS DO PEOPLE WITH IT HAVE?

Perhaps the most urgent need of individuals with Duchenne MD and, to a lesser extent, with other dystrophies is to develop a realistic worldview through which to design and live a rewarding life. Parents and professionals alike should encourage children, youth, and adults with MD to establish short- and long-term personal goals that they themselves find both meaningful and motivating. Similarly, although this should go without saying, parents and professionals should advocate for the individual with MD in his attempts to reach these goals.

The fact that Duchenne MD in particular is a relentlessly progressing and invariably fatal condition can easily lead to despair both by the affected individual and by those around him. Indeed, some professionals, notably medical doctors, have resisted use of life-saving and life-enhancing technologies and methods out of a misguided sense that the individual does not have enough of a chance for a fulfilling life. For example, Bach (1996) reported that assisted ventilation is hotly controversial among physicians and clinic directors. Assisted ventilation is supported, however, by "every patient without exception," for which reason, Bach concluded, "clinicians should be cognizant of their inability to gauge disabled patients' life satisfaction and restrain from letting inaccurate and unwarranted judgment of these subjective factors affect patient management decisions."

WHAT SPECIAL-EDUCATION AND RELATED SERVICES MAY HELP?

In muscular dystrophy, physical and occupational therapy are supportive rather than restorative. Although both services help individuals with MD to function better, neither is particularly effective in arresting or halting the relentless degeneration characteristic of the condition. Physical therapist Mary Beth Deering (1996a) recommends daily stretching exercises. She urges early intervention, beginning soon after the condition is diagnosed, to stretch focal muscle groups and to enhance muscle coordination. Beginning as early as age 2, stretching sessions are needed two to three times weekly. During the 4–7 age range, when some tightness develops, four to seven sessions each week are necessary. Playing a musical instrument and swimming can help with breathing. Because many boys with MD resist exercising, Deering urges parents and professionals to be creative and to use varying means to accomplish the same objectives. Particularly helpful are swimming and bicycle riding. Deering (1996b) adds that "objective research in this area is desperately needed" to answer such questions as what kinds of therapy should be used, on what schedules, and over what durations.

Generally, physical therapy aims to prevent contractures, for example, often painful positioning of joints due to shortened and weakened muscles around those joints. Physical therapists also work with individuals who have MD on the effective use of residual strength and on standing, ambulation, and transfer. Occupational therapists can help with positioning and support of the arms and hands for writing, combing hair, brushing teeth, etc. (Deering, 1996a). Physical and occupational therapists may also prescribe, fit, and monitor use of orthoses (devices that supplement a body part). Stretching exercises often are recommended for alleviation of contractures. Strengthening exercises, however, are controversial; the MDA (1997) says they are "usually of limited help, and the patient with muscle disease should always be cautioned against overexertion." Hayes and Williams (1996) disagree, reporting positive results in a study of running by mice that have muscular dystrophy-like conditions.

Because MD specifically affects motor activity, special-education services that focus upon intellectual activities may be appropriate. The emphasis should be upon helping the child to develop his strengths and talents. A preoccupation with alleviating the weaknesses is misplaced. Parents, educators, and therapists must always bear in mind that children and youth with MD are individuals with abilities. The MDA (1997) recommends against overprotection of individuals with MD because it leads to isolation and dependence. Rather, the MDA suggests that honest expectations be set and adhered to, insisting that the individual perform those tasks he realistically can do.

WHAT OTHER INTERVENTIONS CAN BE EFFECTIVE?

Now that a gene associated with Duchenne MD has been identified, it is possible that at some time in the near future genetic interventions will alleviate or even eliminate the effects of the disease. Clemens (1997) noted that efforts to deliver dystrophin into the bodies of people with MD have been complicated by a number of factors. Gene transfer, or the delivery of the gene that codes for dystrophin, may be accomplished with the use of a virus that has been altered to (1) carry the dystrophin gene and (2) not cause disease (i.e., not replicate). It is possible to inject the vector (virus + dystrophin) directly into muscles, although this would require many hundreds of injections to affect a sufficient number of muscles. An alternative would be to use the body's vascular system to transport the vector throughout the body, although it is not in the nature of viruses to enter muscles through the vascular system. A third problem is overcoming the body's immune response, which both attacks the virus as foreign and mobilizes to attack any second administration of the virus (Haecker, Stedman, Balice-Gordon, Smith, & Greelish, 1996). For these reasons, genetic therapy may be a number of years off. Until such a time as dystrophin can be delivered into the body, physical therapy to slow down muscle atrophy and occupational therapy to help the child cope with muscle weaknesses are the principal interventions.

In part because of the difficulties researchers are having with gene therapy and dystrophin, interest has grown in a similar protein known as "utrophin." Studies with mice have suggested that utrophin might help to compensate for the missing dystrophin. One advantage is that utrophin is already present in the bodies of boys and young men with MD; the need is to accelerate the body's production of this protein (Cooke, 1996).

Some studies have suggested that the steroid prednisone slows the muscle deterioration. Boys taking prednisone did not need wheelchairs until about 3 years after boys not taking it did. Steroids, however, have serious side effects—including high blood pressure, cataracts, diabetes, and significant weight gain (it can be a particular problem for boys with weakened muscles to carry extra weight). Researchers are now trying to identify the active ingredient in prednisone that slows MD to isolate it in the hope that they can offer help without the side effects. The research is being funded by the MDA, the group for whom Jerry Lewis holds his Labor Day telethons.

WHAT ASSISTIVE TECHNOLOGIES AND SERVICES CAN HELP?

Assistive technology devices can enable the child to do things that he no longer can do alone, including sitting upright and moving independently with the assistance of braces, crutches, and a wheelchair. Particularly important is proper positioning in the wheelchair, since children and youth with MD spend so much time sitting (Deering, 1996a). Other assistive technology devices, notably pointing and switching products, help individuals with MD in fine-motor control functions. Raised chairs and toilet seats, grab bars, bathtub benches, high stools, and footboards for wheelchairs are among the assistive technology devices recommended by the MDA (1997). Hydraulic, electric, and mechanical lifts for transferring to and from bed and bath are also recommended.

It is particularly important in MD that physical and occupational therapists, as well as parents and educators, very carefully monitor the boy's needs for assistive technology. These needs are likely to change, often dramatically, over time. Thus, adjustments to and replacements for assistive technology devices are required periodically.

WHAT ARE THE PROSPECTS FOR POSTSECONDARY EDUCATION?

For individuals with Duchenne MD, limited experience exists upon which to draw because so many young men with this condition have died in their early 20s. If the research now being conducted should result in prolonging of life for individuals with Duchenne MD, there would be little reason to expect anything other than good prospects for postsecondary education. Today, virtually all colleges and universities in the United States are accessible to one degree or another so that persons using manual or electric wheelchairs can get around campus readily and easily. With respect to Becker or other dystrophies that cause less severe muscle weaknesses, all indications are that prospects for postsecondary education should be bright.

WHAT ARE THE EMPLOYMENT PROSPECTS?

We have little experience to point to with respect to employment of individuals with Duchenne MD, simply because death occurs prior to the age at which people usually begin employment. Therapies emerging from today's research on dystrophin may change that, in which case employment prospects will depend upon (1) the individual's training and talents, (2) nondiscrimination laws and regulations, and (3) reasonable accommodations on the job. With gene therapy of dystrophin appearing to be on the threshold of becoming reality, parents and professionals may want to place increasing emphasis upon vocational training for individuals with Duchenne MD, especially those who are still young boys. The kinds of vocational goals that once were sadly unthinkable may soon become quite feasible if the research lives up to its promise.

WHAT ARE THE PROSPECTS FOR INDEPENDENT LIVING?

Assistive technology devices and services today make it possible even for individuals with very limited muscle strength to live semiindependently, at least until the final stages of Duchenne MD. These are, in many instances, the same kinds of assistive devices that are helpful with spinal cord injury, spina bifida, and multiple sclerosis.

Arthritis

Nineteen-year-old amateur tennis player Justin Hertzberg of Boca Raton, Florida, has lived with juvenile rheumatoid arthritis (JRA) since he was a young boy. At 6, he had to hold onto a handrail to walk down a flight of stairs. "I fight through it," he told journalist Jason Molinet. "There are days when it's real hard to roll out of bed. Normally, it gets better by midafternoon. And there will be times when I'm fine. I can go a week where I don't have a problem, and then out of nowhere I'll wake up and it's back. That's the tough part."

JRA causes inflammation in the joints, the tissue around joints, and other body organs. Justin usually cannot touch his shoulders with his fingers, for

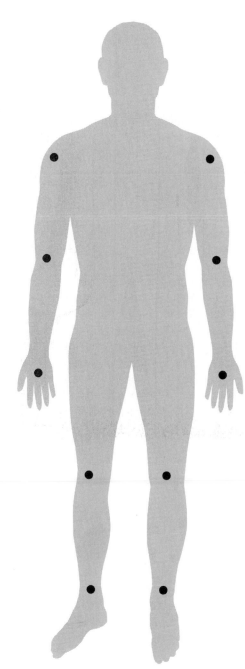

example. His most reliable relief comes from hot showers, which he takes twice or more often a day. Justin also uses naprosyn (an antiinflammatory drug), methotrexate (an anticancer drug that has been reported to prevent progressive joint atrophy), and a third pill to counter the nausea side effects of methotrexate. Even with these drugs, playing competitive tennis is a struggle: "By tonight," he said during a recent tournament, "I'll be a cripple. It won't happen during a match because I stay loose. But once my body gets rested, that's when I start to swell up" (Molinet, 1998).

WHAT IS IT?

The term *arthritis* encompasses a variety of autoimmune (the body fighting itself) conditions that affect joints, cartilage, and bones. The Arthritis Foundation (1997) recognizes more than 100 forms of arthritis and related disorders. For example, JRA, once thought to be one type, is now recognized as comprising at least six separate diseases (Fink, Fernandez-Vina, & Stastny, 1995). Arthritis in its various forms has in common the fact that it causes pain and stiffness, usually because of inflammation. In fact, *arthritis* means 'inflammation of the joint'.

WHAT CAUSES IT? CAN IT BE PREVENTED? IF SO, HOW?

No definitive cause or causes have been identified. A relation of some kind exists between certain kinds of arthritis and weight, and people who lose as much as 10 pounds may reduce their risk of getting some forms of arthritis, particularly those involving the knees, by as much as half. There does seem to be a genetic disposition to some kinds of arthritis; people who have close relatives with arthritis are more likely to get it. One study suggested that the genetic factor involved may reside on the 22nd chromosome (Sullivan et al., 1997). Another study found that production of an insulin-like growth factor was impaired in children with JRA (Davies, Jones, Reeve, Camacho-Hubner, Charlett, Ansell, Preece, & Woo, 1997). In addition, people who sustain joint injuries in accidents tend to have higher risks than others (Arthritis Foundation, 1997).

HOW PREVALENT IS IT? WHAT IS THE INCIDENCE?

Arthritis is very common, affecting 1 American in every 7, or some 40 million people in this country. Slightly more than half are women (Arthritis Foundation, 1997). The most common form is osteoarthritis, which usually occurs after the age of 45. Much less common are forms of JRA, which is rather arbitrarily defined as arthritis that begins prior to age 16. JRA occurs most frequently in the 1- to 3-year age range and again in the 8- to 10-year age period. According to the Arthritis Foundation (1997), 2.9 per 1,000 children, or 285,000 American children, have some form of arthritis, usually a variation of JRA. Adult-onset arthritis is commonly thought of as a condition primarily affecting older people; however, about one third of individuals with arthritis are under 36 years of age (Pharmaceutical Information Network, 1997).

WHAT EFFECTS CAN IT HAVE?

Most people who have arthritis are able to function independently despite the condition. In a significant minority, however, it becomes severe, so much so that arthritis is one of the biggest causes of disability today. It limits the daily activities of about 7 million Americans (Arthritis Foundation, 1997). These people have difficulty dressing, climbing stairs, doing paid work or schoolwork, and even getting out of bed in the morning. Pain is a constant part of the lives of many individuals with arthritis. People with arthritis may also have stiffness in their joints, and some have swelling in or around the joints. This pain and stiffness may make everyday tasks, including climbing stairs and opening jars, difficult. One measure of the impact of arthritis is the Arthritis Foundation's (1991) estimate that rheumatic disease costs the American economy some $35 billion each year in direct and indirect expenses.

Among the types of juvenile rheumatoid arthritis are polyarticular JRA, which affects five or more joints (*poly* means 'many' and *articular* means 'joint'); pauciarticular JRA, which affects four or fewer joints (*pauci* means 'few'); and systemic JRA, which affects both joints and internal organs. These forms of arthritis are characterized by joint inflammation (when pain and stiffness occur in the lining of the joint, known as the synovium), joint contracture (when tendons tighten and shorten), joint damage (when joint surfaces erode as a result of long-lasting inflammation), and altered growth

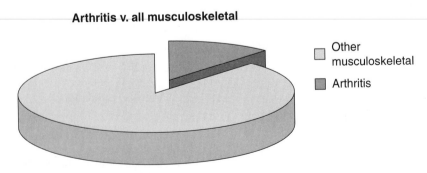

Arthritis v. all musculoskeletal

Other musculoskeletal

Arthritis

Figure 8.2
Population Estimates: Arthritis As Compared to All Musculoskeletal Physical Disabilities

(when inflammation either speeds up or slows down the growth centers in bones) (Arthritis Foundation, 1997). Most commonly (50% of the cases), several joints are affected, although in 30% of the instances, only one joint (usually the knee) is involved. In addition, muscle strength and thickness are reduced in some forms of arthritis (Lindehammar & Backman, 1995).

WHAT SECONDARY CONDITIONS ARE COMMON?

Eye disease, fatigue, and low-grade fevers often accompany arthritis, especially JRA forms. Older individuals with arthritis may also have limitations of hearing or vision, both of which are common among senior citizens. Some people have hip-girdle involvement and need surgical replacements of the hip. Many people with JRA have abnormal digestive or bowel functions.

WHAT NEEDS DO PEOPLE WITH IT HAVE?

The major need is for medication to reduce inflammation, especially in the joints, and to relieve pain.

WHAT SPECIAL-EDUCATION AND RELATED SERVICES MAY HELP?

Adaptive equipment, notably low-tech assistive technology devices, can be very helpful. Fortunately, a wide variety of these are available, often at general merchandise and home furnishing stores such as Home Depot. Such items as bottle and can openers that require much less pressure and twisting and wide-handled knives, forks, and spoons can make a big difference in everyday life. With respect to personal computer use, adaptations that are used to prevent or treat repetitive strain injury (RSI) also help with arthritis. They include ergonomic keyboards or Dvorak keyboards. Also helpful are adaptive technology services, notably training in techniques of avoiding prolonged stress on the nerves of the fingers, hands, and wrists.

WHAT OTHER INTERVENTIONS CAN BE EFFECTIVE?

Physical therapy is almost always indicated, particularly because exercise is known to help in the management of arthritis. Physical therapists can help people to keep muscles from weakening and joints from stiffening. Strengthening exercises that increase muscle strength and stretching exercises that keep joints flexible should be done daily. Among the activities recommended by experts on arthritis are swimming, bicycling, jogging, and hand exercises. Swimming, in particular, is highly recommended because it puts so little pressure on joints. Some people like to apply heat to their aching joints before exercising and cold afterwards. Occupational therapy, especially to learn alternative ways of doing things so that pressure on affected joints is lessened, is also widely recommended. Occupational therapists can fit people with splints and other devices to help reduce stress on joints. As Hackett,

Johnson, Parkin, and Southwood (1996) pointed out, the literature on physical and occupational therapy contains a paucity of research studies on these interventions with people who have arthritis. Accordingly, there are few guidelines available to indicate which protocols and how much of each should be used.

Diet is another kind of intervention; the focus is upon getting enough calcium into the body while keeping sugar and fat intake down. Many people with arthritis take medication, notably antiinflammatories that reduce pain and swelling. Some who have severe cases of arthritis take corticosteriods for the same reasons; these, however, can have serious side effects. Prednisone, a steroid, may be used for brief periods. The most commonly used treatment is aspirin. People with arthritis often take large doses of aspirin. Teachers, counselors, and family members should be alert to side effects of such large amounts of aspirin, including hearing loss, nausea, vomiting, stomach upset, and irritability.

About half of all children and youth who have JRA take methotrexate, an anticancer drug. While the long-term effects and side effects of this drug remain unknown, short-term results appear promising. Many young children who had regressed to crawling because of pain and stiffness in the legs are able to resume walking, running, and even dancing because of methotrexate.

A new class of drugs, known as "COX-2 inhibitors," is being introduced by Monsanto's G.D. Searle unit and Merck. These drugs are much less likely to produce side effects than are other drugs, including Relafen and Lodine XL, and even than aspirin or Advil. The latter work by blocking an enzyme known as cyclo-oxygenase, or COX, which appears to be involved in inflammation but also acts to protect the stomach lining. The COX-2 inhibitors, by contrast, work on a second enzyme, called COX-2, which seems to be more directly involved in the body's inflammation but not to have any role in the stomach (Barrett & Melcher, 1998).

WHAT ASSISTIVE TECHNOLOGIES AND SERVICES CAN HELP?

For some people, braces, crutches, or even a wheelchair can make walking easier by reducing stress on the knee joints. Splints may be used to hold joints in the proper position; they will need to be adjusted when inflammation levels change and, of course, as children grow. As noted earlier, a wide variety of low-tech products, such as utensils, pencils, and pens, that are equipped with larger handles can make housework, writing, and other activities easier.

Follow-up studies of people with arthritis after discharge from the hospital suggest that assistive technology devices are not used as much as expected. Some people discard the products after they recover functioning abilities, while others abandon the devices as stigmatizing. Particularly needed by people with arthritis, according to a study by Mann, Hurren, and Tomita (1995), are reachers, remote controls, lift chairs, cordless phones, magnifying glasses, bathroom grab bars, and jar openers.

WHAT ARE THE PROSPECTS FOR POSTSECONDARY EDUCATION?

If the necessary pain- and inflammation-reducing medications are taken properly, nothing about arthritis should limit anyone's participation in post-secondary education.

WHAT ARE THE EMPLOYMENT PROSPECTS?

These, too, should not be limited by arthritis. The Americans with Disabilities Act requires employers to make reasonable accommodations on the job for qualified workers. Such accommodations can include ergonomic keyboards, ergonomic chairs, and other adjustments that can limit the deleterious effects of arthritis.

WHAT ARE THE PROSPECTS FOR INDEPENDENT LIVING?

Again, given the use of proper medication and adaptive devices, independent living should not be restricted just because someone has arthritis.

Amputation

John D. Kemp (1949–), who is president and CEO of Very Special Arts, a not-for-profit organization that sponsors and celebrates creative work by people with disabilities, was born without arms or legs. These limb deficiencies have never stopped John. At the age of 10, he was an Easter Seals poster boy. When I first met him in the 1970s, he was an attorney advising corporations on their equal employment opportunity obligations. Later, he became executive director of United Cerebral Palsy Associations Inc., the position he held before going to Very Special Arts. He is also active in the Amputee Coalition of America. John uses two hooks for hands, wielding them expertly to do anything I can do with my hands and fingers. After a few minutes with him, most visitors all but forget the artificial limbs because John's quiet dignity puts them at such ease. It is this unflappability and cultured smoothness of manner that is his greatest strength and makes him such an effective executive and fund raiser. In 1997, New Mobility magazine named him its Person of the Year (Maddox, 1998).

WHAT IS IT?

Amputation is the surgical removal of all or part of a limb. It usually occurs as a life-saving measure after disease, but it may also follow an accident. In some instances, limbs are amputated for survival reasons, as when a bone is cancerous; we refer to these as adventitious. Although adventitious amputations are different from congenital limb deficiencies, the practical effects of the differences in treatment of children, youth, and adults often are insignificant. For this reason, amputations and limb deficiencies will be discussed together here. Limb deficiencies among young children are more likely, by a

3-to-1 or 4-to-1 ratio, to be congenital than adventitious (Jones, 1988). After the age of 10, trauma (as in accidents) and tumors (as in cancer) are the most common causes (Jain, 1996).

WHAT CAUSES IT? CAN IT BE PREVENTED? IF SO, HOW?

Worldwide, the number one cause of amputation is landmines. The Landmine Survivors Network was one of the charities favored by the late Diana, Princess of Wales (White, 1997). Within the United States, the major causes of limb deficiencies are vascular disease (particularly with diabetes mellitus),

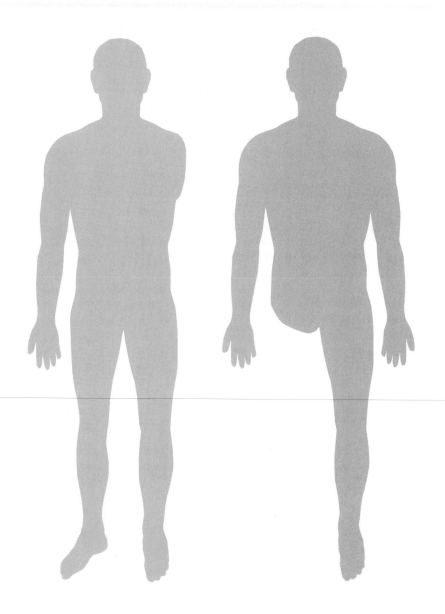

cancer, infection, birth defects, and trauma, especially from accidents. In approximately 60% of the cases, a precise cause for missing limbs cannot be identified. Single-gene mutations account for approximately 20% of missing-limb deficiencies (Scott, 1989). In the fetus, a maternal infection, a disease, or exposure of the fetus to drugs may be at cause. Some women take medicinal drugs before they know they are pregnant; others, despite knowing they are pregnant, take legal or illicit illegal drugs. Rubella (German measles) and other diseases may also cause congenital conditions. Acquired limb deficiencies (amputations) in children typically occur because of automobile or motorcycle accidents, power-tool injuries, and gunshot wounds. Such therapeutic amputations are more frequent among boys than girls, as boys tend to be physically more adventurous and have more accidents (Jones, 1988). Finally, tumors are frequent in the 10- to 20-year-old range; amputations are done to save the young person's life.

Good prenatal care, including education of pregnant women about side effects of medication, can prevent many congenital limb deficiencies. Child safety precautions and use of protective equipment in sporting events and bicycle or motorcycle use similarly can reduce the incidence of traumatic acquired amputations. With respect to diabetes, control of blood glucose and blood pressure can limit the number of individuals who need amputations (Selby & Zhang, 1995).

HOW PREVALENT IS IT? WHAT IS THE INCIDENCE?

At the estimated prevalence of 1.5 amputees per 1,000 people in the United States, the number of Americans with amputation is about 400,000. The National Association for the Advancement of Orthotics and Prosthetics (1995) has estimated the prevalence at a much higher, 2 million, level. Lower-limb amputations are by far the most common; including partial foot amputations, lower-limb amputations account for about 91% of all amputations. Among lower-limb amputations, below-knee amputations are more common than

Amputation v. all musculoskeletal

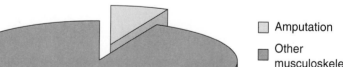
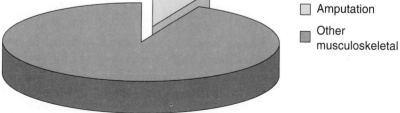

☐ Amputation
■ Other musculoskeletal

Figure 8.3
Population Estimates: Amputation As Compared to All Musculoskeletal Physical Disabilities

are above-knee amputations; similarly, among upper-limb amputations, below-elbow amputations are more common than above-elbow amputations (Northwestern University, 1996). I have not found incidence reports in which I have confidence. Recognizing the same problem, the Amputee Coalition of America, in cooperation with the Centers for Disease Control and Prevention, recently launched the National Limb Loss Information Center, which will collect and report incidence and prevalence information.

WHAT EFFECTS CAN IT HAVE?

Given good artificial limbs, amputation should have few effects on everyday life. There is always the risk of irritation of residual joints and skin and of infection. Proper fitting and regular checking of the artificial limbs should contain those problems, however.

WHAT SECONDARY CONDITIONS ARE COMMON?

Phantom limb sensation and phantom pain are felt by as many as 70% of people with amputations. Phantom limb sensation is the feeling that the limb is still there, while phantom pain is perceived pain from the limb that is no longer there. In both cases, the nerves in the residual limb continue to generate impulses that traverse over the central nervous system to the brain and the spinal cord. Usually, both sensation and pain diminish over time; those that persist for 6 months or longer, however, are difficult to treat (Esquenazi & Meier, 1996).

WHAT NEEDS DO PEOPLE WITH IT HAVE?

The energy required to accomplish a given task with a prosthesis is considerably higher than the energy needed to do the same thing with unimpaired limbs. Between 40% and 100% more energy is expended with an artificial limb than without (Czerniecki, 1996; Esquenazi & Meier, 1996). In addition, especially for people with newly fitted devices, more time is required to do things. For these reasons, educators and employers alike should allow additional time in testing and in other activities as a reasonable accommodation.

WHAT SPECIAL-EDUCATION AND RELATED SERVICES MAY HELP?

People with limb deficiencies or amputations should need no special education as such, but occupational therapy to learn effective use of artificial limbs and physical therapy to build and maintain muscle strength in residual limbs are important. When the lower limbs are deficient or amputated, getting around may take a bit longer than usual; thus, releasing a child a few minutes prior to the end of a class or otherwise allowing a child a little more time for travel can help. Similarly, when upper limbs are deficient or amputated, and especially when artificial limbs are new, allowing additional time for taking tests or otherwise doing paperwork is a reasonable accommodation.

WHAT OTHER INTERVENTIONS CAN BE EFFECTIVE?

My former student James Billy, who has an artificial arm and hand, has alerted me to a problem I had not anticipated. James, who lives in the Bronx, often has difficulty hailing a cab because taxi drivers sometimes regard his hook as a weapon and refuse to accept his request for transportation. This is a rather extreme example of ways in which community education about disability can improve the everyday lives of people with limb deficiencies or amputations. Children may tease people with artificial limbs. As is often true, a few minutes of orientation and instruction about the disability can alleviate such teasing by making children more comfortable with the need for and function of artificial limbs.

WHAT ASSISTIVE TECHNOLOGIES AND SERVICES CAN HELP?

An amazing variety of artificial limbs is now available. These prostheses may be fitted to children as young as 3 to 9 months of age. They come with small passive hands, mitts, or feet in infant sizes. Rapid fitting is important because if it is delayed, children develop compensatory mechanisms that meet their immediate needs. For this reason, these children may reject the prosthesis when it is introduced as being less effective and efficient than their makeshift approaches (Atkins, 1997). They may also reject it as offering less sensory input and feedback than the residual limb. For whatever reason, rejection of prostheses may cause children not to meet or to be seriously delayed in meeting important developmental milestones. In the long run, today's prostheses likely will prove more helpful in ways of doing things than are idiosyncratic adjustments.

Children often outgrow their prostheses. Signs that a prosthesis may need replacement include skin irritation, failure of the residual limb to fit into the socket, and irregularities in walking or using upper limbs. Jain (1996) has reported that "[c]hildren usually require a new lower limb prosthesis annually up to age 5, every other year from ages 5 to 12, then once every 3 years up to age 21" (p. S-12). As this suggests, prostheses and orthoses need to be custom-designed, custom-fitted, and regularly inspected. Myoelectric arms and legs pick up signals from muscles in the residual limb and convert them into signals that tell the prosthesis what to do. These limbs are much favored by parents because they look so natural, yet they are about twice as expensive as body-powered units, require precise socket fitting, and need almost constant maintenance. For these reasons, plus the fact that children tend to care more about functionality than about appearance, some occupational therapists recommend body-powered over myoelectric prostheses (Puig, 1997).

Children who never had (or who have no memory of having) the missing limb adjust more readily to the condition than children who lose the limb later in childhood. They more quickly accept braces, artificial limbs, and assistive technology devices and services. By contrast, people who remember life before amputation often resist the introduction of artificial devices and aids; this is similar to what happens with many individuals with spinal cord injuries.

In recent years, people with limb deficiencies, whether congenital or adventitious, have expressed ever-greater interest in following or resuming an active lifestyle. For this reason, research in orthotics and prosthetics increasingly has focused on ways to make artificial limbs that support running, jumping, and participation in such sports as tennis and basketball. Czerniecki (1996) has offered a good summary of the findings from that research. Other advances in form and function add yet more sophistication to today's artificial limbs (Schuch, 1996).

Artificial hands come in two categories: passive and powered. A passive hand (mitt) has no grasping capability. Powered hands may be body-powered, or they may be myoelectric. Body-powered hands are more cosmetically attractive but lack the pinch force and precision of movement of today's myoelectric hands. Myoelectric hands derive power from the small electrical charges in muscles. They come in two varieties: hands and hooks. Of the two, hooks continue to offer greater precision of movement and manipulation of objects, while hands are expensive and heavy and require frequent maintenance. Some people wear hooks by day and hands by night (Northwestern University, 1996).

WHAT ARE THE PROSPECTS FOR POSTSECONDARY EDUCATION?

Nothing about limb deficiencies or amputations should limit in any significant way the prospects of a student in a college or university.

WHAT ARE THE EMPLOYMENT PROSPECTS?

There is no good reason why limb deficiencies or amputations should restrict employment opportunities. Given that job applicants and workers make the effort to put employers and coworkers at ease and to demonstrate how the work can be done, people with limb deficiencies or amputations should be able to do most any job.

It is worth noting that the Americans with Disabilities Act and Title V of the Rehabilitation Act of 1973, as amended, require reasonable accommodations by employers on behalf of people with disabilities. With respect to people who use artificial limbs, the laws require that repair and replacement of the artificial body parts be treated much as is surgery on natural body parts. This might include a period of time for the fitting and adjustment to the daily use of artificial limbs.

WHAT ARE THE PROSPECTS FOR INDEPENDENT LIVING?

Again, there are no good reasons why these should be limited in any meaningful ways. Particularly with today's assistive technology devices and services, individuals with limb deficiencies and amputations should be able to accomplish virtually every task of independent living, including driving (perhaps with hand controls), housework (perhaps with the assistance of an environmental control unit), and all the other often mundane tasks that go into everyday life.

Little People

My first encounter with Little People of America (LPA) came in 1977 when LPA leader Lee Kitchens approached me in a hotel in Washington, D.C. At the time, I was executive director of a national lobby organization representing people with all kinds of physical, mental, and sensory disabilities. Thus, I was accustomed to individuals with different disabilities wanting to be sure that I understood their particular needs so that I could advocate for them in Congress and at the White House. Lee Kitchens, however, surprised me. The first words out of his mouth were, "What's your position on water fountains?" I was a bit taken aback, so I resorted to humor ("I'm for them!"). Lee was not deterred. He went on to articulate the need for lowered water fountains, pay

Steps that help users of wheelchairs to gain access (e.g., ramps, elevators, lowered cabinets, automatic doors, etc.) also help little people.

phones, bank counters, etc. In fact, he said, a general rule is that anything you do for people using wheelchairs most likely will also help little people. It's a good rule, one I've never forgotten.

WHAT IS IT?

Little People of America (LPA, 1997) has defined dwarfism as an adult height of 4 feet, 10 inches or less, in both men and women, as a result of a genetic or medical condition. LPA, founded in 1957 by the actor Billy Barty, has estimated that there are more than 100 different genetic causes of dwarfism, or skeletal dysplasia. Terms acceptable to LPA include *dwarfs, little person* or *people,* and *person of short stature; midget,* however, is regarded as being a derogatory term. Most little people are 4 feet or less in height (Human Growth Foundation, 1996).

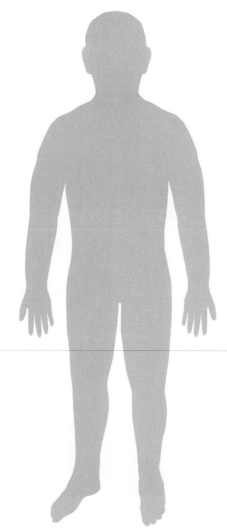

WHAT CAUSES IT? CAN IT BE PREVENTED? IF SO, HOW?

Virtually all instances of dwarfism are genetically caused. The most common form is *achondroplasia,* which usually leads to an adult height of 4 feet. The gene for this condition was identified in 1994 by scientists at the University of California at Irvine. It primarily affects growth of the long bones. In most instances, the genetic mutation is spontaneous; both parents are of normal height, and neither carries a dwarfism gene (American Academy of Pediatrics, 1995; Human Growth Foundation, 1996). Less common is *osteogenesis imperfecta,* characterized by fragile bones that fracture easily.

Dwarfism results from dominant genes. Persons with achondroplasia have one dwarfism gene and one nondwarfism gene. Children born to two adults with achondroplasia would have a 25% chance of being of normal height (inheritance of two nondwarfism genes), a 50% chance of being a dwarf (inheritance of one dwarfism gene and one nondwarfism gene), and a 25% chance of "double dominant" inheritance (inheritance of two dwarfism genes), which invariably leads to an early death (LPA, 1997).

LPA has become deeply concerned about genetic testing of unborn fetuses. Its leaders worry that a society that approves of abortion to prevent dwarfism might also look with disfavor upon little people who are already alive. The association does support genetic testing when both parents have achondroplasia, and the testing is performed to ascertain the likelihood that the fetus would be born with double dominance (LPA, 1997). In these, as in many other ways, the "culture" of little people resembles that of the deaf community: Little people often insist that they do not have disabilities but rather are just different; they resist genetic or medical "cures"; they often intermarry. Two highly readable accounts of their culture appear in John Richardson's

1998 *Esquire* article, "Dwarfs: A Love Story," and in David Berreby's 1996 piece in *The New Republic* that quoted one little person as exclaiming, "If there were a magic pill that would make me wake up tomorrow and be tall, I would not take it." This is very similar to what many people who are deaf say.

HOW PREVALENT IS IT? WHAT IS THE INCIDENCE?

Little People of America has 5,000 members, half of whom are normal-height family members. LPA has suggested that its 2,500 dwarf members represent 10% of the nation's population of little people (LPA, 1997). That would support a prevalence estimate of 25,000. The Human Growth Foundation (1996), however, has estimated that just 10,000 Americans of all ages have achondroplasia, the most common form of skeletal dysplasia, and that it occurs in about one per 25,000 live births. For our purposes, we will compromise at a prevalence of 20,000 and an incidence rate of 500 new cases annually.

WHAT EFFECTS CAN IT HAVE?

Children with achondroplasia typically reach motor milestones late (e.g., walking at 24–36 months versus 12–15 months for most children). They often get ear infections because of inadequate drainage of the eustachian tube. The spine may become curved and the legs bowed; surgery usually repairs the former, and braces (with or without surgery) the latter (Human Growth Foundation, 1996).

Children, youth, and adults who are little people typically have normal intelligence and can participate in normal, age-appropriate activities. Little people generally are healthy individuals with near normal life expectancies. They may, however, require surgery—sometimes multiple surgeries—to correct structural, postural, and other problems. As is true of people with any disability, they will function better if their general health is good. Exercise (particularly swimming and bicycling) is recommended by LPA, but running

Little people v. all musculoskeletal

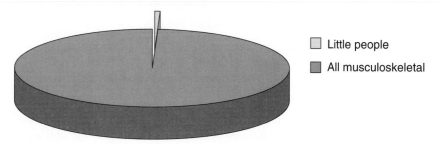

Figure 8.4
Population Estimates: Little People As Compared to Persons with All Kinds of Musculoskeletal Physical Disabilities

and long-distance walking are discouraged by the association on the grounds that constant pounding can be harmful (LPA, 1997).

WHAT SECONDARY CONDITIONS ARE COMMON?

According to LPA (1997), several secondary complications are possible but not likely. One is compression of the foramen magnum, or brain stem at the top of the spinal cord, because it is too small to accommodate the spinal cord. Hydrocephalus, or excess fluid on the brain, is also possible. As with other cases of hydrocephalus, a shunt may be implanted to drain off the excess fluid. A third possibility is obstructive apnea, where an infant's airways are too small or improperly shaped; about 3% of infants or toddlers with achondroplasia die of unexpected infant death syndrome (American Academy of Pediatrics, 1995). Each of these secondary problems is treatable medically (LPA, 1997). In addition, overcrowding of teeth may occur (Human Growth Foundation, 1996).

WHAT NEEDS DO PEOPLE WITH IT HAVE?

With very young children, the skull should be measured monthly to monitor for hydrocephalus. Sleep studies are important, too, to avoid sudden infant death. Curvature of the spine can be minimized by giving support to the young child until sufficient thoracic strength has been achieved to permit unsupported sitting. In fact, parents are urged to help their child avoid unsupported sitting for the first year of life (American Academy of Pediatrics, 1995). An important need is to curb the tendency of other children to tease short-statured children. People need to be aware that achondroplasia and other skeletal dysplasias are genetic conditions and cannot be caught by other people. Another need is weight control: Little people must exercise care on a lifelong basis to avoid becoming overweight.

WHAT SPECIAL-EDUCATION AND RELATED SERVICES MAY HELP?

Physical and occupational therapy, especially to fit seat supports or other special devices, can be important. Given the necessary assistive devices (discussed later), individuals of short stature should be able to participate fully in school and on the job.

WHAT OTHER INTERVENTIONS CAN BE EFFECTIVE?

If there is a choice about schools to attend, LPA (1997) suggests that parents select a smaller, preferably single-level school. Careful scheduling of classes so that they are within short distances of each other and releasing a short-statured child 5 minutes prior to the bell are other steps that can help. These reduce the amount of walking and stair climbing necessary and the danger that hordes of running children might trample the short-statured child. School buses should be equipped with seat belts; as an alternative, removable seat belts can be used that wrap completely around the child's seat and that may be stored in the child's backpack after each use. An advantage of removable seat belts is that the child is not limited to always riding in any one bus or in any one seat. Although relatively few school buses come equipped with seat belts, many schools will add seat belts upon request; some will provide removable seat belts. Also helpful during the school years is a double set of schoolbooks. This removes the necessity for the child to carry books to and from school every day.

Choosing (or altering, if necessary) the right clothes can make a big difference in children's independence. This is especially true when young children need to use rest rooms. Helpful are Velcro (instead of zippers or shoelaces) for fastening clothes or shoes. Belts should be soft, loose fitting, and not wide or stiff. Shirts and pants should be of one or closely related colors rather than of contrasting colors; lines should be vertical rather than horizontal. Keeping colors monotone and lines vertical helps to give an illusion of greater height (Little People of America, 1997).

LPA strongly opposes limb-lengthening surgeries, believing that they are both medically unnecessary and potentially harmful because they weaken the limbs. However, LPA has also conceded that some of its own members have had this surgery and are pleased with the results. Growth hormones and other drug therapies usually are ineffective with this population (American Academy of Pediatrics, 1995).

WHAT ASSISTIVE TECHNOLOGIES AND SERVICES CAN HELP?

Adaptations in schools, workplaces, and homes that meet the needs of people using wheelchairs usually will also respond to the special needs of people of short stature. Stools (every room should have at least one), lowered faucets and light switches, and adapted toys can be very helpful. Danny Black, who has a family member who is of short stature, has assembled a useful Web page of products useful for little people: home.sprynet.com/sprynet/dblack/dwrfprod.htm. These products include stools of various kinds, custom-designed clothing, custom bicycles, and pedal extensions for automobile driving. Some people of short stature prefer using car hand controls rather than pedal extensions; the major car rental companies make hand-control-equipped vehicles available with a 24- or 48-hour advance notice. In addition, General Motors and Chrysler offer cash reimbursements or incentives to help in purchasing new car adaptations. Classroom interventions include allowing extra time to write (because of short fingers) and permitting the use of a tape recorder to reduce the amount of note taking required.

WHAT ARE THE PROSPECTS FOR POSTSECONDARY EDUCATION?

These are excellent. Virtually every college and university in the United States has made itself program accessible for individuals using wheelchairs. In most instances, this means at least minimal accessibility for little people as well.

WHAT ARE THE EMPLOYMENT PROSPECTS?

These are quite good. LPA has adopted the motto "Think Big" to reflect, in part, its conviction that virtually all occupations are open to little people. Employment is not limited to Walt Disney or Dream Works movies, circuses, or other entertainment jobs related directly to short stature, although that was true half a century ago. Today, for example, LPA members hold a wide variety of jobs ranging from lawyer to government human services specialist to engineer.

WHAT ARE THE PROSPECTS FOR INDEPENDENT LIVING?

These are excellent. In general, barrier-removal steps that help people using wheelchairs also assist little people. Many other accessibility problems can be resolved simply by placing step stools in most rooms of the house.

Questions for Reflection and Discussion

1. What are some of the first symptoms of Duchenne muscular dystrophy (MD)?

2. If Duchenne MD is caused by the absence of the protein dystrophin, why have scientists yet to succeed with the obvious "cure"—injecting dystrophin into the body?

3. What should counselors do to help children and youth with Duchenne MD deal with their worries about morbidity and mortality?

4. What kinds of physical therapy are recommended for MD?

5. What secondary conditions often are found with arthritis?

6. What kinds of low-tech products can help people who have arthritis?

7. Why might giving breaks from work or schoolwork help people who have amputations?

8. Why did Lee Kitchens say that "virtually anything you do for people using wheelchairs is good for little people"?

9. Why would many dwarfs refuse a cure if offered?

10. What considerations should govern selection of clothing for little people?

Where is more information available?

Amputee Coalition of America
900 E. Hill Avenue, Suite 285
Knoxville, TN 37921
1-888-AMP-KNOW
1-423-524-8772
E-mail: ACAOne@aol.com

American Amputee Foundation
P.O. Box 250218
Hillcrest Station
Little Rock, AR 72225
1-501-666-8367

Arthritis Foundation
1330 West Peachtree Street
Atlanta, GA 30309
1-404-872-7100 or
800-283-7800
www.arthritis.org

American Juvenile Arthritis
Organization
1314 Spring Street N.W.
Atlanta, GA 30309
1-404-872-7100

Billy Barty Foundation
929 West Olive Avenue #C
Burbank, CA 91506
1-818-953-5410

Landmine Survivors Network
700 13th Street NW, Suite 905
Washington, DC 20005

Little People Research Fund
3010 Olympia Way
Longview, WA 98632
1-360-636-0276
E-mail: jacobsen@aone.com

Muscular Dystrophy
Association
3300 East Sunrise Drive
Tucson, AZ 85718
1-800-572-1717
1-520-529-2000
www.mdusa.org

National Amputee Foundation
73 Church Street
Malverne, NY 11365
1-516-887-3600

National Institute of
Neurological Disorders
and Stroke
National Institutes of Health
Bethesda, MD 20892
www.ninds.nih.gov

9

HEALTH IMPAIRMENTS

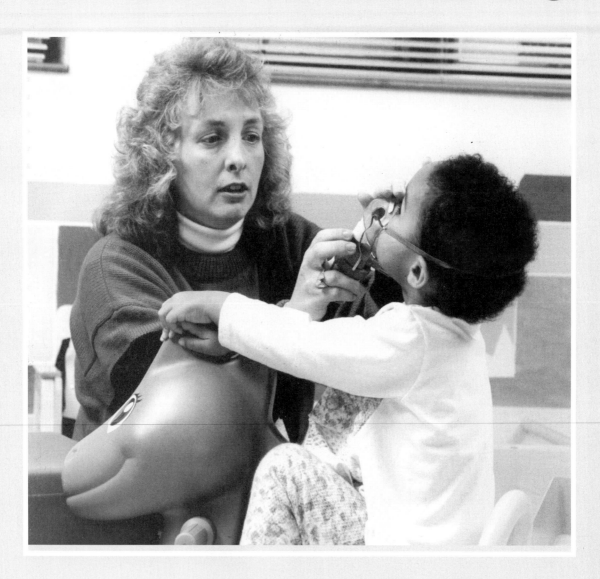

This chapter discusses nine important health disabilities: HIV/AIDS, asthma, cancer, cardiac conditions, child abuse/neglect, cystic fibrosis, diabetes, medical fragility/technology dependence, and sickle-cell disorders. These often are considered to be "other health impairments" with respect to eligibility under the Individuals with Disabilities Education Act (IDEA). They also may qualify people for protection against discrimination on the basis of disability under Section 504 of the Rehabilitation Act.

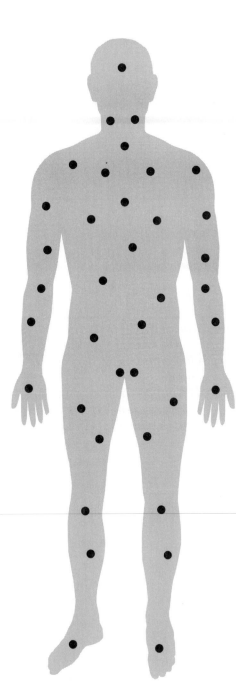

HIV/AIDS

Perhaps no one better personified AIDS than did Ryan White (1971–1990). In his 6 years as a person with AIDS, Ryan White confronted the outright bigotry and thoughtless treatment that characterized both Indiana and the United States as America first came to grips with this deadly disease. His hometown school in Kokomo, Indiana, refused to allow him to attend classes. His erstwhile "friends" avoided, ridiculed, and harassed him. Throughout all of this, Ryan White stood tall. He understood the fears of those around him with a maturity that belied his years. He appeared on television and made many presentations before audiences all over the country, patiently talking about AIDS and calming those irrational fears. Ryan White lived just 18 years, yet he taught the nation a great deal about this disease and, just as important, about the dignity to which we as human beings can aspire (White, 1997).

WHAT IS IT?

The human immunodeficiency virus (HIV) is the virus that causes acquired immune deficiency syndrome (also known as auto immune deficiency syndrome), or AIDS. People who test positive for the presence of antibodies that fight HIV are called "HIV-positive." Many people who are HIV-positive appear to be asymptomatic; that is, they show no outward symptoms. AIDS, by contrast, is a condition in which symptoms are undeniably present. To date, despite the availability of so-called miracle drugs, including protease inhibitors that interfere with the virus's ability to self-replicate and thus spread throughout the body, there is no way to cure someone of AIDS.

Is HIV-positive status a disability? The U.S. Supreme Court ruled in June 1998 that it is. Writing for a 5–4 majority in *Bragdon v. Abbott* (No. 97-156), Justice William Kennedy said, "In light of the immediacy with which the virus begins to damage the infected person's white blood cells and the severity of the disease, we hold that it is an impairment from the moment of the infection."

The Court thus sided with the U.S. Department of Justice (DoJ), the main federal agency carrying out the Americans with Disabilities Act, in interpreting the ADA's three-part definition of the word *disability*. This definition requires people to satisfy only one of the three prongs; of course, some individuals meet two, or even three, parts of the definition.

The first prong of the definition is that people have a permanent medical condition that significantly limits them in major life activities such as working, going to school, and doing housework. People with AIDS satisfy that condition; many who are HIV-positive do not. In *Bragdon,* the Supreme Court determined that Ms. Abbott did, because, the Court said, reproduction is a major life activity. The second prong is that they have a record of having had such a medical condition, since both people who are HIV-positive and those who have AIDS have medical records that unscrupulous employers, insurers, or others could use to discriminate against them. The third prong is that they are falsely treated by employers, educators, or others as if they have a disability; people who are HIV-positive, even those who have no evident symptoms, often are treated as if they have a disability.

WHAT CAUSES IT? CAN IT BE PREVENTED? IF SO, HOW?

The HIV virus is transmitted person to person through bodily fluids, such as blood or semen. It can be contracted by means of blood transfusions, unprotected sex, or exposure to the blood of affected persons who use drugs or drug products. It is also transmittable perinatally from an infected mother during pregnancy, birth, or breast feeding. AIDS, in turn, is caused by the HIV virus. It typically takes 8 to 10 years for someone who has the HIV virus to contract full-blown AIDS. Life expectancy for people who have AIDS varies according to the treatment used, but recently it has ranged from 1 to 4 years.

Prevention measures are obvious. The Centers for Disease Control and Prevention's (CDC) universal precautions should be followed by anyone who might come into contact with another person's bodily fluids. Individuals should engage in safe sex. People using needles for whatever purpose should never share them; only sterile needles should be used. Ideally, people who believe they may have been exposed should be screened; a simple preliminary screening costs about $5 per person, and a follow-up test, if needed, is about $50 per person. By being tested, people can get treatment earlier; meanwhile, they can protect their sexual partners from contracting the condition. Such measures, combined with the growing use of improved medications, plus continuing efforts to educate the general public about AIDS, have contributed to a declining number of individuals who are dying of AIDS, at least in the United States (Suris, 1997).

Longer term, the ability of some individuals to avoid AIDS may hold promise of offering others immunity as well. A gene that protects people from the virus was recently identified by Stephen O'Brien, a National Cancer Institute (NCI) geneticist, working from clues offered by University of California virologist Jay Levy. If the unique features of the gene can be isolated and ways found to give them to others, as University of Maryland researcher Robert Gallo (famous for his research on HIV when he was with the NCI) is trying to do, a long-sought cure may at last appear (Radetsky, 1997).

HOW PREVALENT IS IT? WHAT IS THE INCIDENCE?

Worldwide, at least 30 million people carry the virus that causes AIDS. The worldwide incidence is 3 million new cases annually. Both figures are

HIV v. all health disabilities

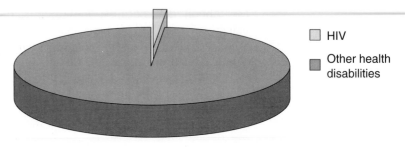

☐ HIV

▨ Other health
disabilities

Figure 9.1
Population Estimates: HIV As Compared to All Health Disabilities

for people who are HIV-positive, not for individuals who actually have AIDS. More than 700,000 Americans are HIV-positive (the prevalence), according to CDC, and the number grows by about 40,000 annually (the incidence).

Among young adults in the United States, HIV infection is most common in African Americans and Hispanic Americans; some 70% of all 18- to 29-year-old Americans who are infected are members of those two minority groups, a proportion far greater than their 27% representation among Americans in that age range. Of Americans testing positive, more than one-quarter million have developed AIDS; about half have died from it. The virus remains the principal cause of death in the United States among persons aged 24 to 44 years (O'Brien & Dean, 1997). The numbers are far higher in many developing countries than they are in the United States or Europe. For example, in Sub-Saharan Africa in 1997, more than 4 million people became HIV-infected for the first time, compared to just 44,000 in North America (Cooke, 1998b).

The incidence, or number of new instances, of AIDS has been declining in recent years in the United States. In large part, this is due to the development and use of a cocktail of drugs, including the drug zidovudine, commonly known as AZT, in combination with protease inhibitors that interfere with the reproduction of the virus, such as saquinavir, and such new medications as 3TC. In addition, women with AIDS who take AZT while they are pregnant reduce the risk that their children will get the disease.

With all these numbers looming large, it is important to bear in mind that very few children in the United States are HIV-positive or have AIDS. Just 1% of new AIDS cases reported annually to CDC are of young children perinatally infected—about 7,000 children in all since the CDC began collecting data (Rabin, 1997). As of 1998, only 500 American children per year are being born infected with the virus. With many pregnant women now taking AZT, the number should remain low.

WHAT EFFECTS CAN IT HAVE?

AIDS is perhaps best understood today as a chronic condition. Once people acquire it, they must contend with the condition for life. No drugs, surgery, or other intervention can as yet cure people of AIDS.

Many HIV-positive individuals live for a number of years, perhaps 10 or even more, with no noticeable symptoms. However, the virus weakens the human immune system, making it difficult for the person to fight off infections. Thus, being HIV-positive can lead to opportunistic infections that have more severe and longer-lasting effects than the same infections might have on someone who is not HIV-positive. The immune system also helps people to ward off cancers. When AIDS develops, symptoms come quickly. Several of them are severe enough to be classified as disabilities themselves. They can include cancers such as Kaposi's sarcoma as well as fatigue. In addition, the medication people take for AIDS may produce nausea, dizzy spells, and even vision loss.

WHAT SECONDARY CONDITIONS ARE COMMON?

The symptoms of AIDS vary from person to person. Fatigue, frequent fevers, diarrhea, and weight loss all are common consequences of the body's reduced capacity to fight infections. Some people get ear infections, while others have enlarged lymph nodes. If the virus spreads to the brain, memory loss and attention deficits may occur. An important consideration for professionals who work with individuals who are HIV-positive or who have AIDS is that even the cocktail of drugs sometimes does not restore the body's ability to combat infections.

WHAT NEEDS DO PEOPLE WITH IT HAVE?

Since AIDS remains a highly stigmatizing condition, a major need of individuals who are HIV-positive or have AIDS continues to be protection against bias, bigotry, and discrimination. The privacy of these individuals should be respected. If the family elects to inform the school principal, a teacher, or an employer, these professionals should honor the family's desire for confidentiality. Strict observance of universal precaution procedures should suffice to protect other students or workers who are not informed about the individual's condition.

The cocktail of drugs many people need to combat AIDS is very costly (in most cases, about $15,000 to $25,000 annually, or some $55 a day). Those expenses put the combination of drugs beyond the reach of many people. Adequate medical coverage, whether through a private insurance company or through Medicaid, is an obvious need. In 1998, the federal government spent more than $9 billion on HIV/AIDS, mostly to cover drugs under Medicaid. Ironically, protease inhibitors if taken conscientiously restore enough health to many infected persons that they no longer qualify for Medicaid.

Once dropped from the Medicaid rolls, they may stop taking the drugs because they cannot afford them. This leads, inevitably, to the virus again becoming virulent. It is a vicious cycle (Arnst, 1997).

WHAT SPECIAL-EDUCATION AND RELATED SERVICES MAY HELP?

Physical therapy can help in the day-to-day management of AIDS. In particular, myofacial release and craniosacral therapy, as well as ultrasound, transcutaneous nerve stimulation, laser, and counter-irritation techniques have been shown to help to reduce the pain that many people with AIDS experience (Galantino, 1992; O'Dell & Dillon, 1992; Stanton, 1993). Physical therapists can also design and implement exercise programs to help the person to maintain his or her strength. Stanton has suggested that exercise be sufficient to produce endurance and strength benefits but not so prolonged or challenging as to lead to fatigue.

Physical and occupational therapists can help individuals with HIV/AIDS to learn how to conduct daily dressing, washing, feeding, etc., activities despite fatigue or other complications. They can also help people with HIV/AIDS as well as family members and friends to learn the universal precautions that are necessary to prevent transmission of the HIV virus. Caretakers should not assume that a person who is HIV-positive or has AIDS is knowledgeable about and consistently follows universal precautions.

Another service—respite care—can prove to be very helpful for families of children with AIDS. Both emergency and planned respite services are needed. Because caring for someone with the condition is so physically and emotionally draining, many parents and siblings of people with AIDS need the break—whether for a few hours, one day, or a weekend—that respite programs provide. However, some families do not seek respite care because they fear violating the family's privacy. In-home respite services that have the worker come to the family's residence are one way of responding to such concerns. The IDEA, under Part C (Infants and Toddlers), permits respite services as an early-intervention service, while Part B (Children with Disabilities) allows them as related services.

WHAT OTHER INTERVENTIONS CAN BE EFFECTIVE?

The cocktail of drugs featuring protease inhibitors, AZT, and 3TC has been shown to eradicate most signs of the disease in people for whom it is suited. By taking a combination of 20+ pills daily (in some cases, as many as 60), people can reduce the level of HIV in their bodies to the point of undetectability for several years. However, the virus can hide in the body and, once the person stops taking the drugs, can reappear with a vengeance.

Several caveats are associated with the cocktail of drugs. First, it is very expensive. Second, it does not help everyone who is HIV-positive or has AIDS; some experts have estimated that 10% to 30% of people with HIV, particularly those who have been HIV-positive for several years, will not benefit from the cocktail. Third, dosages that are effective with children are not well understood. Experts recommend using all available protease inhibitors (including the most used invirase, norvir, and crixivan) with children, as well as two newly FDA-approved protease inhibitors that are specifically formulated for children (ritonavir and nelfinavir); effective dosage levels are still being developed (McGinley, 1996). In August 1997, President Clinton proposed that new drugs likely to be prescribed for children, including drugs to fight AIDS, should first be tested on children so that appropriate dosages could be developed to guide physicians. This requirement would raise the costs of developing and testing drugs. On the other hand, it would lead to safer and more effective dosages of drugs that children need to combat AIDS (McGinley, 1997). Finally, the protease inhibitors may have significant side effects (e.g., in redistributing body fat), so much so that some people stop taking the cocktail of drugs.

AZT, which has been used to treat AIDS for more than a decade, has an important effect: When taken by pregnant women who are HIV-positive or who have AIDS, AZT dramatically slashes the likelihood that these women's children will be born with the disease. The CDC reported in late 1996 that the number of newborns who contracted AIDS from their mother dropped by more than one quarter (27%) between 1992 and 1995. The odds that any given child of such a mother would be born with AIDS fell by an even more impressive proportion (67%) ("Number of Newborns with AIDS Declined," 1996).

Two recent developments are notable. First, hydroxyurea, a generic, unpatented drug, may help to reduce HIV when used in combination with standard HIV and AIDS drugs (Garrett, 1998). Second, some scientists who observed that about 1% of Americans have a mutation in their chemokine receptors that protect them from becoming infected by HIV have begun exploring the possibility that chemokines might block the virus from gaining entry into cells. Chemokines are small proteins that help "direct traffic" in the immune system. Even if the work is successful and chemokines can be used to prevent HIV from entering cells, chemokines cannot kill the virus already in a cell. For that reason, it will not be a cure (Carey, 1998b).

The holy grail of AIDS research, a vaccine, remains out of reach as of this writing. Much work is being done to establish the necessary knowledge upon which to build a vaccine. However, the whole concept of purposely giving people a potentially fatal virus, however well deactivated it may be, continues to cause many researchers to have serious ethical qualms about an AIDS vaccine.

WHAT ASSISTIVE TECHNOLOGIES AND SERVICES CAN HELP?

AIDS-related complications, including fatigue, vision loss, and other limitations, often can be addressed with assistive technology devices and services. Using a scooter or motorized wheelchair instead of walking long distances is a clear example.

WHAT ARE THE PROSPECTS FOR POSTSECONDARY EDUCATION?

The new drugs have brought us a generation of young people born HIV-positive yet still alive and relatively healthy at the age of 15 or older (Rabin, 1997). Quite unexpectedly, these young people now confront the prospect of college and, later, gainful employment. Assuming that the condition is controlled medically and the individual has the necessary energy, HIV/AIDS should not prevent anyone from participating in postsecondary education. This includes extracurricular activities, such as sports. In contact sports, universal precautions would call for any player who bleeds for any reason to be removed immediately from the game for treatment. Virtually every college and university in the United States is required by the ADA to prohibit discrimination against people with HIV/AIDS.

WHAT ARE THE EMPLOYMENT PROSPECTS?

These are challenging but much better than just a few years ago. A recent review of data on individuals with HIV (Sebesta & LaPlante, 1996) found that more than half were out of the labor force (neither working nor looking for employment) and the unemployment rate was 11%, or more than double the national rate.* About 1 in 10 of those who did not have jobs reported being fired as a direct result of their HIV status. Those with jobs were far more likely to be male than female.

The Americans with Disabilities Act (ADA) clearly protects people who are HIV-positive or have AIDS against unjust discrimination in employment. Such protection is important because, according to the CDC, 1 out of every 6 employers in America has experience with an employee who is HIV-positive or has AIDS. Employers subject to the ADA may not offer medical or other benefits for people who are HIV-positive or have AIDS that are significantly different from the benefits those employers provide to noninfected workers. A policy that provides less coverage for conditions known to be associated with AIDS than for similar conditions that are not usually related to AIDS might well violate the Act.

In addition, people who are "associated with" (e.g., family members or friends of) people who are HIV-positive or who have AIDS are protected against discrimination on the basis of that association. Thus, the father of an HIV-positive daughter may not be discriminated against by his employer because of that relationship.

WHAT ARE THE PROSPECTS FOR INDEPENDENT LIVING?

Except in the final weeks and months of terminal AIDS, typically a period when the individual is unable to perform even the most mundane household

---

*The unemployment rate is the proportion of persons in the labor force (i.e., working or looking for work) who are looking for employment. The calculation of the rate does not include people who are out of the labor force.

and self-help chores, AIDS should not prevent people from living independently. Indeed, many people who have AIDS treasure their ability to reside in their own home or apartment rather than in an impersonal institution such as a hospital or nursing home.

Asthma and Other Pulmonary Disorders

Olympic gold medalist Amy Van Dyken (1973–) thrilled millions of viewers around the world with her swimming victories in Atlanta in 1996. In addition to using an inhaler (which she keeps by the pool whenever she swims), she takes two prescription drugs to treat her condition: "I have all types of asthma: exercise-induced, allergy-induced, and infection-induced" (quoted in Dowling, 1997, p. 92).

WHAT IS IT?

The bronchi and bronchioles (airways) of all of our lungs may narrow in response to allergens or other irritants. In asthma, these airways are hypersensitive to certain environmental stimuli, known as triggers, that cause them to become blocked or constricted. The body produces excess antibodies in response to pollens or other antigens. This is an allergic reaction to the antigens. In someone with asthma, the antibodies are not effective in combating the antigens but rather trigger production or release of histamines, deleterious chemicals that in turn cause swelling in the airways. This swelling makes breathing difficult and leads to the characteristic wheezing of persons with asthma. The person cannot get enough oxygen, not only in the lungs but also throughout the body.

In addition, exhaling through the obstructed airways is as problematic as inhaling, causing carbon dioxide levels to accumulate in the body, making blood acidic. Asthma thus is best understood as a chronic respiratory disorder primarily affecting the airways in the lungs. It often appears within the first year of life. However, because symptoms may be mistaken as something else (e.g., congenital heart disease), diagnosis may not occur until a child is in preschool.

Asthma may be classified into four stages: mild intermittent, mild persistent, moderate persistent, and severe persistent. In the mildest form, symptoms surface at most twice weekly. In the most severe form, symptoms are continuous and limit physical activity.

WHAT CAUSES IT? CAN IT BE PREVENTED? IF SO, HOW?

Asthma is not inherited, although a tendency toward the condition may be. If one or both parents have asthma or allergies, the likelihood that the children will develop asthma increases dramatically, compared to children neither of whose parents has asthma or allergies. Sometimes, asthma develops following a respiratory infection that is not promptly and thoroughly treated. A viral infection in particular is a common precursor to asthma in young children.

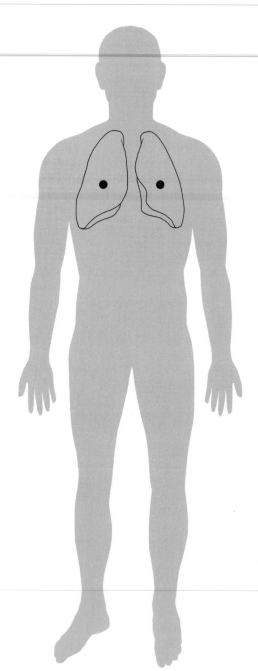

The most frequent triggers of asthma attacks are viruses (e.g., influenza, bronchitis), bacterial infections (including sinus infections), such irritants as pollution or cigarette smoke, exercise, and, for those with allergies, allergens. Probably the most common triggers are exercise and dust.

HOW PREVALENT IS IT? WHAT IS THE INCIDENCE?

Asthma is quite common in children; in fact, some one third of all Americans with asthma are school-age or younger. Among school-age children, asthma is one of the most frequent causes of absenteeism. According to the Centers for Disease Control and Prevention (CDC), about 15 million Americans of all ages have asthma, up from 7 million in 1980; the increase is most notable among girls and women.

In recent years, the number of reported instances of asthma has increased sharply. It is not yet clear how much of this growth is due to more people getting asthma and how much to better reporting of conditions. The rising numbers have highlighted the possibility that today's tightly constructed office buildings and modern apartment buildings (many of which do not have windows that open) are contributing to an increase in the prevalence of asthma. Allergens and triggers such as dust mites and cockroach droppings that once were gently blown out of the house through open windows or otherwise dispersed now accumulate indoors and may reach concentration levels that cause problems for people.

WHAT EFFECTS CAN IT HAVE?

Asthma can be severe. For an affected individual, walking from class to class in a high school may be as exhausting as running a marathon is for a trained distance runner. Asthma directly or indirectly results in 5,000 deaths annually and accounts for some 500,000 days of hospitalization each year. These problems are particularly common in inner cities, where children are as much as 6 times more likely than children in other areas to die from inadequate care of asthma (Goldberg, 1997).

The effects of asthma in children are similar to those of cystic fibrosis. An important difference is that in asthma the obstruction may be alleviated and even reversed, either with medication or spontaneously, hence, the technical name of reversible obstructive airway disease. Asthma often disappears in adolescence because the airways have grown and no longer are blocked by the factors that obstructed their smaller

Asthma v. all health disabilities

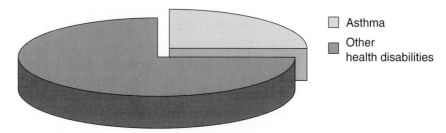

☐ Asthma

■ Other
   health disabilities

Figure 9.2
Population Estimates: Asthma As Compared to All Health Disabilities

airways in childhood. (Unlike asthma, emphysema, another pulmonary disease, is irreversible.)

Psychological and genetic factors are also involved in asthma. Children with emotional difficulties are more prone to asthma; the onset of asthma, in turn, may exacerbate those emotional conditions.

Although technically people do not "grow out of" asthma, as they reach adolescence and adulthood, their airways become larger and somewhat less sensitive. These individuals also learn to avoid the triggers. On the other hand, some people develop asthma for the first time in adolescence or in adulthood in reaction to occupational triggers such as metal, chemicals, and paint.

WHAT SECONDARY CONDITIONS ARE COMMON?

Many people (not all, however) who have asthma also have allergies. Also, people with asthma should exercise care about taking aspirin. For some individuals with asthma, aspirin can be a trigger. Prescription cough suppressants should also be avoided by some people with asthma because they make mucus harder to raise and remove. In addition, medications taken to control asthma may affect a child's ability to concentrate on schoolwork.

WHAT NEEDS DO PEOPLE WITH IT HAVE?

As with other respiratory disorders, people with asthma most need understanding and flexibility in scheduling. Given that frequent absences from school and occasional hospitalization are often necessary, educators and other professionals should give children the opportunity to make up work at convenient times. Excessive absenteeism constrains a child's progress in school and may lead to social and emotional problems because the other children learn not to rely on this child's being there. Children like friends who are reliable and may not form close attachments to children on whose presence they cannot rely.

Educators can work with parents to identify triggers and then remove them from the school and environs, thus reducing the likelihood of asthmatic attacks. Because exercise is one possible trigger, children with asthma should be monitored during physical education classes and recreational sports.

Asthma typically is treated by use of antihistamine inhalers. As chlorofluorocarbon-powered devices, these inhalers pose a risk to the ozone layer. For this reason, in 1997, the U.S. Environmental Protection Agency (EPA) proposed that they be banned (Goldberg, 1997).

WHAT SPECIAL-EDUCATION AND RELATED SERVICES MAY HELP?

Physical therapy can help individuals with asthma and other chronic pulmonary disorders learn correct inhaler techniques, practice bronchial hygiene, maintain proper nutrition, and follow sensible exercise routines. Physical education is recognized as a related service in the Individuals with Disabilities Education Act. Aerobic (resistance) exercise can improve breathing patterns, especially for people with severe pulmonary obstructions. The focus of exercise should be on endurance rather than physical strength (Smith, 1995).

WHAT OTHER INTERVENTIONS CAN BE EFFECTIVE?

In February 1997, the National Heart, Lung, and Blood Institute, part of the National Institutes of Health (NIH), issued guidelines urging physicians to change the ways they treat patients with asthma. Doctors are now urged to attack the condition when it first appears, using an aggressive treatment protocol that features multiple drugs.

Two new drugs—salmeterol (Serevent, from Glaxo-Wellcome) and montelukast (Singulair, from Merck)—offer long-lasting relief from exercise-induced asthma. Both promise all-day relief but in reality last 12 hours or less. For people whose asthma is caused by an allergy, Genentech has developed a genetically engineered antibody, anti-IgE. According to the company, the antibody inhibits inflammation, with few side effects (Knapschaefer, 1997). In addition, leukotriene-blocker drugs are being introduced for children aged 6 and older and for adults. These drugs block leukotrienes, molecules active in the kinds of inflammation common in asthma. They do not have the side effects (stunted growth, glaucoma, etc.), that are common with inhaled steroids, although they may have other side effects (Barrett, 1998).

Specialists now recommend that people with asthma avoid over-the-counter drugs, keep no dogs or cats at home, and develop and follow personal plans for controlling the condition. In addition, for some people, daily lung-capacity tests are strongly recommended.

WHAT ASSISTIVE TECHNOLOGIES AND SERVICES CAN HELP?

Aside from inhalers, people with asthma seldom need assistive technology devices or services.

WHAT ARE THE PROSPECTS FOR POSTSECONDARY EDUCATION?

Nothing about asthma, aside from absenteeism and occasional hospitalization, should prevent someone from attending college. As long as sensible precautions are taken, including moderation in exercise as appropriate, people with asthma should be able to participate in all aspects of postsecondary education. Students may need to borrow notes when classes are missed and to reschedule examinations on occasion; otherwise, the condition should not affect them in college.

WHAT ARE THE EMPLOYMENT PROSPECTS?

People with asthma and other chronic pulmonary disorders that are controlled should encounter few difficulties. Many employers with 15 or more workers are required by the Americans with Disabilities Act (ADA) to make reasonable accommodations in the workplace. This can include taking such steps as allowing the employee to perform certain projects over a period of time; such a project approach allows flexibility in case the person cannot come to work daily.

WHAT ARE THE PROSPECTS FOR INDEPENDENT LIVING?

Nothing about asthma should prevent people from living independently. It would be prudent for individuals with asthma or other chronic pulmonary disorders to remove triggers from indoors and outdoors and to keep the environment clean so as to alleviate symptoms and to reduce the likelihood of attacks.

Cancer

When he was 41 years of age, my friend and colleague at Hofstra, John V. Conti (1937–) learned he had cancer of the colon. For John, this meant a wrenching change. John was a rehabilitation counselor, accustomed to planning rehabilitation services for others; now, he had suddenly become a patient. Eventually, John recovered completely; he long ago passed the 5-year survival threshold. Nonetheless, Dr. Conti vividly recalls how differently people treated him after his diagnosis became known. Sensitive to these attitudes, he launched what became a second career as an activist in cancer organizations, including the American Cancer Society's "CanSurmount" program. Today, when he learns that an acquaintance is newly diagnosed with cancer, John does not hesitate to reach out, saying, "Can I be of assistance?"

WHAT IS IT?

Although we speak of cancer as a single condition, in reality, there are many different forms of cancer. Among children, the most common are leukemia, various brain tumors, soft-tissue sarcomas, and neuroblastoma (Stiller, Allen, & Eatock, 1995). Cancer in children is very distinct from cancer in adults; the

Dr. John Conti, adjunct professor of rehabilitation counseling at Hofstra, is a nationally recognized expert on cancer rehabilitation. He is quick to volunteer when he learns someone has been diagnosed with cancer.

causes differ, as do the conditions themselves; treatments also differ. Children very seldom get cancers of the lung, breast, colon, or stomach, as do adults (Miller, Young, & Novakovic, 1994). Rather, childhood cancers involve white blood cells (leukemia), the brain, the bones, and the lymphatic system.

Leukemia is the most common type of cancer in children. In leukemia, lymphocytes (which protect the body from infection) do not mature properly. They also become too numerous in the blood and bone marrow (the spongy tissue inside the large bones of the body). Leukemia is a condition in which white blood cells proliferate in the blood and bone marrow in numbers far above normal. While normal bone marrow has 5 to 7 tiny blood vessels, cancerous bone marrow may hold 40 or even more blood vessels. The appearance in urine of a growth factor called fibroblast may indicate that cancer is growing or recurring. Measuring fibroblast in urine thus is a way of monitoring leukemia.

Neuroblastoma, one of the most common solid tumors in children, emerges in the abdomen near the adrenal gland. Retinoblastoma, a cancer of the eye, occurs in some children who are under 5 years of age. In this form of cancer, juvenile cells keep replicating because their internal controls are askew. This is an instance in which disruption of the cell's "clock" is at the root of the problem. Normally, the clock prevents overproduction of cells, although when the clock does not function properly, cell division continues long after it should stop.

Brain and spinal cord tumors occur in some children. According to the National Coalition for Cancer Research (1997), about 1 in every 5 cases of

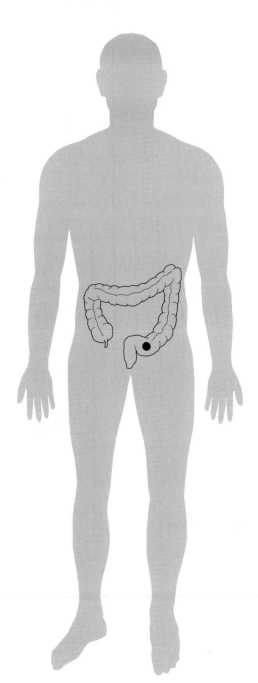

brain tumors occurs in children, somewhat more among boys than among girls. The Coalition reports a peak in incidence between the ages of 5 and 10. Lymphomas (Hodgkin's and non-Hodgkin's) also are relatively common among children and youth. Pediatric lymphomas, diffuse neoplasms that replicate in an aggressive fashion (Shad & Magrath, 1997), are different from adult-onset lymphomas.

WHAT CAUSES IT? CAN IT BE PREVENTED? IF SO, HOW?

Genetic bases are known or suspected in many kinds of cancer; some 10% to 15% of all childhood cancers are suspected to have a genetic component in that they are hereditary or familial (Quesnel & Malkin, 1997). Experts believe, however, that the environment also plays a large role. In particular, diet appears to be involved, especially in childhood cancer. This is why reports of inadequate diet among America's children and youth—particularly the failure to follow nutrition guidelines on dark green and deep yellow vegetables—are disturbing (Munoz, Krebs-Smith, Ballard-Barbash, & Cleveland, 1997).

Most cancers are not automatically terminal. Cure rates (usually defined as survival for 5 or more years) have risen dramatically over the past 2 decades (Draper, Kroll, & Stiller, 1994; Lukens, 1994). Today, more than half of all children who develop leukemia survive; some children have a better than 80% chance of survival (Leukemia Research Fund, 1997). According to the American Cancer Society (1997), 5-year survival rates are 79% for acute lymphocytic leukemia, 61% for neuroblastoma, 61% for brain and spinal cord cancer, and 65% for bone cancer.

There is hope that a new agent, known as endostatin, will stop tumors from growing. Endostatin starves cancer cells by denying them the blood vessels they need to use for nourishment. After repeated doses, even large tumors did not regrow, according to Judah Folkman of Children's Hospital in Boston (Cooke, 1997). The treatment contrasts with chemotherapy, which is sometimes limited because cancer cells become resistant to it. Folkman's work is an example of a promising approach, known as antiangiogenesis, that involves starving cancer cells by blocking the growth of blood vessels (Arnst, 1998; Cooke, 1998a).

Genetic therapy is another possible approach to cancer, although caution is in order with respect to the prospects for cures based on biogenetics. Although genes associated with different kinds of cancer are being discovered on a regular basis, the path from gene discovery to treatment is long and torturous (Waldholz, 1997). Thus, although tests to determine whether someone carries genes that potentially may lead to cancer are becoming widely available, the truth is that at this time there is little doctors can do to actually prevent such cancers (Brenner, 1997).

Finally, some experts point to experimental drugs known as antineoplastons. The Food and Drug Administration has not approved these drugs for use with patients, for which reason doctors who prescribe them and even patients who use them may be subject, at least in theory, to prosecution by federal authorities (Blevins, 1997).

HOW PREVALENT IS IT? WHAT IS THE INCIDENCE?

Some 8 million Americans of all ages have a history of a cancer diagnosis; some 1 million are diagnosed annually (Brennan, DePompolo, & Garden, 1996; Marciniak, Sliwa, Spill, Heinemann, & Semik, 1996). Childhood cancer is very rare. Only 1 in every 600 children under the age of 15 develops any kind of cancer (Stiller, 1992). About 11,000 children in the United States have cancer. The American Cancer Society (1997) estimated that 1,700 deaths due to cancer occurred in American children in 1997, one third of them because of leukemia.

Of the childhood cancers, leukemia is by far the most prevalent, accounting for about one third of cancers in children under the age of 15. About one fifth of childhood cancers are brain tumors (Kun, 1997). Hodgkin's-type lymphomas are more common among boys than girls.

The National Cancer Act of 1971 requires the collection of data on prevention, diagnosis, and treatment of cancer. This work is conducted by the Surveillance, Epidemiology, and End Results Program at the National Cancer Institute. The data indicate dramatic reductions in recent years in childhood cancer rates and correspondingly strong increases in survival rates (Ries et al., 1997). To illustrate: Some 70% of children with leukemia now survive, as against just 5% in the late 1960s. This is indicative of work on cancer in general: People hold a great deal of optimism that a corner has been turned.

Cancer v. all health disabilities

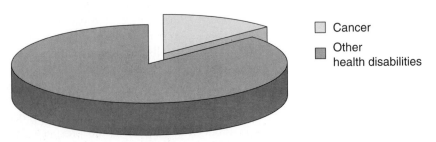

Figure 9.3
Population Estimates: Cancer As Compared to All Health Disabilities

WHAT EFFECTS CAN IT HAVE?

Cancer can and does kill. Even if one ultimately does survive, receiving the diagnosis of cancer alters the self-concept for many individuals. Cancer is a shocking diagnosis. Children and youth who previously thought of themselves as all but invincible are suddenly confronted with their mortality. Even after one passes the 5-year survival timeline, the sense of vulnerability may remain (Conti, 1989). Depression is a common consequence (Frank, Blount, & Brown, 1997).

Treatment of cancer is time-consuming. Hospital stays of several weeks to a month or longer may be necessary soon after diagnosis. Thereafter, depending on the course of treatment that is adopted, several hours must be devoted to treatment each month. People who are treated with chemotherapy may experience a loss of energy (a need to nap at or about midday or a general, continuous feeling of tiredness).

WHAT SECONDARY CONDITIONS ARE COMMON?

Children who are undergoing chemotherapy are especially prone to infections. Parents and teachers should be alert to keep such children away from other children who have infectious diseases. Commonly, there is a loss of hair (which does grow back after the treatment ceases). Children may also experience variable appetites and some moodiness.

When radiation is used to treat childhood cancers, learning problems may result. Intelligence may be lowered in children with leukemia and non-Hodgkin's lymphoma who undergo radiation treatment (Van Dongen-Melman, De Groot, Van Dongen, Verhulst, & Hahlen, 1997). Chemotherapy potentially has a vast number of serious side effects. A pamphlet published by the National Cancer Institute, "Chemotherapy and You" (1996), for example, lists infections, anemia/fatigue, nausea and vomiting, hair loss, diarrhea, and constipation among possible side effects.

WHAT NEEDS DO PEOPLE WITH IT HAVE?

Children and youth who have been diagnosed with cancer need an understanding and supportive environment. They need to learn coping skills. It is also important that they understand why they developed cancer and to learn how to attribute their feelings about the disease (e.g., external vs. internal attribution). Because many children with cancer miss some time at school to complete treatment protocols and may have less energy when they are physically present in the classroom, it is important that teachers be flexible about assignments and permit delayed completion of work on an as-needed basis (Deasy-Spinetta, 1993).

Now that more than half of all persons diagnosed with cancer survive for 5 or more years, cancer should be considered to be a chronic illness rather than a terminal one. The needs are for assistance in daily living tasks so as to increase personal independence. This includes self-care, locomotion (walking or using a wheelchair), and transfers (as from a wheelchair to a toilet).

Rehabilitation services provided to cancer patients can markedly increase their independence in these areas, irrespective of the specific cancer diagnosis (Marciniak et al., 1996).

WHAT SPECIAL-EDUCATION AND RELATED SERVICES MAY HELP?

Perhaps most important for children, youth, and families is information combined with supportive counseling (Conti, 1989). As Dr. Conti put it: "The central issue is that of support, particularly verbal support, for persons diagnosed as having cancer, as well as for their families" (p. 3).

WHAT OTHER INTERVENTIONS CAN BE EFFECTIVE?

Chemotherapy, the use of powerful drugs to kill cancer cells, commonly is used to treat childhood cancers. Bone marrow transplantation may also be used. A new type of bone marrow transplantation, called "autologous," involves taking bone marrow from a patient, treating it with drugs, and freezing it. The patient then is given chemotherapy to destroy all remaining marrow in the body. Finally, the frozen marrow is thawed and then reinserted.

The typical treatment for leukemia takes about 3 years and involves several admissions to the hospital, although most treatment is on an outpatient basis. Chemotherapy is given about once a month and requires some 2 hours per session.

Neuroblastoma remains hard to treat, and outcomes continue to be poor compared to other common childhood cancers (Castleberry, 1997). Colon cancers may be treated with aspirin. Research reported in the journal *Cell* in mid-1998 suggests that aspirin inhibited the growth of blood vessels in mice who had colon cancer. Further research is being done to see whether the same effect occurs outside the test tube and in humans as well as in mice.

WHAT ASSISTIVE TECHNOLOGIES AND SERVICES CAN HELP?

Most people with cancer will not need assistive devices. Some, however, will, especially with respect to locomotion (getting around) during periods of intense illness. Practical devices that assist with wheelchair-to-bed mobility and with other day-to-day physical tasks may help if the individual is feeling particularly weak. Otherwise, assistive technology is not particularly suited for persons with cancer.

There are a few exceptions. One is people whose voice has been lost to cancer. That happened to disc jockey Dan Lawrence, who works for KHUM-FM in Ferndale, a Northern California town. "Digital Dan" is the only DJ in America to use an electronic voice—Digital Equipment Corporation's DECtalk, a highly regarded speech synthesizer. He broadcasts music and commentary on Thursday and Friday nights. The Vietnam veteran blames Agent Orange for his cancer.

WHAT ARE THE PROSPECTS FOR POSTSECONDARY EDUCATION?

Given that most Americans now survive cancers of all kinds and that improved intervention lessens side effects, participation in postsecondary programs should not be limited for individuals who have cancer.

WHAT ARE THE EMPLOYMENT PROSPECTS?

The major obstacle for individuals with cancer and for persons who have survived cancer is the attitudes of others, especially employers and coworkers (Conti, 1989). The Americans with Disabilities Act (ADA), in Title I, bars discrimination on the basis of disability both for people who have conditions (cancer) and for persons who have a record of such a condition but are not currently affected by it. This legislation is enormously important. However, as Dr. Conti has pointed out, attitudes are difficult to change. The reality is that many people who have or survive cancer will continue to be confronted by negative attitudes. These people's best approach is to continue to do the job and, if necessary, to pursue remedies under the ADA.

WHAT ARE THE PROSPECTS FOR INDEPENDENT LIVING?

Most people who have cancer and virtually all persons who have survived cancer can live independently in the community. Significant amounts of care from others is usually required only temporarily, if at all, while the person is undergoing treatment. Even during such times, institutionalization or hospitalization is rarely required.

Cardiac Conditions

My father died of a heart attack in 1983 at the age of 65. For 20 years prior to that, he had been taking medication to thin his blood because his arteries were clogged by atherosclerosis. Looking back, I suspect his health problems were due to not following good nutrition guidelines in his daily diet, smoking, and drinking. They may also be attributed, as may his poor eyesight, to his years of service in Europe as a soldier during World War II.

WHAT ARE THEY?

Cardiac conditions include coronary artery disease (CAD), in which arteries become clogged by waxy deposits. CAD is the biggest cardiac problem in the United States today, responsible for more deaths than any other cardiac condition. Hypertension, or high blood pressure, is another form. Also included is congestive heart failure (CHF), or a reduction in cardiac function, usually associated with old age, and congenital heart disease (CHD), a weakness in heart function with which children are born.

WHAT CAUSES THEM? CAN THEY BE PREVENTED? IF SO, HOW?

Experts estimate that at least half of all heart disease in the United States could be prevented if more Americans would follow good nutrition guidelines, cease smoking, and engage in more exercise.

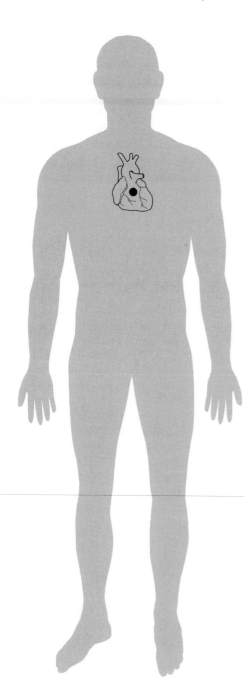

Diabetes is a major cause of cardiac conditions. People with diabetes typically are overweight, have high cholesterol, and have high blood pressure (hypertension)—all risk factors for cardiac conditions. Heart disease may also result from a sedentary lifestyle (especially if accompanied by overeating). Similarly, cardiac problems are common in persons who have spinal cord injuries (SCI) of more than 30 years standing and for those who are over 60 years of age. To illustrate, Justin W. Dart, Jr., the disability rights advocate most responsible for convincing Congress to enact the Americans with Disabilities Act, suffered a heart attack in late 1997 at the age of 67; he had used a wheelchair for 50-odd years after contracting polio in his youth. The connection between SCI and cardiac conditions seems to relate to insulin resistance among many persons with SCI.

Cardiac conditions have also been tied to cigarette smoking and to family history (genetics). Recently, a gene suspected to cause ventricular fibrillation in young people, such that they would have heart attacks without warning and without a prior history of heart problems (so-called idiopathic cardiac conditions), was identified by Wang and his colleagues (Chen et al., 1998). People with this gene have a characteristic electrocardiographic pattern, making detection possible in advance of a heart attack. It is possible that this gene was involved in the sudden cardiac arrests of well-known basketball players who had no prior history of heart problems.

A famous *60 Minutes* segment on heart disease publicized the fact that residents of the Italian village of Limone sul Garda, many of them descendants of an 18th-century resident named Giovanni Pomaroli, have a genetic mutation that protects them from heart disease. This suggests that in the future, genetic therapy might make the benefits of those genes available to all of us.

HOW PREVALENT ARE THEY?
WHAT IS THE INCIDENCE?

Heart conditions are America's leading cause of death, killing about 1 million persons every year. Thirteen million Americans have CAD; the number of people in the United

Cardiac conditions v. all health disabilities

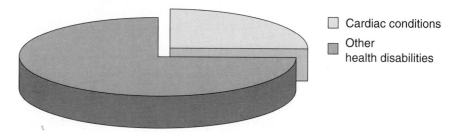

☐ Cardiac conditions

☐ Other
health disabilities

Figure 9.4
Population Estimates: Cardiac Conditions As Compared to All Health Disabilities

States who are living with CHF has tripled since the late 1970s. Looking at 35 countries in the Americas, cardiovascular diseases and strokes are the leading cause of death in 31 (InterAmerican Heart Foundation, 1998). CHD, however, is relatively rare.

WHAT EFFECTS CAN THEY HAVE?

Heart conditions of all kinds produce a feeling of fatigue. People with CHF, for example, may not have the energy to walk across a room. This is because their heart must work far harder than normal to support any given level of activity.

WHAT SECONDARY CONDITIONS ARE COMMON?

The conditions that often coexist with heart disease are those that contribute to the cardiac condition rather than result from it. Thus, diabetes, hypertension, and overweight are frequently associated with heart disease.

WHAT NEEDS DO PEOPLE WITH THEM HAVE?

Heart disease is best treated by a combination of nutrition, medication, and exercise. Using polyunsaturated fats (e.g., olive oil, peanut oil) instead of saturated fats (e.g., butter, coconut oil), reducing salt intake, and maintaining sensible body weight are all steps people with cardiac conditions should take. Exercise lowers cholesterol levels and increases heart capacity. Medications such as antihypertensives (which lower blood pressure), diuretics (which help the body to eliminate unneeded water), and vasodilators (which enhance blood flow through blood vessels) also help.

Appropriate diets that children will accept and follow have proven to be difficult to find. Kersting and Schoch (1992) proposed diets that meet American Recommended Daily Allowance standards and yet were accepted by German children and adolescents (aged 1–14 years). Such diets include avoidance of fatty meats and meat products, reduction of fatty foodstuffs and foodstuffs having a high sucrose content, and increase of whole grain cereal products, potatoes, and vegetables.

WHAT SPECIAL-EDUCATION AND RELATED SERVICES MAY HELP?

Physical and occupational therapy may assist people with cardiac conditions by guiding them through a sensible routine of exercise, monitoring their cardiac functioning, and providing information about healthy lifestyle choices. Hertanu and Moldover (1996) offered cardiac rehabilitation programs suitable for use with people having different kinds of cardiac conditions. Their approaches feature cardiac exercise programs to enhance physical functioning while reducing exercise heart rate, sensible diets, cessation of smoking, and measures to help people to manage stress.

WHAT OTHER INTERVENTIONS CAN BE EFFECTIVE?

The best interventions may be the simplest: Follow good nutrition guidelines, avoid smoking, and engage in moderate exercise on a regular basis. One or two aspirins daily may help to prevent a second heart attack. Science is making progress in offering other interventions, but even the most advanced technology likely will help little in the absence of such low-tech approaches as eating the right foods.

A wide range of surgical and technological advances promises to help people to survive cardiac conditions. Pacemakers are becoming more sophisticated. A device called a "stent" can keep arteries open that had been clogged by fatty deposits, lessening the risk of a heart attack. Artificial hearts are expected to become feasible shortly after the turn of the century; these new machines are far better than the first devices like the pioneering "Jarvik 7" heart of 1982.

Pashkow (1996) reviewed a wide range of outcome studies with cardiac patients. She reported that recent advances in cardiac rehabilitation have led to higher quality-of-life outcomes among persons who have had heart attacks or heart disease. Patients report greater ability to perform self-care, mobility, and other activities and to enjoy higher self-esteem than did patients in earlier years who received different treatments.

WHAT ASSISTIVE TECHNOLOGIES AND SERVICES CAN HELP?

Cardiac patients may benefit from devices that minimize physical labor in completing necessary tasks. An obvious example is an electric wheelchair, which makes moving around far less strenuous than walking. Other examples are machines that manipulate, lift, or carry heavy objects.

WHAT ARE THE PROSPECTS FOR POSTSECONDARY EDUCATION?

Assuming the individual has sufficient energy to move around campus and to concentrate on studies, nothing about cardiac conditions should prevent him or her from participating in postsecondary education activities.

WHAT ARE THE EMPLOYMENT PROSPECTS?

They are excellent, particularly because more and more jobs in today's economy involve the collection, interpretation, and reporting of information. These jobs tend to be sedentary occupations, in contrast to the heavily physical nature of factory, field, and mining jobs.

WHAT ARE THE PROSPECTS FOR INDEPENDENT LIVING?

With a few exceptions, heart disease should not limit one's ability to live independently. People who are recovering from a heart attack or surgery should not engage in unsupervised exercise without a doctor's permission. Those with CHF should limit physical activity, including housework, as directed by a physician.

Child Abuse and Neglect

America's most famous child abuse victim is talk show hostess Oprah Winfrey (1954–). Born in Kosciusko, Mississippi, Oprah lived in Milwaukee with her mother from age 6 to age 13, suffering abuse and molestation. She then lived with her father, a strict disciplinarian, who required her to write weekly book reports—the precursors of today's famous Oprah Book Club broadcasts. Since 1978, she has hosted talk shows, first in Baltimore, later in Chicago. Her production company, HARPO Productions, has owned and produced The Oprah Winfrey Show since 1986 and has made Winfrey one of America's wealthiest people.

WHAT ARE THEY?

Child abuse includes physical abuse, sexual abuse, and emotional abuse; neglect includes emotional neglect and malnutrition. Also included in child abuse and neglect are fetal alcohol syndrome, fetal alcohol effect, and substance abuse by parents or caretakers.

Physical abuse is nonaccidental, nonsexual, and physical injury to a child by a caretaker. An example of physical abuse is "shaken baby syndrome." Indications include bleeding in the eyes and in the membranes just above the brain (between the scalp and the brain); these symptoms are usually found, regrettably, at autopsy. Sexual abuse encompasses inappropriately touching a child and being touched as well as forcing a child to observe sexual activities. Emotional abuse may accompany physical and sexual abuse or may stand alone as a caretaker's use of fear, humiliation, and shame to control a child. Neglect is failure to provide a child with needed nutrition, shelter, medical care, or supervision (Lowenthal, 1996).

Fetal alcohol syndrome (FAS) is the complex of physical and learning conditions caused by alcohol use before and during pregnancy. The syndrome has three components: characteristic facial features, growth retardation, and learning difficulties. Fetal alcohol effect (FAE) involves two of the three kinds of outcomes. In most instances, FAS and FAE result from alcohol

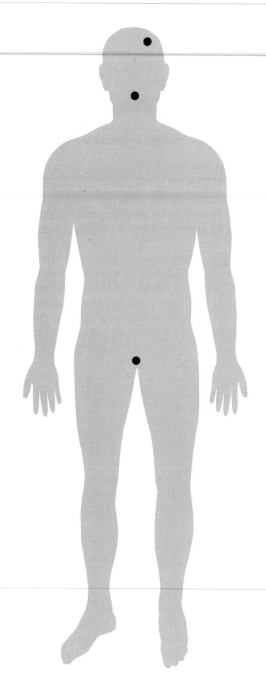

abuse by pregnant women; occasionally, however, use of alcohol by the father just prior to conception is a contributing factor.

WHAT CAUSES THEM? CAN THEY BE PREVENTED? IF SO, HOW?

Child abuse frequently results from frustration among caregivers, particularly parents. Babies and very young children are particularly susceptible to child abuse. They cry frequently and may persist despite caregiver attempts to comfort them. Most child abuse occurs in the home and involves very young children. Despite the amount of publicity given to it, only about half as many cases occur in child-care facilities, including early-childhood centers. Parents and other caregivers can, and often do, claim that abuse did not occur and that the injuries are, instead, the result of accidents. Child protective service (CPS) personnel can, at times, disprove those claims by pointing to the nature of the injuries or by calling upon independent witnesses; at other times, however, CPS staff can only suspect rather than document abuse.

Prevention has three levels. First, prompt reporting of suspected incidents can prevent further abuse or neglect. Professionals responsible for caring for children, including teachers, counselors, and day-care providers, are required by state law (all 50 states have such a law) to report cases of suspected abuse or neglect. These reports are requests to CPS staff to investigate; the teacher or counselor is under no obligation to prove or document abuse or neglect but rather is required to report reasonable suspicions. In fact, most state laws expressly give immunity to teachers and other child-care workers from lawsuits concerning reports of child abuse as long as those reports are made in good faith. Despite this fact, just 10% of such reports are made by school personnel (Fossey, 1995). Second, education for parents and prospective parents, as well as for other caregivers, can help to prevent abuse and neglect. Training in anger management is particularly important (Marshall et al., 1996). Finally, professionals can help children and youth to surmount abuse and neglect by identifying and striving to reach lifetime goals (Bloom, 1996). This involves supporting the child in his or her personal, academic, and social growth.

Since there is no known safe level of alcohol consumption during pregnancy, doctors now recommend that women avoid alcohol altogether throughout the pregnancy as a way to prevent FAS and FAE.

HOW PREVALENT ARE THEY? WHAT IS THE INCIDENCE?

More than 3 million children were reported to have been abused or neglected in 1994, or about 1 instance per 500 children in the United States. Reports were provided to CPS agencies in the 50 states. Because child abuse and neglect are well-known to be underreported, the figure certainly understates the problem (Sedlak, 1990). Of the children alleged to have been abused or neglected, one third, or 1 million children, were substantiated by CPS agencies to have actually been abused or neglected (Wiese & Daro, 1995). The prevalence, or number of children who have been abused or neglected (including instances from prior years), can only be estimated, but it is most likely well in excess of 10 million American children and youth. One study, for example, estimated that 9 million children and youth in the United States have been affected by substance-abusing parents or caregivers (Woodside, 1988).

According to reported incidents, more boys than girls are physically abused or neglected, while more girls than boys are sexually abused. When boys have disabilities, they are particularly susceptible to abuse or neglect (Sobsey, Randall, & Parrila, 1997). The Westat Corporation, under a contract from the National Center on Child Abuse and Neglect, has estimated that children with disabilities are abused or neglected twice as often as are children with no disabilities (Westat, 1993). However, Margaret Nosek, an expert on women with disabilities, disagrees, reporting that women and girls with disabilities are not more abused than are women and girls without disabilities but rather tend to be abused over longer periods of time (Nosek, Howland, & Young, 1997).

Overall, neglect (49%), physical abuse (21%), and sexual abuse (11%) are most common, according to the 1994 survey (Wiese & Daro, 1995); the percentages are proportions of all reported instances filed with CPS agencies in 1994. The National Center on Child Abuse and Neglect reported similar figures for 1993: 49% neglect, 24% physical abuse, and 14% sexual abuse (National Center on Child Abuse and Neglect, 1995).

Child abuse v. all health disabilities

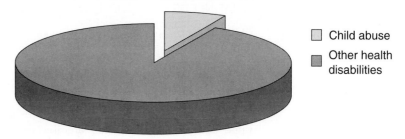

□ Child abuse
■ Other health disabilities

Figure 9.5
Population Estimates: Child Abuse As Compared to All Health Disabilities

Fetal alcohol syndrome affects about 5,000 infants each year—or 7% of all American newborns. Some 50,000 children have fetal alcohol effect (National Organization on Fetal Alcohol Syndrome, 1997).

These are the most credible statistics the author could find on abuse/neglect and substance abuse. The two fields are notoriously prone to exaggerated statistics (see, for example, Kaminker, 1997; and Stossel, 1997).

WHAT EFFECTS CAN THEY HAVE?

Child abuse and neglect can result in death. The 1994 study (Wiese & Daro, 1995) suggested that as many as three children die each day as a direct result of abuse or neglect. CPS agencies confirmed in 1994 a total of 1,271 deaths in children for these reasons (Wiese & Daro). Most often, these children are under the age of 5. Abuse and neglect can also result in disabilities, such as traumatic brain injury. Abused children may become withdrawn, lose friends, and demonstrate difficulty in problem solving (Fossey, 1995).

Fetal alcohol syndrome produces children who are small—their heights are in the lowest tenth of children their ages. They also have eyes that appear to be too far apart, a flat nose, and a flat midface.

WHAT SECONDARY CONDITIONS ARE COMMON?

One fast-growing secondary condition associated with child abuse is traumatic brain injury (TBI). Spinal cord injuries can also result from abuse. Neglect, particularly in the form of malnutrition, can lead to mental retardation. One estimate is that 25% of all developmental disabilities (those occurring during childhood or adolescence and resulting in multiple needs for different kinds of services) may be caused by child abuse and neglect (Baladerian, 1994).

Fetal alcohol syndrome is one of the leading causes of mental retardation; it is also known to result in learning disabilities. Shaken baby syndrome can produce cerebral palsy, blindness, and other disabilities, including brain damage. About 25% of infants with the syndrome die, usually within weeks or months.

WHAT NEEDS DO PEOPLE WITH THEM HAVE?

Children and youth who have been or are susceptible to being abused or neglected often are taught the "No-Go-Tell" strategy of dealing with abuse or neglect (Say No, Go Home, Tell an Adult). The National Resource Center for Respite and Crisis Care Services has noted, however, that this strategy may not be particularly helpful for many children who have disabilities. Such children commonly are taught to obey figures in authority, and ironically, those same authority figures often are the very persons doing the abusing or neglecting.

Children with FAS and FAE may need simplified, concrete instruction if, as often happens, maternal alcohol abuse led to mental retardation, learning disabilities, or both. The children may demonstrate immature or inappropriate social skills, an inability to learn cause and effect, and difficulty generalizing (applying what is learned in one location or setting to a different location/setting). An excellent introduction to the needs of children with FAS is Michael Dorris's *The Broken Cord* (1989).

WHAT SPECIAL-EDUCATION AND RELATED SERVICES MAY HELP?

Perhaps the most urgent such services are formal reporting of instances of suspected abuse and neglect. Teachers in the public schools are required to report such instances. In addition, occupational therapists and other personnel who work in the schools and in other settings frequented by children and youth should report instances of suspected child abuse or neglect (Davidson, 1995).

Weinberg (1997) has argued that in actual practice, professional responsibilities of teachers and related-services personnel too often cease with observation and report. The special-education and related-services needs of the children often are not met by CPS agencies, which are concerned more with finding placements that are safe for the children than they are with meeting the children's special needs.

With respect to FAS and FAE, special education may be necessary as a result of mental retardation or learning disabilities. In particular, children with FAS and FAE may not understand cause and effect; they may need to be trained, not just taught, about how one action leads to another. Teachers may need to give cues to prompt correct answers, avoid discussing abstract ideas without concrete examples, and physically demonstrate what is desired.

Respite care may be required to give parents or caregivers a break. Respite care services—where an early-intervention program takes care of the child for a day or two so that parents can enjoy a stress-free period—are authorized by the IDEA's Part C as early-intervention services. They are less frequently seen as related services under IDEA Part B.

WHAT OTHER INTERVENTIONS CAN BE EFFECTIVE?

Identification of abused or neglected children is primary. Educators, counselors, and others should be alert to frequent or unexplained injuries or bruises, unusual fears, fear about going home, unusual knowledge about sex, and behavior that is uncommonly aggressive or withdrawn.

State protection-and-advocacy (P&A) agencies are a major resource for children who have been abused or neglected. The typical P&A agency is staffed with litigation experts, lawyers who specialize in representing vulnerable children. Each state has at least one such agency. These agencies have joined together as members of the National Association of Protection and Advocacy Systems.

Teachers, counselors, and others working with children can follow straightforward guidelines on appropriate ways of interacting with children. For example, tell the child what you are going to do before you touch him or her; as needed, ask permission first. Physical contact should be limited to those occasions where it is necessary. Teach the child the name and function of different body parts and identify private parts of the body as those covered by underwear. Respect and support children if they choose not to hug or kiss adults.

WHAT ASSISTIVE TECHNOLOGIES AND SERVICES CAN HELP?

Special software that offers support, or scaffolding, as it leads a child through a unit of instruction may help some children with FAS or FAE. Otherwise, adaptive technology is not particularly well-suited for these populations.

WHAT ARE THE PROSPECTS FOR POSTSECONDARY EDUCATION?

Adolescents and adults who were victims of child abuse or neglect usually can continue on to college, and many do. Severe FAS or FAE, however, often produces such profound learning problems that postsecondary education is not feasible.

WHAT ARE THE EMPLOYMENT PROSPECTS?

There is no inherent limitation in employment for persons who were abused or neglected as children. For individuals with FAS or FAE, however, employment prospects may be limited to those jobs calling for repetitive tasks on which the individual can be thoroughly trained. This includes entry-level jobs in hotels, restaurants, and other service-sector occupations.

WHAT ARE THE PROSPECTS FOR INDEPENDENT LIVING?

For people who were abused or neglected, these are excellent. For many individuals with FAS or FAE, however, they are guarded unless these people are painstakingly trained to follow safety rules and to avoid dangerous situations.

Cystic Fibrosis

Gunnar Esiason, son of former quarterback for the NFL Cincinnati Bengals and New York Jets Boomer Esiason, has cystic fibrosis. To raise funds to fight the disease, to support the Boomer Esiason Foundation, and to finance the Gunnar H. Esiason Scholarship Fund at Hofstra University, the former all-star quarterback annually hosts a football game at Hofstra, where the Jets hold their preseason camps each year.

WHAT IS IT?

Cystic fibrosis is an inherited condition in which breathing, digestion, and reproduction are affected by the body's inability to manufacture a complete version of a key protein. A protein called the cystic fibrosis transmembrane

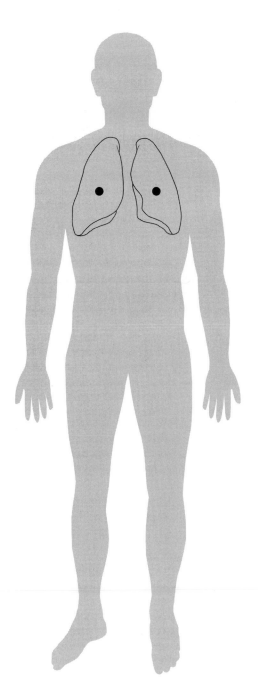

regulator (CFTR), which governs the transport within the body of chloride (which with sodium makes up salt), does not function properly in people with cystic fibrosis. These people's CFTR lacks an amino acid necessary for chloride to enter and leave cells. For this reason, the sweat of people with cystic fibrosis is unusually salty; this is one of the first clinical indications of the condition. The lungs become covered with a sticky mucus that makes them more susceptible to infection. People with cystic fibrosis also get chronic digestive disorders.

Most people with the condition die from it. Indeed, cystic fibrosis is the most common fatal genetic disease in America, according to the Cystic Fibrosis Foundation (1998). The Foundation reports that life expectancy is now 31 years of age; a quarter century ago; it was just 8 years of age. The disease was named in 1938 by Columbia University's Dorothy Andersen, who first noticed its effects on the lungs and body organs.

WHAT CAUSES IT? CAN IT BE PREVENTED? IF SO, HOW?

The condition is caused by a recessive gene that is carried by 1 American in every 23, according to the Cystic Fibrosis Foundation (1998). This gene was discovered in 1989. People with one defective gene are carriers; those with two get cystic fibrosis. The gene makes the protein CFTR. Because it is an autosomal recessive gene, two carrier parents have a 1-in-4 chance of having a child with cystic fibrosis, a 1-in-2 chance of having a child who is also a carrier, and a 1-in-4 chance of having a child with two normal versions of the gene.

Current understanding is that inflammation in the lungs, caused by airway obstruction and bronchial infection, gradually destroys the lungs. This inflammation apparently begins in infancy, even though babies show no signs of illness. This suggests that the inflammation may unexpectedly precede infection. For these reasons, experts believe that antiinflammatory treatments should begin at diagnosis and continue throughout life (Konstan & Berger, 1997).

HOW PREVALENT IS IT? WHAT IS THE INCIDENCE?

About 30,000 Americans have cystic fibrosis, according to the Cystic Fibrosis Foundation (1998). That is the prevalence. According to the Foundation, the incidence is 1,000 new cases annually. The Foundation also estimates that cystic fibrosis occurs about once every 3,300 live births. The condition is much more common among whites (notably people of

Cystic Fibrosis v. all health disabilities

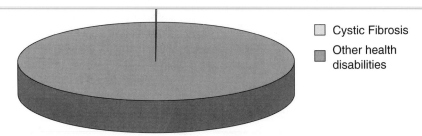

Cystic Fibrosis

Other health disabilities

Figure 9.6
Population Estimates: Cystic Fibrosis As Compared to All Health Disabilities

Northwestern European ancestry) than other races. According to the Foundation, some 10 million Americans are carriers of the gene but display no symptoms. There is some evidence that one recessive gene offers protection against typhoid fever, which was a scourge of Northwestern Europe several centuries ago. Thus, as with sickle-cell disease (discussed later in the chapter), there seems to be some survival value in inheriting one gene, while inheriting two genes can be fatal.

WHAT EFFECTS CAN IT HAVE?

The first and often the most noticeable symptom of cystic fibrosis is very salty-tasting skin. In fact, a sweat test is the standard way the condition is initially diagnosed. Other symptoms include excessive coughing, a large appetite but no commensurate accompanying weight gain, and bulky stools (Cystic Fibrosis Foundation, 1998).

People with cystic fibrosis need frequent hospitalization, heavy doses of antibiotics, and enzyme supplements to fight infections. Lung impairments account for about 90% of the disability and death associated with the condition (Welsh & Smith, 1995). The vast majority of males with cystic fibrosis are infertile because the ducts in the reproductive organs become clogged by mucus to the point of not transporting sperm. Individuals with cystic fibrosis typically are underweight, but many are of normal height.

Although cystic fibrosis is usually diagnosed in childhood, in some instances it is not diagnosed until adulthood. A recent study suggested that adult-onset cystic fibrosis is mild compared with childhood-onset conditions (Gan, Geus, Bakker, Lamers, & Heijerman, 1995).

WHAT SECONDARY CONDITIONS ARE COMMON?

Since cystic fibrosis gradually destroys the pancreas, diabetes is a frequent secondary condition. Liver disease and pancreatic disease also are common. Osteoporosis occurs frequently, especially among females.

WHAT NEEDS DO PEOPLE WITH IT HAVE?

People with cystic fibrosis need to understand the nature of the condition. This is a serious concern, according to one recent study that found that patient knowledge about key aspects of cystic fibrosis (even among persons who have had the condition for years) was spotty at best (Conway, Pond, Watson, & Hamnett, 1996). This is why scientists at the University of Texas developed a Cystic Fibrosis Family Education Program. The curriculum, a print-based intervention, teaches cystic fibrosis patients and their families about the condition, effective interventions, and self-management techniques. Preliminary evidence suggests that this increased knowledge has positive outcomes (Bartholomew et al., 1997).

In addition, people with cystic fibrosis often expend more energy per unit of activity than do other people, mostly because of reduced lung capacity. For this reason, they need more frequent rest from physically demanding work.

WHAT SPECIAL-EDUCATION AND RELATED SERVICES MAY HELP?

Physical therapy is necessary on a daily basis. This includes chest pounding to loosen the mucus and prevent its buildup.

WHAT OTHER INTERVENTIONS CAN BE EFFECTIVE?

People with cystic fibrosis need to eat frequent, high-calorie meals, usually with pancreatic enzyme supplements that facilitate digestion. With such supplements, affected persons can eat much the same kinds of food that other people eat. Early intervention, started immediately after diagnosis, is essential (Dankert-Roelse & te Meerman, 1995), especially to establish dietary routines and to introduce dietary supplements. Regular exercise is important because it helps to loosen mucus and to maintain breathing and muscle strength. Aerobic and anaerobic exercises both help.

Standard treatment includes the intravenous drug tobramycin, which usually is given in a hospital. The drug is of limited help; even with it, patients typically lose about 2% of lung function each year. It also has side effects—tobramycin can cause deafness and damage the kidneys.

In late 1997, an advisory panel for the Food and Drug Administration (FDA) recommended approval of an inhaled antibiotic called TOBI™ (tobramycin for inhalation). Preliminary tests had suggested that the antibiotic seemed to increase lung function by about 12% after 6 months of treatment. The manufacturer is PathoGenesis Corporation (Associated Press, 1997). According to the Cystic Fibrosis Foundation (1998), the major benefit of TOBI is that it can be delivered directly to the site of lung inflammations at much higher concentrations than are possible with other drugs.

An inhaled drug called DNase, which first appeared in 1993, appears to be an effective treatment because it breaks up mucus by digesting the DNA of dead cells that clog the lungs of individuals with cystic fibrosis (Welsh & Smith, 1995). The drug was introduced by Genentech under the name Pulmozyme. This drug, one of the first biotechnology drugs to appear on the market, reduces future damage; it does not, however, repair existing tissue, nor can it cure the condition. Contributors to the CYSTIC-L E-mail listserv have frequently commented that Pulmozyme must be refrigerated; if left unrefrigerated for 24 hours, the drug should be discarded. The medication costs about $1,000 per month.

Another treatment option is gene therapy. In this approach, normal CTFR-making genes would be delivered to the cells that need it. Although promising, gene therapy to date has been problematic. The cells of the epithelium die and are replaced every few months, making gene therapy administration necessary several times a year (Welsh & Smith, 1995). In addition, the usual tactic in gene therapy is to attach the normal DNA to a vector, or carrier; adenoviruses, which usually cause common colds, are the vector of choice. In individuals with cystic fibrosis, however, adenovirus infections are common, which means the body has mobilized itself to combat them (Rosenecker, Harms, Bertele, Pohl-Koppe, Mutius, Adam, & Nocolai, 1996). This may be why recent clinical trials with specially modified adenoviruses have failed to alleviate symptoms (Knowles, Hoeneker, Zhou, Olsen, Noah, Hu, Leigh, Englehardt, Edwards, & Jones, 1995). For these reasons, the attention of researchers recently has turned to efforts to correct the defective protein itself rather than the gene (Carey, 1998a).

WHAT ASSISTIVE TECHNOLOGIES AND SERVICES CAN HELP?

Few assistive devices appear to be indicated with cystic fibrosis. One possibility, if lung inflammation is severe, is motorized wheelchairs or scooters for conserving strength and maintaining endurance.

WHAT ARE THE PROSPECTS FOR POSTSECONDARY EDUCATION?

Nothing about cystic fibrosis should limit a person's ability to participate in postsecondary education, although periodic hospitalizations and other absences from classes are necessary.

WHAT ARE THE EMPLOYMENT PROSPECTS?

According to the CYSTIC-L E-mail listserv's "Frequently Asked Questions" page, 33% of adults with cystic fibrosis are employed full-time and another 17% part-time. Some 21% are not employed. The others are students or homemakers.

WHAT ARE THE PROSPECTS FOR INDEPENDENT LIVING?

These are not materially affected by cystic fibrosis.

Diabetes
My brother-in-law Mark Schwartz (1947–) has Type 2 diabetes, as did his father. Mark has to monitor his eating habits; in particular, he must eat at regular intervals throughout the day. This is an injunction Mark finds difficult to obey: His job as an executive of a computer services company requires him to respond to unpredictable crises at client companies almost daily. A few years ago, Mark had cardiac surgery, in large part because of diabetes. While Mark is always conscious of his condition, he is not limited by it in any meaningful way. He works longer hours than I do, under more pressure, and consistently at a high level of competence. Diabetes is more of a bother for Mark than a disability.

WHAT IS IT?

Diabetes is the name given to a variety of chronic conditions that limit the body's ability to make or use insulin. Insulin is a hormone made in the pancreas, a gland near the stomach; it is used by the body to burn glucose, a form of sugar produced when starches and sugars are digested. If the body lacks insulin, it cannot burn glucose, and eventually, the person would die. Because it results in too high or too low levels of insulin in the body, diabetes can affect many different organs and body functions.

Diabetes has two main types. In **Type 1** diabetes, also known as **juvenile,** or early-onset, diabetes, the body stops producing insulin. People with Type 1 diabetes must inject themselves daily with insulin. They cannot take insulin in oral forms (pills or liquid) because acid in the stomach destroys all or most of that insulin before it can be used. (The term *insulin-dependent diabetes mellitus,* or IDDM, is no longer in use; the American Diabetes Association in mid-1997 recommended that the condition be referred to as Type 1, or juvenile, diabetes.)

In **Type 2** diabetes, also known as adult-onset diabetes, the body continues to produce insulin but becomes unable to use the insulin properly. It most frequently develops after age 40, usually in people who are overweight and physically inactive. A blood sugar reading of 126 or higher in two separate readings on different days can lead to a diagnosis of Type 2 diabetes. A simple 5-dollar blood test is used. (Prior to mid-1997, the American Diabetes Association recommended use of a blood-sugar reading of 140 or higher. The Association recommended the new, lower level at the same time it advised against continued use of the term *non-insulin-dependent diabetes mellitus,* or NIDDM.)

WHAT CAUSES IT? CAN IT BE PREVENTED? IF SO, HOW?

The causes of diabetes are not well understood. In Type 1 diabetes, the beta cells in the pancreas are destroyed, usually in childhood but occasionally in adolescence (Field & Tobias, 1997). Because beta cells occur in the islet of Langerhans, they often are called islet cells. Some experts believe that a malfunction in the immune system is responsible for the death of the beta

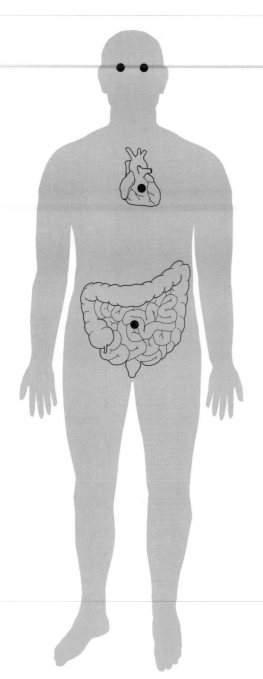

cells (Juvenile Diabetes Foundation [JDF], 1997). Other cases of Type 1 diabetes have no known etiologies, or causes. Type 2 diabetes seems to be triggered by obesity and lack of exercise, although it is not clear *how* those factors lead to diabetes. Current theories are that people who have genes making them susceptible to diabetes develop the condition if an outside influence, such as a virus, triggers it. There are suspicions that dioxin, a chemical widely used in pesticides, may be one such outside influence in Type 2 diabetes.

Diabetes is not an infectious disease; classmates and coworkers of individuals with diabetes are not at risk of acquiring the condition. No cure for diabetes is yet known. Treatments help people to manage the condition but do not prevent it; the goal, rather, is to forestall further deterioration.

Insulin resistance is common among persons with spinal cord injury (SCI), resulting in a number of metabolic and blood pressure problems in this population that can, in turn, lead to atherosclerotic types of heart disease (Bauman & Spungen, 1994).

One step that experts agree could help to prevent diabetes is regular physical exercise. Walking, jogging, or playing tennis or other sports can strengthen the heart, lungs, and blood vessels; it can also help to control blood-glucose levels and to reduce cardiovascular problems. Physical activity can help to prevent both Type 1 and Type 2 diabetes. With respect to individuals with SCI, however, it should be noted that height-weight charts (commonly used to determine whether someone is overweight) often are of little use with people who have SCI: The charts significantly underestimate obesity among persons with SCI. A better measure is body composition testing. Notwithstanding these facts, healthy eating and exercise remain of great value in preventing cardiac conditions among individuals who have SCI.

HOW PREVALENT IS IT? WHAT IS THE INCIDENCE?

Type 1 diabetes affects some 700,000 to 800,000 Americans, according to the American Diabetes Association (1997) and the JDF (1997). Type 2 diabetes is far more common, affecting an estimated 16 million Americans (American Diabetes Association, 1997), a sixfold increase from 1958. Thus, Type 1 diabetes accounts for about 5% of all persons with diabetes, and Type 2 for some 90% to 95%. Daneman and Frank (1996) estimate that the incidence of Type 1 diabetes is 10 to 15 new cases annually per 1,000 population under age 20; stated differently, about 1 out of every 500 high school seniors has Type 1 diabetes. Type 2 diabetes has grown 9% annually in the past decade. Overall, we can estimate the preva-

Diabetes v. all health disabilities

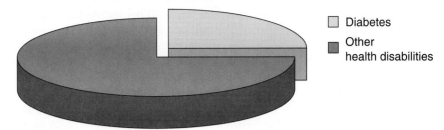

☐ Diabetes
■ Other
health disabilities

Figure 9.7
Population Estimates: Diabetes As Compared to All Health Disabilities

lence of diabetes at 17 million Americans and the incidence at about one-half million new cases annually. Worldwide, some 125 million people have some kind of diabetes, according to the World Health Organization.

WHAT EFFECTS CAN IT HAVE?

There was a time in the 1920s and even before that what was then known as diabetes mellitus was a rapidly fatal disease (Sinnock & Most, 1986). Today, however, given proper care, diabetes usually does not produce permanent limitations in major life activities. People with diabetes can eat just about anything other people can eat (the major exception being candies or other high-sugar-content foods). In fact, the American Diabetes Association estimated that half of the American population of 16 million people who had Type 2 diabetes did not even know it. That was one reason the Association changed its guidelines in 1997.

A question then arises: Is controlled diabetes still a disability? A U.S. Court of Appeals addressed that question in late 1997 in the case of *Gilday v. Mecosta County*. Mecosta County, Michigan, had fired Mr. Gilday from his job as an emergency medical technician in August 1994. Gilday then sued, claiming that his diabetes, diagnosed 3 years earlier, was behind the termination. Writing for the court, Judge Karen Moore explained that people who have conditions that are controlled with medication or ameliorated with technology are still people with disabilities. Judge Ralph G. Guy added that as long as Mr. Gilday exercises, eats at regular intervals, and takes his medication, he may "rarely require any accommodation, but his achievement should not leave him subject to discrimination based on his underlying disability."

WHAT SECONDARY CONDITIONS ARE COMMON?

Diabetes is a major cause of several other disabilities. In most instances, secondary conditions worsen over time; that is, the longer someone has lived with diabetes, the worse those other effects generally are. Diabetes is the fourth leading cause of death in America. It is also the major cause of blindness and vision impairment in adults under 75 years of age; most people with diabetes, however, will not notice any changes in vision. Diabetes is also the major cause of end-stage renal (kidney) disease; 40% of people with Type 1 diabetes will develop renal problems within 10 years of the onset of diabetes. And more than half of all leg amputations in America are due to diabetes (JDF, 1997). Overall, the cost in America to treat Type 2 diabetes is $92 billion annually (Carey, 1997), about 15% of all health-care spending and 25% of Medicare allocations. In most instances, the secondary conditions of diabetes that drive up costs can be prevented with monitoring and self-treatment.

Also common in diabetes is neuropathy, or damage to the nervous system. This manifests in the inability of many people with diabetes to feel sensations with their fingers or feet. Neuropathy is why individuals who become blind from diabetes often are unable to learn or use Braille. It is also why people with diabetes must inspect their feet daily; failure to do so may lead to infections that become so serious that leg amputations are necessary. According to the JDF (1997), some 70% of people with diabetes will have some kind of neuropathy. Those who do are at increased risk of strokes and heart attacks. In fact, people with diabetes are two or more times as likely to have strokes or heart attacks as are people without diabetes.

WHAT NEEDS DO PEOPLE WITH IT HAVE?

Children, youth, and adults with diabetes require understanding of their need to self-medicate. This is particularly true during adolescence, when hormonal changes may aggravate the condition despite the youth's best, most conscientious efforts to control it. The JDF speculates that a growth hormone acts as an antiinsulin agent. When a diabetic teen's blood sugar drops, this triggers release of adrenaline, which in turn stimulates release of stored blood glucose. The result is unpredictable falls and rises in blood sugar levels. It is important to remember that the young person is not to blame for these irregularities.

Constant monitoring is necessary because eating causes glucose levels to rise; by contrast, insulin and exercise make those levels fall. Life for someone with diabetes is an unending effort to maintain stability of glucose by balancing food, exercise, and insulin. If too much insulin is taken into the body, an **insulin reaction** can occur. This is also known as insulin shock, or hypoglycemia (too low levels of glucose). An insulin reaction can lead to loss of consciousness. Insulin reactions are the most common and potentially the most dangerous side effects of insulin therapy. Indications of an oncoming insulin reaction include shallow breathing, faintness, rapid pulse, and sweating. To counter an insulin reaction, children need immediate food; milk, orange juice, and even candy can help. Once the symptoms subside, the child should have more slowly digested food, perhaps a sandwich with milk (JDF, 1997).

Hyperglycemia (too high levels of glucose) is much less common. Insulin reactions can produce hyperglycemia for a period of several hours after the crisis begins because the body responds to the reaction by releasing stored glucose, which then combines with the sugar taken by the individual to counter the reaction. Where symptoms have been ignored and treatments are not taken, a **diabetic coma** may result. This is a medical emergency that can lead to death. Indicators that it may be approaching include dry, hot skin; excessive thirst and urination; drowsiness; and elevated sugar levels (JDF, 1997). For all of these reasons, regular visits to a doctor and annual checkups by ophthalmologists and podiatrists are essential.

WHAT SPECIAL-EDUCATION AND RELATED SERVICES MAY HELP?

It can take 1 to 3 hours daily for an individual with diabetes to perform the necessary self-monitoring and self-medication tasks. Teachers, counselors, employers, and others need to allow the individual the time and the privacy to perform these essential tasks. In addition, it is very important for people with diabetes to eat at regularly scheduled times. Teachers and other school personnel should supervise younger children in their monitoring and self-medicating activities; this includes reminding children of the need to eat at scheduled times. Older children may not require such reminders. As for adults, one reasonable accommodation in employment is to permit individuals to work regular-shift hours with consistent break times for eating.

WHAT OTHER INTERVENTIONS CAN BE EFFECTIVE?

Diabetes requires active monitoring and management by the individual himself or herself. Children, youth, and adults with Type 1 diabetes must inject themselves with insulin as many as two to six times daily; they must also monitor their blood sugar levels as many as eight times each day (JDF, 1997). According to the JDF (1997), "Children don't just receive treatment, they have to learn to be their own nurse. They need to constantly monitor their blood sugars, watch what they eat and schedule exercise programs, all of which requires a high level of discipline."

Type 2 diabetes usually is treated by a combination of diet and exercise to reduce weight and occasionally by oral drugs. Rezulin (troglitazone) can reduce the need for people with Type 2 diabetes to inject themselves from three times to just one time daily. However, because of liver-related deaths, the Food and Drug Administration (FDA) raised serious questions about Rezulin in 1998. Glucophage (metformin), another widely used drug, can lead to lactic acidosis, or acid buildup in the blood, which is a signal of organ failure. This, too, must be closely monitored by physicians.

Some new treatments are on the horizon. Islet cell transplantation is an obvious one; here the beta cells that were destroyed in Type 1 diabetes would be replaced. Research in this area is active. However, immune system rejection or destruction of the implanted cells has stymied efforts to date (JDF, 1997).

Rezulin does not work for people with Type 1 diabetes. For these people, a possible new treatment using a hormone that helps to control sugar levels, called amylin, has been developed by Amylin Pharmaceuticals (Alpert, 1997). In addition, Pfizer has announced a device that permits diabetes patients to inhale rather than inject insulin (Tanouye, 1997).

In late August 1997, President Clinton announced an intensified search for cures for diabetes. Calling diabetes "the country's seventh leading killer," President Clinton said that the balanced-budget legislation he had just signed into law included provisions that "will take us a tremendous step forward in our fight against diabetes." The law expands Medicare coverage for senior citizens with diabetes by more than $2 billion and allocates $150 million for new research (Holland, 1997).

WHAT ASSISTIVE TECHNOLOGIES AND SERVICES CAN HELP?

People with diabetes who are also blind or have low vision frequently benefit from the same assistive devices and services that people who lose their vision from other causes use. The major exception, as noted earlier, is that individuals with diabetes often cannot feel sensations in the fingers well enough to be able to read Braille. Similarly, individuals who have amputations because of diabetes complications may be helped by the same assistive technologies as those used by other people with amputation, including prostheses and orthoses.

Other than these measures for diabetes-related secondary conditions, few accommodations usually are necessary. Indeed, several federal courts have ruled that insulin-dependency diabetes is not a disability under terms of the Americans with Disabilities Act because diabetes does not routinely limit major life activities to a substantial extent.

WHAT ARE THE PROSPECTS FOR POSTSECONDARY EDUCATION?

Nothing about diabetes should limit or prevent people from pursuing a college education. Many individuals with diabetes, in fact, do well at universities because the disability has taught them to become responsible and self-reliant. Those who have secondary conditions such as blindness or amputation will benefit from the accommodations colleges and universities routinely make for blind and low-vision students and for students with physical disabilities, including materials in appropriate media (e.g., on tape, on disk, in large type) and architectural accessibility on campus.

WHAT ARE THE EMPLOYMENT PROSPECTS?

People with diabetes can become effective employees in virtually any occupation. Among the few jobs that might cause problems for people with diabetes are positions that require work on rotating shifts or otherwise odd hours. This is because eating and self-medication must occur at regular, predictable times. Many employers, particularly larger companies, have become accustomed to meeting these needs of people with diabetes and to making such reasonable accommodations as assigning the individual to a regular shift of work.

WHAT ARE THE PROSPECTS FOR INDEPENDENT LIVING?

Nothing about diabetes should prevent or even limit someone's ability to live independently. The major exception obviously is someone who is in a diabetic coma because that condition is imminently life-threatening and requires hospitalization.

Medical Fragility/ Technology Dependence

Edward V. Roberts (1939–1995) used an iron lung (a body-length machine that made it possible for him to breathe) every night and a respirator every day as a result of contracting polio at the age of 14. In 1962, as a student at the University of California—Berkeley, he was humiliated to be forced to use the campus hospital as his dorm. As a result, after graduating in 1966, Ed founded the world's first independent-living center—the now famous Center for Independent Living (CIL) in Berkeley. I got to know him in the 1970s and worked with him in the 1980s on a wide variety of disability rights issues. Although he was in actuality dependent on technology to live, I have never met a less dependent human being. That speaks volumes for the strength and integrity of Ed's spirit.

WHAT IS IT?

The category of "medically fragile/technology-dependent" children and youth comprises a broad range of rare disorders that until recently required almost continuous hospitalization. Medically fragile or technology-dependent children require use of one or more pieces of equipment to prevent death or to forestall further disability. Until recently, such children usually died within hours or days of birth. If they did survive, they lived in hospitals, often in intensive care units (ICUs), for years; for some, the ICU was the only home they ever knew.

Recently, the development of sophisticated and portable equipment has allowed many children and youth to be discharged from the hospital to the home and to the public schools. Included in this category are children who need one or more of the following:

ventilator or other oxygen machine
tracheostomy suctioning
ostomy care
urethral catheterization
dialysis
IV feeding
nasal/oral gastric tube feeding

These devices monitor the children's health and sustain the children with food and oxygen when they cannot eat or breathe on their own.

Examples of children who may be medically fragile/technology-dependent include some

infants on an apnea monitor (e.g., those in danger of sudden infant death syndrome)

children with special breathing problems

children in body casts (spica casts)

children with specialized feeding problems (e.g., an inability to retain food or extended feeding schedules)

In addition, some children with fetal alcohol syndrome, diabetes, asthma, or seizure disorders may be medically fragile and technology-dependent if their conditions are severe.

WHAT CAUSES IT? CAN IT BE PREVENTED? IF SO, HOW?

In addition to a large number of rare genetic disorders, most of which until recently were usually fatal, prematurity can cause children to become medically fragile/technology-dependent. From the preceding list, however, it should be evident that a wide variety of causes is involved.

HOW PREVALENT IS IT? WHAT IS THE INCIDENCE?

The U.S. Congress Office of Technology Assessment (OTA) estimated in 1987 that between as few as 17,000 and as many as 100,000 children and youth were technology-dependent. (The OTA later was abolished by Congress.) No more precise estimate has since been published to the author's knowledge. For our purposes, we can make some "guesstimates": a prevalence of 50,000 and an incidence of 1,000 new cases annually, both for the

Medically fragile v. all health disabilities

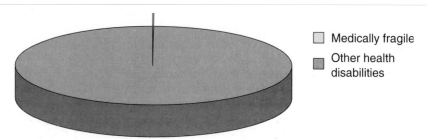

☐ Medically fragile

▨ Other health disabilities

Figure 9.8
Population Estimates: Persons Who Are Medically Fragile As Compared to People with All Kinds of Health Disabilities

United States. It is important, however, that these numbers be understood as gross estimates.

WHAT EFFECTS CAN IT HAVE?

Medically fragile/technology-dependent individuals are susceptible to sudden death. For that reason, they often have one-to-one nursing care; they also must use technology round the clock. The effects of the conditions are numerous and diverse; the one commonality is that without the machine (working properly!), many of these children would not survive. If you think about it for a few minutes, this continuous accompaniment by a nurse and by a machine likely will have pervasive effects upon the individual. Obvious are the effects upon the person's social life. Another common effect is a preoccupation with feelings of morbidity and mortality. Yet another is learned helplessness—the person may decline to perform tasks he or she can do, feeling that such efforts are pointless.

WHAT SECONDARY CONDITIONS ARE COMMON?

An important one is depression. The child soon discovers that he or she is one of only a few people in the community whose life is so constrained. As a teenager, the impossibility of privacy can cause despair. A second category of accompanying problems is *experiential deprivation*. The child literally cannot affect the environment by doing things to it, for which reason he or she has a hard time learning cause and effect. In addition, many health problems can emerge from the individual's vulnerability to environmental factors. Devices used to keep the person alive may harbor bacteria or viruses, leading to pneumonia and other complications. Some individuals also have epilepsy-like seizures.

WHAT NEEDS DO PEOPLE WITH IT HAVE?

A written medical care plan, in addition to an IEP, is required for these children or youth. This plan should include emergency procedures, including rehospitalization if necessary. School personnel, especially school nurses, require training before the child can be released to the public schools. Ideally, a year or more of advance planning by hospital and school personnel would precede the child's admission to the school (Haynie, Porter, & Palfrey, 1989).

One issue that may arise is how to handle "Do Not Resuscitate" (DNR) orders. These orders may be issued by parents for use if the child's death appears imminent. They may take the form of an Advance Directive to a Physician or of a Durable Power of Attorney for Health Care. How these orders are handled varies from state to state. In some states, state law makes it a crime not to comply with a DNR, while in other states, it is a crime *to* follow the DNR's directives (Haynie, Porter, & Palfrey, 1989; Leff & Walizer, 1992).

WHAT SPECIAL-EDUCATION AND RELATED SERVICES MAY HELP?

Respite care for the family members is an essential early-intervention or related service. The pressure upon family members to monitor the child's well-being 24 hours a day can be overwhelming. Even when medically fragile children begin attending school, family relief may be short-lived. Schools may challenge the family's obligation under the IDEA to provide nursing or other monitoring during program hours. The family may need to exercise its due process rights to establish that responsibility. Otherwise, the family would need to secure private health insurance or Medicaid coverage, which may also require time-consuming and emotionally draining fights with health-care organizations or the government.

The fact that these children have constant one-on-one adult monitoring limits their independence and may slow social and emotional growth. One solution to this problem is to place the child in a specialized setting where child-care workers and early-childhood special educators are trained in maintaining the equipment and caring for the child (Beck, Hammond-Cordero, & Poole, 1994). Such programs may not be geographically convenient, however, meaning that such placement would separate family and child.

WHAT OTHER INTERVENTIONS CAN BE EFFECTIVE?

Close working relationships between school, hospital, and home are essential. Leff and Walizer (1992) have offered useful guidelines for creating and sustaining such partnerships. Technology-dependent children may need machines for ventilation or for feeding. Child-care workers must monitor the child virtually every minute of the school day, as the family must at home. Focusing on early-intervention and preschool special-education programs that feature closer family-professional ties than do K–12 public schools, Shelton and Stepanek (1994) observed that this requirement for 24-hour monitoring creates tremendous needs on the family's part for respite care. The extensive support system required for monitoring may begin to fail over time as the demands of employment, care for other children, and other deferred or delayed needs resurface.

Renee Waissman (1993) of the Centre de Recherche Medicine in Paris has commented that many parents who decide to accept responsibility to raise technology-dependent children, including children with chronic illnesses, "behave with conviction and a sense of responsibility when they decide to treat their child at home. However, they don't necessarily consider all possible consequences of their decision" (p. 29). Helping parents to explore those possible outcomes is the responsibility of the professional. One aspect of that role is assisting parents to overcome what Waissman calls the "guilt of being healthy and being unable to transmit that health" (p. 30).

WHAT ASSISTIVE TECHNOLOGIES AND SERVICES CAN HELP?

A landmark report from the now defunct OTA, *Technology-Dependent Children: Hospital v. Home Care: A Technical Memorandum* (1987), was instrumental in speeding up work on the national and state levels to discharge children with chronic illnesses from hospital to home. (Copies are still available from the U.S. Government Printing Office, Washington, DC 20401.) The importance of the report was in its consensus among a broad range of experts that technology had reached the point of being able to sustain the lives of many children and youth outside the hospital. In the years since, the number and sophistication of the devices have improved notably, making hospital-to-school transition even more feasible for many technology-dependent children and youth.

According to Lantos and Kohrman (1992), complex life support devices not only must be selected, acquired, and operated but also must be maintained and, at times, repaired. This requires schools to have on staff, or readily available, not only medical personnel such as school nurses but also rehabilitation engineers or other technology experts.

WHAT ARE THE PROSPECTS FOR POSTSECONDARY EDUCATION?

The Americans with Disabilities Act (ADA) and Section 504 of the Rehabilitation Act, as amended, provide that virtually all colleges and universities in the United States will make what they consider to be reasonable accommodations enabling qualified individuals to enroll, take courses, and otherwise participate in postsecondary programs.

WHAT ARE THE EMPLOYMENT PROSPECTS?

The ADA and Section 503 of the Rehabilitation Act both require that employers provide reasonable accommodations to job applicants and workers who qualify for employment. Since there are limits to what the laws consider to be "reasonable," some companies may decline to provide some kinds of medical services or devices. Some may permit and pay for attendant care services at the workplace, while others will not. Each instance must be judged on its own.

WHAT ARE THE PROSPECTS FOR INDEPENDENT LIVING?

Medically fragile/technology-dependent individuals who live to adulthood frequently will need attendant care services at home. Their attendants not only would perform household and personal chores, including cooking and bathing, but also would monitor the equipment upon which the individual's life depends.

Sickle-Cell Disease

In his The Wisdom of the Body, *Yale surgery professor Sherwin Nuland (1997) wrote about the sickle-cell disease of Mural Penn, known as Kip: "Before Kip told me his story, I could not have imagined the havoc wrought on a man's life by a single incorrect amino acid placed in error by one infinitesimal defective gene" (p. 112). Penn, a 35-year-old African American, has had to visit the Yale-New Haven Hospital several hundred times for pain medication and to deal with sickle-cell crises. Whereas most people have blood that is about 42% comprised of red blood cells, Penn's usually is 24% and sometimes as low as 18% when he has a crisis. Commented Nuland: "This means not only that he has no reserve for exertion but also that his tissues are always getting less oxygen than they need. As with so many sicklers, the low oxygenation has resulted in a degree of impaired growth. Kip is five seven and weighs 131 pounds" (p. 112).*

WHAT IS IT?

Sickle-cell disease is a group of inherited disorders of the red blood cells, which carry oxygen to all parts of the body. The red blood cells use hemoglobin to transport the oxygen. The most common type of sickle-cell disease is sickle-cell anemia, a condition in which hemoglobin synthesis goes awry: The gene that produces the hemoglobin molecule creates one erroneous polypeptide. This stretches the cell membrane, making the whole cell resemble a sickle. Individuals become anemic because the red blood cells lose their natural deformability and clump together, blocking the flow of oxygen to tissues. The blockage produces pain that can be extremely severe; this is known as a "sickle-cell crisis." Because blood vessels exist throughout the body, serving virtually all organs and tissues, the effect can be widespread. The spleen is particularly susceptible to such blockage. Gradually losing its blood supply over the years, it shrinks and becomes incapable of effectively fighting off infection (Nuland, 1997).

WHAT CAUSES IT? CAN IT BE PREVENTED?
IF SO, HOW?

The condition is an inherited one; its cause is a recessive gene, meaning that an individual must have two such genes for the condition to manifest itself. People having only one such gene are said to have **sickle-cell trait,** a condition that rarely produces symptoms. Because sickle-cell disease is autosomal recessive, if both parents carry the gene, the chance of a fetus inheriting the condition is 1 in 4; the likelihood of the fetus becoming a carrier is 1 in 2; and the chance that the fetus will be neither a carrier nor affected is 1 in 4.

HOW PREVALENT IS IT? WHAT IS THE INCIDENCE?

Sickle-cell anemia is most common among African Americans. Some 100,000 people in the United States, most of them African Americans, have sickle-cell anemia. About 1 in every 375 African American children, youth, and young adults have sickle-cell anemia. For our purposes, we can estimate the incidence at about 1,000 per year in the United States. The origin of the condition appears to be central Africa, where malaria is widespread. Since people who are carriers of sickle-cell anemia genes rarely get malaria, the

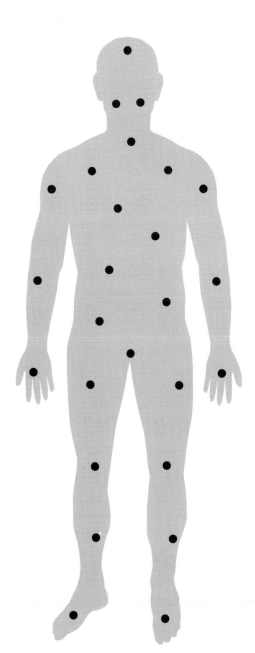

condition confers evolutionary benefits. Individuals of Northern European origin, by contrast, derive no such benefit because malaria is rare in that region. While having sickle-cell trait (being a carrier) has some advantages, no such gains accompany sickle-cell disease (being affected). That is, there is no evolutionary or other benefit associated with inheriting two recessive genes.

WHAT EFFECTS CAN IT HAVE?

Nuland reported: "For most patients afflicted with it, sickle-cell disease is ceaselessly and interminably the dominating fact of each hour lived" (1997, p. 112). This is both because of the pain and because of the uncertainty about when another sickle-cell crisis may appear. Nuland continued: "Any illness, any hot summer's day, any overexertion can bring on a grueling agony of pain that lasts for days and requires astonishingly large amounts of narcotic to ease it" (p. 112).

In children, the primary effect of sickle-cell disease is the ever present danger of infection. Because virtually any infection can produce a severe illness, absenteeism is common. However, sickle-cell anemia is fatal much less often than it once was. Davis, Schoendorf, Gergen, and Moore (1997), examining mortality rates among children with sickle-cell disease, found that survival was much more common in 1992 than it was in 1968.

WHAT SECONDARY CONDITIONS ARE COMMON?

Individuals with sickle-cell anemia often have to have operations to remove their gallbladders because disintegrating red blood cells discharge substances that collect into stones. These individuals also are susceptible to pneumonia because the spleen cannot act effectively to fight the infection. Typically, people with sickle-cell anemia are small physically. Men, for example, tend to reach mid-five-foot heights and to have very low body weights. Because they so often need drugs to control pain, many people with sickle-cell anemia become addicted to narcotics. In some individuals, infections in the throat necessitate a tracheostomy, an opening in the windpipe that allows a person to breathe (Nuland, 1997).

Almost 1 in every 5 (17%) individuals with sickle-cell anemia will have a stroke. Children between 5 and 17 years of age are particularly susceptible; those with sickle-cell disease are 300 times more likely than children without it to suffer a stroke. Those who have a stroke and survive it have a 70% chance of having a second stroke, often within 3 years (Serjeant & Graham, 1992).

Sickle cell disease v. all health disabilities

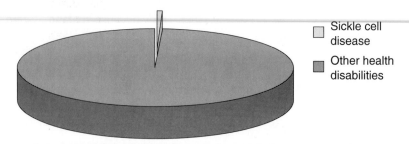

Sickle cell disease

Other health disabilities

Figure 9.9
Population Estimates: Sickle-Cell Disease As Compared to All Health Disabilities

In addition, painful bone infarction is frequent in people with sickle-cell disease. According to Thaddeus Kelly (1997), such infarctions are the most frequent cause of absenteeism attributable to sickle-cell disease.

WHAT NEEDS DO PEOPLE WITH IT HAVE?

Frequent absences from school or work are common with sickle-cell anemia; people may spend weeks at a time in the hospital, heavily medicated, often with Demerol and methadone. These recurrent painful episodes are the number one disabling feature of sickle-cell anemia because they interfere with education, work, and independent living.

Good health care is probably the biggest need people with sickle-cell anemia have. These people must avoid dehydration, cold, and physical overexertion. According to Singhal, Davies, Wierenga, Thomas, and Serjeant (1997), avoidance of physical activity is likely a compensatory mechanism in children who have sickle-cell disease. Although such children seem to eat as much and as well as other children, "[t]he low weight, low height-for-age, delayed skeletal maturation, and retarded puberty in children with homozygous sickle cell disease are consistent with chronic malnutrition" (p. 386). In other words, these children, despite adequate diet, function as if they lack energy.

WHAT SPECIAL-EDUCATION AND RELATED SERVICES MAY HELP?

Because sickle-cell disease so often leads to absenteeism and even hospitalization, educators, employers, and others need to accommodate the individual's need to be permitted to make up for lost time. In school and in work, this may take the form of a "contract" under terms of which the individual agrees to perform certain work over a rather extended period of time. Whether that work is done evenly over time or sporadically as necessitated by illness would be essentially irrelevant.

WHAT OTHER INTERVENTIONS CAN BE EFFECTIVE?

Most states screen newborns for sickle-cell disease. If the disease is found, oral penicillin is given immediately and continues to be administered at least until the child is 5 years of age and often throughout the school years (Kelly, 1997). Vaccinations against hepatitis B and other diseases should be administered between 2 months and 2 years of age.

Hydroxyurea (HU), an oral chemotherapeutic drug that stimulates the body to make more hemoglobin, can reduce the frequency and severity of sickle-cell crises by as much as 50% (National Heart, Lung, and Blood Institute, 1995). Sold in the United States under the name "Droxia" by Bristol-Myers Squibb, hydroxyurea was approved by the Food and Drug Administration (FDA) in March 1998 for use with people who have sickle-cell anemia. Research suggests that it can be effective in helping patients to deal with pain, although its long-term effects in children remain unknown (Ballas, 1997; deMontalembert, Belloy, Bernaudin, Gouraud, Capdeville, Mardini, Philippe, Jais, Bardakdjian, Ducrocq, Maier-Redelsperger, Elion, Labie, & Girot, 1997). People on hydroxyurea should have blood tests every 2 weeks to assure that their blood count is not depressed.

Bone marrow transplantation is another possible intervention. Walters (1966) found that transplantation of bone marrow from matched siblings can cure people of sickle-cell anemia, although side effects, including infertility and heightened risk of other conditions, remain severe. For that reason, the researchers recommended the procedure only for individuals who otherwise would have poor prognoses. Hydroxyurea, unlike transplantation, can be discontinued and has short-term and reversible side effects.

WHAT ASSISTIVE TECHNOLOGIES AND SERVICES CAN HELP?

No assistive technology devices as such are required in the case of sickle-cell disease, although products that reduce the individual's need for physical exertion do help in preventing sickle-cell crises. An example of a non-technological aid would be a teacher's allowing someone the time necessary to walk, rather than run, from class to class.

WHAT ARE THE PROSPECTS FOR POSTSECONDARY EDUCATION?

In general, sickle-cell disease should not limit someone's opportunities in college. This is because instructors are accustomed to rescheduling exams for students who miss tests and allowing papers to be handed in early or late because of extenuating circumstances. Nuland (1997) explained that Kip Penn's most vexing moments with the condition occurred during the college years when he had to visit emergency rooms as often as three times a month, with each crisis lasting 3 to 4 days. If a student who has sickle-cell disease and experiences this kind of episode were to encounter resistance from a particular instructor, it may help to call upon the college's special-services staff to explain the need to the instructor.

WHAT ARE THE EMPLOYMENT PROSPECTS?

People with sickle-cell anemia can work, and many do, but they must exercise precautions, such as avoiding extremes of heat and cold as well as too much physical exercise (Sickle Cell Disease Association of America, 1997).

WHAT ARE THE PROSPECTS FOR INDEPENDENT LIVING?

People with sickle-cell disease usually can live independently. However, life expectancies are shorter than normal because of the susceptibility to infection.

Questions for Reflection and Discussion

1. What are the three prongs of the definition of *disability* in the Americans with Disabilities Act?

2. Why is it important for pregnant women who have AIDS to take AZT?

3. What is respite care? For people with which disabilities discussed in this chapter do you think it could be important?

4. Contrast asthma to cystic fibrosis.

5. Why is there so much optimism now among cancer specialists?

6. Cardiac conditions are common corollaries of what disabilities discussed in this chapter?

7. People with which two disabilities discussed in this chapter expend more energy per unit of activity than do other people?

8. Diabetes may cause which of the disabilities discussed in this chapter?

9. What is the significance of *Gilday v. Mecosta County* (1997) for individuals who have medication-controlled conditions?

10. One condition reviewed in this chapter is most common among blacks; another among whites. Which is which?

Where is additional information available?

American Academy of Otolaryngic Allergy
8455 Colesville Road, #743
Silver Spring, MD 20910.
E-mail: AAOA@aol.com

American College of Allergy & Immunology
85 West Algonquin Road, #550
Arlington Heights, IL 60005
1-708-427-1200

American Diabetes Association
1660 Duke Street
Alexandria, VA 22314
1-800-232-3472
1-703-549-1500
www.diabetes.org.

American Medical Association
515 North State Street
Chicago, IL 60610
1-312-464-5000
www.ama-assn.org

Association for the Care of Children's Health
7910 Woodmont Avenue, #300
Bethesda, MD 20814
1-301-654-6549
www.acch.org

Center for Research on Women with Disabilities
Department of Physical Medicine
and Rehabilitation
Baylor University College of Medicine
3440 Richmond Avenue, Suite B
Houston, TX 77046
1-713-960-0505

Cystic Fibrosis Foundation
6931 Arlington Road
Bethesda, MD 20814
1-800-FIGHT-CF
1-301-951-4422
E-mail: info@cff.org
www.cff.org

Cystic Fibrosis Research Inc.
560 San Antonio Road, #103
Palo Alto, CA 94306-4349
1-650-326-1038
E-mail: cfri@ix.netcom.com
www.cfri.org

Diabetic Research Foundation
120 Wall Street
New York, NY 10005-4001

The Family Village
Waisman Center
University of Wisconsin at Madison
1500 Highland Avenue
Madison, WI 53705-2280
www.familyvillage.wisc.edu

Juvenile Diabetes Foundation International
Diabetes Research Foundation
120 Wall Street
New York, NY 10005-4001
1-800-JDF-CURE
www.jdfcure.com

InterAmerican Heart Foundation
7272 Greenville Avenue
Dallas, TX 75231-4596
1-972-706-1218
www.interamericanheart.org

National AIDS Clearinghouse
P.O. Box 6003
Rockville, MD 20849-6003
1-800-458-5231

National Association of Protection
and Advocacy Systems
900 Second Street, N.E., Suite 1401
Washington, DC 20002
1-202-408-9514
E-mail: hn4537@handsnet.org

National Cancer Institute
Office of Cancer Communications
31 Center Drive, MSC 2580
Bethesda, MD 20892-2580
1-800-4-CANCER
www.icic.nci.nih.gov

National Center for Child Abuse and Neglect
c/o Clearinghouse on Child Abuse
and Neglect Information
P.O. Box 1182
Washington, DC 20013
1-800-394-3366
E-mail: nccanch@calib.com or prevent@calib.com
www.calib.com/nccanch

National Childhood Cancer Foundation
440 East Huntington Drive, Suite 300
P.O. Box 60012
Arcadia, CA 91066-6012
1-800-458-6223

National Coalition on Abuse and Disability
P.O. Box "T"
Culver City, CA 90230-3366
1-310-391-2420

National Organization for Rare Disorders
P.O. Box 8923
New Fairfield, CT 06812-8923
1-800-999-6673
1-203-746-6518
www.nord-rdb.copm/~orphan

National Organization on Fetal Alcohol Syndrome
1819 H Street, Suite 750
Washington, DC 20006
1-800-66-NOFAS
www.nofas.org

National Pediatric HIV Resource Center
15 South Ninth Street
Newark, NJ 07017
1-800-362-0071

National Resource Center for Respite
and Crisis Care Services
Chapel Hill Training-Outreach Project
800 Eastowne Drive, Suite 105
Chapel Hill, NC 27514
1-800-473-1727
www.chtop.com/archbroc.htm

Sickle Cell Disease Association of America
200 Corporate Point, #495
Culver City, CA 90230-7633
1-800-421-8453

SCDAA Educational Program
220 Milam Street, #9
Shreveport, LA 71103
1-318-226-8975

Totally Kids Specialty Healthcare
1720 Mountain View Avenue
Loma Linda, CA 92354
1-909-796-6915

10

SECONDARY CONDITIONS: COGNITIVE, VISION, AND HEARING

This chapter surveys three kinds of conditions that frequently accompany physical or health disabilities. In order, they are (1) cognitive impairments (attention deficit disorders, learning disabilities, and mental retardation), (2) vision impairments (including blindness), and (3) hearing impairments (including deafness). These disabilities are important in their own right. They are called secondary conditions in this text because they often appear with some of the physical and health disabilities described in earlier chapters. The resources for further information and the questions for reflection/discussion for all three areas appear at chapter's end.

Cognitive Impairments (Attention Deficits, Learning Disabilities, and Mental Retardation)

My former student Claudia Gisonda has told me many stories about how learning disabilities complicate her life. Her husband does the food shopping because she becomes so overwhelmed with all the information coming at her in a supermarket that she even forgets that she has her children with her. For similar reasons, she really disliked Netscape Navigator the first several times she used it to surf the Net: There was just too much information and too many choices on the screen. As is often the case (some learning disabilities have a genetic component), Claudia's son also has learning disabilities, plus he has attention deficit hyperactivity disorder (ADHD). Claudia finds him to be impulsive and often defiant; she hopes that much of this is due to his age (he is a teenager) rather than to his conditions.

WHAT ARE THEY?

To learn, we must first *attend* to information. We notice sights and sounds in our environment, and often we pick out specific aspects (e.g., color, size, pitch) that capture our interest or that we consider to be relevant. We might, for example, listen for the voice of a child playing outside or look for a taxicab. Other sights and sounds we ignore, often because we have become habituated to them (e.g., the sight of many people hurrying along the sidewalk in the city, the sound of crickets in the country).

In **attention deficit disorder (ADD),** people do not take in the same information that others do. Children, youth, and adults who have ADD *do* attend to stimuli but often not to what the rest of us consider to be the relevant ones (e.g., they may feel overwhelmed by the sight of thousands of people rushing by or by the sound of crickets). Thus, they may not attend to the child's voice or to the approaching taxicab. If these people also are hyperactive, they may have **attention deficit hyperactivity disorder (ADHD).** Individuals with ADHD often are so preoccupied with physical activity that they fail to attend to academic or work-related information.

ADD, with or without hyperactivity, is controversial because it seems to be so prevalent. As with learning disabilities (discussed later), diagnosis largely is a matter of testing the child for other conditions or problems. No one test exists for ADD or ADHD. The *Diagnostic and Statistical Manual of Mental Disorders-IV (DSM-IV)* (American Psychiatric Association, 1994) recognizes three kinds of disorders: ADD, hyperactivity/impulsivity, and a combined ADHD. The *DSM-IV* looks for symptoms to appear prior to age 6 or 7.

If information is in fact attended to, the next stage in cognition is that of *perception.* When we perceive sights or sounds, we make sense of them. That is, we interpret them in terms that are meaningful to us. We may hear two people speaking in a foreign language, but because we do not know that language, we do not perceive what they are saying: What is said holds no meaning for us. This is true of many things young children hear, such as when adults converse about inflation or politics. In some instances, however, the brain itself seems to mess up the message. This is what's known as **learning disability (LD).** Thus, words on a page may seem to be reversed or even to float across the page. In the case of sounds, the individual may wonder: *Did I just hear bait or mate, or was it paste?* Learning disabilities often affect metacognition, the ability to understand one's own thinking processes and adjust them so as to do better in school or at work.

Another way of saying the same thing is to observe that much of learning disability is a problem in handling phonology, that is, the sounds of language as they are represented on the printed page. Sally Shaywitz of the Yale School of Medicine and her colleagues (1998), using functional magnetic resonance imaging, examined the brains of people with and without dyslexia, an important learning disability, They found real differences in the parts of the brain that people with dyslexia activate when performing phonological tasks from the brain sections that people without dyslexia activate when doing these

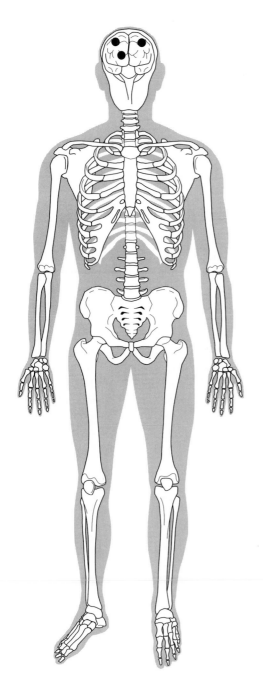

sound-based assignments. Apparently, then, dyslexia (and probably other learning disabilities as well) seems to have a neurological component; this component is specific to the mapping of sounds onto printed words.

Mental retardation (MR) is significantly subaverage intelligence (2 or more standard deviations below the mean, or an IQ lower than 70) together with behavior that is characteristic of younger persons. It occurs during the developmental years (prior to age 18). If a traumatic brain injury or other incident produces retardation after the age of 18, a term other than mental retardation (i.e., brain-injured) is used.

Attention deficits appear to emerge from neurological problems that lead to chemical imbalances that affect attention (Lerner et al., 1995). Learning disabilities also are presumed to be caused by neurological deficits. That is, the problem is not in one's ability to hear or to see but rather in the brain's ability to make sense of what is heard or seen. People with LD may have problems separating "signal" from "field" or the words of interest from surrounding words, images, or pictures. In the case of auditory-based LD, the difficulty may be in distinguishing between the voice of a teacher, boss, or spouse and background sounds. (This also is called "figure-ground segregation.") Mental retardation is a general lowering of intellectual functioning that manifests itself across the board in all kinds of activities.

None of these are conditions that people grow out of. That is, these are permanent disabilities. Many people do, however, learn to compensate, and others benefit from environmental changes, including information in multiple modalities and steps to reduce ambient stimuli. Intensive early intervention can ameliorate much mental retardation.

WHAT CAUSES THEM? CAN THEY BE PREVENTED? IF SO, HOW?

Attention deficits, learning disabilities, and mental retardation may be inherited. Most of these conditions seem to have genetic components, as was illustrated with Claudia Gisonda and her son. I have met many adults with ADD/ADHD or learning disabilities whose children have somewhat different forms of the same conditions, as was the case, again, with Claudia. Also thought to cause at least some of these disorders is the use of alcohol, particularly when a women drinks heavily throughout pregnancy. Maternal use of other drugs during pregnancy may also account for some instances of these conditions (Miller, 1997). Exposure to lead is recognized as a cause of LD and of mental retardation. Prematurity or low birth weight appears to be associated with these three kinds of cognitive limitations. Many instances, however, are of unknown origin.

As for prevention, other than advising women to avoid alcohol and illicit drugs during pregnancy and monitoring lead levels in homes, it is not clear how these conditions can be prevented. No cure for ADHD has been found. The treatment most substantiated by research is the use of stimulant medications such as Ritalin, Dexedrine, and Cylert. Applied behavior analysis often is recommended first before stimulants are tried. Generally, medication is weaned after self-control is learned. Good prenatal medical care, adequate nutrition, and sufficient intellectual stimulation during early childhood may prevent many cases of mental retardation.

HOW PREVALENT ARE THEY? WHAT IS THE INCIDENCE?

Attention deficits appear to be very common, affecting as many as 3% to 5% of all school-age children and youth (Lerner, Lowenthal, & Lerner, 1995). We do not have good statistics on adults with attention deficits. Learning disabilities are the most common of all conditions among school-age children, accounting for 51% of all children aged 6–21 who had any disability at all, with about 2.6 million children being identified with this disability during the 1995–1996 school year (U.S. Department of Education, 1997). LD is also frequently reported among children under school age but in much smaller numbers. Some 109,000 children from birth to 6 years of age, or about 13% of children in that age range who have any disability at all, were identified as having LD (Bowe, 1995c). About 5 million Americans of all ages have mental retardation.

WHAT EFFECTS DO THEY HAVE?

Attention deficits affect learning by limiting the person's ability to acquire needed information. When hyperactivity is part of the equation, the individual may also be restricted from pursuing gainful activity, particularly in jobs

Cognitive disabilities in K-12 students

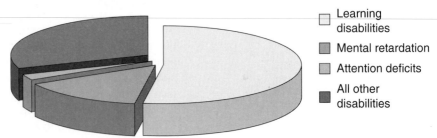

Learning disabilities

Mental retardation

Attention deficits

All other disabilities

Figure 10.1
Population Estimates: Cognitive Limitations As Compared to Other Disabilities Among School-age Children and Youth

Source: U.S. Department of Education (1997)

that require sustained attention to specific information. When people with ADHD are predominantly attention-deficit, they literally may not register sensory input; the condition seems to make them unavailable for learning. By contrast, persons who are predominantly hyperactive/impulsive display low frustration tolerance, frequent outbursts or aggressive behavior, unpredictability, and short attention spans. Individuals with the combined condition (ADHD) exhibit several of these effects.

Learning disabilities affect acquisition and use of listening, speaking, reading, writing, reasoning, or mathematical abilities. People may be unable to process information coming in to more than one part of the brain at one time. Claudia Gisonda, for example, tells her children not to talk to her until she has finished the dishes. She's unable to process auditory stimuli while she is also attending to tactual and visual information.

Mental retardation greatly affects short-term memory; it is very hard for many mentally retarded individuals to master new material. Once they do, however, they tend to remember it; that is, their long-term memory is comparatively good.

WHAT SECONDARY CONDITIONS ARE COMMON?

People with epilepsy who take medication may develop ADHD as a side effect of the medication (sedatives or anticonvulsant) they take to control seizures (Ariel, 1992). In addition, ADHD sometimes results from traumatic brain injuries (TBI).

Learning disabilities often accompany cerebral palsy, spina bifida, TBI, epilepsy, and fetal alcohol syndrome, as indicated in the earlier chapters that described those conditions. Although learning disabilities differ from attention deficits, some people have both conditions.

Mental retardation is a common secondary condition to cerebral palsy. It can also be caused by hydrocephalus, a condition often found with spina bifida.

WHAT NEEDS DO PEOPLE WITH THEM HAVE?

Individuals with attention deficits need assistance from others in identifying what information is worth attending to and what is not. Over time, they should internalize these priorities so as to train themselves to attend to important stimuli and to disregard competing stimuli. Similarly, those who are hyperactive first need external reinforcers to stay on task and later need to internalize those reinforcers.

People with learning disabilities also need external help for a time, after which they should develop their own coping strategies. Some people with learning disabilities, for example, have great difficulty dialing phone numbers. One solution is to get a rotary phone, which seems to be much easier for many of these individuals to use than touch-tone phones.

Many individuals with mental retardation need considerable assistance from others throughout the day in virtually all of their daily activities. Others, however, can learn to lead relatively independent lives and to assume responsibility for much of what they do, including self-care. Some hold down paying jobs, commute independently between work and home, and manage their own rooms or apartments.

WHAT SPECIAL-EDUCATION AND RELATED SERVICES MAY HELP?

In the case of attention deficits, teachers, counselors, and others can call attention to specific kinds of information ("Notice the color here"), thus helping people with ADD or ADHD to attend to the "relevant" information. Teachers can also train children and youth with attention deficits to "force themselves" to attend to some stimuli and to ignore others.

The work of Shaywitz and her colleagues (1998) supports the use of direct instruction in phonics, that is, of teaching phonological awareness and decoding skills, with people who have dyslexia. Other interventions for people with LD include multimedia, computer-based programs. With dyslexia, listening to information rather than (or in addition to) reading it can help. Research suggests that when people listen to computer speech synthesis, they understand better than they do the same sounds in human speech. This is because the computer can artificially stretch out (slow down) the similar sounding letters, making it possible for children with LD to distinguish between, say, the *b* and *d* sounds.

The computer may be programmed to present synthesized speech at variable rates of speed. Initially, a slow rate might be selected so that the child can understand speech. Over time, however, it is important to speed up the rate so that eventually it approximates that of conversation. Computers and the programs they run are infinitely patient; they will run for any length of time, repeating as necessary. Today's programs also often are interactive; they require children to make responses, and the programs in turn react to the answers given. This makes for individualization of instruction to an extent only imaginable with real-world teachers and therapists.

More generally, learning disabilities seem often to be problems in handling rapidly changing information. Thus, teachers should slow down in the classroom and repeat information frequently. Claudia Gisonda told me that she had to decide between listening to my lecture and taking notes on what I said and looking at what I wrote on the blackboard and taking notes on that: She could not do both simultaneously.

The same strategy of slowing down and repeating works with some people who have ADD or ADHD. In that case, you are giving the individual more opportunities to attend to information you regard as important.

Many of these techniques also work with people who have mental retardation. Breaking activities down into small parts (task analysis), repetition, multisensory modes of input, and modeling desired behavior are a few approaches that can be very helpful with people who are mentally retarded.

Helpful related services include speech and language pathology, which can include use of sensitive diagnostic instruments, individualized treatment protocols, and suggestions both for professionals (teachers, counselors, et al.) and for individuals themselves.

WHAT OTHER INTERVENTIONS CAN BE EFFECTIVE?

Early intervention seems to help with all three of these cognitive limitations. The most valuable kinds of intervention appear to be environmental stimulation, good nutrition, and health care, which appear actually to alter the brain's chemistry, particularly with respect to neural circuitry and synaptic connections (Hallet & Proctor, 1996).

Some drugs, notably Ritalin, have been shown to be effective in helping children with ADD/ADHD to attend to academic tasks. Dexedrine is another drug often prescribed for ADD/ADHD. These medications may have side effects such as weight loss, insomnia, and increased blood pressure. For these reasons, medication should be used only after behavioral interventions have been tried and found not to be sufficiently effective. Teachers, counselors, supervisors, and others can help by looking for positive behavior and attending to it when they find it. (Applied behavior analysis was discussed in chapter 4.)

WHAT ASSISTIVE TECHNOLOGIES AND SERVICES CAN HELP?

Some individuals with learning disabilities benefit greatly from being able to listen to material—whether on a personal computer through a speech synthesizer or on a tape recorder or from a teacher or teacher's aide—rather than having to read it. Others, with different kinds of learning disabilities, do better reading than they do listening. In both cases, having information available in multimodal formats is very helpful. People with mental retardation often learn better by seeing (perhaps on a computer program) someone else do what they are expected to do and then having opportunities to practice that behavior. They also tend to benefit from listening to information more than they do from reading it.

WHAT ARE THE PROSPECTS FOR POSTSECONDARY EDUCATION?

These are excellent. Virtually every college and university in the nation must practice nondiscrimination in admissions, teaching, testing, and advancing students. In addition, many colleges and universities have special-services coordinators that provide extensive support for students with learning disabilities or attention deficits. Vocational or trade schools are more appropriate for individuals with mental retardation; they, too, must practice nondiscrimination.

WHAT ARE THE EMPLOYMENT PROSPECTS?

Individuals with learning disabilities or attention deficits who acquire skills in compensating for their limitations will find that their prospects for gainful employment are very good. Increasingly, people with mental retardation are qualifying for, getting, and keeping jobs, particularly jobs calling for repeated performance of a limited set of behaviors, such as custodial services. Virtually every American employer of 20 or more workers must practice nondiscrimination on the basis of disability in interviewing, testing, hiring, placing, assigning, and advancing people in employment.

WHAT ARE THE PROSPECTS FOR INDEPENDENT LIVING?

Individuals with ADD or ADHD sometimes have difficulties in their everyday lives because they do not spend enough time at any given task to complete it satisfactorily. Taken to an extreme, these difficulties could make independent living a real challenge. In some cases, ADD or ADHD can lead to a chaotic life. To illustrate: One individual I know moved from apartment to apartment five times within one year. Most people with mental retardation need at least occasional monitoring and supervision to ensure that they remember to do everything that is important (e.g., paying the rent on time).

Vision Impairment (Blindness and Low Vision)

Eunice Fiorito (1930–) was the first person I got to know well who was blind. By any measure, Eunice is a remarkable person. She learned Braille in 2 weeks. I still cannot comprehend that. Her first job paid 5 cents an hour. That was at a time when blindness was considered to be an insurmountable barrier to employment. From there, she went on to earn a master's degree in social work, and after moving from Chicago to New York City, she began what eventually became a 35-year career of tilting at windmills. She wanted to change the world—and by enlisting the help of thousands of people with disabilities, she did. So impressive was her work that I wrote a short biography of her (Bowe, 1981).

Eunice recently retired after a long career in the U.S. Department of Education, in Washington, D.C. Only in her last few years of work did she benefit from today's technologies that allow someone who is blind to read and write independently with no help from a sighted person. Anyone who watched Eunice Fiorito move mountains despite not having these technologies available could only wonder what she could have accomplished with today's remarkable technologies.

WHAT IS IT?

Blindness is 20/200 vision or tunnel vision where central vision subtends at an angle of 20% or less as measured with corrective lenses. Low vision is

Eunice Fiorito was one of the first people, anywhere in the world, to recognize that the environment is what makes the difference between disabilities and handicaps. When the environment is accessible, people with disabilities can lead fulfilling and rewarding lives; when it is not, however, community barriers limit what these people can do.

20/70 vision, or worse, to 20/200 vision. Normal vision is expressed as 20/20, meaning that the individual standing 20 feet from a chart correctly identifies the letters/symbols the chart displays. Thus, someone with 20/70 vision can see symbols on a Snellen chart at 20 feet that a person with unimpaired vision could see at 70 feet.

The more useful question in education is whether the individual has enough residual vision (functional vision) to be able to use the eyes to learn or whether other senses (notably the ears and the fingers) must be used. Although most blind people do have residual vision, they tend to learn better through their ears and fingers; low-vision people, by contrast, tend to learn better through their eyes. For an extended discussion of these issues, see Teplin (1995).

WHAT CAUSES IT? CAN IT BE PREVENTED? IF SO, HOW?

The causes of vision loss in children often are not known. The most common known cause of blindness in infants continues to be retinopathy of prematurity (ROP), once known as retrolental fibroplasia. ROP is associated with prematurity, affecting about 4% of low birth weight (less than 1000 g) infants

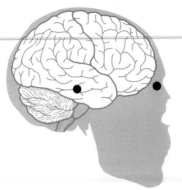

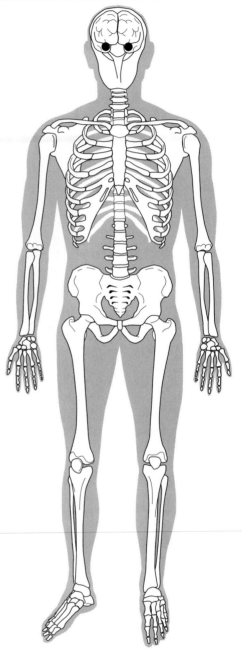

(Glass, 1993). The condition once occurred when premature infants were placed into incubators and given excessive amounts of oxygen. With careful monitoring of oxygen levels, ROP all but disappeared in the late 1960s and 1970s. Now, however, Deitz and Ferrell (1993) have reported, increasing use of newborn life support systems, including 24-hour bright light in the neonatal intensive care unit (NICU), has led to a "new epidemic" of ROP. Glass (1993) commented that ROP now is known to be associated with other predisposing factors, including not only prematurity but also hypoxia. (In hypoxia, body tissues lack sufficient oxygen, usually because of a reduction in the oxygen-carrying capacity of blood.) As more and more babies survive low birth weight and prematurity, many more potentially are at risk for ROP.

Other important known causes of blindness are inheritance and pre-, peri- and postnatal illnesses and accidents that also may cause cerebral palsy, retardation, and other disabilities. Such illnesses and accidents tend to occur prior to age 1, if they happen at all. Diabetes is a major cause of blindness but usually in adulthood rather than in childhood.

HOW PREVALENT IS IT? WHAT IS THE INCIDENCE?

Blindness and vision impairment are relatively rare among children and youth. Only about 25,000 elementary and secondary students in the United States are blind or have low vision (U.S. Department of Education, 1997). Overall, about 1 child per 1,000 in the school-age population is blind or has low vision. Blindness and low vision are not quite half as common as are deafness and hearing loss in the K–12 population. Looking at the entire age range, about 500,000 Americans are blind or have low vision, of whom some 70% are over the age of 65. Among older Americans, the incidence is about 12,000 new cases annually. About 6 million Americans of all ages have low vision (Packer & Kirchner, 1997).

WHAT EFFECTS CAN IT HAVE?

The effects of blindness or low vision on children vary according to age at onset. A congenital condition is likely to cause greater developmental delay than is a later occurring loss. Children who once had good vision have formed mental images of themselves and of their environments. Children who were born blind, by contrast, lack these firsthand mental images and must acquire substitute versions by other means.

Young children who are blind but who have no other major limitations usually will acquire communication competence by the time they enter school. During the early childhood years, however, many are delayed in communication development. With appropriate parental, early-intervention, and special-education assistance, such delays often are temporary. Parents also may restrain the child who is blind from exploratory and independent play, fearing for the child's safety. Such **experiential deprivation** is a major factor in developmental delays among children who are blind.

WHAT SECONDARY CONDITIONS ARE COMMON?

Today's blind or low-vision child is more likely than were children with blindness in the past to have other disabilities. Cerebral palsy is a common accompanying condition. That is not surprising, since illnesses producing high fevers may damage the optic nerve and motor-control areas in the brain. Vision impairment in children with cerebral palsy tends to be of the low-vision variety rather than blindness. As noted in earlier chapters, muscular dystrophy sometimes leads to vision problems because of weakness in eye muscles. Arthritis, too, sometimes is accompanied by eye disease. Of course,

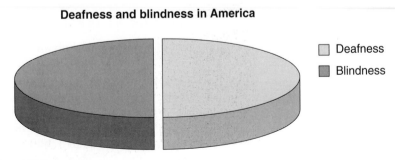

Deafness and blindness in America

☐ Deafness
■ Blindness

Figure 10.2
Population Estimates: Deafness As Compared to Blindness

diabetes is the most common cause of visual impairment and so is a very frequent secondary condition.

WHAT NEEDS TO PEOPLE WITH IT HAVE?

Helen Keller, who was both deaf and blind, was fond of saying that "blindness comes between people and things, and deafness comes between people and people." Updating her insights to today's world, the more significant impact of blindness today is that it comes between people and information. Thus, the greatest need today of people with blindness or low vision is for *appropriate media,* that is, for information in a form they can use. Teachers who prepare handouts on their personal computers, for example, can give the blind child a disk with that handout. The child can then listen to a speech synthesizer speak out loud the material on the disk. Anyone lecturing or speaking to a group should articulate (say out loud) whatever he or she writes on a blackboard or points to on an overhead.

WHAT SPECIAL-EDUCATION AND RELATED SERVICES MAY HELP?

For children diagnosed as blind or having low vision, perhaps the most urgent tasks of educators are to facilitate the development of independent mobility and tactual exploration skills and to introduce the use of modern assistive technology. Helping with this work are **orientation and mobility specialists.** These related-services personnel assist blind and low-vision students to make maximum use of residual vision, to get around the school and neighborhood independently, and to learn through the senses of hearing and touch. If these support services are provided, most blind or low-vision children and youth can be educated in regular public schools or colleges (U.S. Department of Education, 1997, Table AB2).

An excellent overview of orientation and mobility services is offered by Blasch, Wiener, and Welsh (1997), whose 800-page text discusses what we know about perception and control of locomotion, adaptive technologies, and strategies of teaching orientation and mobility skills to people who are blind or have low vision.

WHAT OTHER INTERVENTIONS CAN BE EFFECTIVE?

Assuming that orientation and mobility training has been provided, children who are blind or have low vision should be encouraged to be as independent and self-reliant as possible. In America today, most sighted individuals are only too willing to help blind or low-vision people; such "help" can make these persons needlessly passive and dependent. Teachers, counselors, and parents should insist that the child with blindness or low vision perform all tasks that are expected of sighted children. Blindness experts Elton Moore, Bill Graves, and Jeanne Patterson offer a wealth of other suggestions in their 1997 text *Foundations of Rehabilitation Counseling With Persons Who Are Blind or Visually Impaired.*

WHAT ASSISTIVE TECHNOLOGIES AND SERVICES CAN HELP?

Technology is tremendously important for many children with blindness or low vision. In years past, before modern devices emerged, blind students such as Eunice Fiorito had to depend on sighted volunteers who painstakingly converted printed texts to braille or to speech on a tape recorder. Today, **scanners with optical character recognition** (that is, machines that "read") do the same conversion in minutes with no intervention by sighted persons required. Even easier is **speech synthesis,** an inexpensive technology that "talks"—speaking aloud virtually anything that is on a computer disk, whether hard or floppy. Today's speech synthesis has a natural-sounding rhythm, at least compared to the earlier flat-pitched, monotone voice that pronounced everything in the same machine-sounding way. The user can select from among several voices; typical choices include the voice of a man, a woman, or a child as well as a voice with a Spanish accent.

Television and other video programming can be made accessible to viewers who are blind or have low vision by means of video description. In this technique, brief spoken descriptions of on-screen action are inserted into the video at times when no actors are speaking. In "closed" description, the narration is transmitted over the second audio program (SAP) feature of stereo televisions. The major proponent of closed descriptions is Descriptive Video Service®, pioneered by WGBH Educational Foundation in Boston. "Open" description, by contrast, provides the narration for all viewers; the method is used by Narrative Television Network (NTN) of Tulsa, Oklahoma (Packer & Kirchner, 1997).

Another technology with potentially great value for individuals who are blind or have low vision is global positioning system (GPS) technology. Magellan Systems offers a $99.99 Pioneer, a 6-inch by 2-inch by 1-inch box that receives GPS signals that are emitted by 12 orbiting satellites. The technology runs for 24 hours on two AA batteries. Now all we need is an inexpensive voice chip so that it speaks out precisely where the user is, and it will really help a lot of blind and low-vision travelers. (Contact Megellan Systems, 960 Overland Court, San Dimas, CA 92117; 1-909-394-5000; www.magellangps.com.)

WHAT ARE THE PROSPECTS FOR POSTSECONDARY EDUCATION?

Blind and low-vision persons have the highest rate of college attendance of people in any category of special education (U.S. Department of Education, 1997). Virtually every college and university in the United States is required by the Americans with Disabilities Act (ADA) and by Section 504 of the 1973 Rehabilitation Act to provide appropriate media for blind or low-vision students. In addition, most state vocational rehabilitation agencies offer financial assistance for college attendance.

WHAT ARE THE EMPLOYMENT PROSPECTS?

Individuals who are blind or have low vision can work in virtually any job, provided that they have the necessary education and training *and* that the required technology is supplied, usually by the employer. The Americans with Disabilities Act (ADA) requires many employers of 15 or more workers to offer reasonable accommodations to qualified applicants and employees who have disabilities. For a blind person, this may include a PC equipped with speech synthesis and other assistive technology devices and software.

Although the potential is bright, the reality is quite different. Most adults who are blind do not work at full-time jobs. This is largely due to three factors. First, most people who are blind or have low vision lost their sight at an age when they were already retired or were contemplating retirement; many feel that coping with late-onset blindness is challenge enough and prefer not to also attempt employment. Second, many lack the education they need to qualify for information jobs, that is, the kinds of jobs that best take advantage of today's technologies. Finally, some persons who are blind or have low vision qualify for government benefits that are quite generous compared with those that are available to people with other disabilities and believe that they can do better with entitlements than they could by working.

WHAT ARE THE PROSPECTS FOR INDEPENDENT LIVING?

Vision impairment should not limit someone's ability to live independently. With a minimum amount of help from a sighted person, most people with blindness or low vision quickly learn how to arrange clothing in closets and bureaus so that color coordination is easy to achieve, how to fold and sort paper money so as to differentiate dollar bills from 5-dollar and 10-dollar bills, and how to safely operate kitchen and other household appliances.

Hearing Impairment (Deafness and Hearing Loss)

I became deaf early in life when a sustained temperature well above 100 resulted in damage to my inner ears and to my VIIIth nerve (auditory nerve). I have no conscious memory of being a hearing person. The biggest effect deafness had during my childhood was on my acquisition of language. I needed to know English, and know it well, to learn everything else in school. It was not until I entered ninth grade that I mastered the language well enough to use it to acquire knowledge in academic subjects. Until that time, I struggled mightily to pass from year to year in the Lewisburg, Pennsylvania, public schools.

Today, partly because I know the language so well and partly because of new technologies, deafness is more of an irritant for me than a hindrance. I can communicate with virtually anyone today, using E-mail, fax, and other technologies or with the assistance of an interpreter. With these aids, I can work full-time as a university professor and author. Many television programs and cable movies are captioned, as are a few theatrical movies. What I still cannot do is to have a relaxing, informal conversation with most hearing people; interpersonal communication with such persons demands my full, undivided attention.

WHAT IS IT?

Hearing impairment comes in two basic forms. One is *conductive* hearing loss, which usually involves the middle ear. Generally caused by ear infections, it produces mild to moderate loss of hearing that is often correctable by surgery. The other form is *sensorineural* in nature, so called because it involves nerves. In some instances of sensorineural hearing loss, high temperatures such as those that accompany sustained fevers damage or destroy the small hair cells of the inner ear, including the cochlea. In others, the VIIIth nerve is damaged by oxygen deprivation (as in cerebral palsy), or it never forms properly because of genetic factors. In some cases, damage to both the inner ear and the VIIIth nerve occurs. Sensorineural hearing impairment usually is severe to profound and generally is not medically treatable.

The difference between mild/moderate and severe/profound hearing loss is significant. Individuals with milder forms of hearing impairment usually can hear and understand speech, although they may have difficulty doing so without the assistance of a hearing aid or lipreading (speechreading). These people are sometimes called "hard-of-hearing." Individuals who have hearing loss secondary to cerebral palsy or Down syndrome typically are hard-of-hearing. People with severe or profound hearing loss, by contrast, usually cannot understand speech through the ear alone, even with amplification. We use the term *deaf* to refer to these people.

WHAT CAUSES IT? CAN IT BE PREVENTED? IF SO, HOW?

Hearing loss is congenital (present at birth) or adventitious (occurring after birth). Some children inherit deafness or another hearing impairment, although well over 90% of all children who are deaf have parents who can both hear. The most common causes of hearing loss today are viruses or other agents triggering high body temperature, particularly congenital cytomegalovirus infection (CMV). With respect to genetics, hearing loss usually involves recessive genes; only if both parents have the same gene will some of their children be deaf. However, in some cases, the gene is dominant; in these instances, entire families (over many generations) will be deaf.

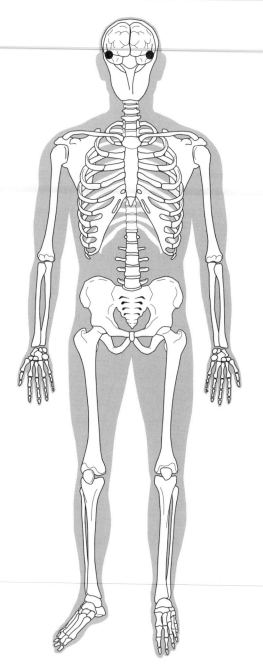

Impairments of hearing that make people hard-of-hearing sometimes can be prevented. Exposure to very loud noise for sustained periods of time is one example. People can avoid such experiences altogether, can limit them to short periods of time, or can wear protective devices.

HOW PREVALENT IS IT? WHAT IS THE INCIDENCE?

Hearing loss is rather uncommon in young children. About 30,000 school-age children and youth in the United States are deaf and need special education services. Another 35,000 K–12 students are sufficiently hard-of-hearing to need such services (U.S. Department of Education, 1997). The incidence of deafness or severe hearing loss among children under 18 is about 5,000 new cases annually. Hearing impairments become sizeable in number as people reach their 60s, 70s, or 80s. Overall, about one-half million Americans are deaf or severely hard-of-hearing, some two thirds of them over the age of 65. The incidence among older persons is about 20,000 new instances annually.

WHAT EFFECTS CAN IT HAVE?

The effects of deafness or other severe hearing impairment in children depend largely on *age at onset*. The earlier the age at onset of the hearing loss, the more significant the effects. Thus, a congenital loss interferes much more in education than does a loss of the same severity that occurs at age 5, and certainly one that happens after that age. This is because children's development of language, speech, and much incidental knowledge occurs principally through the ears during the early childhood years. The second important factor upon which the effects rest is the *degree of hearing loss*. Children who are hard-of-hearing can learn auditorially, although many will need amplification and training in lipreading. By contrast, children who are deaf usually will learn only through the eyes: They must depend upon sign language, finger spelling, and lipreading to understand conversational speech.

For children affected from early childhood, deafness is a major limitation with respect to education. It is a severe disability that requires significant special-education and related services. It also interferes with child-to-child communication. As a result, deafness or severe hearing loss has significant socialization effects. Lesser degrees of hearing loss generally have lesser effects on education. Those effects nonetheless can be important. Consider, for example, that a single word *is* (vs. *isn't*) can change the entire meaning of a teacher's statement.

WHAT SECONDARY CONDITIONS ARE COMMON?

About one out of every three children who are deaf has a secondary disability. Most common is cerebral palsy, although learning disabilities also are frequent. In many cases, the medical condition that caused the deafness also produces the other condition. Thus, oxygen deprivation prior to, during, or just after birth may lead both to cerebral palsy and to deafness. Some children who are deaf or hard-of-hearing also have learning disabilities, and some are mentally retarded. As noted in earlier chapters, some people with traumatic brain injuries have auditory processing problems; such problems, however, rarely rise to the level of constituting deafness.

WHAT NEEDS DO PEOPLE WITH IT HAVE?

Language is mastered by children during the early-childhood years—if hearing is intact. The major need of deaf children, accordingly, is for rapid and effective language development. Without early intervention and preschool special-education instruction in language, children who are deaf or severely hard-of-hearing will enter first grade knowing just a few words—and virtually no grammar, syntax, or other aspects of language. Children who are deaf who learn some language, notably American Sign Language, early in life are known to learn English much better and much more easily than do children who do not master any language before they begin their schooling (Bowe, 1988). Typically, a deaf person will reach high school unable to read above sixth- or seventh-grade level; this fact graphically illustrates how severe an educational disability deafness is.

Hearing aids amplify but also distort speech. It is important for educators, counselors, and others to realize that deaf or hard-of-hearing people do not usually regain anything like "normal" hearing simply by wearing a hearing aid. In addition, children using hearing aids may need visual input to understand conversational speech. For deaf children, substitute the word *will* for *may* in the above sentence.

Because children and youth who are deaf or hard-of-hearing are not just "learning machines" but are human beings, their personal and social development needs attention, too. This may mean providing these children with opportunities to interact with other children who also are deaf or hard-of-hearing, particularly those who sign. This is why the Individuals with Disabilities Education Act Amendments of 1997 (P.L. 105-17) require educators to "consider the [deaf or hard-of-hearing] child's language and communication needs, opportunities for direct communication with peers and professional personnel in the child's language and communication mode, academic level, and full range of needs, including opportunities for direct instruction in the child's language and communication mode" [§614 (d) (e) (3) (iv)].

WHAT SPECIAL-EDUCATION AND RELATED SERVICES MAY HELP?

Education for deaf children and youth is a specialized endeavor, so much so that most states require certification in teaching deaf children rather than a broader certification in special education. It is not enough just to provide a sign-language interpreter. Rather, the deaf child's needs in such areas as language, interpersonal communication, and social and emotional development may be so significant and so pervasive that a comprehensive package of services is necessary.

The child's Individualized Education Program (IEP) should include an explicit statement of the child's communication needs, including personal and parental preferences. Teachers should work closely with speech and language pathologists to carry out the needed steps in the IEP. Rosemary Kerrin (1996) suggested that collaboration between teacher and pathologist is the most effective approach. Such collaboration may include coteaching lessons in the classroom, alternating lessons taught first by one professional and then by the other, and invitation by the teacher to the pathologist to observe the performance of a hearing-impaired student in the special-education classroom. These approaches differ from the traditional pull-out model in which the student is removed from the classroom once or twice weekly for therapy.

The pathologist may suggest ways the teacher can improve in-class communication. Depending on the severity of the student's hearing loss, the pathologist may recommend (1) articulating clearly but without exaggerating lip movement; (2) speaking in a normal tone of voice (hearing aids and other amplification equipment make the voice sound louder, and the teacher need not raise his or her voice); (3) taking great care to write key ideas, especially new terms, on a blackboard or other visual aid; (4) using natural gestures and simple signs to augment vocal communication; and (5) avoiding teacher-to-student questions that can be answered yes or no; questions that can be answered only with a substantive response (e.g., "Does this image look like a heptagon or like a rectangle?") are much better because the student's answer reveals whether or not the student understood the question.

Speech and language pathology services often are needed by deaf and hard-of-hearing students. Pure-tone audiometry measures one kind of hearing. In this method, tones varying from very low in pitch to very high are presented to the child at graduated levels of sound volume. The child raises a hand to report hearing the sound. Results are expressed on an *audiogram*, a graphic display of hearing in terms of both pitch and volume. A better-ear average (BEA) can be calculated by taking the decibel (dB) levels of each of the three speech-range frequencies (500, 1000, 2000) for the left ear and dividing by 3, and doing the same for the right ear. The better (lower) average is the BEA. Generally, averages above 60 are of most concern because hearing loss at or above that level is unusual in humans unless there is inner-ear damage. Lesser degrees of hearing loss still are important. Studies have shown that children with hearing impairment as mild as 20 dB are limited in speech comprehension.

Speech and language pathologists can then determine the child's need for amplification, training in lipreading, or sign language. Options for communicating with children who are deaf include total communication, in which children use speechreading, residual hearing, finger spelling, and sign language together with gestures and facial expressions to communicate. Total communication generally adopts Signed English, because when speech and signs are used simultaneously it is necessary for the signs to track English word order. **American Sign Language (ASL),** a rich, expressive language, usually cannot be used in a total communication environment because it has its own grammar and syntax; it is very different from Signed English.

Finally, speech and language pathologists can offer intensive additional instruction in reading and writing. Such tutoring becomes more and more important as students move from elementary to secondary school: Students' academic success will be a direct function of their mastery of the written language.

WHAT OTHER INTERVENTIONS CAN BE EFFECTIVE?

Without question, early detection, followed by early intervention, is essential for all infants, toddlers, preschoolers, and students who are deaf or hard-of-hearing. In the 1990s, a method of identifying newborns with hearing loss spread throughout the United States. Beginning in Rhode Island, the transient evoked otacoustic emissions (TEOAE) test has been administered to babies even before they leave the hospital. Costs are just $25 per newborn.

One recent development is the adoption by the Centers for Disease Control and Prevention (CDC) of National Institutes of Health (NIH) guidelines for early detection of hearing loss (http://nlm.nih.gov/nih/cdc/www/92txt.html). Despite these efforts, our best estimates are that just 15% of babies born in the United States receive hearing tests and just 40% of those identified as having a hearing loss receive timely follow-up, in-depth assessments, and treatment. Experts hope that the new screening procedures will be adopted nationwide, leading to 100% testing of all newborns by 2000 (Short, 1997).

With so much mainstreaming taking place in K–12 schools and in colleges, interventions that facilitate extracurricular participation by deaf or hard-of-hearing students are becoming ever more important. At a school for deaf children, for example, an aspiring actor can probably get a role in the school play; a deaf child mainstreamed into a regular public school will find that task far more difficult. Accordingly, schools should explore ways for deaf and hard-of-hearing students to be active in social and recreational events. This may mean providing interpreters for extracurricular activities; it may also mean providing sensitivity training for athletic coaches, drama coaches, and faculty advisers for student papers and clubs.

WHAT ASSISTIVE TECHNOLOGIES AND SERVICES CAN HELP?

Because deaf and most hard-of-hearing people communicate visually, such communications technologies as electronic mail (E-mail) and facsimile (fax) are very important. The good news for deaf Americans is that both E-mail and fax have become very widely accepted and are used by hearing people, too, making them ideal technologies for deaf-hearing communication. Also helpful are relay services, in which phone operators (who are hearing) translate the typed words of deaf callers and the spoken words of hearing callers so that deaf and hearing people can communicate with each other in real-time, two-way phone calls.

Certainly, interpreters are an essential related service for many deaf or hard-of-hearing individuals. Deaf students usually prefer sign-language interpreters; some like ASL interpreters, while others prefer Signed English interpreters. Also available (and primarily used by hard-of-hearing people) are oral interpreters—individuals who move their lips and make gestures to help students to understand what is being said in the classroom.

A new technology is the Rear Window™ Captioning System developed by the WGBH Educational Foundation in Boston. This system produces reversed captions (e.g., "snoitpac" for "captions") on a light-emitting diode (LED) text display that is mounted at the rear of a movie theater. Deaf or hard-of-hearing movie patrons use transparent acrylic panels attached to their seats to reflect the captions so that they appear superimposed on the movie screen.

WHAT ARE THE PROSPECTS FOR POSTSECONDARY EDUCATION?

Many deaf and hard-of-hearing students pursue postsecondary education. Some attend specialized institutions such as Gallaudet University (Washington, D.C.) or the National Technical Institute for the Deaf (Rochester, New York). Others who go to "regular" colleges tend to prefer schools with strong support services and sizeable enrollments of deaf students. Although large numbers of deaf students enroll in colleges and universities every year, fewer than half ever graduate (Bowe, 1988)—usually because their reading abilities are not sufficient to enable them to keep up with college texts.

WHAT ARE THE EMPLOYMENT PROSPECTS?

These are excellent. In most offices today, personal computers (PCs) equipped with modems and communications software allow deaf or hard-of-hearing workers to use E-mail and to surf the Internet. Fax machines, whether stand-alone or built into PCs, are also commonplace. For more traditional two-way phone conversations, deaf and hard-of-hearing workers can use TTYs (tele-typewriters) with relay services. All of these technologies, of course, require that deaf or hard-of-hearing users possess good reading and writing skills. Given such abilities, the technologies, added to the use of sign-language interpreters for staff meetings, allow the deaf or hard-of-hearing person to communicate as effectively and as widely as hearing workers.

WHAT ARE THE PROSPECTS FOR INDEPENDENT LIVING?

People who are deaf or hard-of-hearing use simple, low-tech products to live independently. Doorbells and phone signals can be "heard" by flashing lights. Relay services allow deaf and hard-of-hearing people to make and receive phone calls. Captioning makes television viewing enjoyable.

Questions for Reflection and Discussion

1. Contrast "attention" to "perception" and use this difference to distinguish attention deficits from learning disabilities.

2. Some cases of learning disabilities, attention deficits, and mental retardation are due to the same causative factors. Name two such factors.

3. Which of the physical disabilities we have studied in this text often have cognitive limitations as secondary conditions?

4. What interventions does this chapter suggest be used with students who have cognitive limitations?

5. Helen Keller used to say, "Blindness comes between people and things, but deafness comes between people and people." How might this saying be updated for today? Why is the difference important?

6. Which technologies discussed in chapter 5 appear to be most likely to help people with low vision or blindness? Of them, which are also likely to help people with learning disabilities or mental retardation?

7. Give two reasons why hearing loss, including deafness, can be a significant limitation with respect to education.

8. What is the argument in favor of segregated preschool education for young children who are blind? Who are deaf?

9. Why is age at onset such an important factor with respect to deafness? Blindness?

10. What is total communication?

Where is more information available?

American Foundation
for the Blind
11 Penn Plaza, #300
New York, NY 10001
1-212-502-7600
www.afb.org/afb

American Council of the Blind
1155 15th Street NW
Washington, DC 20005
1-202-467-5081
www.acb.org

Children and Adults with
Attention Deficit Disorders
(Ch.A.D.D.)
499 NW 70th Avenue, #101
Plantation, FL 33317
www.chadd.org

Learning Disabilities
Association of America (LDA)
4165 Library Road
Pittsburgh, PA 15234
www.ldanatl.org

Narrative Television Network
5840 South Memorial
Drive, #312
Tulsa, OK 74145-9082
1-918-627-1000

National Association
of the Deaf
814 Thayer Avenue
Silver Spring, MD 20910
1-301-587-1788
www.nad.org

Orton Dyslexia Society
Chester Building, #382
8600 LaSalle Road
Baltimore, MD 21286-2044
www.ods.org

Self Help for Hard
of Hearing People
7910 Woodmont
Avenue, #1200
Bethesda, MD 20814
1-301-657-2249

The Arc [formerly Association
for Retarded Citizens]
500 East Border Street
Arlington, TX 76010
www.thearc.org

WGBH Educational Foundation
125 Western Avenue
Boston, MA 02134
1-617-492-2777, Ext. 3490
www.wgbh.org/dvs

Part Four

The four chapters of Part Four examine the environment. Our focus is sequentially upon the built environment generally (chapter 11), housing (chapter 12), transportation (chapter 13), and employment (chapter 14). In each instance, the landmark federal laws introduced in chapter 2 have resulted in a level of accessibility in the United States that is unknown in most nations of the world.

Chapter 11 explores the different levels of access: program accessibility, physical accessibility, universal design, and barrier-free design. Generally, new buildings that serve the general public are required to be barrier-free (i.e., have no major structural impediments). Existing buildings, by contrast, usually need meet only program accessibility or physical accessibility standards. Those standards provide that there must be a way for someone with a disability to get into, move around in, and exit from a building or facility. Universal design is a new idea. It offers a basic level of physical accessibility but presents this as "visitability" or convenience for all people, not just for individuals with disabilities.

Chapter 12 looks at the bleak reality of housing for individuals with physical and health conditions. Although affordable and accessible housing is the exception rather than the rule in the United States today, there is reason for optimism. This chapter outlines the legal rights of people with disabilities with respect to housing and offers practical suggestions for educators, therapists, and counselors who work with this population.

Chapter 13 examines transportation accessibility in the United States. While the picture here is much brighter than it is with respect to housing, important barriers remain. The legal rights of individuals with disabilities are explained, and practical suggestions for traveling are offered.

Finally, chapter 14 examines the current reality and the future prospects for employment for adults with physical and health disabilities.

Some reviewers of this text while it was in development questioned the need for chapters on housing and transportation in a book aimed at educators, therapists, and counselors. After reading the chapters, however, these reviewers acknowledged the importance of the information provided in Part Four. Professionals seeking to assist individuals with disabilities and their families need to appreciate the many barriers these people face on a daily basis, to know the rights these persons enjoy, and to understand the day-to-day options these individuals may pursue in their efforts to cope with the effects of physical and health conditions.

11

ISSUES OF ACCESSIBILITY

John Callahan, 46, is a nationally syndicated cartoonist. He is also a quadriplegic who lives near Portland, Oregon, and a recovered alcoholic. His cartoons put issues of accessibility into the newspapers Americans read every day. The cartoons have been collected in such books as Freaks of Nature, Do What He Says! He's Crazy!!!, *and* Will the Real John Callahan Please Stand Up? *The artist brings a sardonic sense of humor to his work. The cartoons are resolutely politically incorrect. One, for example, portrays the rear entrance to a restaurant advertising a dinner of frogs' legs. In the foreground are a number of frogs, each leaving the restaurant in a wheelchair. Another depicts three Old West sheriffs on horseback finding an empty wheelchair. Says one sheriff to the others: "Don't worry. He won't get far on foot." Callahan has a hard time imagining life as anything other than a cartoonist (Medgyesi, 1996).*

A vital role of teachers, counselors, therapists, and others who work with individuals having physical or health conditions is that of an advocate for community access. While great strides have been made in recent years to open up America's cities and towns to users of wheelchairs or other mobility aids (refer to chapter 2), much remains to be done. The work generally is "at the margin"—that is, relatively small, incremental steps are needed in most communities because many of the major barriers have already been removed. Further work, however, is required. The major federal laws on accessibility all are *complaint-driven*—that is, they become effective when someone with a disability files a complaint about an inaccessible building or facility. One cannot just wait and expect that in time, barriers will disappear. Rather, individuals with disabilities, family members, and professionals alike must take the step of calling attention to those barriers and asking that they be removed.

When we talk about access to the environment, exactly what do we mean? The answer, it turns out, depends upon whether we are talking about the built environment (existing buildings and other facilities) or planned renovations for such existing buildings or as yet wholly unbuilt facilities (new construction). A much higher standard applies for new buildings and facilities than for existing ones. With respect to structures that were built in years past, we use *accessible* or *program-accessible* as a standard. The *barrier-free* standard applies to renovated parts of such buildings and to all new buildings. A relatively new term, *universal design,* recently has come into use. It calls for barrier-free design, but rather than focus upon disability uses, it suggests that buildings, facilities, and consumer products—as well as educational curricula and materials—be designed for optimal use by all kinds of people—young or old, disabled or not.

Accessible

An accessible environment is one in which someone using a wheelchair or other mobility aid or someone with limited ambulatory abilities can get into the facility, through common areas such as lounges, into meeting rooms, classrooms, etc., and into at least one rest room. The standard is one applying to existing buildings. There must be *one* accessible entrance/exit, *one* accessible rest room for males and one for females, clear pathways through common areas, and access into at least some function rooms. Thus, a four-story building may have just two accessible rest rooms (one for men, one for women) out of eight rest rooms and still be "accessible."

Title III of the ADA sets an "accessible" standard for places of public accommodations (stores, restaurants, hotels, medical offices, etc., as well as private colleges and universities) that use existing buildings and facilities. This standard calls for alterations that are **readily achievable.** The readily achievable standard means "easily accomplishable and able to be carried out without much difficulty or expense" (§301 [9]). Thus, the standard is a relatively low one. However, Title III sees the obligation as a continuing duty: If a needed alteration is not readily achievable under one year's budget, it may be under the following year's. Accordingly, the owner must regularly assess what further steps are necessary and whether they may be accomplished at relatively little expense in any given year.

Section 504 of the Rehabilitation Act of 1973 (PL 93-112, most recently amended by PL 105-220—refer to chapter 2) and the Americans with Disabilities Act (ADA) (PL 101-336) call for **program accessibility** in existing facilities used by private colleges and universities as well as public elementary and secondary schools. This standard means accessibility as previously explained and adds that access may *also* be achieved if programs or activities are moved from inaccessible rooms or buildings to accessible ones. Thus, a school need not make all four floors of an existing building accessible so long as it moves a class for which someone using a wheelchair registers from an inaccessible classroom to an accessible one. The point is that the student gains access to the class.

The program-accessibility standard does call for some modifications in some buildings. In older buildings, ramps often must be constructed. Doors on the ground floor may need to be widened. One male and one female rest room must be made accessible on the accessible floor. Where "accessible" differs from "barrier-free" (discussed next) is in accepting some barriers: This permits some entrances, some floors, and some rooms to remain inaccessible on the basis that costs to alter all of them would be high.

The Individuals with Disabilities Education Act (IDEA) (most recently amended by PL 105-17) does not explicitly require that architectural barriers such as steps and narrow doors be removed from existing public school buildings. The law's mandate, rather, is that educational services be provided to each student who needs them. That is, school districts must make available a free appropriate public education to every child or youth with a disability—either in the neighborhood school buildings or elsewhere, through an out-of-district placement at the expense of the local school district.

Section 504 and the ADA require that public schools provide nondiscriminatory treatment for children and youth with disabilities such that the real test is whether or not individuals receive essentially the same services as persons with no disabilities, which services may or may not involve physical accessibility in public school buildings. That was the issue in *Hendricks v. Gilhool* (709 F. Suppl. 1362, E.D. Pa. 1989). The Carbon-Lehigh Intermediate Unit had placed students with disabilities into buildings and classrooms that were inferior to those used by students with no disabilities. The court decided that both the IDEA and Section 504 prohibited placement of persons with disabilities into objectively inferior settings. The standard, the court held, is one in which students with disabilities are placed into regular school buildings if they can secure an appropriate education there; if separate placements are required, they must be comparable to those used by students with no disabilities.

Be that as it may, for many school districts, it will be far less costly to lower architectural barriers (a one-time capital expense) than to pay special transportation and other expenses at out-of-district alternative placements. Such costs are both high and continuing (year after year).

Barrier-Free New buildings subject to the ADA, Section 504, or the IDEA need to be barrier-free. The barrier-free standard is a much higher standard. It requires that *all* entrances into the building, *all* function rooms, and *all* rest rooms be accessible. If a building is renovated, the altered part of the building must meet the barrier-free standard.

In facilities primarily used by children between the ages of 2 and 12, ramps with slopes between 1:16 (rising 1 inch in height every 16 inches in length) and 1:20 are preferred (vs. no more than 1:12 for adults). The paths themselves should be at least 36 inches wide. If two wheelchairs can pass each other going in opposite directions, paths should be at least 60 inches wide (those dimensions are unchanged from those for adults). If handrails are used, they should be no more than 28 inches in height (vs. 34 inches to 36 inches for handrails intended for adult use); if necessary, a second rail should be installed for children's use. The handrails should be 1 inch to 1.25 inches in diameter (vs. 1.25 inches to 1.5 inches for rails adults will use). Controls, stored items, and other items children must reach are speci-

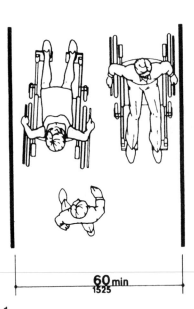

Figure 11.1
Hallway and Walkway Width. Accessible hallways or pathways in newly constructed or recently renovated facilities should be at least 60 inches wide, so as to accommodate two wheelchairs. At least 30 inches is needed to accommodate one wheelchair.

Drawing courtesy U.S. Architectural and Transportation Barriers Compliance Board ("Access Board"), "Americans with Disabilities Act Accessibility Guidelines" (ADAAG), *Federal Register,* January 13, 1998, p. 2034. Reprinted with permission from the Access Board.

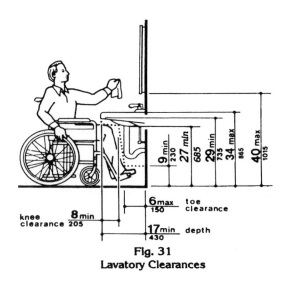

Fig. 31
Lavatory Clearances

Figure 11.2
Sink and Table Heights. Sinks and tables need to be designed so as to allow children, youth and adults both to use the surface top area effectively *and* to be able to fit their legs under the top. About 27 inches of clear space, measured from the floor to the bottom of the sink/table is usually needed. There should also be at least 17 inches of clear space from the protruding edge of the sink/table for leg and toe clearance.

Drawing courtesy U.S. Architectural and Transportation Barriers Compliance Board ("Access Board"), "Americans with Disabilities Act Accessibility Guidelines" (ADAAG), *Federal Register,* January 13, 1998, p. 2080. Reprinted with permission from the Access Board.

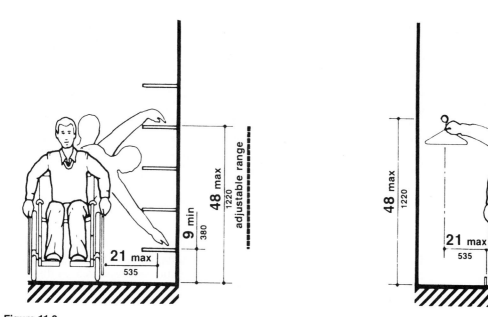

Figure 11.3

Height of Shelves or Closet Racks. Children, youth and adults who use wheelchairs need to be able to reach books and other items that are placed on shelves and to be able to hang clothing on closet racks. Administrators of facilities should consider both how *low* items may be and how *high* they may be. Children, youth and adults themselves should test shelves and closets, measuring side and forward reach.

Drawing courtesy U.S. Architectural and Transportation Barriers Compliance Board ("Access Board"), "Americans with Disabilities Act Accessibility Guidelines" (ADAAG), *Federal Register*, January 13, 1998, p. 2080. Reprinted with permission from the Access Board.

fied in the Architectural and Transportation Barriers Compliance Board "Children's Elements" rules in three age ranges: for 2–4-year-olds, 36 inches (high) and 20 inches (low); for 5–8-year-olds, 40 inches (high) and 18 inches (low), and for 9–12-year-olds, 44 inches (high) and 16 inches (low). Controls and storage items intended for adult use should be 48 inches (high) and 15 inches (low).

All doors used by the general public should have levers rather than doorknobs. The doors themselves should be at least 32 inches wide (36 inches preferable). Door levers and other hardware should be mounted no more than 48 inches above the floor for adults (see preceding for young children).

Drinking fountains intended for children's use should have spouts no more than 36 inches from the floor. (This dimension is the same for adults.) The spout should be located toward the front of the unit and should produce a water stream of at least 4 inches in height (to facilitate filling a glass or cup with water). With respect to drinking fountains, rest room sinks, and other protruding objects, however, it is important to remember that many young children using wheelchairs have footrests that are high relative to those of adults; sufficient clear space under the unit should be allowed for those footrests.

Universal Design

Universal design is a design approach that maximizes useability of products, services, and environments for everyone—young people and old, short people and tall, people with disabilities and those without. The idea is to be as inclusive as possible from the get-go—meaning that only a small minority of users will need "special" accommodations. The concept first arose in design of the built environment, that is, in architecture. It proved to be very successful, for which reason it was then adopted by designers of personal-use products, including kitchen utensils, room temperature controls, and desk lamps. As we saw in chapter 4, the concept of universal design holds great promise in the area of education.

The Center for Universal Design at North Carolina State University has developed seven principles of universal design. The following are the key ideas:

1. The design can be used and marketed to people with diverse abilities. It appeals to all kinds of people. A good example is power doors that open automatically when someone steps on a pressure-sensitive area on the pathway leading to the door.

2. The design incorporates a wide variety of preferences. People have choices as to how they use it. An example is a kiosk or ATM machine that lets people decide whether to read or listen to information.

3. The product or service is easy to understand and use. It avoids unnecessary complexity. A good example is the user manuals that accompany Hewlett-Packard printers—the manuals are very brief, relying more on drawings than on text.

4. It works in all kinds of settings. Even in "eyes-busy" or noisy environments, people can use it with ease. An example is an information system at a train station that offers arrival and departure information both visually and auditorially.

5. The design accommodates error. People can make a mistake or two without disastrous consequences. An example is a kiosk that offers the option of returning to the main menu at every screen.

6. The product or service requires minimal effort to use. Neither intense nor sustained physical effort is required. Door levers are an excellent example—no grasping or twisting motions are required.

7. It accommodates variations in size and position. People can use it while standing, sitting, or reaching. An example is subway turnstiles that present the token or card slot at a height easily reached by people using wheelchairs and young children yet do not require ambulatory adults to crouch.

The beauty of universal design is that it forces product and service designers to *think* about these things. When designers realize that users of all kinds, sizes, and abilities will need this product or service, they come up with solutions—often very creative ones. When business consultant Jim Tobias asked representatives of large companies about how they were using universal design principles, several mentioned print and television advertising that includes people with disabilities on an incidental basis without calling attention to the disability. Others pointed to checklists used by product designers and developers, specifically requiring them to consider how their projected products would be used by very young or very old people, short and tall persons, and left-handers as well as right-handers (Tobias, 1997).

A great deal of material, both printed and electronic, is available to assist educators, program directors, and others to comply with the various access standards.

The U.S. Architectural and Transportation Barriers Compliance Board (ATBCB, or Access Board) has published very helpful materials. It recently issued a "final rule" providing guidance for Title III entities, that is, places of public accommodations. The Access Board's *Accessibility Guidelines for Buildings and Facilities* (1998a) were developed for adoption by the U.S. Department of Justice, which is responsible for enforcement of Title III. The guidelines are part of the Access Board's "Americans with Disabilities Act Accessibility Guidelines" (ADAAG). The ADAAG provides very specific guidance on, for example, the number of "handicap parking" spaces required, the width of walkways, the height of drinking fountains, the dimensions of rest rooms, the height and other features of cafeteria or restaurant tables, the spacing of displays in commercial stores, and the seating arrangements in sports facilities. The guidelines are available without charge from the ATBCB.

Also in 1998, the Access Board issued an addendum, *Building Elements Designed for Children's Use,* another final rule written for consideration of the U.S. Department of Justice for enforcement under the ADA. These guidelines provide for "exceptions" (optional deviations from the ADAAG) that may be adopted by owners of facilities primarily used by children. The "children's elements" rule focuses upon children between the ages of 2 and 12. It provides specifications for such things as drinking fountains, rest rooms, stairs, elevators, ramps, and chairs and tables. The Department of Justice has allowed, since its initial rulemaking on the ADA in 1991, for architects, designers, and facility owners to deviate from the adult specifications in the ADAAG in order to meet different needs of children. However, fearing litigation or Justice investigation, some designers were hesitant to do so. The appearance of the children's elements specifications should go a long way toward relieving such concerns, because the rule explicitly states that dimensions adopted because children need them are "permitted departures from requirements based on adult dimensions" (Access Board, 1998b, p. 2061). The final rule is in the January 13, 1998, issue of the *Federal Register* (pp. 2059–2091).

In 1992, the Center for Universal Design (then known as the Center for Accessible Housing) produced under contract to the Access Board a comprehensive set of *Recommendations for Accessibility Standards for Children's Environments.* This report, available from the Access Board, provides much more detail than does the Board's own children's elements guidelines. One strength of the Center's report is that it pulls together national and individual state standards to explain what options are available for meeting different needs. The Center also publishes materials on how to market universally designed facilities and features. (In the interests of full disclosure, the author of this text is on its advisory board.)

The ATBCB (1997) has issued the final report of its committee on play facilities. That report examines indoor and outdoor play facilities, looking primarily at the needs of children and youth, and offers specific guidance on ramps, paths, and surface coverings. The final report is available both in print and at the Access Board's Web site (www.access-board.gov).

In addition, the private American National Standards Institute (ANSI) continues to offer its widely used ANSI A117.1 accessibility standard. The ANSI standard is a voluntary one, although it has been adopted by many state and local governments. In addition, since the mid-1980s, ANSI and ATBCB have worked hand in hand to make the public and private specifications more consonant with each other so as to reduce confusion and conflicts for architects, designers, and others. The ANSI A117.1 standard is available for purchase from the Institute.

A wealth of information is available on the World Wide Web. The Trace R&D Center at the University of Wisconsin at Madison maintains a "Designing an Accessible World" collection of materials (www.trace.wisc.edu/world/world.html). The Center for Universal Design's site focuses on building design and housing. Adaptive Environments in Boston has a Web site (www.adaptenv.org/) that offers national and international links on universal design, again mostly with respect to the built environment. Also worth a "visit" is www.universaldesign.com—a site focused on the contents of the Universal Design newsletter (6 Grant Avenue, Takoma Park, MD 20912).

Questions for Reflection and Discussion

1. Contrast "accessible" to "barrier-free."

2. What does the text mean by saying that the major federal laws protecting people with disabilities are complaint-driven?

3. What is "readily achievable"? Why do you think the ADA sets such a low standard for existing stores and restaurants?

4. Public schools must meet a program-accessibility standard. What does that standard require?

5. Reread the Center for Universal Design's seven criteria for universal design. Then explain this standard in your own words.

6. How might the 1998 publication of children's elements help to make schools and other settings children often use more accessible?

Resources

American National Standards Institute
11 West 42nd Street
New York, NY 10036
1-212-642-4900
www.ansi.org

Center for Universal Design
North Carolina State University
Box 8613
Raleigh, NC 27695-8613
1-800-647-6777
1-919-515-3082
www.design.ncsu.edu/cud

Trace Research & Development Center
S-151 Waisman Center
University of Wisconsin—Madison
1500 Highland Avenue
Madison, WI 53705-2280
1-608-262-6966
www.trace.wisc.edu/

U.S. Architectural and Transportation Barriers
Compliance Board
1331 F Street NW, #1000
Washington, DC 20004-1111
1-800-USA-ABLE
www.access-board.gov

U.S. Department of Justice
Office of Americans with Disabilities
P.O. Box 66118
Washington, DC 20035-66118
1-202-514-0381
www.usdoj.gov

12

HOUSING

When Gary Dockery (1955–) awoke in the hospital from a coma after sustaining a traumatic brain injury when someone shot him, his first words were: "I don't want to go back to the Village." Dockery was referring to a nursing home that had been his home for 8 years while he was in a coma. He did not get his wish. The insurance company and his doctors, acting "in his best interests" and considering their costs, sent him right back to Alexian Village (Medgyesi, 1997).

Finding accessible and affordable housing is urgent for many people with physical disabilities. Regrettably, it is also a source of enormous frustration for millions of such individuals. Hundreds of thousands of Americans with physical disabilities like Gary Dockery have to live in nursing homes, senior-citizen housing developments, or other institutional environments simply because accessible and affordable housing is not available in their communities. Indeed, the *1994 Report to Congress on Worst Case Housing Needs* (U.S. Department of Housing and Urban Development, 1994) said that people with disabilities are *the* group most likely to live in severely substandard housing. The *1996 Report* added that individuals with disabilities most often pay more than half their income for rent, even though the units they rent are severely inadequate in meeting their needs (U.S. Department of Housing and Urban Development, 1996).

For many individuals with physical disabilities, where they live is an important aspect of how they see themselves. In an insightful study, Kenneth Robey (1997) of the Matheny School and Hospital in northern New Jersey explored how the self-concept of a young man with cerebral palsy related to the man's housing situation. This 31-year-old had lived for 2 years in a nursing home; at the time of the study, he had resided at a home/hospital for about 12 years. Concluded Robey:

> The location of the two identities "myself as one who has a disability" and "myself as one who lives at the hospital" within the same identity class (i.e., association with the same feature classes) might be viewed as reflecting a close association of those identities. More so than for individuals who are residing in community-based residences, identity structure models that have been constructed thus far in pilot work with individuals residing in a hospital suggest an equation of living situation with disability. (p. 98)

This is not surprising. For people who live independently in community-based residences, control over the environment and time is either complete or nearly so. That markedly enhances one's sense of worth. For persons living in nursing homes or other institutional environments, by contrast, control is minimal. These people cannot change their environment and usually cannot control the timing of events within that environment (e.g., when they will arise in the morning, when they will eat lunch). This has a negative impact on their sense of worth.

Features To Create Or Look For

It may seem obvious, but Hewitt (1997) states that the three most important aspects of housing for people with physical or health disabilities are "location, location, location!" She built her home close to a shopping plaza. Within 3 minutes, she can wheel herself to the grocery store, a bank, and a restaurant. Her home is also close to a bus route serviced by lift-equipped buses.

Families with children who have physical disabilities should consider modifying their home to make it more accessible. If in the market for a new home, a family should be alert for access features that will make the new home more livable. Such features not only facilitate independence for the child with a disability but also foster a child's personal growth and independence. Hewitt (1997), for example, notes that putting 10-inch wood pedestals under the washer and dryer and using front-loading machines make doing the laundry much easier. She uses keyless entry systems for main doorways, noting that she need not fumble for keys or worry about being locked out. (The combination is changed frequently, and special codes are used for housekeepers and attendants.)

With respect to altering an existing home or selecting a new home, the National Easter Seals Society (NESS) and Century 21 (1996) have offered an easy-to-use checklist. Posted on NESS's Web site at http://seals.com/publish/achome/c21checklist, the checklist suggests that families look for, among other things:

- Doorways at least 32" wide (Hewitt suggests 36")
- Halls 48" to 60" wide; minimum 42" wide
- At least one bathroom with 5' × 5' turnaround space
- A *U* or *L*-shaped or open-plan kitchen
- Chair-height switches and controls (48" to 54" from the floor). Someone sitting in a chair and reaching forward can manipulate a switch that is 48" from the floor; if the individual approaches from the side and stops the chair parallel to the wall, he or she can reach as high as 54" from the floor. This includes light switches and doorbells.
- Electrical outlets that are 6" higher than standard and electrical controls that are 6" lower than standard.
- In the kitchen, front-controlled range and dishwasher.
- Direct outside emergency exit from the bedroom.

The Access Foundation offers a database on products for home accessibility. The Center for Universal Design at North Carolina State University provides home-modification guides, as does the National Association of Home Builders (NAHB). NAHB's *Directory of Accessible Building Products* costs $3. AbleData has a database of several thousand assistive technology devices. Call 1-800-827-0216 (9 a.m.–6 p.m., Eastern, M–F, except federal holidays) and ask for items by category (e.g., grab bars, levers, slip-resistant bathtub coating). The National Accessible Apartment Clearinghouse (1-800-421-1221) offers data on the location and cost of accessible apartments. In addition, a wide range of electronic products, which together can create a "smart home," is described at www.smarthome.com.

Environmental control units (ECUs) permit on-site control of dozens of home appliances. Virtually anything electric can be remotely controlled by means of X-10 modules, which sell for about $12 from Radio Shack and other hardware stores. A keypad at $25 or a remote keypad at $30 is the only other piece of equipment you'll need. No special wiring is required. Just plug the device (light, coffee maker, etc.) into the X-10 unit, and the X-10 unit into an electrical outlet. IBM offers a $99 software program called Home Director® that enables people to control electrical devices throughout the house, even when the personal computer is turned off. Remote modules attached to lights, heat controls, air conditioners, televisions, toasters, coffee makers, and other products connect these household items to the PC. Using the software, the owner decides what time which products will turn on or off. Madenta Communications offers a similar PROXi environmental control system that can be voice-operated to control some 250 electrical devices as well as an intercom system. As great as the potential of ECUs is, reported Holme, Kanny, Guthrie, and Johnson (1997), occupational therapists prescribe them for relatively few of their clients. Reasons cited by the therapists included costs, lack of available third-party (insurance) reimbursement, and the need for training and more information about ECUs by the therapists themselves.

Light-switch motion detectors are available for about $20 in most hardware stores. They turn lights on when someone enters a room and then turn the lights off after a preset time period when no one remains in the room. Automatic door openers are made by Gentleman Door Company for about $350 (1-302-239-4045). Imaginative Concepts (1-800-269-6566) offers for $45 to $50 sheets with cloth handles that make it easier to shift position or get out of bed. Universally designed kitchen utensils, from knives to plates, are available at reasonable prices at Home Depot and many hardware stores. Adaptations (1-800-688-1758) sells door hinges that let doors swing completely open, allowing an additional 2 inches of clear width. Hinged shelves that drop down to reachable levels are marketed by E-Z Shelf (1-800-755-0066) for about $100 per shelf unit.

Other low-cost, low-tech solutions include a tap turner (that helps to turn faucets on or off), priced by UniTurner™ at about $16; lever-handle doorknobs, widely available for about $15 each, and doorknob extensions (that fit over ordinary doorknobs and turn them into levers), about $6 to $15 each; wall-switch extenders (that lower electrical on/off switches by 12 inches), about $7; and offset door hinges (that widen the effective width of a doorway), about $25. These and many other suggestions are offered by Shelley Schwarz (1998).

Universal Design

Why are so few houses, apartments, and other dwellings built with these kinds of features? A big part of the problem in America is that one's home is regarded in America's popular culture as private and personal—beyond the reach of law. The saying "A man's home is his castle" captures this cultural reality. Thus, federal and state governments have shied away from imposing requirements upon residential housing, especially single-family homes. This is not the case in many Scandinavian countries, such as Sweden and Denmark, where it is very common to find recently constructed homes that are accessible to and useable by people with disabilities (Stone, 1997). In 1998, the United Kingdom (England) passed a law mandating that all new private homes be built with minimal access features, including an entryway without steps, a rest room on the first floor, doorways and hallways that are wide enough to accommodate wheelchairs, and other elements of universal design. The aim is to achieve a "visitable" home. As exciting as this breakthrough is, readers should recognize that much work would remain to be done in a visitable home before it would be accessible to and useable by someone with a physical disability.

Such a law may eventually be passed in the United States. In those few instances where American state legislatures have acted to regulate housing, the mandates they have established tend to be limited in scope and in meaning for people with physical disabilities. One exception is Atlanta, Georgia. Eleanor Smith of Concrete Change, based in Atlanta, successfully advocated for alterations in Atlanta's building ordinances. Thanks to her efforts, the city's code now requires that certain new one-floor homes feature a flat or sloped entrance (no steps, no stairs), wide doors (at least 32 inches wide), adaptable electrical fixtures (that can be raised or lowered), and adaptable bathrooms (featuring built-in wall reinforcements that can accept grab bars). Smith's group has had similar success in other communities.

Despite those efforts, just 2% to 3% of America's housing stock is accessible to individuals with physical disabilities, notably those who use wheelchairs. Virtually all of this stock consists of new (post-1991) apartment, co-op, or condominium units. Making matters worse is the need faced by many people with disabilities for housing that is not only accessible but also affordable. Few federal or state programs offer help in meeting this need for people with disabilities. The rapid rise in home valuations of the 1980s and, to a lesser extent, the late 1990s, has placed many housing units beyond the financial reach of most Americans with physical disabilities.

There are a few hopeful signs that things will improve in the years to come. The most notable of these is the increasing popularity of an architectural approach known as universal design. Universally designed homes and apartment buildings are being marketed as "lifelong" housing units because their accessibility features accommodate the needs of able-bodied persons who become disabled as they get older (see, for example, Usher, 1998). Will enough Americans buy into the concept of lifelong housing that significant numbers of private homes and apartments will become available for people with physical disabilities? Only time will tell.

The arguments are compelling. An estimated 20% of American homes or apartments include at least one person who has a disability. While not all of these people are limited in mobility or other functions necessitating accessibility or adaptability in housing, sizeable numbers of people are. The number should grow in the years to come as an aging America's baby-boom generation enters its 50s and 60s, traditionally the ages during which people are most likely to become disabled. Fueled by the aging of this large generation, by 2010, about 25% of all Americans will be 65 years of age or over; the rate of disability among persons aged 65 to 79 is currently 47% (McNeil, 1997). Thus, people looking for a home, whether a private house or an apartment, condominium, or co-op, may well be interested in accessible units because such housing stock can accommodate disability if it occurs among any family member.

Meanwhile, universally designed housing units look very much like other structures. The accessible entrances, for example, feature gradually sloping sidewalks that terminate flush with the first-floor entrance; no ramp or lift is needed. The wider doors look inviting, too, and show their value and convenience the first time couches or other large pieces of furniture are moved into the home. "Special" design features, such as grab bars in bathrooms, may be removed quickly and easily if not needed, restoring the "normal" look of the room. Universally designed units feature levers in place of doorknobs; levers are unobtrusive and have the additional benefit of being convenient to able-bodied persons. To illustrate, bringing in the week's grocery shopping is far easier with levers. One simply bumps the lever down and enters the building; there is no need, as there is with doorknobs, to put down the packages, open the door, and then pick up the packages again (Center for Universal Design, 1995a).

Miles Homes (Minneapolis), a unit of DeGeorge Home Alliance (Cheshire, Connecticut), is one company that makes universally designed homes as part of its Lifespan Collection (Usher, 1998). Miles Homes is particularly proud of its bathroom designs, which feature roll-in showers, grab bars, lift systems, toilets that vary in height, and levered faucets. Another builder with a strong track record in universal design is Amherst Homes (Cincinnati), where Ron Wietzel has led the way by putting up a model home that showcases the best of universal design.

In Plantation, Florida, "Gizmo House" illustrates how homes may be designed for optimal accessibility (a far higher standard than universal design). Living there are six adults with physical disabilities who previously resided at the nearby Ann Storck Center, a federally funded institution. Gizmo House features controls that are easily reached from wheelchairs. Many appliances are electronically controlled by wireless switches placed on those wheelchairs. The kitchen table may be raised or lowered via such switches. Inch-wide moldings along hallways prevent walls from being scratched by wheelchairs. Although the house is expensive, the Ann Storck Center argues that the costs are actually lower than those required to keep the individuals at the institution.

Home Health Care

Increasingly feasible is delivery of health services in the home. Today, about 6 million Americans (about half of them under 65 years of age) receive home health-care services. In 1995, some 500 million home visits were made by home-care medical workers at an average cost of $63 per visit. This contrasts to $2,000 a day for hospitalization. These services could have kept Gary Dockery out of a nursing home.

Even less costly is "telemedicine," or two-way interactive telecommunications connections through which a remotely located physician or other trained health-care worker can receive and review medical information, including blood pressure, and observe the patient via two-way video. Cardiograms and other vital signs can be transmitted over vast distances via telephone or cable television lines to doctors or other health-care professionals. Sometimes called "modern-day house calls," such connections can cost as little as $35 per "visit" (McDaniel, 1997).

Legislation

The key laws are the Fair Housing Amendments Act of 1988 and the Fair Housing Act of 1937 (including Sections 8, 202, and 811).

FAIR HOUSING AMENDMENTS ACT
(PL 100-430; 42 U.S.C. 3601 ET SEQ.)

The major federal initiative in this area was the Fair Housing Amendments Act of 1988 (FHAA). Final regulations implementing the Act were published by the U.S. Department of Housing and Urban Development (HUD) in the January 23, 1989, *Federal Register*. HUD also published technical guidelines in the March 6, 1991, *Federal Register*. Those rules should be consulted for definitive explanations of the FHAA. Perhaps the most far-reaching change mandated by the Act is that landlords and real estate agents are forbidden from discriminating on the basis of disability against any individual with a disability. For decades, many individuals with visible disabilities were victimized by landlords and real estate agents who told them, falsely, that no homes or apartments were available for purchase or rent. Sometimes this occurred because owners of a real estate property feared that current occupants might feel uncomfortable around someone with a visible limitation. Whatever the reason, such actions are now illegal. (That is not to say they no longer occur; they do. But now victims have recourse. They can file complaints with HUD. Details follow.) Also prohibited by the FHAA is steering, or forcing applicants who have disabilities into segregated or out-of-the-way units or homes. Realtors and agents sometimes steered individuals with visible disabilities away from centrally located housing units out of a misguided desire not to offend the sensibilities of current residents. Again, whether or not this was the prevailing motivation, such actions are now against federal law.

The FHAA requires accessibility in multifamily housing—apartment complexes, co-ops, condominium buildings—that have four or more units and that were constructed for first occupancy after March 13, 1991. Thus, the FHAA imposed no rules at all about single- or two-family homes and few rules about existing apartment or other multifamily housing complexes.

According to the FHAA, newly constructed multifamily housing complexes must have apartments that are both accessible and adaptable. The rules apply to ground-floor units of buildings that do not have elevators and to all units of buildings that do. **Accessibility** means that someone using a wheelchair or other mobility device can get into and around the apartment. This includes an accessible route from outside the apartment building to any ground-floor unit. Accessibility also includes light switches that are positioned on walls so that they may be reached by a person sitting in a wheelchair. **Adaptability** means that the unit is constructed so as to readily accept additional access measures. For example, bathrooms have reinforcements built into walls so that grab bars may be attached easily if needed. Other examples of adaptability include kitchen storage units that may be lowered if needed, as well as bathrooms that are large enough to allow someone using a wheelchair to maneuver comfortably within the space.

Owners of housing stock built for first occupancy on or after March 13, 1991 (the effective date of the FHAA) are required by the FHAA to design the housing stock so as to be accessible and adaptable. In any instance in which such design features were not part of the original construction, owners must make reasonable accommodations, as needed, for renters or other occupants who have special needs. Examples are provision of "handicapped parking" spaces, installation of a ramp leading from the parking area to the building, and wide doors and level flooring to and within common areas, such as laundry rooms or recreation facilities. These should have been part of the original design. If they were not, the owner is responsible to make the changes and to pay for them (Center for Universal Design, 1995b).

The FHAA also requires that renters or other occupants of housing units, such as apartments or condominiums, built for first occupancy *before* March 13, 1991, be permitted to make accessibility modifications at their own expense. Landlords and agents may not refuse reasonable requests for changes, although they may insist that the changes meet building codes. In the event that a particular change will interfere with a subsequent renter's use and enjoyment of the unit, owners may stipulate that the individual restore the original structure upon vacating the apartment or other unit. (In most instances, access changes are unlikely to interfere with a subsequent occupant's use and enjoyment of the unit and thus need not be reversed at the tenant's expense.) Thus, renters with physical disabilities probably will have to pay for making changes to their units and possibly might also have to pay to remove those alterations when they move out. This is an example of how modest the steps the FHAA mandates really are. The law does not require building owners to pay for such changes in structures that predate the effective date of the FHAA.

The FHAA adopted an approach later taken in the area of public transportation by the Americans with Disabilities Act of 1990 (PL 101-336). The idea was to regulate *future* activity, leaving alone existing property and letting time do the essential work of enhancing accessibility. That approach has worked very well with respect to commuter buses and commuter rail services, but it has given us only small gains in the area of housing. This is because most housing stock remains useable for many decades, whereas commuter buses have much shorter lifespans (generally 8 to 10 years). Thus, while most public transit buses now in use were purchased after August 1990 and thus are lift-equipped, most multifamily housing units now occupied by renters or owners were constructed well before the March 13, 1991, effective date of the FHAA and thus are not accessible, because they are exempted from access requirements of the FHAA.

Individuals with disabilities may file complaints alleging noncompliance with the FHAA. See illustration of a complaint form in the nearby box. Official complaint forms may be sent no later than 1 year following the date of the alleged discrimination to HUD, 451 7th Avenue SW, Washington, DC 20410. HUD has 100 days to investigate and respond to the complaint. Within that time period, HUD may refer the complaint to a state or local government agency that has jurisdiction over housing in a particular geographical area. HUD, after looking into the facts of the case, may seek to have the building owner, real estate agent, or other person or entity that manages the housing unit (the respondent) enter into a conciliation agreement with the person who filed the complaint (the complainant). Such agreements must be approved by HUD. They may provide for binding arbitration through which the complainant and the respondent agree to comply with the decision of an impartial third party (the arbitrator).

Unless the complainant chooses to go to court, HUD may arrange for a hearing before an administrative law judge (ALJ). That hearing must take place within 120 days of the issuance of the charge. If the ALJ finds that discrimination did in fact take place or is about to occur, he or she may assess penalties against the respondent. Penalties range up to $10,000 for a first offense, $25,000 for a second offense within a 5-year period, and $50,000 if the respondent has committed two other offenses during the 7-year period ending on the date of the first filing of the charge at issue in the case. If the individual who filed the complaint prevails at the hearing, the ALJ may award him or her reasonable attorney fees and costs. That is because the complainant never should have had to bring the action and thus should not be responsible for the attorney fees associated with it.

In addition, individuals with disabilities who believe they have been the victim of discrimination under the FHAA may go to federal district court for relief. Such courts may award actual and punitive damages and may issue injunctions against further discrimination.

Finally, HUD may refer a complaint to the U.S. Department of Justice (DoJ). The FHAA gives the DoJ the right to file pattern and practice cases against respondents. "Pattern and practice" means that a respondent has engaged in a series of violations, as in constructing several apartment buildings or other complexes over a period of time, in willful disregard of the FHAA's requirements that such structures be accessible and adaptable. Federal courts may award plaintiffs up to $50,000 for a first violation and up to $100,000 for any subsequent violation. Courts may also award attorney fees to the prevailing party, other than the United States.

The Department of Justice successfully sued the developers and architects of five housing complexes in Chicago in late 1997 (U.S. Department of Justice, 1997). The action followed audits that were conducted by "testers" with and without disabilities who posed as prospective buyers. Of the 49 sites tested, 48 were found to be in violation, with 29 significantly out of compliance with the FHAA. In out-of-court settlements with the Department of Justice, the developers agreed to correct most violations in return for not being assessed penalties.

In another case, this one by an Alabama woman whose landlord refused to move her to an accessible apartment, HUD itself acted. The woman was

U.S. Department of Housing and Urban Development
Office of Fair Housing and Equal Opportunity
451 7th Street SW
Washington, DC 20410

Complaints should be signed and dated. They may be mailed to a HUD regional office, to a field office, or to the above address. The "Housing Discrimination Complaint" form includes spaces for the following information. The official form should be used. This example is intended to be used for illustration purposes only.

1. Name of Aggrieved Person   Tel. No. (home)   Tel No. (work)

   _____

   Street Address (City, County, State, and ZIP Code)

   _____

2. Against whom is this complaint being filed? (Last, First, MI)

   _____

   Street Address (City, County, State, and ZIP Code)

   _____

   The party named above is (check one)

   ☐ Builder   ☐ Owner   ☐ Broker   ☐ Salesperson
   ☐ Supt. or Manager   ☐ Bank or Other Lender   ☐ Other

3. What did the persons you are complaining against do? (Check all that apply)

   ☐ Refuse to rent, sell, or deal with you

   ☐ Falsely deny housing was available

   ☐ Discriminate in the conditions or terms of sale or rental occupancy or in services or facilities

   ☐ Discriminate in financing

   ☐ Advertise in a discriminatory way

   ☐ Other

4. Do you believe that you were discriminated against because of your (check all that apply):

   ☐ Race or color   ☐ Religion   ☐ Sex   ☐ Handicap

5. What kind of property was involved?

   ☐ Single-family house   ☐ A house or building for 2 or 3 families

   ☐ A house or building for 4 or more families

   ☐ Other, including vacant land held for residential use

   Did the owner live there? ☐ Yes   ☐ No   ☐ Unknown

   Is the house or property: ☐ Being sold?   ☐ Being rented?

   What is the address of the house or property? (Street, City, County, State)

   _____

unable to enter the bathroom of the apartment she occupied with her teenager daughters because the doorway was too narrow (her daughters had to take care of her needs outside the bathroom). Similarly, the unit lacked a ramp from the front door to the sidewalk; the woman had to roll her wheelchair in the grass, and several times the chair tipped over. In early 1998, HUD announced a settlement with the building's owner and its builder under which they agreed to pay the woman $50,000 to cover costs of making the apartment accessible and to invest another $60,000 to make other units accessible.

HOUSING ACT OF 1937, AS AMENDED
(PL 93-383, 42 USC 1437 ET SEQ.)

Section 8 of this Act authorizes a program of rent subsidies for low-income families, including families with members who have disabilities. The subsidies are intended to make up the difference between fair market value rents and 30% of adjusted family income or 10% of gross family income, whichever is higher. In part because of low fair market value levels, and in part because building owners often wish to avoid becoming subject to federal regulations, Section 8 rent subsidies are most commonly used to pay rent in public housing (i.e., "projects") rather than in private housing. The program has been underfunded for many years (*Opening Doors,* 1996).

HOUSING ACT OF 1959 (PL 86-372, 42 USC 11381 ET SEQ.)

Section 202 of this Act authorizes a program of federal loans to not-for-profit organizations that construct housing units for elderly persons. For many years, the law required that at least 10% of such units be accessible to people with disabilities. However, for a variety of reasons (viz., concerns by advocates of individuals with disabilities that these are "segregated" housing units), Section 202 housing units are now usually "elderly only." Title VI of the Housing and Community Development Act of 1992 (PL 102-550) and Section 10 of the Housing Opportunity Program Extension Act of 1996

(PL 104-120) provide for Section 202 housing units to be designed exclusively for persons 62 years of age and older.

Section 811 takes up where Section 202 leaves off. This Supportive Housing for Persons with Disabilities program offers capital financing (loans bearing no interest) to help finance housing construction or rehabilitation. Repayment of the loan is waived so long as the housing is available for occupancy for 40 years by persons with disabilities who have very low incomes. These loans may be used by not-for-profit organizations to acquire group homes, condominiums, co-operatives, or apartment complexes. It should be evident from this description that Section 811 housing is "segregated" housing, that is, only for people with disabilities.

Rental assistance is also provided under Section 811; these funds make up the difference between HUD-approved operating costs of a unit (apartment, etc.) and 30% of the tenant's adjusted income. Some Section 811 funds are set aside for vouchers and certificates so that eligible people with disabilities may search for suitable quarters, using the vouchers as partial payment of rent.

According to data posted on the HUD Web site (www.hud.gov/fha/mfh/mfh811.htm), the Section 811 program is much smaller than the Section 202 housing program. To illustrate: In federal fiscal year 1996 (ending September 30, 1996), a total of 216 Section 811 projects built 2,700 apartments or other units carrying a mortgage value of $178 million. By contrast, 150 Section 202 (elderly only) projects constructed 7,500 units with a combined mortgage value of $525 million. Thus, three times as much money was spent on housing for older persons as for persons with disabilities. In 1997, HUD spent even less on Section 811 projects: just $95 million, enough to provide housing for just 1,169 individuals with disabilities. The balance of funds set aside for housing for people with disabilities went to fund certificates and vouchers.

Group Homes

Group homes are state-funded and monitored. Some states, notably New York and Michigan, have powerful laws promoting group homes; other states, however, have weak laws or no laws at all. A group home typically is a standard one-family house converted to add more bedrooms. Living in the home are a number (from as few as 6 to as many as 14) of individuals with disabilities, plus a supervisor. Counselors work in the home with the residents but do not themselves reside in the group home. Commonly, residents sign over their Supplemental Security Income (SSI) checks to pay for room and board. They go to a job or day activity center during the day. Earnings from the job or center are the residents' for use as they wish (clothes, recreation, etc.).

Community resistance often accompanies the opening of a group home. Neighbors fear that the group home will result in lower real-estate values, or they are afraid that group-home residents will be dangerous. Typically, such resistance wanes after a few months as neighbors see how well-maintained the group home is and that property values do not decline.

Questions For Reflection And Discussion

1. Why might where someone lives have as great an effect upon one's self-concept as Robey (1997) found in New Jersey?

2. Why does Hewitt (1997) suggest that hallways in private homes be as wide as 60 inches?

3. How might environmental control units (ECUs) make everyday life in an apartment or home much easier for someone with a physical or health disability?

4. Think about quadriplegia, arthritis, and other physical conditions. Then explain why levers are much preferred over doorknobs.

5. What American value conflicts with universal design in private housing?

6. What provisions of the Fair Housing Amendments Act have made it a relatively weak accessibility law?

7. What is "adaptability" in housing design?

8. To which agency does someone file a complaint about discrimination in housing?

9. Why have Section 8 and Section 811 offered relatively little relief to Americans with disabilities who need housing?

10. What has kept group homes from reaching their potential as housing options for people with severe and multiple needs?

Resources

Ann Storck Center
1790 SW 43rd Way
Plantation, FL 33317
1-954-584-8000

Center for Universal Design
North Carolina State University
Box 8613
Raleigh, NC 27695-8613
1-800-647-6777
1-919-515-3082
www.design.ncsu.edu/cud

Concrete Change
concretechange.home.mindspring.com
   This is the Internet home page of
Atlanta's Concrete Change organization.
A related site, that of ADAPT of Georgia, is at
mindspring.com/~adaptgazan/adapt-ga.htm.

IBM Home Director
1-800-426-7235

Madenta Communications
Edmonton, Alberta, Canada
1-800-661-8406

National Accessible Apartment Clearinghouse
1111 14th Street NW, #900
Washington, DC 20005
1-800-421-1221
1-202-842-4811

National Association of Home Builders
400 Prince Georges Boulevard
Upper Marlboro, MD 20772-8731
1-301-249-4000

Office of Fair Housing and Equal Opportunity
U.S. Department of Housing and
Urban Development
451 7th Street SW, Room 5116
Washington, DC 20410
http://www.hud.gov

13
TRANSPORTATION

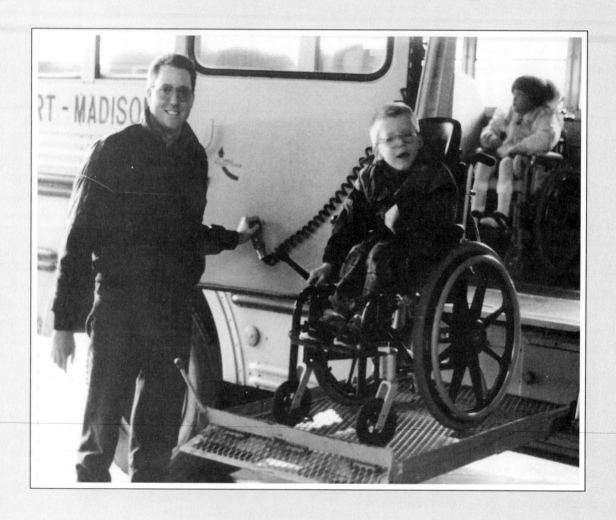

Tom Harper is a 41-year-old student at Hofstra University who traveled four days a week between his home in Melville and the university on Long Island bus routes, using lift-equipped buses. Tom waited for the lift-equipped bus to arrive each afternoon at a bus stop a few feet from a Dunkin' Donuts shop near the campus. He did, that is, until a May 5, 1997, incident dissuaded him. That afternoon, an impatient commuter parked his car right in front of the bus stop and the curb cut and rushed into the Dunkin' Donuts shop. Tom shouted to the man that the only lift-equipped bus for the next hour-plus would be arriving any moment and that he would miss it unless the commuter moved his car. He added the obvious—that Dunkin' Donuts had its own parking lot a few feet away and there were several open parking spaces. The commuter ignored him.

After the bus had come and gone, the commuter returned with his newly purchased coffee and finally spoke to Tom. He called Tom a crybaby and then swore at him and poured his hot coffee over Tom's head. Tom wiped the coffee off but could not keep it from scalding his skin, producing a second-degree burn. The commuter then got into his car and sped away. A few days later, using Tom Harper's description and other eyewitness reports, the local police arrested the commuter. But Tom had had enough—he arranged with a friend to ride to classes that summer in a private car (Vitello, 1997).

Access to transportation is, with accessible housing, one of the most important quality-of-life issues for many Americans with physical disabilities. The 1990 Americans with Disabilities Act (ADA) has made a tremendous difference in the accessibility of public transportation in the United States. Nonetheless, access varies widely from city to city. To illustrate, as of late 1997, just 25% of the bus routes in Houston were accessible, versus 73% in Tucson (Ola, 1997). Access to air travel is uniformly excellent throughout the country; the one area in which exceptions occur is with small, regional air carriers that sometimes still fail to accommodate travelers with physical disabilities.

The December 1997 issue of *New Mobility* magazine carried the feature article "10 Disability-Friendly Cities" (McCoy, 1997). Top-ranked was Denver, which has outstanding public mass transit accessibility in addition to being a relatively flat urban area (notwithstanding the breathtaking mountains clearly visible in the distance!). Berkeley, California, came in second—thanks to the long-standing advocacy of its Center for Independent Living (CIL), one of the nation's oldest and most aggressive such centers. Other top-ranked cities included Seattle, Washington; Sioux Falls, South Dakota; Raleigh, North Carolina; San Jose, California; and Rochester, Minnesota. A common element in every case was an accessible public transit system. (Also important in the rankings were accessible housing and the availability of personal-care assistance services.)

What makes for disability-friendly cities? One key element is the presence of a center for independent living (CIL). These not-for-profit organizations usually are funded by grants from the federal or state government. Some also receive county or local government funding, and a few receive private financing as well. There are more than 500 such centers in the United States today. Their principal purposes are threefold: (1) to offer information and referral services, such as putting people with disabilities in touch with personal assistance services; (2) to provide community advocacy, primarily to urge local government to remove barriers; and (3) to provide direct personal services to individuals with disabilities, including peer counseling and wheelchair repair. Virtually without exception, every city that scored high in the *New Mobility* rankings has a strong CIL.

Two cities that were not ranked were New York City and Los Angeles. New York City has made great progress over the past several years, as exemplified by a 1998 award in a competition sponsored by the National Organization on Disability and United Parcel Service; however, great gaps remain. An obvious example is the city's sprawling subway system. The ADA gives New York City's subway system until 2020 just to make its key stations (points of origination, termination, and transfer) accessible. The long time frame is a recognition of the huge costs that will be involved. Nonetheless, virtually every mass transit bus on the city streets is equipped with a lift, and the city is making good progress with respect to other transit services. Los Angeles is a very different story. The fact that the city is notorious for its utter dependence on private automobiles makes Los Angeles a disability-unfriendly city. There are few lift-equipped buses in the city, lifts often are "broken," and transit personnel frequently are rude (Cromer, 1998).

What can teachers, therapists, counselors, parents, and individuals with disabilities do when they encounter such instances of inaccessibility in transportation? One step is to contact "Project Action," a federally funded effort to improve transportation access by sponsoring and publicizing innovative programs. An example is "Metro Wheels," a project in Los Angeles. As consumers ride the bus, they note its condition, the lift, the actions and attitude of the bus operator, etc. After their ride, they submit their assessments to the LA Metropolitan Transportation Authority (LAMTA) via the Internet. The LAMTA, in turn, creates from these reports daily, weekly, and monthly "report cards" that track what is really happening on the streets of Los Angeles.

Another step is to take advantage of federal laws outlawing discrimination by filing complaints. These laws are "complaint-driven"—that is, the laws take effect in response to complaints filed by people with disabilities. (Suggestions on filing complaints appear later in this chapter.) Especially in rural areas, one may need to rely upon personal vehicles, to which we now turn.

Private Vehicles

Without question, privately owned vehicles are far more convenient than public transportation. The major drawback is cost. Not only do most cars cost more than $20,000 and most customized vans more than $35,000, but insurance, maintenance, and gas and oil add several thousand dollars every year to the cost of owning a vehicle.

If a family or an individual with a physical disability elects to rely primarily upon a privately owned vehicle, the two major choices are cars and vans. Automobiles are fine for people with paraplegia who use folding chairs and for people using crutches and other mobility aids. These aids all can be stored between the front and back seats of most cars or, assuming an ambulatory person is available to assist, in the car's trunk. Automobiles can be equipped with hand controls that permit hand manipulation of gas and brake pedals. People using motorized chairs, however, usually need vans that are equipped with lifts, custom-designed interiors, and, often, raised roofs. Whether one requires customized vans or hand-control-equipped cars, financial assistance is available from the Big Three car companies in Detroit. Each offers rebates that assist both in buying equipment such as lifts and in customizing interiors. The contact points are as follows:

Chrysler Corporation
  Automobility Program
P.O. Box 3124
Bloomfield Hills, MI 48302-3124
1-800-922-3826

General Motors Mobility
  Assistance Program
P.O. Box 901
Detroit, MI 48202-0901
1-800-323-9935

Ford Mobility Motoring
P.O. Box 529
Bloomfield, MI 48303-0529
1-800-952-2248

Beck (1997) offered specific suggestions on van conversions. The key questions, he wrote, are, Can you duck through a van's doorway?, How high do you sit?, and Raise the bridge or lower the river? To explain: If you want to drive the van without leaving your wheelchair, it makes more sense to lower the van's floor than it does to raise the van's roof. This is because one's ability to see clearly is much better with a lowered floor. If the person's eyes while the person is seated in the chair are more than 47 inches from the floor, a raised roof merely gives the person an eye-level view of the van's roof. Also, access to covered parking garages, car washes, and some highways having overpasses is much better when floors are lowered than when roofs are raised.

Intercity Travel: Amtrak Versus Greyhound

It may seem to be paradoxical, but the most accessible means of intercity travel today is by air. Virtually every one of the nation's airports is accessible to and easily used by people with physical or health disabilities, thanks to Section 504 of the Rehabilitation Act of 1973 (refer to chapter 2). Similarly, airplanes are accessible, thanks to the Air Carriers Access Act of 1986, which applied Section 504 to Delta, United, and other air carriers. Even on the ground, access is usually available. Hertz, for example, the nation's largest car rental company, has courtesy buses that kneel to the curb in use in many airports. The buses, made by Gillig Corp., have 16-inch floors and 56-inch-wide doorways. There are times when air travel is not possible or convenient. At such times, travelers with physical or health disabilities often have to rely upon Amtrak or Greyhound.

America's national passenger railroad offers accessibility in every train, with at least one car accessible to people using wheelchairs, most stations accessible by ramps or elevators, and special accommodations on sleeping cars on the long-distance Superliners and Viewliners. Amtrak provides a 15% discount on fares both for individuals with disabilities and for their traveling companions. Reservations for bedrooms on trains are available *only* to persons with disabilities up to 14 days prior to departure, at which time reservations are opened to anyone requesting them. Amtrak's intent is to make sure that people who need accessible bedrooms will get them. Amtrak serves some 500 communities throughout the United States.

For many years, the major alternative to Amtrak for long-distance travel, Greyhound Van Lines, has been another story altogether (see Americans with Disabilities Act, discussed next). Over-the-road buses—featuring elevated passenger decks, forward-facing seats, below-seat storage areas, and onboard rest rooms—are used not only by Greyhound but also by many private charter and tour operators. Beginning in 2000, new over-the-road buses and the terminals they use are to be accessible (small charter and tour companies have until 2001 to make their vehicles accessible), according to plans announced in 1998 by the U.S. Department of Transportation. If all goes as planned, individuals with physical disabilities will find over-the-road buses an attractive alternative to Amtrak for intercity transportation.

Legislation

AMERICANS WITH DISABILITIES ACT
(PL 101-336, 42 USC 12101 et seq.)

Titles II and III of the ADA give persons with disabilities certain civil rights in, respectively, public and private transportation. Title II requires affirmative steps by public transit agencies, while Title III governs private companies that provide transportation services.

As of August 26, 1990, public agencies subject to Title II may purchase or lease lift-equipped new buses only for fixed-route systems (established bus routes that do not vary on a daily basis). They are allowed to buy or lease used buses that do not have lifts, but only after making a good-faith effort to acquire lift-equipped ones. These rules have produced, at the time this text was written, a nationwide fleet of lift-equipped buses. This is because urban mass transit buses have a useful life of about 8 to 10 years. Thus, the fact that the ADA set no requirements for buses in use at the time of enactment (July 26, 1990)—that is, existing buses—is almost irrelevant. Through the "magic" of time and at minimal cost, fleets of thousands of mass transit systems have been equipped with lifts.

Each transit system is required by Title II to offer a comparable paratransit system for people who cannot use even lift-equipped mass transit buses. These "dial-a-ride" services are intended only to complement the fixed-route system. Notably, the ADA does not provide financing for any transportation service or vehicle. It is strictly a civil rights law. Paratransit services, accordingly, are modest in scope and size.

Eligibility to use these dial-a-ride services is restricted to individuals with disabilities that prevent them from safely using mass transit buses even when those buses are lift-equipped. These individuals include, for example, some persons who have chronic fatigue or people who have cognitive limitations such that they cannot remember or follow directions.

Also eligible are individuals whose disabilities in conjunction with other factors prevent them from getting to and from transit stations or bus stops. An example is someone using a wheelchair or crutches who can get to a bus stop in summer but cannot safely do so in the midst of a snowstorm. Distance and the presence of architectural barriers on the route to or from the transit station or bus stop alone are not sufficient to qualify someone with a disability under this category. Congress intended for local government to continue to remove barriers and to install curb cuts and did not want to lessen pressure on those units of government.

Dial-a-ride eligibility has a third category—people who need lifts but who are traveling along a route that does not have any lift-equipped buses in service. By the time this chapter was written, very few such routes remained, so the category is, for all intents and purposes, a void one at this point.

The ADA requires that fares for paratransit be no more than double the regular fixed-route bus fare. Personal care attendants whose presence is needed by an eligible rider travel free. In addition, assuming room is available, a friend or colleague of the eligible rider may also travel for the same fare the eligible rider pays.

It is worth emphasizing the safety-net nature of paratransit services. Such door-to-door or curb-to-curb services are, understandably, popular with many people. They are undeniably convenient. At double-fare rates, each ride costs about $2 in most cities and counties. (Private taxis, by contrast, could charge as much as $10 to $30 for rides of similar distances.) Not surprisingly, then, many individuals with disabilities have sought to gain eligibility for dial-a-ride service.

Paratransit is the number-one area about which complaints have been filed with the U.S. Department of Transportation (Federal Transit Administration, 1997). Thus, a reminder is in order: The ADA provides no funding for paratransit services and limits eligibility rather sharply only to persons who cannot use fixed-route systems. Even so, the cost of paratransit services for people with disabilities is widely expected to exceed $700 million by 2000 (Ola, 1997).

Transit agencies must make their new bus stations and bus stops accessible to individuals with disabilities and shall make other stations accessible as they are renovated over time. The intent is that the station, when viewed as a whole, including path of travel to ticket offices, rest rooms, and waiting areas, is accessible to and useable by people with disabilities. As of August 26, 1990, rapid rail and light rail agencies are required by the ADA to purchase or lease only accessible new rail cars. As with buses, used rail cars that are not accessible may be purchased or leased, but only after a good-faith effort has first been made to acquire accessible cars. At least one car in each train must be accessible. Rail agencies also are required to make accessible all new stations or bus stops as well as key stations. The legislation defines "key stations" as starting and ending points, transfer points, and heavily trafficked points along the routes serviced by the agency. Key stations had to be made accessible no later than mid-1993. Similar rules apply to commuter rail and intercity rail systems.

The Act gave private intercity bus systems far more latitude. Private and intercity bus services are governed by Title III, under which Greyhound was exempted from compliance with the key provisions of the ADA for more than 8 years. The company successfully argued before the Congress that it was bankrupt, gaining a statutory 7-year delay. Later, Greyhound secured for itself another 2-year delay by getting Congress to attach an amendment to a transportation bill. Title III even exempted Greyhound from making its bus stations accessible. In 1998, the U.S. Department of Transportation, together with the U.S. Architectural and Transportation Barriers Compliance Board, finally began writing rules for Greyhound and other over-the-road bus companies, such as tour or charter bus companies. Those rules require Greyhound to buy only lift-equipped buses starting in 2000 and to provide a lift-equipped bus to any prospective passenger who requests one at least 48 hours in advance. Greyhound complained loudly that these measures would cost it more than $100 million.

Private taxi services are required by the ADA to purchase or lease lift-equipped vans or buses *only* if they acquire vans or buses (they may purchase or lease only cars and be in compliance with the law). However, taxi drivers may not refuse to give a ride to an individual with a disability strictly on the basis of disability. That would be discrimination.

Finally, the ADA, in Section 503, expressly bans retaliation, coercion, intimidation, interference, and threatening of persons who are enjoying or are attempting to enjoy their civil rights. This encompasses the all too frequent instances in which bus drivers pass by would-be passengers in wheelchairs, declining to carry them because "the lift doesn't work" and using similar tactics. The U.S. Department of Transportation's regulation carrying out the ADA clearly requires a system of regular and frequent maintenance checks of lifts. The system must be sufficient to determine whether the lifts are operative. Inoperative lifts must be reported immediately and repaired before the buses with those lifts are put back into service. If an inoperative lift is discovered and reported on a fixed route and the next available vehicle will arrive more than 30 minutes later, alternate transportation must be promptly provided for persons with disabilities who require a lift (§37.163). The Department admits that "the requirement to provide back-up transportation is not widely implemented, nor are there regular and frequent checks of lifts as required" (Federal Transit Administration, 1997, p. 2).

The Act gives the U.S. Department of Transportation the right to enforce the public transportation provisions of Title II and, with the U.S. Department of Justice, Title III. Individuals with disabilities may file complaints in writing to U.S. Department of Transportation, Federal Transit Administration, Office for Civil Rights, 400 7th Street SW, Room 7412, Washington, DC 20590. An illustration of the complaint form appears in the nearby box.

U.S. Department of Transportation

Office of Civil Rights

400 7th Street SW

Washington, DC 20590

Complaints should be signed and dated. They may be mailed to the above address. The "ADA Complaint Form" includes spaces for the following information. It also asks whether a lawsuit has been filed and whether a prior complaint has been made by the same person to the Department of Transportation. The official form should be used. This example is intended to be used for illustration purposes only.

Section I

Your Name   Tel. No. (home)   Tel No. (work)

_____

Street Address (City, County, State, and ZIP Code)

_____

Electronic Mail Address: _____

Accessible Format Requirements?   Large type   _____

                                    Audio tape   _____

                                    TDD   _____

                                    Other   _____

Section II

Name of the transit provider complaint is against:

_____

Contact person: _____   Title: _____

Telephone number: _____

On separate sheets, please describe your complaint. You should include specific details such as names, dates, times, route numbers, witnesses, and any other information that would assist us in our investigation of your allegations. Please also provide any other documentation that is relevant to this complaint.

May we release a copy of your complaint to the transit provider?

     Yes _____   No _____

May we release your identity to the transit provider?

     Yes _____   No _____

Please sign here:

_____

(Note: We cannot accept your complaint without a signature.)

Date: _____

Air carriers may use "boarding chairs" to assist people who use wheelchairs. Boarding chairs are much narrower and lighter than wheelchairs. They are not designed to be used independently (note absence of wheels).

The U.S. Department of Transportation (DOT) considers persons with temporary disabilities to be eligible for using both fixed-route and dial-a-ride services for the duration of their disability status. It requires that local transit agencies set an expiration date after which the person, presumably recovered from the injury or illness, is again able to travel independently without need for lifts or special vehicles. Similarly, DOT requires local transit agencies to provide services to visitors or nonresidents on a time-limited basis, in this case, for 21 days in any given calendar year (U.S. Department of Transportation, 1996).

DOT says that "discrimination is hard to prove" (Federal Transit Administration, 1997), for which reason it encourages complainants to work out an agreement with the local transit authority. "Occasionally, we disagree with the transit provider's determination. In several complaints from areas with severe winters, we have non-concurred with the transit providers' decision to deny eligibility and have encouraged them to grant conditional eligibility under Category 3" (Federal Transit Administration, 1997, page 1).

AIR CARRIERS ACCESS ACT (49 USC 1301)

This Act (passed in 1986 as PL 99-435) requires that air carriers (American, Delta, United, etc.) treat passengers and would-be passengers with disabilities on the same basis (nondiscrimination) as they treat persons without disabilities. The Act in effect extended Section 504 of the Rehabilitation Act of 1973 to the airlines. Section 504 itself applies to airports, virtually all of which received federal funding for construction. Determining that airlines benefit from the federal airport construction funding, PL 99-435 requires airlines to protect the civil rights of individuals with disabilities in much the same ways that airports must do under Section 504.

The U.S. Department of Transportation's regulations (1990) interpret the Air Carriers Access Act as enabling individuals with disabilities to enjoy nondiscriminatory policies, practices, and facilities. Would-be passengers with disabilities may not be denied transport on the basis of disability. Motorized wheelchairs are to be transported on the same flight as the traveling user. Passengers with disabilities are to be assigned seats they can access and use. And people who are blind may receive a seat next to a sighted passenger who helps them during the flight.

Questions For Reflection And Discussion

1. What makes for a disability-friendly city?

2. How do people with paraplegia and others with manual wheelchairs use automobiles well enough that they do not need customized vans?

3. What kinds of buses are regulated by Title II of the ADA, and which types by Title III?

4. What do many adults with disabilities not understand about the ADA's dial-a-ride, or paratransit, program rules?

5. What are the federal rules about accessibility in taxicabs?

6. Why do you think many Americans with disabilities resent the "Greyhound amendment"?

7. What is the significance of the ADA's insistence not only that buses be equipped with lifts but also that those lifts work?

8. What is the importance of the 1986 Air Carriers Access Act?

Resources

National Easter Seals
Society, Inc.
230 West Monroe Street,
Suite 1800
Chicago, IL 60606
(800) 221-6827
(312) 726-6200
E-Mail: nessinfo@seals.com
www.seals.com

Project Action
National Easter Seals Society
700 13th Street NW, #200
Washington, DC 20005
1-800-659-6428
E-Mail: project_action@
nessdc.org
www.projectaction.org

U.S. Department
of Transportation
Federal Transit Administration
Office for Civil Rights
400 7th Street SW, Room 7412
Washington, DC 20590
(202) 366-9306
www.fta.dot.gov

EMPLOYMENT

Suleyman Gokyigit, 19, a college sophomore at the University of Toledo (Ohio), works part-time as a computer programmer at the Toledo office of IntelliData, a 70-million-dollar software company based in Herndon, Virginia. Because he is blind, Suleyman uses speech synthesis at school and at work. The synthesizers speak out loud what appears on the screen. While using a computer, Suleyman bends his head slightly to listen to the synthesizer. More significant, he allows nothing to distract him. This total concentration, plus a prodigious memory, led his colleagues to nickname him "Suleyman the Magnificent," after the 16th-century Ottoman Empire king. He is the only IntelliData employee who is on call 24 hours a day. What his story tells us is that companies will hire individuals who have the knowledge and skills they need—no matter what the disability. That has not always been true in our country's history. Today it is (Berton, 1997).

Employment is the "holy grail" of public services for Americans with disabilities. Our Congress and our state legislatures have authorized a universally available public education through high school for every child and youth who has a disability, at a cost of over $30 billion a year in state and federal spending (that is, our tax dollars). Congress has also acted to protect individuals with disabilities who seek employment by outlawing unjust discrimination. And Congress has insisted that all new public transit vehicles, as well as all new places of public accommodation such as stores and restaurants, be accessible to and useable by people with disabilities.

These laws were passed by elected officials—acting by overwhelming majorities—because they believed that these statutes would pave the way to employment for hundreds of thousands, if not millions, of Americans with disabilities. When people with disabilities work, they pay taxes—and lose eligibility for many taxpayer-supported entitlement programs. The impact on the bottom line of state and federal governments would be massive.

As I argued some 20 years ago (Bowe, 1978, 1980), each person who works instead of receiving entitlement monies saves taxpayers substantial sums of money. First, more than $10,000 per year in subsistence checks and medical coverage would no longer be provided to this individual by state and federal governments. In addition, the person would pay state and federal income taxes of several thousand dollars each year. If 100,000 adults with disabilities were to leave entitlement rolls and enter payrolls, the annual net gain for U.S. taxpayers would exceed $1.5 billion. Meanwhile, these adults would be able to live far more rewarding lives because with their pay they could buy the housing, transportation, and disability accommodations they needed plus, of course, the many discretionary items that help make up "the good life."

The exciting reality is that there never has been in our nation's history a better time for someone with a disability to seek gainful employment. This is so for many reasons. First, the nation's unemployment rate fell to 4.2 percent in Spring 1999 and is likely to remain near that historic low. To understand the meaning of a 4.2 percent unemployment rate, consider that the unemployment rate includes all people temporarily between jobs as well as those who voluntarily leave the labor force for one reason or another. Significantly, the rate does *not* count people who are out of the labor force, that is, people who are neither working nor actively seeking employment. When unemployment rates are very low, as they have been recently, employers have little choice but to reach out to people who are not in the labor force. We are seeing high-tech firms hiring retired programmers, for example, or college sophomores like Suleyman Gokyigit because they cannot find enough software writers in the active labor market. This bodes well for people with disabilities who are in this out-of-the-labor-force group.

Second, there has never before been a time when jobs have placed fewer physical demands on workers than is the case today. This is a major factor for jobseekers and workers who have physical or health disabilities. The nature of work has changed to the point where it now features reading, writing, calculating, and planning. There are not many heavy-lifting jobs in the American economy today.

Third, adults with disabilities today are better educated, on the average, than ever before. The IDEA guarantees an education through high school. The Rehabilitation Act and the ADA both make postsecondary education far more available for today's young people than was the case 25 or more years ago.

Fourth, the so-called work disincentives built into the big entitlement programs—Social Security Disability Insurance (SSI) and Supplemental Security Income (SSI)—are lower than at any time since they were created in 1956 and 1972, respectively. Steps were taken in 1981, in 1986, and again in 1998, to make it easier for people to leave the SSDI and SSI rolls, especially for those who worry about obtaining adequate medical care. We will return to this issue later in the chapter.

Fifth, more than was the case in the recent past, rehabilitation agencies today must acknowledge the vocational potential of clients. The 1992 Amendments to the Rehabilitation Act outlawed the practice, common among many state agencies, of supporting clients only toward entry-level jobs. The federal Rehabilitation Services Administration (RSA) issued a memorandum to this effect in August 1997 ("Policy Directive").

Despite these encouraging developments, the gainful employment levels of Americans with disabilities continue to be very low. As recently as 1998, only 3 out of every 10 (29%) working-age (16 to 64 years of age) adults with disabilities held full- or part-time jobs. To appreciate this statistic, compare it to the 79% rate of employment in full- or part-time jobs among American working-age adults who have no disabilities (N.O.D./Harris, 1998). Similar data, from the 1994–1995 SIPP (McNeil, 1997), appear in Table 14.1. As the table shows, just 1 out of every 4 (26%) adults aged 21–64 who had a severe disability was employed in late 1994 or early 1995, compared to better than 4 out of every 5 Americans in that age range who had no disabilities.

These differences are unacceptable to anyone who believes that people with disabilities are people with abilities. To illustrate, imagine yourself as a teacher in a classroom having ten 14-year-old students with disabilities. If current trends were to continue, only three of your students would get a job after finishing high school or college; the other seven would not. You would be appalled at such prospects. In fact, they might make you seriously question your choice of profession. Now multiply these results by several millions

Table 14.1 Employment Among Adults Aged 21–64 With and Without Severe Disabilities

	Total	Employed Number	Percent
	(in 000's)	(in 000's)	
No disability	119,902	98,396	82.1
Severe disability	14,219	3,707	26.1

Source: McNeil (1997), Table 2.

of adults with disabilities: The dimensions of this national tragedy become unavoidably apparent.

Worse, the employment rates have not changed much since 1970, when we first started tracking jobs among Americans with disabilities. In fact, proportionally more adults with disabilities worked that year than did 10 years later (1980)—and that worked as recently as 1998 (Bowe, 1990; N.O.D./Harris, 1998). This amazes many people. Consider that in 1970 Americans with disabilities had zero federally enforced employment rights, zero rights to a free public education, zero computer-based accommodations, and just one, virtually meaningless, barrier-removal law (the Architectural Barriers Act of 1968). The intervening years, meanwhile, saw the enactment of the Rehabilitation Act of 1973, the Individuals with Disabilities Education Act of 1975, and the Americans with Disabilities Act of 1990. Why have these laws made so little difference in the employment of adults with disabilities?

There are reasons. First, federal and state entitlement programs—notably SSI and Medicaid—were enacted in 1974 and took effect shortly thereafter. Medicaid is the federal medical insurance program for poor people and is routinely offered to SSI beneficiaries. These programs (discussed in detail in chapter 2) grew exponentially in the 1970s, 1980s, and early to mid-1990s. It is human nature to feel that one has a "right" to entitlements—and to want to "get what's coming to me." When one has such low self worth as to believe that a better life is not attainable, SSI and Medicaid seem attractive.

Second, during this same 1970–1998 period, many of the jobs that people with disabilities could get were minimum-wage jobs. (Previous generations, including that of my father, could get well-paying jobs with just a high-school diploma.) The reality is that today's entry-level jobs pay less in real (i.e., after-tax) dollars than is offered by the entitlement programs.

Third, many of these jobs provide no health insurance or very limited health care. Many people who have severe disabilities face the ever present threat of very major medical expenses. Understandably, then, they would be afraid to accept such a job because it would mean giving up much more comprehensive state and federal medical insurance. The 1994–1995 SIPP study (McNeil, 1997) showed that Americans aged 21–54 who had severe disabilities were vulnerable on this issue. Table 14.2 contains proportions of those with private health insurance (i.e., from one's own or a family member's job), government health insurance (e.g., Medicaid), and no health insurance. Fear of loss of government health insurance is a very significant work disincentive according to research conducted by the Social Security Administration (Daniels, 1998).

Finally, it takes time for federal civil rights laws to create social change. As happened earlier with the Civil Rights Act of 1964, the people who benefited during the law's first years were individuals who *already* had jobs. It is only much later that one begins to see significant benefits for people who are entering the labor force for the first time.

Table 14.2 Health Insurance Among Adults Aged 21–64 With and Without Severe Disabilities: Percentages With Coverage

	Source of Insurance		
	Private	*Government*	*None*
No disability	80%	3%	17%
Severe disability	44%	40%	17%

Source: McNeil (1997), Table 3.

In an effort to accelerate the impact of the ADA's Title I, President Clinton signed an executive order on March 13, 1998, creating a National Task Force on Employment of Adults with Disabilities that he charged with identifying and removing barriers to full employment among working-age persons who have disabilities. Members of the task force include top officials of many federal agencies, in recognition of the fact that barriers to employment are found in many different areas (e.g., health care, housing, transportation). The task force is to issue its final report on July 26, 2002, the tenth anniversary of the ADA.

Transition   These realities help us to understand what we must do in our roles as educators, therapists, and counselors. First, we must educate young people who have physical and health disabilities to recognize the reality that they should aim to qualify for and get "good" jobs. These young people must set their goals high. Only such positions carry with them the high salaries and the comprehensive medical insurance that people with severe disabilities need to do better than they can under entitlement programs (N.O.D./Harris, 1998). A job paying at least $20,000 per year with a good health-care policy is probably necessary to enable people to do better than they would on the entitlement rolls. That level of compensation is roughly twice the minimum wage (which is about $11,000 per year).

Second, we must impress upon these young people that such jobs are within their reach—if they prepare themselves by getting the education and training that these jobs require. In many instances, that means not just a high-school diploma but also a postsecondary degree—either an associate of arts (A.A.) degree from a community college in a fast-growing field (finance, leisure, office and factory automation, elder care, etc.) or a bachelor of arts or sciences (B.A. or B.S.) degree. This, in turn, means taking the right courses during high school and in postsecondary programs.

Krause (1996), examining employment among persons who had lived with spinal cord injuries for at least 20 years, discovered that just 3% of those who lacked even a high-school diploma were employed at the time of his survey and only 38% had worked at any time since sustaining the injury. By contrast, 70% of those with a college diploma were working at the time of the survey and 95% had worked at any time since becoming injured.

An as yet unpublished longitudinal study by the federal Rehabilitation Services Administration (RSA) shows that people with all kinds of disabilities earn about 40% more when they have at least a high-school diploma than when they do not. Similarly, former rehabilitation agency clients who could read at 12th-grade reading level earned, on an average, 36% more than those with poor reading skills, and those who had at least 12th-grade math skills made 50% more than those with poor math abilities (Schroeder, 1998). These data dramatically illustrate the importance of education to the ability of people to make a good living.

To become well-paid employees, people with disabilities need not only education but also skills. People who need augmentative communication devices must be trained in their use. For people who are deaf or severely hearing-impaired, this means, above all else, the ability to read and write—very well. Machines that hear are readily available, but they give the user information in print. The individual must be able to read it; otherwise, the technology is useless. That's why helping people who are deaf to learn the English language is the highest priority of deafness education. Individuals who are blind need to know how to use today's technologies (refer to chapter 5).

Third, we must teach these young people what their rights are. Even as late as 1998, many Americans with disabilities did not know what civil rights they enjoyed (N.O.D./Harris, 1998). It is essential for adolescents and young adults to understand these rights to accurately assess their employment prospects. This means recognizing not only job-related rights but also rights in transportation, housing, and community access. When one comprehends the reach and scope of these laws, it becomes clear that employment and independent living are in fact achievable goals.

The IDEA authorizes transition services for young people who have disabilities. These services are to be free to the individuals and to their families, are to begin no later than the person's 14th birthday, and must include services that are "appropriate," meaning that they meet the student's needs. They must be spelled out in the youth's Individualized Education Program (IEP) at age 14 and annually thereafter until the person is graduated from high school or "ages out" upon reaching 22 years of age. Beginning no later than the year in which the young person turns 16, school officials must establish the interagency relations needed to carry out the transition plan. In many instances, this means forging ties with state vocational rehabilitation counselors, a topic to which we now turn.

Rehabilitation

Each state has one or more rehabilitation agencies that work with adults who have disabilities, helping them to prepare for and get paying jobs. There are 84 such agencies in the 50 states, Puerto Rico, Virgin Islands, the District of

Columbia (Washington, D.C.) and some Pacific Islands. About 30 of these agencies serve only clients who are blind or have low vision. Vocational rehabilitation services are funded primarily by the federal government, which pays about 80% of the costs; the states pick up the other 20%.

It is important for readers of this book to understand some significant differences between vocational rehabilitation and special education. First, special education is much better funded. For this reason, schools can spend far more for each child with a disability than rehabilitation agencies can spend for each adult client. Second, special-education and related services that a particular child needs, as spelled out in the child's IEP, are guaranteed to be provided to that child. There are no guarantees when it comes to vocational rehabilitation. Third, special-education and related services are guaranteed to be free to the child and to the family. Some vocational rehabilitation services—notably diagnosis, preparation of the Individualized Plan for Employment (IPE), and counseling—are free to clients and their families, but other services may be paid for both by the agency and by the client/family or may be 100% funded by the client and the family. Finally, needed special-education and related services must be made available immediately (usually within 30 days). Vocational rehabilitation services, by contrast, may become available the following year, when funds to pay for them become available. These are all examples of effects of what is called "aging out" from IDEA services.

The fact that services listed in a child's IEP are fully funded by special-education agencies suggests that rehabilitation counselors and allied workers should become involved with young people at or even before they turn 16 (refer to previous section, "Transition"). Beginning this early also is advisable because decisions made at this time are critical and because rehabilitation counselors can convince these teens that they can live a much richer, more rewarding life if employed than if receiving entitlement benefits. As suggested earlier, the best advice a counselor could give to a young person with a disability is to become well-educated and well-trained. Employers are most willing to make accommodations for such workers.

Any services needed beyond high school may be written into an IPE, which contains several elements. First, the client's employment goal is identified. Services that are needed to qualify the individual for the job are then spelled out. The plan will explain who will be responsible for paying for these services (the agency, the client, both). The IPE has a section where the client may explain how and to what extent he or she was personally involved in selecting the goal(s) and in approving the services. Attached to the plan is an explanation of the client's rights to appeal decisions made by the vocational rehabilitation counselor.

Perhaps the most important part of the IPE is the section on goals. Counselors must encourage individuals with disabilities to pursue vocations more because of abilities, talents, and interests than because of disability. Companies need productivity. They will get it if they hire and place based on ability, then make the needed accommodations. Today, we have newspaper editors who are blind and traveling salespeople who use wheel-chairs. This makes sense if you think of these individuals as people with skills and talent.

Jack Cooney, a former disability/veterans equal employment staff member for Bell Atlantic in Boston, thought that way. He was a national leader in accommodating people with disabilities on the job. What made Jack Cooney's work significant? Jack began with the job his company needed to fill, not with the candidate's disability. His thinking went like this: "The job requires X, Y, and Z. We have an applicant for this job who has all those attributes. People object that this kind of job has never been filled by some-one who uses a wheelchair. Some people even tell me it can't be. But I can find a way."

Many hundreds of times, Jack Cooney hired people who had the mix of skills and talents that his company needed—and then, and only then, did he focus on the disability. He identified the accommodations those people needed to perform the job. And then he made the placement. Jack Cooney's approach worked because his company got qualified workers and because the workers got jobs that tapped their talents, interests, and ambitions. These are the ideal outcomes of the hiring process. Not surprisingly, then, the com-pany tends to keep these workers—and the employees tend to stay with the company.

Rehabilitation counselors may be most challenged when they seek to help an individual who first became disabled well into adulthood. Krause and Anson (1996) found that people who were in their 50s when they sus-tained spinal cord injuries were unlikely to return to work unless their former employers brought them back. These adults may find early retirement more appealing unless counselors can convince them of the personal, social, and economic benefits of continuing to work.

Regardless of the jobseeker's age, getting and doing a job requires accessibility across the spectrum. Housing must be affordable, accessible, and located near the workplace. Transportation must be available. For these reasons, counselors must push for full enforcement of the nation's nondis-crimination laws. As noted in earlier chapters, barriers in transportation and in housing will finally be removed only if people file complaints. It is, regrettably, true that if an insurmountable barrier exists anywhere along the spectrum from housing to transportation to office accommodations, the individual cannot do the job. This is true no matter how well-trained he or she is on the actual job tasks. That is why rehabilitation professionals can-not limit themselves to job training but rather must advocate for barrier removal.

Counselors will need to work with clients to think through the routes and barriers to employment. Research shows us that too many people with severe physical or health disabilities give up on employment because they do not understand how achievable it is (Krause & Anson, 1996) and how much employment contributes to overall adjustment to the disability (Krause, 1996). Individuals who sustain traumatic brain injuries are particularly unlikely to return to gainful employment unless they receive extraordinary assistance, such as the help of a supported employment job coach (Wehman, 1994). In supported employment, a rehabilitation worker, known as a job coach, works side by side with the individual who has a disability until that individual masters the work.

Legislation

AMERICANS WITH DISABILITIES ACT
(PL 101-336, 42 USC 12101 ET SEQ.)

Title I of the ADA bars discrimination on the basis of disability in employment by companies having 15 or more workers. The real significance of Title I is that it covers private companies that previously were not subject to any federal disability nondiscrimination law. The Rehabilitation Act of 1973 (discussed next) covered only those private companies (usually very large ones) that had contracts with federal agencies.

The protection offered by the ADA's Title I is broadly based. It encompasses interviews, testing, hiring, placement, benefits, promotion, training, and termination. In each of these employment processes, the employer must provide individuals with disabilities with the same or essentially equal services. The employer may not use disability as a basis for action in any of those processes. For example, employers ensure that office buildings, especially employment interview and testing rooms, are accessible to and useable by people with physical or health disabilities. Position descriptions must be written to require only those abilities the job actually calls for. Phrases such as "prepares reports" are to be used rather than "types reports" because reports may not actually have to be typed. This is a major advantage for job-seekers who have disabilities.

Employers must offer the same benefits packages to workers who do have disabilities as to those who do not. If medical examinations are given, they may be administered only *after* a job offer has been extended (to ensure that medical factors play no role in the actual hiring decision). Employers must provide the same job-related training to workers with as to workers without disabilities. They must make promotions to better, higher-paying jobs equally available. And they must use the same job-related factors—not the disability—as a basis for any termination.

Who enjoys protection under these ADA employment provisions? Title I defines a "qualified individual with a disability" as someone who can do a job with or without a reasonable accommodation. That is, only people who meet the job specifications enjoy nondiscrimination protection. This is why education and training are so critical for people who have physical or health disabilities. If these people do not qualify for jobs for which they have applied, the ADA does nothing for them.

Employers are required to offer reasonable accommodations to qualified individuals with disabilities. A reasonable accommodation is any change in the way a job is done so that someone who is fully qualified to do the job but needs that change in order to do it can, with the accommodation, perform the work. Many hundreds of thousands of reasonable accommodations have been devised over the years. To find examples, point your Web browser to http://janweb.icdi.wvu.edu/pubs/accommodationidealist.html.

The ADA, in Title I, goes a step further: It protects jobseekers and employees from discrimination on the basis of a relationship with someone who has a disability. For example, an employer may not decline to hire someone who has a child with a severe medical condition, nor may the employer extend less than equal medical benefits to such an employee.

Title I of the ADA is carried out by the U.S. Equal Employment Opportunity Commission (EEOC). For comprehensive information on ADA rules about employment, contact the EEOC to request its *Technical Assistance Manual on the Employment Provisions of the Americans with Disabilities Act,* which was first issued in 1992 and has since been updated periodically.

As is the case with other aspects of disability rights, the employment protections in Title I of the ADA generally become effective when people with disabilities file complaints alleging discrimination. A simple complaint, which can take the form of a letter, is all that is required to begin the process. The complaint should identify the individual (including address, phone, and other contact information), the employer (in as much detail as possible), the allegations (specifically what happened, when, and where), and the relief sought (whether the complainant seeks reinstatement, back pay, etc.). A nearby box outlines the contents of a complaint letter. The EEOC will review the complaint and, if necessary, contact the individual for more information. Within 180 days (6 months), the EEOC will either decide to take on the case or give the complainant a "right to sue" letter, which lets the individual pursue the case through legal channels. The lawsuit is to be filed within 90 days after receipt of the right to sue letter.

While complaints to the EEOC are quite easy, litigation is another matter altogether. The decision to file a lawsuit against an employer is not one that should be entered into lightly. Litigation tends to be lengthy, costly, and very draining emotionally (Trapp, 1998; see also Mudrick & Asch, 1996).

REHABILITATION ACT (29 USC 706–794)

The Rehabilitation Act of 1973 (PL 93-112, most recently amended by PL 105-220) was, until the ADA Title I provisions took effect in 1992, the major federal law protecting jobseekers and workers with disabilities against unjust discrimination. It is not going too far to say that had the Act's Title V not been enacted in the 1970s and had it not proven to be successful, Congress would not have extended nondiscrimination protection to private employers in the ADA Title I (Bowe, 1990).

Section 501 of the Rehabilitation Act bars federal agencies—such as the U.S. Department of Health and Human Services, the U.S. Department of Education, and the U.S. Department of Defense—from discriminating against jobseekers and employees who have disabilities. Section 501 is important because it was the first disability employment law to take effect. As such, Section 501 paved the way for other statutory protections for Americans with

U.S. Equal Employment Opportunity Commission

1801 L Street NW

Washington, DC 20507

Complaints should be signed and dated. They may be mailed to the above address. People may also file the initial complaint over the phone and follow up by mail. As noted in the text, people may file complaints with other federal agencies (e.g., with the U.S. Department of Education if it is alleged that a public school discriminated in employment on the basis of disability). Those agencies have work-sharing agreements with the EEOC that may result in the complaints being referred to the Commission. The complaint letter should include the following information:

1. The complainant's name, address, and phone number. [If someone else is filing the complaint on behalf of an individual with a disability, his/her identity may remain confidential unless a court demands it.]

2. The name, address, phone number, and number of employees [if known] of the employer.

3. The basis of discrimination [here, disability].

4. The employment process involved [e.g., failure to hire, failure to promote, failure to offer reasonable accommodation].

5. The date of the alleged discrimination.

6. Descriptive information explaining what happened, where it happened, and who was involved.

7. Identity of any witnesses who can be called upon to verify key aspects of the allegations.

disabilities. Section 501 requires the following of federal agencies: (1) job descriptions must accurately describe what the job actually requires (i.e., the position descriptions may not call for abilities that are not used on the job); (2) tests must measure people's job skills, and not their disabilities; (3) people with disabilities who satisfy the job requirements and pass any necessary test must be given as much chance at the job as anyone else; (4) people with disabilities who receive a job offer must be asked whether they need and want a reasonable accommodation.

Section 501 was much more important in the mid-1970s, when federal agencies were still growing in size, than it has been in recent years, when federal employment has been stable and even declining in some areas. It was also critical in paving the way for other nondiscrimination provisions: It required the federal government to serve as a model for other employers, showing that disability nondiscrimination was feasible and demonstrating how reasonable accommodations could be made on behalf of individuals with a broad range of disabilities.

Section 503 of the Act applies to private companies that do business with federal agencies. For example, IBM sells computers to such agencies as the U.S. Department of Defense, while AT&T offers telecommunications services to such agencies as the U.S. Department of Agriculture. As with Section 501, employers must ensure that all employment processes, from initial interviews to eventual retirement or other termination, are accessible to and useable by people with disabilities. Section 503 is carried out by the U.S. Department of Labor. However, because many of the requirements are similar to those of the ADA, the U.S. Department of Justice accepts Section 503 complaints and will, as needed, forward them to the Labor Department.

Section 504 of the Rehabilitation Act applies to not-for-profit organizations as well as to government agencies on the basis that the programs and activities of these groups and agencies receive or benefit from federal financial assistance (grants). Covered are schools, libraries, colleges and universities, hospitals, airports, and federal agencies. (Title I of the ADA covers many of the same not-for-profit groups; it exempts federal agencies from coverage because Section 501 of the Rehabilitation Act already covers those agencies.) Section 504 requires covered organizations to make all of their programs and activities, including employment, equally available to people with and people without disabilities. Each federal agency has its own Section 504 regulations, which discuss employment, among other matters. Most have interagency agreements with the EEOC such that employment-related complaints may be forwarded to the EEOC for investigation and enforcement.

Questions For Reflection And Discussion

1. What nondisability factors strongly affect the employability of adults with disabilities?

2. What factors should, at least in theory, help adults with disabilities to find jobs in today's economy?

3. Contrast 1970 to 1998 with respect to civil rights for people with disabilities.

4. Which federal agency handles most employment discrimination cases?

5. What is the historical significance of Section 501?

6. How does the ADA define "qualified" individuals with disabilities? How does that definition affect the work of a teacher or counselor?

7. What key facts are required for a complete complaint alleging employment discrimination?

8. Why should counselors become advocates for barrier removal in the community?

Resources

U. S. Department of Justice Civil Rights Division
P.O. Box 66738
Washington, DC 20035-6738
1-800-514-0301
www.usdoj.gov
(The DoJ is responsible for implementing much of the Americans with Disabilities Act as well as much of Section 504.)

U.S. Equal Employment Opportunity Commission
1801 L Street NW
Washington, DC 20507
1-800-669-4000
(ADA questions)
1-800-669-3362
(ADA publications)
www.eeoc.gov

Resources

Keeping Current

This text contains the most accurate and current information available to me at the time of publication. However, our knowledge about individuals with disabilities is growing very rapidly. A tremendous amount of medical research is being conducted, some of which produces data that significantly alter our understanding of certain disabilities. Similarly, new means of intervention and treatment continually appear, some of which represent valuable additions to the state of the art in special education and rehabilitation. An excellent way to keep up with these developments is to make regular and extensive use of the World Wide Web. The Web is a connected fabric linking many thousands of servers (large computers). People browse the Web by pointing such browsers as Netscape Navigator®, Microsoft Internet Explorer®, and Lynx to Web sites, or home pages, that are provided by organizations and companies around the world.

Readers of this text who wish to expand their knowledge are well-advised to exercise caution on the Web. Creating and posting a home page is very easy to do. Many people have done so to offer information about disabilities, education, and rehabilitation. Regrettably, not all of these creators of Web pages are reputable experts about disability. Thus, it is possible for the unwary Web surfer to be seriously misled. There is, for example, a Web home page about multiple sclerosis (MS) (discussed in Part Three) that purports to explain this often mysterious disability and to offer "cures." Similarly, there is a Web home page that promotes the use of "facilitated communication" (refer to Chapter 5) despite the fact that virtually all credible research on the technique has shown that it is both unreliable and dangerous when used with people who have autism.

For these and other reasons, a few suggestions on using the Web appear to be appropriate. First, when looking for information about any particular condition, the reader should start the search at the Web home page of a reputable national organization specializing in that disability. For example, a good starting point for information about cerebral palsy is www.ucpa.org—the home page of United Cerebral Palsy Associations (UCPA). Upon visiting this site, the surfer will find hyperlinks, or instant connections to many other sites. The likelihood is very good that these connected sites are also reputable.

Similarly, when examining fields of study such as special education, a good way to start is by visiting the Web pages of professional associations in that field. With respect to special education, for instance, a good beginning site is www.cec.sped.org—the home page of the Council for Exceptional Children (CEC). Again, the surfer will find many hyperlinks to other reliable home pages. The May/June 1998 issue of *Teaching Exceptional Children* (published by CEC) has a lot of good information about the Web and special education.

Finally, home pages of federal agencies are a good place to begin. For example, the home page of the U.S. Department of Housing and Urban Development (www.hud.gov) offers good information and also has hyperlinks to other reputable sites.

With respect to medical information in particular, a good place to begin is the home page of the National Institutes of Health (NIH), www.nih.gov. Other Web sites include

American Academy of Pediatrics: www.aap.org
American Medical Association: www.ama-assn.org
Centers for Disease Control and Prevention: www.cdc.gov
Intellihealth: www.intellihealth.com
Mayo Clinic: www.mayo.ivi.com
Medscape: www.medscape.org
MedicineNet: www.medicinenet.com
Sapient Health Networks: www.shn.net

Intellihealth offers the opportunity to ask questions of medical doctors and provides "zones" (electronic rooms) on different disabilities. Medscape offers searchable, full-text medical articles, while MedicineNet provides an "Ask the Experts" feature. Sapient Health Networks cosponsors, with the University of California at San Francisco, an online medical chat room moderated by physicians and nurses.

Another resource is *Internet Disability Resources for 98* (Barrow-Bailey & Boyd, 1998). Yet another is the home page of the *New England Journal of Medicine* (NEJM). Upon visiting www.nejm.com, one finds a hyperlink to MedLine, a very helpful search tool for securing abstracts of medical literature. The surfer may use MedLine to locate abstracts on any medical topic.

National Resources

Most internet addresses have "www" prefixes although some do not. Many browsers will assume the "www" prefix if you do not type it in.

American Academy of
Otolaryngic Allergy
8455 Colesville Road #743
Silver Spring, MD 20910
E-mail: AAOA@aol.com

A professional society providing information about asthma.

American Amputee Foundation
P.O. Box 250218
Hillcrest Station
Little Rock, AR 72225-0218
(501) 666-8367

A grant-making foundation that supports research about amputation.

Amputee Coalition of America
900 E. Hill Avenue, Suite 285
Knoxville, TN 37921
(888) AMP-KNOW
(423) 524-8772
E-mail: ACAOne@aol.com

A self-help consumer organization.

American College of Allergy
& Immunology
85 West Algonquin Road #550
Arlington Heights, IL 60005
(708) 427-1200

A professional society offering information about asthma.

American Council of the Blind
1155 15th Street NW
Washington, DC 20005
(202) 467-5081
www.acb.org

One of the nation's oldest membership organizations of and for people who are blind or have low vision.

American Diabetes Association
1660 Duke Street
Alexandria, VA 22314
(800) 232-3472
(703) 549-1500

A major information resource about diabetes and related conditions, including blindness.

American Foundation
for the Blind
11 Penn Plaza, #300
New York, NY 10001
(212) 502-7600
www.afb.org/afb

A major information source on low vision and blindness.

American Juvenile Arthritis
Organization
1314 Spring Street N.W.
Atlanta, GA 30309
(404) 872-7100

This resource specializes in early-onset arthritis.

American Medical Association
515 North State Street
Chicago, IL 60610
(312) 464-5000
www.ama-assn.org

The major association of physicians in the United States. The AMA publishes the *Journal of the American Medical Association* (popularly called *JAMA*), a valuable source of information in many fields of medicine.

American Occupational
Therapy Association (AOTA)
P.O. Box 31220
Bethesda, MD 20824-1220
(301) 652-2682
www.etown.edu/home/ot/aota.
html

The national professional association of occupational therapists.

American Physical Therapy
Association (APTA)
1111 North Fairfax Street
Alexandria, VA 22314
(800) 999-2782
(703) 684-2782
E-mail: practice@apta.org
www.apta.org

The national association of physical therapists. [Note that there is another APTA, the American Public Transit Association, which represents local bus operating authorities.]

American Speech-Language-
Hearing Association (ASHA)
10801 Rockville Pike
Rockville, MD 20852
(800) 638-8255
(301) 897-5700
E-mail: webmaster@asha.org
www2.asha.org/asha/

The major professional organization of speech and language pathologists. The initials stand for its old name (American Speech and Hearing Association) before the profession added "language" to the group's name.

American Therapeutic
Recreation Association
P.O. Box 15215
Hattiesburg, MS 39404-5215
(601) 264-3413
E-mail: atta@accessnet.com
www.atra-tr.org

This organization brings together physical education professionals, physical therapists, and others interested in the therapeutic uses of recreation (e.g., swimming).

ARCH National Resource
Center for Respite and Crisis
Care Services
Chapel Hill Training-
Outreach Project
800 Eastowne Drive, Suite 105
Chapel Hill, NC 27514
(800) 473-1727
(800) 773-5433 (National
Respite Locator Service)
(919) 490-5577
E-mail: HN4735@
connectinc.com
chtop.com/archbroc.htm

The ARCH offers information about and referral to local sources for respite care and similar services. Respite care is an allowable early-intervention service under the IDEA, Part C. It provides much needed breaks for family members from round-the-clock care for an individual with serious health needs.

Arthritis Foundation
1330 West Peachtree Street
Atlanta, GA 30309
(404) 872-7100
(800) 283-7800
www.arthritis.org

This organization supports research and offers information about all kinds of arthritis, particularly adult-onset types.

Association for the
Advancement of Rehabilitation
Technology (RESNA)
1700 N. Moore Street,
Suite 1540
Arlington, VA 22209-1903
(703) 524-6686
E-mail: natloffice@resna.org
www.resna.org/resna/reshome.
htm

RESNA (the initials stand for its old name, the Rehabilitation Engineering Society of North America) brings together engineers and inventors interested in technology for individuals with disabilities.

Association for the Care of
Children's Health (ACCH)
7910 Woodmont Avenue,
Suite 300
Bethesda, MD 20814-3015
(800) 808-2224
(301) 654-6549
E-mail: acch@clark.net
acch.org

This organization advocates for families, especially poor families, that have children with special health needs.

Attention Deficit Disorder
Association (ADDA)
P.O. Box 972
Mentor, OH 44061-0972
(216) 350-9595
(800) 487-2282 (to request
information packet)
E-mail: NATLADDA@aol.com
www.add.org

This organization offers information about and referral to local services for children,
youth, and adults with ADD or ADHD.

Brain Injury Association
(formerly the National Head
Injury Foundation)
1776 Massachusetts Avenue
NW, Suite 100
Washington, DC 20036
(202) 296-6443
www.biausa.org

This organization specializes in traumatic brain injury.

Center for Research on Women
with Disabilities
Department of Physical
Medicine and Rehabilitation
Baylor University College
of Medicine
3440 Richmond Avenue,
Suite B
Houston, TX 77046
(713) 960-0505

This center, affiliated with Baylor University, is headed by a woman who is herself a person with disabilities. It focuses upon the special needs of girls and women who have disabilities, providing both research and training.

Centers for Disease Control
and Prevention
Office on Disability and Health
4770 Buford Highway, F-29
Atlanta, GA 30341
(770) 488-7081
E-mail: lrbl@cdc.gov

This office focuses upon prevention of disability and promotion of health. It sponsors occasional conferences on these topics.

Children and Adults with Attention Deficit Disorders (Ch.A.D.D.)
499 NW 70th Avenue, Suite 101
Plantation, FL 33317
(954) 587-3700
(800) 233-4050 (to request information packet)
www.chadd.org

This association unites people who have ADD or ADHD, as well as members of their families. Major funding for the group's activities has been provided for many years by a drug company that makes and sells Ritalin.

Council for Exceptional Children (CEC)
1920 Association Drive
Reston, VA 20191-1589
(703) 620-3660
E-mail: cec@cec.sped.org
www.cec.sped.org/home.htm

The major professional association for special-education teachers. It has units concentrating on early childhood, physical disability, and other segments of the broad field of special education.

Cystic Fibrosis Foundation
6931 Arlington Road
Bethesda, MD 20814
(800) FIGHT-CF
(301) 951-4422
E-mail: info@cff.org
www.cff.org

One of two major organizations providing information about cystic fibrosis.

Cystic Fibrosis Research, Inc.
560 San Antonio Road, #103
Palo Alto, CA 94306-4349
(650) 326-1038
E-mail: cfri@ix.netcom.com

The other major information source about cystic fibrosis.

Diabetic Research Foundation
120 Wall Street
New York, NY 10005-4001

Another information source on diabetes.

Epilepsy Foundation of America (EFA)
4351 Garden City Drive, 5th Floor
Landover, MD 20785-4941
(800) 332-1000
(301) 459-3700
E-mail: postmaster@efa.org
www.efa.org

The major resource on epilepsy, EFA has a large library of materials on seizures and provides answers by physicians to questions about the disorder.

Family Village
Waisman Center
University of Wisconsin—Madison
1500 Highland Avenue
Madison, WI 53705-2280
www.familyvillage.wisc.edu/

This electronic resource, reachable by the Internet, provides information for families and hyperlinks to other sites of interest to people who are related to or who work with children who have disabilities.

HEATH Resource Center (National Clearinghouse on Postsecondary Education for Individuals with Disabilities)
One Dupont Circle NW, Suite 800
Washington, DC 20036-1193
(800) 544-3284
(202) 939-9320
E-mail: heath@ace.nche.edu
ace-info-server.nche.edu/ Programs/HEATH/home.html

As the name implies, this clearinghouse specializes in accommodations at colleges and universities. The host institution is the American Council on Education (ACE).

Hydrocephalus Association
870 Market Street, #955
San Francisco, CA 94102
(415) 732-7040
E-mail: hydroassoc@aol.com
neurosurgery.mgh.harvard.edu/ha/

This group focuses upon hydrocephalus, a common secondary condition of spina bifida.

Independent Living Research Utilization Project
The Institute for Rehabilitation and Research
2323 South Sheppard, Suite 1000
Houston, TX 77019
(713) 520-0232
E-mail: ilru@bcm.tmc.edu
www.bcm.tmc.edu/ilru

The major information source about local centers for independent living. There are about 500 such advocacy, service, and referral centers in the United States. Their addresses, phone numbers, and other contact information change very frequently, a fact that makes ILRU's annual directory an indispensable tool for anyone interested in the daily lives of adults with disabilities.

InterAmerican Heart
Foundation
7272 Greenville Avenue
Dallas, TX 75231-4596
(972) 706-1218
www.interamericanheart.org

This organization focuses upon heart-related issues in Latin America and the United States.

Juvenile Diabetes Foundation
International
c/o The Diabetes Research
Foundation
120 Wall Street
New York, NY 10005-4001
(800) JDF-CURE
www.jdfcure.com

This organization sponsors research and provides information about juvenile diabetes.

Learning Disabilities
Association of America (LDA)
4156 Library Road
Pittsburgh, PA 15234
(412) 341-1515
E-mail: ldanatl@usaor.net
www.ldanatl.org

A major national organization of persons interested in learning disabilities. Its former name was Association for Children with Learning Disabilities (ACLD).

The Lighthouse
111 East 59th Street
New York, NY 10022-1202
(212) 821-9482
E-mail: info@lighthouse.org
www.lighthouse.org

A major national resource on blindness and low vision, the Lighthouse is headquartered in a universally designed building in mid-Manhattan.

March of Dimes Birth
Defects Foundation
1275 Mamaroneck Avenue
White Plains, NY 10605
(914) 428-7100
E-mail: resourcecenter@
modimes.org
www.modimes.org

The organization that sponsors the March of Dimes fundraising campaign. It is an important information source on birth defects and genetic syndromes.

The Miami Project
to Cure Paralysis
University of Miami
School of Medicine
1600 Northwest 10th Avenue,
#R-48
Miami, FL 33136
(800) STAND-UP
(305) 243-6001
www.cureparalysis.org

A not-for-profit organization dedicated, forthrightly, to "cure" spinal cord injury.

Muscular Dystrophy
Association (MDA)
3300 East Sunrise Drive
Tucson, AZ 85718
(800) 572-1717
(520) 529-2000
E-mail: mda@mdausa.org
www.mdausa.org or mda.org

The organization that sponsors the Labor Day telethon with Jerry Lewis. Proceeds fund a wide variety of activities, some for persons with physical disabilities other than muscular dystrophy.

Myelin Project
1747 Pennsylvania Avenue
NW, #950
Washington, DC 20006
(202) 452-8994
E-mail: myelin@erols.com
www.myelin.org

This organization supports research into the causes and treatment of multiple sclerosis.

Narrative Television Network
5840 South Memorial Drive,
#312
Tulsa, OK 74145-9082
(918) 627-1000

This organization sponsors video description for people who are blind or have low vision.

National AIDS Clearinghouse
P.O. Box 6003
Rockville, MD 20849-6003
(800) 458-5231

A major information source about AIDS.

National Arthritis and
Musculoskeletal and Skin
Diseases Information
Clearinghouse
1 AMS Circle
Bethesda, MD 20892-3675
(301) 495-4484
www.nih.gov/niams

This clearinghouse is sponsored by the National Institutes of Health, a federal agency.

National Association
of the Deaf
814 Thayer Avenue
Silver Spring, MD 20910
(301) 587-1788
www.nad.org
A national membership association of people who are deaf; it also has state chapters throughout the country.

National Association of
Protection and
Advocacy Systems
900 Second Street NE,
Suite 1401
Washington, DC 20002
(202) 408-9514
E-mail: hn4537@handsnet.org
Virtually every state has protection and advocacy (P&A) agencies that are supported by federal and state grants. These P&A agencies advocate on behalf of individuals with multiple and severe needs in education, rehabilitation, and independent living.

National Cancer Institute
Office of Cancer
Communications
31 Center Drive, MSC 2580
Bethesda, MD 20892-2580
(800) 4-CANCER
www.icic.nci.nih.gov
A federal agency, part of the National Institutes of Health.

National Center for Child
Abuse and Neglect
c/o Clearinghouse on Child
Abuse and Neglect Information
P.O. Box 1182
Washington, DC 20013-1182
(800) 394-3366

E-mail: nccanch@calib.com or
prevent@calib.com
www.calib.com/nccanch
One of the few resources specifically focused on child abuse and neglect.

National Center for Learning
Disabilities (NCLD)
381 Park Avenue South,
Suite 1401
New York, NY 10016
(212) 545-7510
(888) 575-7373
www.ncld.org
An important information source about learning disabilities.

National Childhood
Cancer Foundation
P.O. Box 60012
Arcadia, CA 91066-6012
(800) 458-6223
As the name suggests, this foundation supports research and offers information about cancers that occur in children.

National Clearinghouse
for Professions
in Special Education
Council for
Exceptional Children
1920 Association Drive
Reston, VA 20191-1589
(800) 641-7824
(703) 264-9474
E-mail: ncpse@cec.sped.org
www.cec.sped.org/cl-
menu.htm
As the name suggests, the focus of this clearinghouse is on information about supply and demand in the overall field of special education.

National Coalition on Abuse
and Disability
P.O. Box "T"
Culver City, CA 90230-3366
(310) 391-2420
This resource specializes in abuse of children who have disabilities. As the text explained, such children are at greater risk than able-bodied children to be abused or neglected.

National Easter Seals
Society, Inc.
230 West Monroe Street,
Suite 1800
Chicago, IL 60606
(800) 221-6827
(312) 726-6200
E-Mail: nessinfo@seals.com
www.seals.com
A national organization that has hundreds of local chapters that offer direct services to individuals with physical and other disabilities.

National Health
Information Center
P.O. Box 1133
Washington, DC 20013-1133
(800) 336-4797
(301) 565-4167
E-mail: nhicinfo@health.org
nhic-nt.health.org
This resource contains links to other health-related Web sites as well as to organizations, articles, and other sources of information.

National Information Center
for Children and Youth
with Disabilities (NICHCY)
P.O. Box 1492
Washington, DC 20013-1492
(800) 695-0285
(202) 884-8200

E-mail: nichcy@aed.org
www.nichcy.org

A federally funded clearinghouse. The initials stand for its old, presensitive-language name (National Information Center for Handicapped Children and Youth).

National Information Center on Deafness (NICD)
Gallaudet University
800 Florida Avenue NE
Washington, DC 20002-3695
(202) 651-5051
E-mail:
nicd@gallux.gallaudet.edu
www.gallaudet.edu/~nicd

This information center specializes in information about deafness and hearing loss. Gallaudet University is the world's oldest college specifically for students who are deaf.

National Institute of
Neurological Disorders
and Stroke
National Institutes of Health
Bethesda, MD 20892
www.ninds.nih.gov

A major information source on muscular dystrophy.

National Maternal and Child
Health Clearinghouse
2070 Chain Bridge Road,
Suite 450
Vienna, VA 22182-2536
(703) 821-8955,
ext. 254 or 265
E-mail: nmchc@circsol.com

This clearinghouse offers information about the federal- and state-funded maternal and child health programs that provide services for poor families.

National Multiple
Sclerosis Society
733 Third Avenue
New York, NY 10017
(212) 986-3240
(800) 344-4867
www.nmss.org

The major national resource on MS.

National Organization
on Disability
910 16th Street NW
Washington, DC 20006
(202) 293-5968
www.nod.org

A private group promoting employment of adults with disabilities. NOD is the source for the reports on the 1994 and 1998 Harris surveys on Americans with disabilities.

National Organization on Fetal
Alcohol Syndrome
1819 H Street, Suite 750
Washington, DC 20006
1-800-66-NOFAS
www.nofas.org

The major resource on fetal alcohol syndrome (FAS) and fetal alcohol effect (FAE).

National Organization
for Rare Disorders (NORD)
P.O. Box 8923
New Fairfield, CT 06812-8923
(800) 999-6673
(203) 746-6518
E-mail: orphan@nord-rdb.com
www.nord-rdb.com/~orphan

When you can't find information anywhere else about an unusual genetic syndrome, illness, or other condition, try NORD. NORD is also a very

helpful resource on orphan drugs (i.e., medications helping people with very unusual conditions).

National Parent Network
on Disabilities
1727 King Street, Suite 305
Alexandria, VA 22031
(703) 684-6763
E-Mail: npnd@cs.com
www.npnd.org

An important organization of parents of children with disabilities. The NPND supports local chapters of parents throughout the nation.

National Parent to Parent
Support and Information
System, Inc.
P.O. Box 907
Blue Ridge, GA 30513-0907
(800) 651-1151
(706) 632-8822
E-mail: Judd103w@
wonder.em.cdc.gov
www.nppsis.org

Another parent group network.

National Pediatric HIV
Resource Center
15 South Ninth Street
Newark, NJ 07017
(800) 362-0071

An important resource for professionals working with families in which a young child is HIV-positive or has AIDS. As noted in the text, very few American children are HIV-positive. However, those who are, and their families, often need considerable support and assistance.

National Rehabilitation
Information Center (NARIC)
8455 Colesville Road,
Suite 935
Silver Spring, MD 20910-3319
(800) 346-2742
(301) 588-9284
www.naric.com/naric

NARIC provides "off line" (i.e., your requests for information are handled after you log off rather than while you are online) information about thousands of low-tech and high-tech products and services for people with disabilities.

National Resource Center for
Respite and Crisis Care Services
Chapel Hill Training-
Outreach Project
800 Eastowne Drive, Suite 105
Chapel Hill, NC 27514
(800) 473-1727
www.chtop.com/archbroc.htm

A national information and referral source on respite care, an early-intervention service under the IDEA's Part C.

National Spinal Cord
Injury Association
8300 Colesville Road,
Suite 551
Silver Spring, MD 20910
(800) 962-9629
(301) 588-6959
E-mail: nscia2@aol.com
www.spinalcord.org

An important resource about spinal cord injury and about self-help and support groups in different states.

Orton Dyslexia Society
Chester Building #382
8600 LaSalle Road
Baltimore, MD 21286-2044
www.ods.org

A major information source on learning disabilities.

Osteogenesis Imperfecta
Foundation
804 Diamond Avenue,
Suite 210
Gaithersburg, MD 20878
(800) 981-BONE
E-mail: bonelink@aol.com
users.aol.com/bonelink

This foundation supports research and offers information about musculoskeletal conditions.

President's Committee's Job
Accommodation Network
West Virginia University
P.O. Box 6080
Morgantown, WV 26506-6080
(800) 526-7234
(800) 232-9675 (information on the ADA)
E-mail: jan@.iedi.wvu.edu
janweb.icdi.wvu.edu

A federally funded resource specializing in reasonable accommodations on the job for jobseekers and employees who have disabilities.

Project Action
National Easter Seals Society
700 13th Street NW, #200
Washington, DC 20005
1-800-659-6428
E-Mail: project_action@
nessdc.org
www.projectaction.org

Project Action offers technical assistance project grants and publicizes the innovations these grants produce in a federally funded effort to spur creativity in accessible transportation.

Recording for the Blind
and Dyslexic
The Anne T. Macdonald Center
20 Roszel Road
Princeton, NJ 08540
(800) 221-4792
(609) 452-0606
www.rfbd.org

This organization offers talking books and other materials for people who have difficulty reading or cannot read because of vision impairment or dyslexia. The focus on dyslexia is new; for generations, Recording for the Blind specialized in serving only people who were blind or had low vision.

Research and Training Center
on Family Support and
Children's Mental Health
Portland State University
P.O. Box 751
Portland, OR 97207-0751
(800) 628-1696
(503) 725-4040
E-mail: stepheb@rri.pdx.edu
www.adm.pdx.edu/user/rri/rtc

One of several federally supported centers on families and children with disabilities (in this case, mental and emotional conditions).

Self Help for Hard
of Hearing People
7910 Woodmont Avenue,
#1200
Bethesda, MD 20814
(301) 657-2249

A membership organization for people who are hard-of-hearing; it also has state and substate chapters.

Sibling Information Network
A.J. Pappanikou Center
University of Connecticut
249 Glenbrook Road, U64
Storrs, CT 06269-2064
(860) 486-5035

This organization is one of only a few resources specifically geared toward helping brothers and sisters of children and youth who have disabilities. Such siblings often feel taken for granted or otherwise overlooked because the sibling with a disability commands so much time and attention.

Sickle Cell Disease Association
of America
200 Corporate Point, #495
Culver City, CA 90230-7633
(800) 421-8453

A major information source about this genetic disorder.

Social Security Administration
Office of Disability
6401 Security Boulevard
Baltimore, MD 21235
(410) 965-1414
www.ssa.gov/odhome

The federal agency administering Supplemental Security Income (SSI) and Social Security Disability Insurance (SSDI).

Special Olympics International
1325 G Street NW, Suite 500
Washington, DC 20005
(202) 628-3630
E-mail: specialolympics@msn.com
www.specialolympics.org/

This organization supports the annual Special Olympics athletic events in which athletes with mental, physical, and other disabilities compete.

Spina Bifida Association
of America
4590 MacArthur Boulevard
NW, Suite 250
Washington, DC 20007-4226
(800) 621-3141
(202) 944-3285
E-mail: spinabifda@aol.com
www.infohiway.com/spinabifida

This organization is one of only a handful of resources for information about spina bifida.

Technical Assistance
to Parent Programs (TAPP)
Federation for Children
with Special Needs
95 Berkeley Street, Suite 104
Boston, MA 02116
(617) 482-2915
E-Mail: fcsnifo@fcsn.org
www.fcsn.org/tapp/home.htm

As the name implies, this organization supports parents of children with disabilities.

Trace Research &
Development Center
S-151 Waisman Center
University of
Wisconsin—Madison
1500 Highland Avenue
Madison, WI 53705-2280
(608) 262-6966
www.trace.wisc.edu/

A major international resource on technology and disability. The Web site offers a tremendous array of hyperlinks to other resources in the United States and other countries.

United Cerebral Palsy
Associations, Inc.
1660 L Street NW, Suite 700
Washington, DC 20036

(202) 776-0406
(800) 872-5827
E-Mail: ucpnatl@ucpa.org
www.ucpa.org

The major advocacy organization for people with cerebral palsy and the national headquarters for hundreds of local chapters throughout the nation.

U.S. Architectural and
Transportation Barriers
Compliance Board
1331 F Street NW, #1000
Washington, DC 20004-1111
(800) USA-ABLE
www.access-board.gov

The Access Board is an important source of information on accessibility in the built environment and transportation.

U.S. Bureau of the Census
Room 2312
Washington, DC 20233
(301) 763-8300

The source for the Census Bureau's disabilities reports, including the Survey of Income and Program Participation (SIPP) reports, on the number of Americans with disabilities. (The office is located in suburban Maryland, hence the "301" area code; however, the mailing address is in Washington, D.C.)

U.S. Department of Education
Office of Special
Education Programs
400 Maryland Avenue SW
Washington, DC 20202
(202) 205-5465
www.ed.gov

The source for the *Nineteenth Annual Report to Congress on Implementation of the*

Individuals with Disabilities Education Act (1997) and other documents about education for children and youth with disabilities.

U.S. Department of Justice
Office on the Americans
with Disabilities Act
P.O. Box 66738
Washington, DC 20035-6738
1-800-514-0301 (toll-free ADA information number)
1-202-514-0381
www.usdoj.gov
[for ADA information:
www.usdoj.gov/crt/ada/
adahom1.htm]
The main implementation and enforcement office of the Americans with Disabilities Act, Titles II and III.

U.S. Department
of Transportation
400 7th Street SW
Washington, DC 20590
(202) 366-9306
www.fta.dot.gov
The main federal office providing funds for transportation and implementing some ADA Title II provisions.

U.S. Equal Employment
Opportunity Commission
1801 L Street NW
Washington, DC 20507
1-800-669-4000
(ADA questions)
1-800-669-3362
(ADA publications)
www.eeoc.gov

The federal agency responsible for carrying out Title I (employment) of the Americans with Disabilities Act.

WGBH Educational Foundation
125 Western Avenue
Boston, MA 02134
(617) 492-2777 Ext. 3490
www.wgbh.org/dvs
A major national resource on captioning and video description.

Glossary

Absence seizures. In epilepsy, short-term seizures formerly called petit-mal seizures.

Accessible. In building design, a standard applying to existing facilities that requires that at least one of each critical element (entrance, rest room, etc.) be present.

Acquired. As contrasted to congenital, this means that a given condition was first contracted after birth.

Acquired immune deficiency syndrome. AIDS, or the full-symptom condition caused by the HIV virus. Sometimes called auto immune deficiency syndrome or acquired immunodeficiency syndrome.

Adaptability. In newly constructed housing, this means that critical features (switches, cabinets, etc.) may be adjusted readily and inexpensively to make them useable by someone with a physical or health condition.

Advocacy. Goal-directed activities aimed at achieving social change, such as legislation or barrier removal.

Afferent. In neurology, nerves that carry messages *to* the brain; contrasted with efferent.

Age at onset. How old the person was when the condition first appeared.

Alternative keyboard. In technology, a specially designed keyboard that has extra-large buttons or areas on a pad.

American Sign Language. A manual communication system that has its own grammar and syntax; contrasted to Signed English, a manual system following English rules.

Americans with Disabilities Act. The landmark civil rights act of 1990.

Amputation. A condition in which one or more extremities are missing or truncated, whether from birth, illness (e.g., cancer), or an accident.

Antecedent. In applied behavior analysis, the event or situation that immediately precedes a given behavior.

Applied behavior analysis. A form of "behavior modification," this approach teaches that we may alter behavior by changing its consequences, its antecedents, or both.

Appropriate. In special education, specially designed services that meet a child's unique needs, carry out the child's Individualized Education Program (IEP), and are good enough so that child passes from year to year.

Art therapy. Noninstructional services designed to help individuals with disabilities to express their feelings and to accomplish something positive despite their limitations.

Arthritis. An autoimmune condition in which the joints and the tissues around joints become inflamed.

Assistive technology devices. In technology, hardware, software, and firmware products that meet the unique needs of people with disabilities.

Assistive technology services. In technology, the acquisition, customization, installation, repair, etc., of assistive technology devices.

Asthma. A health condition in which the lungs become filled with mucus. Believed to be triggered by environmental factors (e.g., dust) or by exercise.

Attention deficit disorder (ADD).   A health condition in which a person is "unavailable for learning" because he or she is not attending effectively to the education being provided.

Attention deficit hyperactivity disorder.   ADD accompanied by hyperactivity.

Augmentative communication.   The use of assistive technology devices to help an individual with a disability, especially someone with cerebral palsy, to communicate expressively in an effective manner.

Autonomic nervous system.   The part of the peripheral nervous system that controls involuntary muscles and glands that operate independent of human thought.

Barrier-free.   In building design, a facility that has access features in each critical element (e.g., all entrances are wheelchair accessible). Applies to newly constructed buildings.

Becker muscular dystrophy.   The less severe form of MD as compared to Duchenne MD.

Blindness.   Severe visual impairment in both eyes, generally resulting in 20/200 vision or worse.

Cancer.   The term used to describe many different conditions (some fatal, some not) in which cells grow uncontrollably.

Cardiac conditions.   Congenital or acquired heart problems.

Central nervous system.   In neurology, the system that transmits messages to and from the brain. Contrasted to the peripheral nervous system. In the human, CNS nerve cells do not regenerate.

Cerebral palsy.   The physical disability in which damage to the motor cortex of the brain results in incomplete control of the body's muscles.

Child abuse *see also* Neglect.   Nonaccidental, nonsexual, but physical or emotional injury to a child by a caretaker.

Children with disabilities.   In the Individuals with Disabilities Education Act (IDEA), children aged 3 to 18 or 21 who have one or more of a list of conditions and who for that reason require special education and related services.

Closed head injury.   A traumatic brain injury in which the skull is not penetrated; contrasted to open head injuries.

Collaborative teaching.   In education, the joint efforts of regular and special-education teachers.

Conductive education.   A controversial approach developed in Hungary that emphasizes physical activities directed by an adult called the conductor.

Congenital.   Occurring prior to or at birth; contrasted to acquired.

Counseling.   Noninstructional services designed to assist individuals with disabilities to adjust to their limitations, identify appropriate vocational and other life goals, and design strategies and tactics to reach those goals.

Cystic fibrosis.   An inherited condition in which breathing, digestion, and reproduction are affected by the body's inability to manufacture a complete version of the protein cystic fibrosis transmembrane regulator (CFTR).

Deafness.   Severe hearing loss in which comprehension of the spoken word through the ear alone does not occur.

Developmental.   Referring to conditions that occur prior to the age of 18 (sometimes 22); that is, these conditions are present during the person's developmental years.

Diabetes.   A health condition, usually involving problems with insulin, that can have numerous and serious secondary effects, including blindness and heart disorders.

Disability.   A permanent health condition producing significant effects upon such major life activities as working and attending school.

Distance learning.   In technology, education in which the teacher and the students are geographically separated but are linked through telecommunications.

Duchenne muscular dystrophy.   The most severe, usually fatal, version of muscular dystrophy. Believed to be related in some way to the less severe Becker MD.

Early intervention.   Services provided, usually at no cost to families, under Part C of the IDEA.

Efferent.   In neurology, nerves that carry signals *from* the brain; contrasted to afferent.

Empowerment.   An approach to working with individuals who have physical or health conditions in which these persons themselves make the key decisions.

Epilepsy.   A health condition that produces seizures in the brain.

Experiential deprivation.   A situation in which a person with a physical or health condition has not experienced some important developmental activities (living away from home, swimming, or doing other things without adult supervision).

Fair Housing Amendments Act.   The 1988 federal law that banned some, but far from all, discrimination on the basis of disability in housing.

Fetal alcohol syndrome (FAS).   A health condition usually caused by maternal use of alcohol during pregnancy. It is characterized by three kinds of symptoms (facial, mental, and growth).

Frontal lobe.   The part of the brain believed to handle self-monitoring and planning activities. Sometimes damaged in traumatic brain injuries.

Generalized seizures.   In epilepsy, seizures that originate in both hemispheres. Contrasted to partial seizures.

Handicap.   An environmental factor that limits or prevents movement by an individual with a disability.

High-tech.   In technology, devices that have more than one moving part, are electronic in nature, or both. Contrasted to low-tech products.

Human immunodeficiency virus (HIV).   The virus that causes AIDS.

Hydrocephalus.   Buildup of cerebrospinal fluid in the brain. Sometimes a characteristic of spina bifida.

Incidence.   In demographics, the number of new instances of something in a given year. Contrasted to prevalence.

Infants and toddlers.   In the Individuals with Disabilities Education Act (IDEA), children under the age of 3 who have developmental delays or disabilities.

Individualized Education Program (IEP).   The written plan that is prepared for children with disabilities aged 3 to 18 (21).

Individualized Family Services Plan (IFSP).   The written plan that is prepared for infants and toddlers (birth to 36 months of age) and their families.

Individualized Plan for Employment (IPE).   The written plan that is prepared for adult clients of state vocational rehabilitation agencies.

Individuals with Disabilities Education Act (IDEA).   The nation's most important special education law, the IDEA authorizes free and appropriate services up to the point of high-school graduation or aging out at 21 years of age.

Keyguard.   In technology, a plastic sheet with holes that fits over the keyboard.

Learning disabilities.   Limitations in learning thought to be caused by neurological lesions or damage.

Little people.   The preferred term, with "dwarfs," for people who are under 4 feet, 10 inches in height or are expected to reach no more than that height in adulthood.

Low-tech.   In technology, devices that have no or at most one moving part and usually are not electronic.

Magnification programs.   In technology, software programs that enlarge images for individuals with low vision.

Medicaid.   The federal-state medical insurance program for Americans who are poor.

Medically fragile/technology-dependent.   A host of health conditions that render individuals very dependent upon technology to survive.

Medicare.   The federal medical insurance program for older Americans and for some under-65 persons who have disabilities.

Mental retardation. Significantly subaverage intelligence combined with behavior that is typical in much younger persons. If this level of intellectual functioning begins prior to age 18, we use the term *mental retardation;* if, however, it first appears after age 18, another term (i.e., *brain injury*) is used to preserve the developmental nature of the category of persons with mental retardation.

Metacognition. Thinking about thinking, or awareness of one's cognitive processes. This is sometimes a problem for people who have learning disabilities.

Modeling. In applied behavior analysis, the process through which learning occurs after observation of models.

Modified curricula. In this text, adapting standard academic curricula and materials so that individuals with disabilities may learn the material effectively.

Multiple sclerosis. A common neurological condition in which the body attacks the central nervous system.

Muscular dystrophy. A condition in which the body is incapable of producing enough dystrophin, the protein that muscles require.

Musculoskeletal. A category of physical disabilities in which the problems people have are due to lesions in the muscles, bones, or skeleton; contrasted to neurological conditions.

Myelomeningocele. The most severe form of spina bifida.

Neglect *see also* **Child abuse.** Denying a child needed nutrition, shelter, medical care, or supervision.

Neurological. The category of physical disabilities in which the problems people have are due to the central nervous system; contrasted to musculoskeletal conditions.

Occupational therapy. Noninstructional services designed to assist individuals with disabilities to perform goal-directed activities of a sensorimotor, cognitive, or psychosocial nature, including gross- and fine-motor coordination, problem solving, self-control, and self-expression.

Open head injury. In traumatic brain injury, instances in which the skull is penetrated by an external object; contrasted to closed head injuries.

Orientation and mobility specialists. Professionals who teach orientation (where you are) and mobility (how to get where you are going) skills to individuals who are blind or have low vision.

Orthopedic impairments. In the IDEA, the term used to refer to cerebral palsy and other physical disabilities.

Orthosis. An artificial body part. Contrasted to prosthesis.

Other health impaired. In the IDEA, the category used for such health impairments as AIDS and cancer; the category is dominated by attention deficit disorders, which sharply limits the category's use in counting physical and health disabilities in school-age children.

Parallel curriculum. In this text, the teaching of self-help and related skills to school-age children and youth who also take academic coursework.

Paraplegia. A term used in spinal cord injury, cerebral palsy, and some other conditions to refer to limitations in the legs. Contrasted to quadriplegia.

Partial seizure. In epilepsy, a seizure that originates in one hemisphere (although it may spread to the other). Contrasted to generalized seizures.

Peer counseling. Advice and counseling offered by a person who has the same or a similar disability.

Peripheral nervous system. Motor, sensory, and other bodily systems other than the brain and the spinal cord. Contrasted to the central nervous system.

Personal care attendants. People who feed, dress, and otherwise perform personal services for individuals with severe disabilities.

Physical accessibility. Buildings and other structures that are accessible to individuals using wheelchairs or other mobility devices. Contrasted to program accessibility.

Physical therapy. Noninstructional services designed to assist individuals with disabilities to retain or improve gross-motor function and to prevent muscle atrophy.

Prediction software. Software that predicts what word or phrase a user intends to write after the user enters the first few letters.

Presentation punishment. In applied behavior analysis, punishment that involves administration of an unwanted consequence. Contrasted to removal punishment.

Presentation reinforcement. In applied behavior analysis, reinforcement that involves administration of a desired consequence. Often called "positive reinforcement." Contrasted to removal reinforcement.

Pressure sores. Decubitus ulcers that develop if a person does not change position or otherwise move body parts.

Prevalence. In demographics, the number of individuals in a population who have a given characteristic. Contrasted to incidence.

Program accessibility. The term used where activities are accessible to individuals with disabilities even if the overall building or facility is not. For example, a course may be moved from a second-floor to a first-floor room to make that course accessible. Contrasted to physical accessibility.

Prosthesis. A device that supplements a body part. Contrasted to orthosis.

Quadriplegia. In spinal cord injury, cerebral palsy, and other physical disabilities, involvement of all four extremities. Contrasted to paraplegia.

Readily achievable. Doable without much expense or effort.

Rehabilitation Act. The major federal legislation on helping adults with disabilities to become employable. Contains the landmark civil rights provision Section 504.

Related services. In the IDEA, noninstructional services that are needed by children and youth with disabilities so that they may benefit from educational services.

Removal punishment. In applied behavior analysis, punishment that involves removal of a desired consequence. Contrasted to presentation punishment.

Removal reinforcement. In applied behavior analysis, reinforcement that involves removal of an unwanted consequence. Contrasted to presentation punishment.

Scanners. Machines that "read" printed materials. Those with optical character recognition can speak out printed words.

Screen readers. Software programs that help people who are blind or have low vision to navigate a computer screen. Often used together with speech synthesizers.

Section 504. The brief but very important civil rights provision of the Rehabilitation Act that bars recipients of federal funds from discriminating against people who have disabilities.

Shunt. A device used to drain fluid from the brain so as to prevent hydrocephalus. Sometimes used when a person has spina bifida.

Sickle-cell disease. An inherited condition in which blood "sickles" or stretches and clumps together. The person with sickle-cell disease becomes anemic.

Social Security Disability Insurance (SSDI). The federal medical insurance program for people under the age of 65 who develop disabilities that prevent them from working.

Special education. In the IDEA, specially designed (custom-designed) instructional services.

Speech and language pathology. Noninstructional services designed to help individuals with disabilities to develop or improve oral and other expressive communication.

Speech recognition. Software programs that "understand" the spoken word.

Speech synthesis. Software and hardware combinations that speak printed words out loud.

Spina bifida. The spinal-cord-injury-like condition that is present at or shortly after birth.

Spinal cord injury. The disability resulting from damage to the spinal cord.

Substantial gainful activity. This Social Security Administration term refers, in effect, to minimum-wage-level earnings.

Supplemental Security Income (SSI). The federal-state guaranteed minimum-income program that offers supplementary checks intended to bring an individual up to the poverty level.

Supported employment. A service program authorized by the Rehabilitation Act in which job coaches go on the job side by side with individuals with disabilities and stay there until the individual masters the job.

Teamwork. Cooperation between professionals from different disciplines so that their efforts complement each other and benefit individuals with disabilities.

Telecommunications Act of 1996. A massive federal law that contains, among many other things, provisions requiring that broadcast and cable television programs as well as video movies be captioned and that new telecommunications products and services be accessible to and useable by individuals with disabilities.

Temporal lobe. The part of the brain that is believed to be involved in the storage of new information. It is sometimes the site of the lesion in traumatic brain injury.

Tonic-clonic seizures. Major seizures, formerly called grand-mal seizures, that usually result in loss of consciousness.

Transition. In the IDEA, services intended to smooth the move from one program to another (e.g., early intervention to preschool).

Traumatic brain injury. The disability resulting from severe open or closed head injuries.

Type 1 diabetes. Juvenile diabetes, with onset prior to age 16.

Type 2 diabetes. Adult-onset diabetes.

Universal design. In architecture, education, and other areas, the design of a building or program from the beginning to make it accessible to all kinds of people.

Virtual reality. Computer software that creates real-seeming artificial realities. In computer talk, something that is "virtual" does not exist.

References

Abrams, A. (1996, November 14). Far from home. *Newsday*, pp. B3–B5.

Albright, A.L., Cervi, A., and Singletary, J. (1991). Intrathecal baclofen for spasticity in cerebral palsy. *Journal of the American Medical Association, 265,* 1418–1422.

Alpert, B. (1997, November 10). Sweet prospects? Amylin's diabetes drug could be effective, despite inconclusive test findings. *Barron's*, p. 24.

American Academy of Pediatrics. (1995). Health supervision for children with achondroplasia. *Pediatrics, 95*(3), 443–451.

American Cancer Society. (1997). Cancer facts and figures—1997. cancer.org/97childr.html.

American Congress of Rehabilitation Medicine, Head Injury Interdisciplinary Group, Mild Traumatic Brain Injury Committee. (1993). Definition of mild traumatic brain injury. *Journal of Head Trauma Rehabilitation, 8*(3), 86–87.

American Diabetes Association. (1997). Diabetes monitor: ADA and WHO announce new classification and diagnostic criteria for diabetes. mdcc.com.

American National Standards Institute. (1998). *ANSI A117.1 accessibility standard.* New York: Author.

American Psychiatric Association. (1994). *Diagnostic and statistical manual of mental disorders* (4th ed.) (DSM-IV). Washington, DC: Author.

Annegers, J., Grabow, J., Groover, R., Laws, E., Elveback, L., & Kurland, L. (1980). Seizures after head trauma: A population study. *Neurology, 30,* 683–689.

Anson, C., & Shepherd, C. (1996). Incidence of secondary complications in spinal cord injury. *International Journal of Rehabilitation Research, 19,* 55–66.

Archer, D., Cuddon, P., Lipsitz, D., & Duncan, L. (1997). Myelination of the canine central nervous system by glial cell transplantation: A model for repair of human myelin disease. *Nature Medicine, 3*(1), 54–59.

Ariel, A. (1992). *Education of children and adolescents with learning disabilities.* New York: Merrill.

Arnst, C. (1998, April 27). Starving tumors to death. *Business Week*, pp. 64–65.

Arnst, C. (1997, June 23). Pulling back an AIDS lifeline. *Business Week,* p. 46.

Arthritis Foundation. (1991). *Arthritis Foundation media fact guide.* Atlanta, GA: Author.

Arthritis Foundation. (1997). Arthritis Research. arthritis. org.

Assistive technology devices and home accessibility features: Prevalence, payment, need, and trends. (1994). *Advance Data from Vital and Health Statistics,* No. 217.

Associated Press. (1997, November 22). A breath of relief in cystic fibrosis. *Newsday,* p. A6.

Atkins, D. (1997). Early fitting is key to success. *In Motion, 7*(1), 36–37.

Bach, J. (1996). DMD respiratory management. Presentation to the Parent Project's and DMD Research Center's conference. mgen.pitt.edu/res21lay/otherres.

Bach, J., & Moldover, J. (1996). Cardiovascular, pulmonary, and cancer rehabilitation. 2. Pulmonary rehabilitation. *Archives of Physical Medicine and Rehabilitation, 77,* S-45–S-51.

Bachrach, S.J., & Miller, F. (1995). *Cerebral palsy: A complete guide for caregiving.* Bethesda, MD: The Johns Hopkins University Press.

Baladerian, N. (1994). Abuse and neglect of children with disabilities. *ARCH Factsheet Number 36.* National Resource Center for Respite and Crisis Care Services. chtop.com/archfs36.htm.

Ballas, S. (1997). Management of sickle pain. *Current Opinions in Hematology, 4*(2), 104–111.

Barrett, A. (1998, March 9). Merck holds its breath: A new asthma pill has the potential to be a blockbuster. *Business Week* p. 42.

Barrett, A., & Melcher, R. (1998, February 16). A revolution in pain relief? *Business Week,* pp. 71, 73.

Barros-Bailey, M., & Boyd, D. (1998). *Internet disability resources for 98.* White Plains, NY: Ahab Press.

Barth, J., & Macciocchi, S. (Eds.) (1993). Mild traumatic brain injury. *Journal of Head Trauma Rehabilitation, 8*(3), 1–120.

Bartholomew, L., Czyzewski, D., Parcel, G., Swank, P., Sockrider, M., Mariotto, M., Schidlow, D., Fink, R., & Seilheimer, D. (1997). Self-management of cystic fibrosis: Short-term outcomes of the cystic fibrosis family education program. *Health Education and Behavior, 24*(5), 652–666.

Battle, D., Dickens-Wright, L., & Murphy, S. (1998). How to empower adolescents: Guidelines for effective self-advocacy. *Teaching Exceptional Children, 30*(3), 28–33.

Bauman, W., & Spungen, A. (1994). Disorders of carbohydrate and lipid metabolism in veterans with paraplegia or quadriplegia: A model of premature aging. *Metabolism, 43,* 949–956.

Beakley, B., & Yoder, S. (1998). Middle schoolers learn community skills. *Teaching Exceptional Children, 30*(3), 16–21.

Beck, K. (1997, January). Cars and vans: Decisions, decisions, decisions. *New Mobility,* p. 32.

Beck, L., Hammond-Cordero, M., & Poole, J. (1994). Integrated services for children who are medically fragile and technology dependent. *Infants and Young Children, 6*(3), 75–83.

Bensen, E., Jaffe, K., & Tarr, P. (1996). Acute gastric dilation in Duchenne muscular dystrophy. *Archives of Physical Medicine and Rehabilitation, 77,* 512–514.

Berreby, D. (1996, April 29). Up with people: Dwarves meet identity politics. *New Republic,* pp. 14–19.

Berton, L. (1997, August 15). A young, blind whiz on computers makes a name in industry. *Wall Street Journal,* p. B1.

Bigge, J. (Ed.). (1991). *Teaching individuals with physical and multiple disabilities.* Columbus, OH: Merrill/Macmillan.

Blasch, B., Wiener, W., & Welsh, R. (Eds.). (1997). *Foundations of orientation and mobility* (2nd ed.). New York: American Foundation for the Blind.

Blevins, S. (1997, June 2), Fighting cancer—and the FDA. *Wall Street Journal,* p. A22.

Bloom, M. (1996). *Primary prevention practices.* Thousand Oaks, CA: Sage.

Blosser, J., & Pearson, S. (1997). Transition coordination for students with brain injury: A challenge schools can meet. *Journal of Head Trauma Rehabilitation, 12*(2), 21–31.

Bochel, C., and Bochel, H. (1994). Researching disability: Insights from and on the social model. *International Journal of Rehabilitation Research, 17,* 82–86.

Boschen, K. (1996). Correlates of life satisfaction, residential satisfaction, and locus of control among adults with spinal cord injury. *Rehabilitation Counseling Bulletin, 39*(4), 230–243.

Bowe, F. (1978). *Handicapping America: Barriers to disabled people.* New York: Harper & Row.

Bowe, F. (1980). *Rehabilitating America.* New York: Harper & Row.

Bowe, F. (1981). *Comeback: Six remarkable people who triumphed over disability.* New York: Harper & Row.

Bowe, F. (Ed.). (1988). *Toward equality: Education of the deaf.* Final report of the U.S. Congress Commission on Education of the Deaf. Washington, DC: U.S. Government Printing Office.

Bowe, F. (1990). Into the private sector. Rights and people with disabilities. *Journal of Disability Policy Studies, 1*(1), 87–99.

Bowe, F. (1995a). *Birth to five: Early childhood special education.* Albany, NY: Delmar Publishers.

Bowe, F. (1995b). "Is it medically necessary?" The political and economic issues that drive and derail assistive technology development. *Generations, 19*(1), 37–40.

Bowe, F. (1995c). Population estimates: Birth-to-5 children with disabilities. *Journal of Special Education, 28*(4), 461–471.

Bowe, F. (2000). *Birth to five: Early childhood special education* (2nd ed.), Albany, NY: Delmar Publishers.

Bracken, M., Shepard, J., Collins, W., Holford, T., Baskin, D., Eisenberg, H., Flamm, E., Leo-Summers, L., Maroon, J., Marshall, L., et al. (1992). Methylprednisolone or naloxone treatment after acute spinal cord injury: 1-year follow-up data: Results of the second national acute spinal cord injury study. *Journal of Neurology, 77*(2), 324–325.

Brand, C. (1997). Meeting the needs of people with disabilities through federal technology transfer. Testimony before the House Committee on Science, July 15. For copies, contact the Committee, U.S. House of Representatives, Washington, DC 20515.

Braunstein, M. (1997). Homeward bound—And wishing they weren't." *New Mobility, 8*(48), 32–37.

Brennan, M., DePompolo, R., & Garden, F. (1996). Cardiovascular, pulmonary, and cancer rehabilitation. 3.

Cancer rehabilitation. *Archives of Physical Medicine and Rehabilitation, 77,* S-52–S-58.

Brenner, M. (1997). Emerging applications of gene transfer in the hematopoietic cancers. *Journal of Pediatric Hematology and Oncology, 19*(1), 1–6.

Brink, J., Imbus, C., & Woo-sam, J. (1980). Physical recovery after severe closed head trauma in children and adolescents. *Journal of Pediatrics, 97,* 721–727.

Budoff, C. (1998, May 17). Training the disabled to lift an eyebrow and open worlds. *New York Times.*

Bullock, R., Chestnut, R., Clifton, G., Ghajar, J., Marion, D., Narayan, R., Rosner, M., & Wilberger, J. (1995). *Guidelines for the management of severe head injury.* San Francisco: Brain Trauma Foundation, Inc.

Carey, J. (1997, December 15). Rezulin: The FDA made the right call. *Business Week,* p. 39.

Carey, J. (1998a, June 8). A new weapon against cystic fibrosis. *Business Week,* p. 68.

Carey, J. (1998b, January 26). A way to lock out AIDS? *Business Week,* pp. 62–63.

Castleberry, R. (1997). Biology and treatment of neuroblastoma. *Pediatric Clinics of North America, 44* (4), 919–937.

Cedar Rapids Community School District v. Garrett F., March 3, 1999, No. 96–1793.

Center for Universal Design. (1995a). *Fair housing accessibility requirements: How to make them a marketing advantage.* Raleigh: North Carolina State University.

Center for Universal Design. (1995b). *Rights and responsibilities of tenants and landlords under the Fair Housing Amendments Act.* Raleigh: North Carolina State University.

Centers for Disease Control and Prevention. (1992, September 11). Recommendations for the use of folic acid to reduce the number of cases of spina bifida and other neural tube defects. *Morbidity and Mortality Weekly Report, 41,* (RR-14).

Chen, Q., Kirsch, G., Zhang, D., Brugada, R., Brugada, J., Brugada, P., Potenza, D., Moya, A., Borggrefe, M., Breithardt, G., Ortiz-Lopez, R., Wang, Z., Antzelevitch, C., O'Brien, R., Schulz-Bahr, E., Keating, M., Towbin, J., and Wang, Q. (1998). Genetic basis and molecular mechanism for idiopathic ventricular fibrillation. *Nature, 392,* 293–296.

Chaplin, D., Deitz, & Jaffe, K. (1993). Motor performance in children after traumatic brain injury. *Archives of Physical Medicine and Rehabilitation, 74,* 161–164.

Charlton, J. (1998). *Nothing about us without us: Disability oppression and empowerment.* Berkeley: University of California Press.

Clemens, P. (1997). Dystrophin delivery. Presentation at the Parent Project DMD Conference, Pittsburgh, PA, June 28. mgen.pitt.edu/res2lay/meetings/conf97.

Coalition for Consumer Rights. (1997). *Annual survey of Illinois voters.* Available from Council for Disability Rights, 205 West Randolph, Suite 1650, Chicago, IL 60606.

Commission for Accreditation of Rehabilitation Facilities. (1994). *CARF standards manual and interpretive guidelines for organizations serving people with disabilities.* Tucson, AZ: Author.

Conway, S., Pond, M., Watson, A., & Hamnett, T. (1996). Knowledge of adult patients with cystic fibrosis about their illness. *Thorax, 51*(1), 34–38.

Conti, J. (1989). *Counseling persons with cancer.* Springfield, IL: Charles Thomas.

Cook, J. (1991). Higher education: An attainable goal for students who have sustained head injuries. *Journal of Head Trauma Rehabilitation, 6,* 64–72.

Cooke, R. (1996, November 28). Hope for muscular dystrophy. *Newsday,* p. A24.

Cooke, R. (1997, November 27). Study: Starving tumors succeeds. *Newsday,* p. A60.

Cooke, R. (1998a, January 6). Cancer; New keys opening molecular doorways. *Newsday,* pp. C4–C5, C10.

Cooke, R. (1998b, January 20). Fears of a deadlier HIV strain in Africa. *Newsday,* p. C7.

Cooley, E., Glang, A., & Voss, J. (1997). Making connections: Helping children with acquired brain injury build friendships. In Glant, A., Singer, G., & Todis, B. (Eds.), *Students with acquired brain injury: The school's response* (pp. 255–275). Baltimore: Paul H. Brookes Publishing.

Creek, J. (Ed.) (1997). *Occupational therapy and mental health.* Edinburgh, U.K.: Churchill Livingstone.

Cromer, M. (1998). Wheelchairs, trains, & buses: Investigating L.A.'s public transportation. *New Mobility, 9*(52), 22–26.

Crowley, C. (1998, August 25). Summary of Jeffords/Kennedy Work Incentives Improvement Act Substitute Legislation to H.R. 3433. Unpublished material available from the office of Senator Jim Jeffords, U.S. Senate, Washington, DC 20510.

Cruickshank, W. (Ed.) (1976). *Cerebral palsy: A developmental disability* (3rd ed.). Syracuse, NY: Syracuse University Press.

Cystic Fibrosis Foundation. (1998). Facts about cystic fibrosis. www.cff.org/factsabo.htm.

Czerniecki, J. (1996). Rehabilitation in limb deficiency. 1. Gait and motion analysis. *Archives of Physical Medicine and Rehabilitation, 77,* S-3–S-8.

Damiano, D.L., Kelly, L.E., & Vaughn, C.L. (1995). Effects of quadriceps femoris muscle strengthening on crouch gait in children with spastic diplegia. *Physical Therapy, 75,* 658–667.

Daneman, D., & Frank, M. (1996). The student with diabetes mellitus. In Haslam, R., & Valletutti, P. (Eds.), *Medical problems in the classroom* (pp. 97–113). Austin, TX: Pro-Ed.

Daniels, S. (1998). Personal communication, February 25.

Dankert-Roelse, J., & te Meerman, G. (1995). Long term prognosis of patients with cystic fibrosis in relation to early detection by neonatal screening and treatment in a cystic fibrosis centre. *Thorax, 50*(7), 712–718.

Davidson, D. (1995). Physical abuse of preschoolers: Identification and intervention through occupational therapy. *American Journal of Occupational Therapy, 49*(3), 235–243.

Davies, U., Jones, J., Reeve, J., Camacho-Hubner, C., Charlett, A., Ansell, B., Preece, M., & Woo, P. (1997). Juvenile rheumatoid arthritis. Effects of disease activity and recombinant human growth hormone on insulin-like growth factor 1, insulin-like growth factor binding proteins 1 and 3, and ostocalcin. *Arthritis & Rheumatism, 40*(2), 332–340.

Davis, H., Schoendorf, K., Gergen, P., & Moore, R. (1997). National trends in the mortality of children with sickle cell disease, 1968 through 1992. *American Journal of Public Health, 87*(8), 1317–1322.

Deasy-Spinetta, P. (1993). School issues and the child with cancer. *Cancer, 71*(10 Suppl), 3261–3264.

Deering, M. (1996a). Current management of Duchenne muscular dystrophy. Presentation to the Parent Project's and DMD Research Center's Conference, 1996. mgen.pitt.edu/res21ay/meetings/deerconf.htm.

Deering, M. (1996b). Q&A: Effectiveness of physical therapy. www.mgen.pitt.edu/res2ay/faq.

Deitz, S., & Ferrell, K. (1993). Early services for young children with vision impairment: From diagnosis to comprehensive services. *Infants and Young Children, 6*(1), 68–76.

deMontalembert, M., Belloy, M., Bernaudin, F., Gouraud, F., Capdeville, R., Mardini, R., Philippe, N., Jais, J., Bardakdjian, J., Ducrocq, R., Maier-Redelsperger, M., Elion, J., Labie, D., & Girot, R. (1997). Three-year follow-up of hydroxyurea treatment in severely ill children with sickle cell disease. The French Study Group on sickle cell disease. *Journal of Pediatric Hematology and Oncology, 19*(4), 313–318.

Dijikers, M. (1996). Quality of life after spinal cord injury. *American Rehabilitation, 22*(3), 18–24.

Dillard, D. (1989). *National study on abandonment of technology* (1989 annual report on the National Rehabilitation Hospital's Rehabilitation Engineering Center's evaluation of assistive technology, Cooperative Agreement No. H133E0016). Washington, DC: National Institute on Disability and Rehabilitation Research.

Dinklage, D., & Barkley, R. (1992). Disorders of attention in children. In S. Segalowitz and I. Rapin (Eds.), *Child Neuropsychology* (Vol. 7, pp. 279–308). Amsterdam: Elsevier.

DiScala, C., Osberg, J., & Savage, R. (1997). Children hospitalized for traumatic brain injury: Transition to postacute care. *Journal of Head Trauma Rehabilitation, 12*(3), 1–10.

Doelling, J., & Bryde, S. (1995). School reentry and educational planning for the individual with traumatic brain injury. *Intervention in School and Clinic, 31*(2), 101–107.

Dormans, J., & Pellegrino, L. (Eds.). (1998). *Caring for children with cerebral palsy.* Baltimore: Paul H. Brookes.

Dorris, M. (1989). *The broken cord.* New York: Harper Perennial.

Dowling, C. (1997, May). An epidemic of sneezing and wheezing. *Life,* pp. 76–84, 89, 92.

Draper, G., Kroll, M., & Stiller, C. (1994). Childhood cancer. In: Trends in cancer incidence and mortality. *Cancer Surveys, 19,* 493–517.

Duhaine, A., Alario, A., Lewander, W., Schut, L., Sutton, L., Seidl, T., et al. (1992). Head injury in very young children: mechanisms, injury types, and ophthalmologic findings in 100 hospitalized patients younger than 2 years of age. *Pediatrics, 90,* 179–185.

Elliott, T., & Frank, R. (1996). Depression following spinal cord injury. *Archives of Physical Medicine and Rehabilitation, 77,* 816–823.

Emery, A. (1994). *Muscular dystrophy: The facts.* New York: Oxford University Press.

Epilepsy Foundation of America. (1997). Frequently asked questions. www.efa.org.

Epilepsy Foundation of America. (1997). Facts and figures. www.efa.org.

Ervin, M. (1998). Lifetime achievement award: Evan Kemp. *New Mobility, 9*(52), 44.

Esquenazi, A., & Meier, R. (1996). Rehabilitation in limb deficiency. 4. Limb amputation. *Archives of Physical Medicine and Rehabilitation, 77,* S-18–S-28.

Ewing-Cobbs, L., Duhaime, A., & Fletcher, J. (1995). Inflicted and noninflicted traumatic brain injury in infants and preschoolers. *Journal of Head Trauma Rehabilitation, 10*(5), 13–24.

Fair Housing Amendments Act. Public Law 100-430. 42 U.S.C. 3601 et seq.

Federal Transit Administration. (1997). *FTA ADA Newsletter.* Issue Number 1. Washington, DC: U.S. Department of Transportation.

Feigenbaum, R. (1998, February 17). Behind the Section 8 ball. *Newsday,* p. A19.

Field, L., & Tobias, R. (1997). Unravelling a complex trait: The genetics of insulin-dependent diabetes mellitus. *Clinical Investigations in Medicine, 20*(1), 41–49.

Fink, C., Fernandez-Vina, M., & Stastny, P. (1995). Clinical and genetic evidence that juvenile arthritis is not a single disease. *Pediatric Clinics of North America, 42*(5), 1155–1169.

Finnie, N. (1994). *Handling the young cerebral palsied child at home.* New York: McGraw-Hill.

Forest, S. (1997, August 4). Epilepsy: The advance of the century. *Business Week,* p. 36.

Forkosch, J., Kaye, H., & LaPlante, M. (1996). *The incidence of traumatic brain injury in the United States.* Disability Statistics Abstract #14. San Francisco: University of California at San Francisco, Disability Statistics Center.

Fossey, R. (1995). The physically or sexually abused child: What teachers need to know. *Harvard Education Letter, 11*(2), 4–7.

Fralish, K., & McMorrow, M. (1998). *Innovations in head injury rehabilitation.* White Plains, NY: Ahab Press.

Frank, N., Blount, R., & Brown, R. (1997). Attributions, coping, and adjustment in children with cancer. *Journal of Pediatric Psychology, 22*(4), 563–576.

Fries, K. (Ed.). (1997). *Staring back: The disability experience from the inside out.* New York: Plume/Penguin.

Frost, P. (1996). Choice and daily activities for people with disabilities. *International Journal of Rehabilitation, 19,* 89–91.

Galantino, M. (1992). *Clinical assessment and treatment of HIV: Rehabilitation of a chronic illness.* Thorofare, NJ: Slack.

Gallagher, H. (1997). Evan Kemp: 1937–1997. *New Mobility, 8*(49), 14.

Gan, K., Geus, W., Bakker, W., Lamers, C., & Heijerman, H. (1995). Genetic and clinical features of patients with cystic fibrosis diagnosed after the age of 16 years. *Thorax, 50*(12), 1301–1304.

Garber, S., Rintala, D., Rossi, C., Hart, K., & Fuhrer, M. (1996). Reported pressure ulcer prevention and management techniques by persons with spinal cord injury. *Archives of Physical Medicine and Rehabilitation, 77,* 744–749.

Gerales, E., & Ritter, T. (Eds.). (1991). *Children with cerebral palsy: A parent's guide.* Rockville, MD: Woodbine House.

Garrett, L. (1998, February 6). Generic drug found to cut HIV. *Newsday,* p. A26.

Gervasio, A., & Kreutzer, J. (1997). Kinship and family members' psychological distress after traumatic brain injury: A large sample study. *Journal of Head Trauma Rehabilitation, 12*(3), 14–26.

Getch, Y., & Neuharth-Pritchett, S. (1999). Children with asthma: strategies for educators. *Teaching Exceptional Children, 31*(3), 30–36.

Glang, A., Todis, B., Cooley, E., Wells, J., & Voss, J. (1997). Building social networks for children and adults with traumatic brain injury: A school-based intervention. *Journal of Head Trauma Rehabilitation, 12*(2), 32–47.

Glass, P. (1993). Development of vision function in preterm infants: Implications for early intervention. *Infants and Young Children, 6*(1), 11–20.

Glickman, L., Deitz, J., Anson, D., & Stewart, K. (1996). The effect of switch control site on computer skills of infants and toddlers. *American Journal of Occupational Therapy, 50*(7), 545–553.

Gliedman, J., & Roth, W. (1980). *The unexpected minority: Handicapped children in America.* New York: Harcourt Brace Jovanovich.

Goldberg, R. (1997, September 19). EPA to asthmatic kids: Hold your breath. *Wall Street Journal,* p. A14.

Goldhaber, M. (1998, May 29). Ronald Gordon, 32, crusader for rights of disabled. *Newsday,* p. A77.

Gorman, J. (1997). *The seeing glass.* New York: Riverhead Books.

Grimby, G., Andren, E., Holmgren, E., Wright, B., Linacre, J., & Sundh, V. (1996). Structure of a combination of functional independence measure and instrumental activity measure items in community-living persons: A study of individuals with cerebral palsy and spina bifida. *Archives of Physical Medicine and Rehabilitation, 77,* 1109–1114.

Guilday v. Mecosta County. U.S. Court of Appeals for the Sixth Circuit. CA 6, No. 96-1571. (September 2, 1997).

Hackett, J., Johnson, B., Parkin, A., & Southwood, T. (1996). Physiotherapy and occupational therapy for juvenile chronic arthritis: Custom and practice in five centres in the UK, USA, and Canada. *British Journal of Rheumatology, 35*(7), 695–699.

Haecker, S., Stedman, H., Balice-Gordon, R., Smith, D., & Greelish, J. (1996). In vivo expression of full-length human dystrophin from adenoviral vectors deleted of all viral genes. *Human Gene Therapy, 7*(15), 1907–1914.

Hahn, H. (1985). Towards a politics of disability: Definitions, disciplines and policies. *Social Science Journal, 22*, 87–105.

Hallett, T., & Proctor, A. (1996). Maturation of the central nervous system as related to communication and cognitive development. *Infants and Young Children, 8*(4), 1–15.

Hanf, B., & Feinberg, E. (1997). Toward the development of a framework for determining the frequency and intensity of early intervention services. *Infants and Young Children, 10*(1), 27–37.

Hari, M. (1990). The history of conductive education and the educational principles of the Peto System. Paper delivered at the World Congress on Conductive Education, Budapest, Hungary.

Hari, M., & Akos, K. (1988). *Conductive education.* London: Rutledge.

Harris, J., & DePompei, R. (1997). Provision of services for students with traumatic brain injury: A survey of Ohio colleges. *Journal of Head Trauma Rehabilitation, 12*(2), 67–77.

Hayes, A., & Williams, D. (1996). Beneficial effects of voluntary wheel running on the properties of dystrophic mouse muscle. *Journal of Applied Physiology, 80*(2), 670–679.

Haynie, M., Porter, S., & Palfrey, J. (1989). *Children assisted by medical technology in educational settings: Guidelines for care.* Boston: Project School Care, Children's Hospital.

Healthy eye muscles are clue to cause of muscular dystrophy. (1996, April 10). Press release, Johns Hopkins University.

Heath, T. (1998, February 12). Judge rules in golfer's favor: Disabled pro can compete using a cart. *Washington Post,* Article 305306.

Heller, K., Fredrick, L., Dykes, M., Best, S., & Cohen, E. (1999). A national perspective of competencies for teachers of individuals with physical and health disabilities. *Exceptional Children, 65*(2), 219–234.

Heriza, C., & Sweeney, J. (1994). Pediatric physical therapy: Part I. Practice, scope, scientific basis, and theoretical foundation. *Infants and Young Children, 7*(2), 20–32.

Heriza, C., & Sweeney, J. (1995). Pediatric physical therapy: Part II. Approaches to movement dysfunction. *Infants and Young Children, 8*(2), 1–14.

Hertanu, J., & Moldover, J. (1996). Cardiovascular, pulmonary, and cancer rehabilitation. 1. Cardiac rehabilitation. *Archives of Physical Medicine and Rehabilitation, 77*, S-38–S-44.

Hewitt, J. (1997). Designing for personal freedom. *New Mobility, 8*(48), 58–62.

Hill, J.L. (1999). *Meeting the needs of students with special physical and health care needs.* Upper Saddle River, NJ: Merrill/Prentice Hall.

Hockenberry, J. (1995). *Moving violations.* New York: Hyperion.

Holicky, R. (1996). Lawsuits: Look before you leap. *New Mobility, 7*(39), 56–59.

Holland, S. (1997, August 8). Clinton announces $2.4 billion war on diabetes. Reuters news story.

Holme, S., Kanny, E., Guthrie, M., & Johnson, K. (1997). The use of environmental control units by occupational therapists in spinal cord injury and disease services. *American Journal of Occupational Therapy, 51*(1), 42–48.

Hopkins, H., & Smith, H. (Eds.). (1993). *Willard and Spackman's occupational therapy* (8th ed.). Philadelphia: Lippincott.

Human Growth Foundation. (1996). Achondroplasia. Booklet available from HGF, 7777 Leesburg Pike #202 S, Falls Church, VA 22043.

Ingersoll, B. (1997, August 19). FDA approves implant that may help quadriplegics regain use of one hand. *Wall Street Journal,* p. B7.

InterAmerican Heart Foundation. (1998). Epidemiology and statistics. www.interamericanheart.org/Epidem.html.

International classification of diseases. Clinical Modification, Vol. 1, 9th rev. (1989). Geneva, Switzerland: World Health Organization.

Irving Independent School District v. Tatro, 468 U.S. 883, 104 S. Ct. 3371 (1984).

Jacobs, S. (1997, July 15). Testimony before the house Committee on Science. [See Brand, above.]

Jaffe, K., Polissar, N., Fay, G., & Liao, S. (1995). Recovery trends over three years following pediatric traumatic brain injury. *Archives of Physical Medicine and Rehabilitation, 76*, 17–26.

Jain, S. (1996). Rehabilitation in limb deficiency. 2. The pediatric amputee. *Archives of Physical Medicine and Rehabilitation, 77*, S9–S-13.

Johnson, M. (Ed.). (1992). *People with disabilities explain it all for you.* Louisville: Avocado Press.

Jones, L. (1988). The free limb scheme and the limb-deficient child. *Australian Paediatric Journal, 24*(5), 290–294.

Juvenile Diabetes Foundation. (1997). Information about diabetes. jdfcure.com.

Kaminker, L. (1997). No exceptions made: Violence against women with disabilities. *New Mobility, 8*(49), 48–52, 54.

Keller, H. (1903). *The story of my life.* New York: Doubleday, Page & Co.

Kelly, T. (1997). The role of genetic mechanisms in childhood disabilities. In Haslam, R., & Valletutti, P. (Eds.), *Medical problems in the classroom* (pp. 125–159). Austin, TX: Pro-Ed.

Kendall, E., Shum, D., Halson, D., Bunning, S., & Teh, M. (1997). The assessment of social problem-solving ability following traumatic brain injury. *Journal of Head Trauma Rehabilitation, 12*(3), 68–78.

Kerrin, R. (1996). Collaboration: Working with the speech-language pathologist. *Intervention in School and Clinic, 32*(1), 56–59.

Kersting, M., & Schoch, G. (1992). Achievable guidelines for food consumption to reach a balanced fat and nutrient intake in childhood and adolescence. *Journal of American Colleges of Nutrition, 11 Suppl,* 74S–78S.

Knapschaefer, J. (1997, December 15). The end of asthma as we know it? *Business Week,* p. 107.

Knowles, M., Hohneker, K., Zhou, Z., Olsen, J., Noah, T., Hu, P., Leigh, M., Englelhardt, J., Edwards, L., & Jones, K. (1995). A controlled study of adenoviral-vector-mediated gene transfer in the nasal epithelium of patients with cystic fibrosis. *New England Journal of Medicine, 333,* 823–831.

Koch, L., Merz, M., & Lynch, R. (1995). Screening for mild traumatic brain injury: A guide for rehabilitation counselors. *Journal of Rehabilitation, 61*(4), 50–56.

Konstan, M., & Berger, M. (1997). Current understanding of the inflammatory process in cystic fibrosis: Onset and etiology. *Pediatric Pulmonology, 24*(2), 137–142.

Kornblith, A., LaRocca, N., & Baum, H. (1986). Employment in individuals with multiple sclerosis. *International Journal of Rehabilitation, 9,* 155–163.

Kozma, I., & Balogh, E. (1995). A brief introduction to conductive education and its application at an early age. *Infants and Young Children, 8*(1), 68–74.

Kraus, J., Rock, A., & Hemyari, P. (1990). Brain injuries among infants, children, adolescents, and young adults. *American Journal of Disorders in Children, 144,* 684–691.

Krause, J. (1996). Employment after spinal cord injury: Transition and life adjustment. *Rehabilitation Counseling Bulletin, 39*(4), 244–255.

Krause, J., & Anson, C. (1996). Employment after spinal cord injury: Relation to selected participant characteristics. *Archives of Physical Medicine and Rehabilitation, 77,* 737–743.

Kreutzer, J., & Witol, A. (1996). Supported employment as an option for return to competitive employment. *i.e. Magazine, 4*(1), 8–11.

Kreutzer, J., Doherty, K., Harris, J., & Zasler, N. (1990). Alcohol use among persons with traumatic brain injury. *Journal of Head Trauma Rehabilitation, 5*(3), 9–20.

Krousop, T. (1983). A synthesis of the factors that contribute to pressure sore formation. *Medical Hypothesis, 62,* 300–306.

Kuhn, T. (1962). *The structure of scientific revolutions.* Chicago: University of Chicago Press.

Kun, L. (1997). Brain tumors. Challenges and directions. *Pediatric Clinics of North America, 44*(4), 907–917.

Landwehr, L., & Boguniewicz, M. (1996). Current perspectives of latex allergy. *Journal of Pediatrics, 128,* 305–312.

Lantos, J., & Kohrman, A. (1992). Ethical aspects of home care. *Pediatrics, 89,* 920–924.

LaPlante, M., Hendershot, G., & Moss, A. (1992, September 16). Assistive technology devices and home accessibility features: Prevalence, payment, need, and trends. *Advance Data from Vital and Health Statistics, 217.* Hyattsville, MD: National Center for Health Statistics.

LaPlante, M., Kennedy, J., Kaye, H., & Wenger, B. (1996). *Disability and employment.* Disability Statistics Abstract #11. San Francisco: University of California at San Francisco, Disability Statistics Center.

Lary, J., & Edmonds, L. (1996, April 19). Prevalence of spina bifida at birth—United States, 1983–1990. A comparison of two surveillance systems. *Morbidity and Mortality Weekly Report, 45,* Number SS-2.

Lees, D., & LePage, P. (1995). Will robots ever replace attendants? Exploring the current capabilities and future potential of robots in education and rehabilitation. *International Journal of Rehabilitation Research, 17,* 285–304.

Leff, P., & Walizer, E. (1992). *Building the healing partnership: Parents, professionals, and children with chronic illnesses and disabilities.* Cambridge, MA: Brookline Books.

Lenihan, J. (1976/1977, November 1976–January 1977). Disabled Americans: A history. *Performance* (Entire issue). [Only a very limited number of copies remain available. Contact the President's Committee on Employment of People with Disabilities, 1331 F Street NW, Washington, DC 20036 for photocopies.]

Lerner, J., Lowenthal, B., & Lerner, S. (1995). *Attention deficit disorders: Assessment and teaching.* Pacific Grove, CA: Brooks/Cole Publishing Company.

Leukemia Research Fund. (1997). Coping with childhood leukemia. www.leukaemia.demon.co.uk/coping.htm.

Levin, H. (1995). Neurobehavioral outcome of closed head injury: Implications for clinical trials. *Journal of Neurotrauma, 12*(4), 601–609.

Levy, T. (1996). Joe Hayward: Coaching trust. *New Mobility, 7*(35), 63.

Lindehammar, H., & Backman, E. (1995). Muscle function in juvenile chronic arthritis. *Journal of Rheumatology, 22*(6), 1159–1165.

Little People of America. (1997). Dwarfism: Frequently asked questions. www.bfs.ucsd.edu/dwarfism/lpa.htm.

Logan, K., & Malone, D. (1998). Comparing instructional contexts of students with and without severe disabilities in general education classrooms. *Exceptional Children, 64*(3), 343–358.

Lowenthal, B. (1996). Educational implications of child abuse. *Intervention in School and Clinic, 32*(1), 21–25.

Lukens, J. (1994). Progress resulting from clinical trials: Solid tumors in childhood cancer. *Cancer, 74,* 2710–2718.

Luthy, D., et al. (1991). Cesarean section before the onset of labor and subsequent motor function in infants with meningomyelocele diagnosed antenatally. *New England Journal of Medicine, 324,* 662–666.

Lutkenhoff, M., & Oppenheimer, S. (1996). *SPINAbilities: A young person's guide to spina bifida.* Bethesda, MD: Woodbine.

Maddox, S. (1997). Q stands for cure. *New Mobility, 8*(40), 50–51.

Maddox, S. (1998). NewMobility's person of the year: John Kemp. *New Mobility, 9*(52), 34–40, 42.

Malian, I., & Love, L. (1998). Leaving high school: An ongoing transition study. *Teaching Exceptional Children, 30*(3), 4–10.

Mann, W., Hurren, C., & Tomita, M. (1995). Assistive devices used by home-based elderly persons with arthritis. *American Journal of Occupational Therapy, 49*(8), 810–820.

Manton, K., Corder, L, and Stallard, E. (1997, March 18). *Proceedings of the National Academy of Sciences.*

Marciniak, C., Sliwa, J., Spill, G., Heinemann, A., & Semik, P. (1996). Functional outcome following rehabilitation of the cancer patient. *Archives of Physical Medicine and Rehabilitation, 77,* 54–57.

Marini, I., Rogers, L., Slate, J., & Vines, C. (1995). Self-esteem differences among persons with spinal cord injury. *Rehabilitation Counseling Bulletin, 38*(3), 198–206.

Marshall, E., Buckner, E., Perkins, J., Lowry, J., Hyatt, C., Campbell, C., & Helms, D. (1996). Effects of a child abuse prevention unit in health classes in four schools. *Journal of Community Health and Nursing, 13*(2), 107–122.

Martin, J., Marshall, L., & Maxson, L. (1993). Transition policy: Infusing self-determination and self-advocacy into transition programs. *Career Development for Exceptional Individuals, 16,* 53–61.

Massagli, T., Dudgeon, B., & Ross, B. (1996). Educational performance and vocational participation after spinal cord injury. *Archives of Physical Medicine and Rehabilitation, 77,* 995–999.

Mayall, J., & Deshamais, G. (1995). *Positioning in a wheelchair: A guide for professional caregivers of the disabled adult.* Thorofare, NJ: Slack, Inc.

McCoy, C. (1997). 10 disability-friendly cities: Where to live and why. *New Mobility, 8*(51), 19–25.

McDaniel, C. (1997, July/August). High-tech home medical care. *Consumer's Digest,* pp. 81–82.

McGinley, L. (1996, November 15). In the line for AIDS drugs, children are last. *Wall Street Journal,* p. B1.

McGinley, L. (1997, August 13). Clinton will call for drug testing on children. *Wall Street Journal,* p. B1.

McLean, D., Kaitz, E., Keenan, C., Dabney, K., Cawley, M., & Alexander, M. (1995). Medical and surgical complications of pediatric brain injury. *Journal of Head Trauma Rehabilitation, 10*(5), 1–12.

McNeil, J. (1993). *Americans with disabilities: 1991–1992. Data from the survey of income and program participation.* Current Population Reports, P70-33. Washington, DC: U.S. Department of Commerce, Bureau of the Census.

McNeil, J. (1997). *Americans with disabilities: 1994–1995.* Current Population Reports, P70-61. Washington, DC: U.S. Department of Commerce, Bureau of the Census.

Medgyesi, V. (1996). Candidate Callahan. *New Mobility, 7*(35), 76–81.

Medgyesi, V. (1997). Gary Dockery: The man human rights forgot. *New Mobility, 8*(40), 27–30.

Meythaler, J. (1996). The management of severe head injury. *Archives of Physical Medicine and Rehabilitation, 77,* 628–629.

Miller, A. (1997). Current and investigational therapies used to alter the course of disease in multiple sclerosis. *Southern Medical Journal, 90*(4), 367–375.

Miller, H. (1997). Prenatal cocaine exposure and mother-infant interaction: Implications for occupational therapy intervention. *American Journal of Occupational Therapy, 51*(2), 119–131.

Miller, R., Young, J., & Novakovic, P. (1994). Childhood cancer. *Cancer, 75,* 395–405.

Mistreet, S., & Lane, S. (1995). Using assistive technology for play and learning: Children from birth to 10 years of age. In W. Mann & J. Lane (Eds.), *Assistive technology for persons with disabilities* (pp. 129–164). Bethesda, MD: American Occupational Therapy Association.

Mitiguy, J., Thompson, G., & Wasco, J. (1993). *Understanding brain injury: Acute hospitalization, a guide for families and friends.* Boston: J.R. Publishing.

Mocellin, G. (1992). An overview of occupational therapy in the context of American influence on the profession: Part 2. *British Journal of Occupational Therapy, 55*(2), 55–59.

Molinet, J. (1998, May 24). Serving lessons in fortitude. *Newsday,* p. C23.

Moore, J., Graves, W., & Patterson, J. (Eds.). (1997). *Foundations of rehabilitation counseling with persons who are blind or visually impaired.* New York: American Foundation for the Blind Press.

Mudrick, N., & Asch, A. (1996). Investigation and enforcement of a disability discrimination statute. *Journal of Disability Policy Studies, 7*(2), 21–41.

Munoz, K., Krebs-Smith, S., Ballard-Barbash, R., & Cleveland, L. (1997). Food intakes of U.S. children and adolescents compared with recommendations. *Pediatrics, 100*(3)(Pt 1), 323–329.

Murdick, N., & Gartin, B. (1996). The inclusion controversy: Emerging patterns in case law. *Journal of Disability Policy Studies, 7*(2), 43–55.

Muscular Dystrophy Association. (1997). 101 FAQ (frequently asked questions). www.mda.org.

National Cancer Institute. (1996). *Chemotherapy and you: A guide to self-help during treatment.* NIH Publication No. 96-1136. Bethesda, MD: Author.

National Center on Child Abuse and Neglect. (1995). *Child maltreatment 1993: Reports from the states to the National Center on Child Abuse and Neglect.* U.S. Department of Health and Human Services. Washington, DC: U.S. Government Printing Office.

National Coalition for Cancer Research. (1997). Facts about childhood cancer. nccf.org/nccf/facts.htm.

National Council on Disability. (1998). *Access to multimedia technology by people with sensory disabilities.* Washington, DC: Author.

National Council on Disability. (1993). *Study on the financing of assistive technology devices and services for individuals with disabilities.* Washington, DC: Author.

National Easter Seals Society and Century 21. (1996). Easy access housing for easier living. seals.com/publish/achome.

National Easter Seals Society. (1997). Understanding spina bifida. seals.com/publish/understanding/usb.html.

National Head Injury Foundation Task Force. (1988). *An Educator's manual: What educators need to know about students with traumatic brain injury.* Framingham, MA: National Head Injury Foundation.

National Heart, Lung, and Blood Institute. (1995, January 30). Clinical alert—Drug treatment for sickle cell anemia. Washington, DC: National Institutes of Health.

National Information Center for Children and Youth with Disabilities. (1997). General information about spina bifida. www.nichcy.org.

National Institute of Neurological Disorders and Stroke. (1997). Multiple sclerosis: Hope through research. ninds.nih.gov/healinfo/disorder/ms.

National Multiple Sclerosis Society. (1997). MS information. nmss.org/info.html.

National Organization on Disability. (1994). *Closing the gap: Expanding the participation of Americans with disabilities.* Washington, DC: Author (910 16th Street NW, Washington, DC 20006).

N.O.D./Louis Harris & Associates. (1991). *Public attitudes toward people with disabilities.* Washington, DC: National Organization on Disability.

National Organization on Fetal Alcohol Syndrome. (1997). Fetal alcohol syndrome fact sheet. www.nofas.org/stats.html.

National Orthotics and Prosthetics Association. (1995). Written testimony regarding fraud and abuse in health care programs. Submitted to U.S. Senate Special Committee on Aging, Washington, DC, March 21. www.oandp.com/organiza/naaop/naaop6.htm.

National Spinal Cord Injury Association. (1997). Factsheet #1: Common questions about spinal cord injury. www.spinalcord.org.

National Spinal Cord Injury Statistical Center. (1997). Spinal cord injury statistical information. www.cureparalysis.org/faq.

Neistadt, M. (1995). Methods of assessing clients' priorities: A survey of adult physical dysfunction settings. *American Journal of Occupational Therapy, 49*(5), 428–436.

Nelson, K., & Grether, J. (1995). Can magnesium sulfate reduce the risk of cerebral palsy in very low birth weight infants? *Pediatrics, 95,* 263.

Newroe, K. (1997). A tribute to personal assistants. *New Mobility, 8*(40), 43–47.

Nicholson, L. (1998, January 25). Adaptive devices open up technology to the disabled. *San Jose Mercury News.* www.sjmercury.com/newslibrary.

1998 N.O.D./Harris survey of Americans with disabilities. (1998). Washington, DC: National Organization on Disability.

Northwestern University. (1996). Prosthetic information page. pele.repoc.nwu.edu/nupoc.

Nosek, M., Howland, C., & Young, M. (1997). Abuse of women with disabilities: Policy implications. *Journal of Disability Policy Studies, 8*(1,2), 157–175.

Nuland, S. (1997). *The wisdom of the body.* New York: Knopf.

Number of newborns with AIDS declined. (1997, November 25). *Wall Street Journal,* p. B7.

O'Brien, S., & Dean, M. (1997). In search of AIDS-resistant genes. *Scientific American, 277*(3), 44–51.

O'Dell, M., & Dillon, M. (1992). Rehabilitation in adults with human immunodeficiency virus-related diseases. *American Journal of Physical Medicine and Rehabilitation, 71*(3), 183–188.

O'Hanlon, A. (1997, December 28). School "nurse" increasingly is a layman: Hiring lag gives staff, teachers more duties. *Washington Post,* Article No. 301761.

Ola. (1997, Summer). ADA. . .The bus stops here. *Project Action Update,* pp. 10–11. Washington, DC: National Easter Seals Society.

Opening doors: Recommendations for a federal policy to address the housing needs of people with disabilities. (1996). Washington, DC: The Arc.

Paciello, M. (1993, December). Accessibility by any other name is. . .usability. *Computer Engineer News.*

Packer, J., & Kirchner, C. (1997). *Who's watching? A profile of the blind and visually impaired audience for television and video.* New York: American Foundation for the Blind.

Palisano, R., Jolobe, T., Haley, S., Lowes, L., & Jones, S. (1995). Validity of the Peabody developmental gross motor scale as an evaluative measure of infants receiving physical therapy. *Physical Therapy, 75*(11), 939–951.

Paradis, L. (1998). Disability rights laws: No better than their enforcement. *New Mobility, 9*(52), 47–50.

Parette, H. (1997, December). Assistive technology devices and services. *Education and Training in Mental Retardation and Developmental Disabilities,* pp. 267–280.

Parette, H., & Angelo, D. (1996). Augmentative and alternative communication impact on families: Trends and future directions. *Journal of Special Education, 30*(1), 77–98.

Pashkow, P. (1996). Outcomes in cardiopulmonary rehabilitation. *Physical Therapy, 76,* 643–656.

Pelka, F. (1997). *The ABC-CLIO companion to the disability rights movement.* Santa Barbara, CA: ABC-CLIO, Inc.

Peloquin. S. (1990). The patient-therapist relationship in occupational therapy: Understanding visions and images. *American Journal of Occupational Therapy, 44,* 13–22.

Pharmaceutical Information Network. (1997). Frequently asked questions about arthritis. pharminfo.com/arthritis.

Puig, L. (1997). A many-sided approach to kids with limb deficiencies. *In Motion, 7*(1), 26–35.

Quesnel, S., & Malkin, D. (1997). Genetic predisposition to cancer and familial cancer syndromes. *Pediatric Clinics of North America, 44*(4), 791–808.

Radetsky, P. (1997). Immune to a plague. *Discover, 18*(6), 61–67.

Rabin, R. (1997, December 29). Keeping hope alive. *Newsday,* pp. A3, A18.

Rapport, M. (1996). Legal guidelines for the delivery of special health care services in schools. *Exceptional Children, 62*(6), 537–549.

Reeve, C. (1998). *Still me.* New York: Random House.

Rehabilitation Services Administration. (1997, August 19). Policy Directive RSA-PD-97-04, Employment goals for an individual with a disability. Washington, DC: Author.

Reid, A. (1997, June 4). Metro adopts new safeguard for blind on subway platforms. *Washington Post,* electronic edition, n.p. www.washingtonpost.com.

Reid, S., Strong, G., Wright, L., Wood, A., Goldman, A., & Bogen, D. (1995). Computers, assistive devices, and augmentative communication aids: Technology for social inclusion. *Journal of Head Trauma Rehabilitation, 10*(5), 80–90.

Repetto, J., & Correa, V. (1996). Expanding views on transition. *Exceptional Children, 62*(6), 551–563.

Richardson, J. (1998). Dwarfs: A love story. *Esquire, 129*(2), 74–81, 121.

Ricks, D. (1998, March 3). The germ theory of heart disease. *Newsday,* pp. C4–C5.

Ries, L., Kosary, C., Hankey, B., Miller, B., Harras, A., & Edwards, B. (Eds.). (1997). *SEER Cancer Statistics Review, 1973–1994.* NIH Publication No. 97-2789. Washington, DC: National Cancer Institute.

Robey, K. (1997). Structural examination of identity in an individual with severe physical disabilities. *Journal of Developmental and Physical Disabilities, 9*(2), 91–100.

Roizen, N. (1997). New advancements in medical treatment of young children with down syndrome: Implications for early intervention. *Infants and Young Children, 9*(4), 36–42.

Rosenberg, G. (1993). An overview of conductive education in the United States. Paper delivered at the Birmingham Institute for Conductive Education, Birmingham, England.

Rosenecker, J., Harms, K., Bertele, R., Pohl-Koppe, A.; v. Mutius, E., Adam, D., & Nicolai, T. (1996). Adenovirus infection in cystic fibrosis patients: Implications for the use of adenoviral vectors for gene transfer. *Infection, 24,* 1, 5–8.

Rosenthal-Malek, A., & Greenspan, J. (1999). A student with diabetes is in my class. *Teaching exceptional children, 31*(3), 38–43.

Ross, M. (1995, October 4). Pediatric epilepsy patients benefiting From ketogenic diet, now offered at UF. Press release.

Rourk, J. (1996). Roles for school-based occupational therapists: Past, present, future. *American Journal of Occupational Therapy, 50*(9), 698–700.

Rowley-Kelly, F., & Reigel, D. (Eds.). (1993). *Teaching the student with spina bifida.* Baltimore: Paul H. Brookes.

Runnebaum v. NationsBank of Maryland, U.S. Court of Appeals for the Fourth Circuit, CA 4, No. 94-2200 (August 15, 1997).

Samuels, R. (1994). Urban Destination—New York City. *New Mobility, 5*(17), 22.

Sanders, J. (1997). Bone marrow transplantation for pediatric malignancies. *Pediatric Clinics of North America, 44*(4), 1005–1020.

Savage, R., & Mishkin, L. (1994). A neuroeducational model for teaching students with acquired brain injuries. In R. Savage & G. Wolcott (Eds.), *Educational dimensions of acquired brain injury* (pp. 393–412). Austin, TX: PRO-ED.

Scheck, A. (1997). The swank "MS Diet." *New Mobility, 8*(40), 16.

Schendel, D., Berg, C., Yeargin-Allsopp, M., Boyle, C., & Decoufle, P. (1996). Prenatal magnesium sulfate exposure and the risk for cerebral palsy or mental retardation among very low birth weight children aged 3 to 5 years. *Journal of the American Medical Association, 276,* 1843–1844.

Schneider, E., Glass, S., Henke, M., & Overton, J. (1997). Distance learning in gerontology: The future is here. *Generations, 21*(3), 46–49.

Schroeder, F. (1998). Bureaucracy and the individual: The plan for rehabilitation in the twenty-first century. Speech given to the annual conference of the National Federation of the Blind, July 8. Also published in the August-September 1998 issue of *Braille Monitor.* www.nfb.org.

Schuch, C. (1996). Prosthetic knees aid active amputees. *In Motion, 6*(3), 19, 21.

Schwarz, S. (1998, January/February). Creating an accessible home with projects under $100. *Enable,* pp. 52–53.

Schwartz, C., Coulthard-Morris, L., & Zeng, Q. (1996). Psychosocial correlates of fatigue in multiple sclerosis. *Archives of Physical Medicine and Rehabilitation, 77,* 165–170.

Scott, C. (1989). Genetic and familial aspects of limb defects with emphasis on the lower extremities. In Kalamchi, A. (Ed.), *Congenital lower limb deficiencies* (pp. 46–57). New York: Springer-Verlag.

Sebesta, D., & LaPlante, M. (1996). *HIV/AIDS, disability and employment.* Disability Statistics Report (9). Washington, DC: U.S. Department of Education, National Institute on Disability and Rehabilitation Research.

Sedlak, A. (1990). *Technical amendments to the study findings—National incidence and prevalence of child abuse and neglect: 1988.* Rockville, MD: Westat.

Seelman, K. (1997, July 15). Testimony before the house Committee on Technology. [See Brand, above.]

Segalowitz, S., & Lawson, S. (1995). Subtle symptoms associated with self-reported mild head injury. *Journal of Learning Disabilities, 28,* 309–319.

Selby, J., & Zhang, D. (1995). Risk factors for lower extremity amputation in persons with diabetes. *Diabetes Care, 18*(4), 509–516.

Serjeant, S., & Graham, R. (1992). *Sickle cell disease.* New York: Oxford University Press.

Shad, A., & Magrath, I. (1997). Non-Hodgkins lymphoma. *Pediatric Clinics of North America, 44*(4), 863–890.

Shaer, C. (1997). The infant and young child with spina bifida: Major medical concerns. *Infants and Young Children, 9*(3), 13–25.

Shaywitz, S., Shaywitz, B., Pugh, K., Fulbright, R., Constable, R., Mencl, W., Shankweiler, D., Lieberman, A., Skudlarksi, P., Fletcher, J., Katz, L., Marchione, K., Lacadie, C., Gatenby, C., & Gore, J. (1998). Functional disruption in the organization of the brain for reading in dyslexia. *Proceedings of the National Academy of Sciences, 95,* 263–2641.

Shelton, T., & Stepanek, J. (1994). *Family-centered care for children needing specialized health and developmental services.* Bethesda, MD: Association for the Care of Children's Health.

Short, L. (1997). Early screening: A promise for the future. *Hearing Health, 13*(5), 26–27.

Sickle Cell Disease Association of America. (1997). Sickle cell anemia. Los Angeles: Author (3345 Wilshire Blvd. #1106, Los Angeles, CA 90010-1880).

Simpson, J. (1997). *Telecommunications and people with cerebral palsy.* Washington, DC: United Cerebral Palsy Associations, Inc. (Available from: UCPA, 1660 L Street NW, Washington, DC 20036.)

Singhal, A., Davies, P., Wierenga, K., Thomas, P., & Serjeant, G. (1997). Is there an energy deficiency in homozygous sickle cell disease? *American Journal of Clinical Nutrition, 66*(2), 386–390.

Sinnock, P., & Most, R. (1986). Diabetes mortality and morbidity data. In Davidson, J. (Ed.), *Clinical diabetes mellitus: A problem oriented approach.* New York: Thieme.

Smith, J. (1995). Pulmonary rehab. *REHAB Management, 8*(1), 35–36, 39, 41, 132.

Sobsey, D., Randall, W., & Parrila, R. (1997). Gender differences in abused children with and without disabilities. *Child Abuse and Neglect, 21*(8), 707–720.

Sosin, D., Sniezek, J., & Waxweiler, R. (1995). Trends in death associated with traumatic brain injury. *Journal of the American Medical Association, 272,* 1778–1780.

Spiegel, G., Cutler, S., & Yetter, C. (1996). What every teacher should know about epilepsy. *Intervention in School and Clinic, 32*(1), 34–38.

Spivack, F. (1995). Conductive education perspectives. *Infants and Young Children, 8*(1), 75–85.

Springer, J., Farmer, J., & Bouman, D. (1997). Common misconceptions about traumatic brain injury among family members of rehabilitation patients. *Journal of Head Trauma Rehabilitation, 12*(3), 41–50.

Stanton, P. (1993). AIDS: The physical therapist's role in rehabilitation. *American Rehabilitation, 19*(3), 10–11.

Starkloff, M. (1997). Spinal cord injury and centers for independent living. *American Rehabilitation, 23*(1), 7–10.

Stiller, C. (1992). Aetiology and epidemiology. In Plowman, P., & Pinkerton, C. (Eds.), *Paediatric oncology: Clinical practice and controversies.* London: Chapman and Hall Medical.

Stiller, C., Allen, M., & Eatock, E. (1995). Childhood cancer in Britain: The national registry of childhood tumours and incidence rates 1978–1987. *European Journal of Cancer, 31A,* 2028–2034.

Stone, K. (1997). *Awakening to disability.* Volcano, CA: Volcano Press.

Stossel, J. (1997, January 9). Overcoming junk science. *Wall Street Journal,* p. A12.

Stover, S. (1996). Facts, figures, and trends on spinal cord injury. *American Rehabilitation, 22*(3), 25–32.

Sullivan, K., McDonald-McGinn, D., Driscoll, D., Zmijewski, C., Ellabban, A., Reed, L., Emanuel, B., Zackai, E., Arthreya, B., & Keenan, G. (1997). Juvenile rheumatoid arthritis-like polyarthritis in chromosome 22q11.2 deletion syndrome. *Arthritis & Rheumatism, 40*(3), 430–436.

Surgery for epilepsy. (1990, March 19–21). *NIH Consensus Statement, 8*(2), 1–20.

Suris, O. (1997, February 28). AIDS deaths drop significantly for first time. *Wall Street Journal,* p. B1.

Sutton, A. (1993). The new world of conductive education. Paper presented at the Conductive Education Conference, Toronto, Canada, May 28–29.

Talan, J. (1997, December 2). Unraveling the MS mystery. *Newsday,* pp. C3, C8.

Tanouye, E. (1997, October 31). Pfizer stock gets early lift from news on impotence drug, other treatments. *Wall Street Journal,* p. B10.

Teplin, S. (1995). Visual impairment in infants and young children. *Infants and Young Children, 8*(1), 18–51.

They are the inspiration for tonight's Jerry Lewis telethon. (1997, August 31). *Parade,* pp. 4–5.

Thomas, D., & Botterbusch, K. (1997). The vocational assessment protocol for school-to-work transition programs. *Journal of Head Trauma Rehabilitation, 12*(2), 48–66.

Timothy W. v. Rochester School District (D.N.H., 1988); 875 F.2d 954 (1st Cir. 1989), *cert. denied,* 493 U.S. 983 (1989).

Tobias, J. (1997). Universal design applied to business practices. *Technology and Disability, 7,* 63–71.

Toy, A. (1994). Stigma. *New Mobility, 5*(18), 11–12.

Trapp, G. (1998, March 6). A time to heal. *JOB Bulletin, 180* (Job Opportunities for the Blind; 1-800-638-7518.)

Tyson, P. (1995, April). High-tech help for the blind. *Technology Review,* at web.mit/edu/techreview/ www/articles/apr95.

UCP Research & Educational Foundation. (1996). Aging and cerebral palsy. www.ucpa.org.html/research/aging/html.

UCP Research & Educational Foundation. (1997). Impact of cerebral palsy. www.ucpa.org/html/research/impact.htm.

Understanding epilepsy/seizures: A guide for educators. (1997). Albany: New York State Commission on Quality of Care (99 Washington Avenue, Suite 1002, Albany, NY 12210-2895).

United Cerebral Palsy Associations. (1998). Augmentative communication. www.ucpa.org/text/advocacy/augmentative.

United Cerebral Palsy Associations. (1997). Cerebral palsy: Facts and figures. Pamphlet (and web posting at www.ucpa.org). Washington, DC: Author.

United Cerebral Palsy of Washington. (1997). Cerebral palsy fact sheet. www.weber.uwashington.edu.

U.S. Architectural and Transportation Barriers Compliance Board. (1998a, January 13). Americans with Disabilities Act (ADA) accessibility guidelines for buildings and facilities. *Federal Register,* pp. 2016–2058. www.access-board.gov/bfdg/adaag.htm.

U.S. Architectural and Transportation Barriers Compliance Board. (1998b, January 13). Americans with Disabilities Act (ADA) accessibility guidelines for buildings and facilities: Building elements designed for children's use. Final rule. *Federal Register,* pp. 2059–2091.

U.S. Architectural and Transportation Barriers Compliance Board. (1992). *Recommendations for accessibility standards for children's environments.* Technical Report. Center for Accessible Housing, North Carolina State University. Washington, DC: Author.

U.S. Architectural and Transportation Barriers Compliance Board. (1997). Regulatory negotiation committee on accessibility guidelines for play facilities. Final report. http://www.access-board.gov/pubs/playrpt.htm.

U.S. Congress Office of Technology Assessment. (1987). *Technology-dependent children: Hospital v. home care: A technical memorandum.* Washington, DC: U.S. Government Printing Office.

U.S. Department of Education. (1992, September 29). Assistance to states for the education of children with disabilities program and preschool grants for children with disabilities. Final rule. *Federal Register,* 44794–44852.

U.S. Department of Education. (1999). Assistance to states for the education of children with disabilities and the early intervention program for infants and toddlers with disabilities. Final Regulation. *Federal Register,* March 12, 12404–12672.

U.S. Department of Education. (1998). *Twentieth Annual Report to Congress on Implementation of the Individuals with Disabilities Education Act.* Washington, DC: Author.

U.S. Department of Education. (1996). *Eighteenth annual report to Congress on implementation of the Individuals with Disabilities Education Act.* Washington, DC: Author.

U.S. Department of Education. (1997). *Nineteenth annual report to Congress on implementation of the Individuals with Disabilities Education Act.* Washington, DC: Author.

U.S. Department of Housing and Urban Development. (1994) *1994 report to Congress on worst case housing needs.* Washington, DC: Author.

U.S. Department of Housing and Urban Development. (1996) *1996 report to Congress on worst case housing needs.* Washington, DC: Author.

U.S. Department of Justice. (1995). Questions and answers: The Americans with Disabilities Act and persons with HIV/AIDS. December 6 factsheet (U.S. Department of Justice, Civil Rights Division, 10th Street and Constitution Avenue NW, Washington, DC 20036).

U.S. Department of Justice. (1997). U.S. Department of Justice information: US DoJ files suits re housing. Washington, DC: Author.

U.S. Department of Transportation. (1990, March 6). Nondiscrimination on the basis of disability in air travel. Final Rule. *Federal Register,* 8009 et seq.

U.S. Department of Transportation. (1996, May 21). Transportation for individuals with disabilities. Final rule. *Federal Register,* 25409–25416.

Usher, B. (1998, January/February). Universal design: Homes of the future. *Enable,* pp. 44–45, 48–51.

Van Dongen-Melman, J., De Groot, A., Van Dongen, J., Verhulst, F., & Hahlen, K. (1997). Cranial irradiation is the major cause of learning problems in children treated for leukemia and lymphoma: A comparative study. *Leukemia, 11*(8), 1197–1200.

Van Reusen, A., Bos, C., Schumaker J., & Deshler, D. (1994). *The self-advocacy strategy for education and transition planning.* Lawrence, KS: Edge Enterprises.

Vitello, P. (1997, June 3). A hot cup of coffee without hospitality. *Newsday,* p. A7.

Waissman, R. (1993). Ethical issues in home care treatment of a chronic illness: Analysis of the notion of responsibility. *Disability Studies Quarterly, 6*(3), 21–32.

Wald, J. (1989). Severe head injury and its stages of recovery explored through art therapy. In Wadeson, H., Durkin, J., & Perach, D. (Eds.), *Advances in art therapy.* New York: Wiley.

Waldholz, M. (1997). *Curing cancer: The story of the men and women unlocking the secrets of our deadliest illness.* New York: Simon & Schuster.

Walters, M., Patience, M., Leisenring, W., Eckman, J., Scott, J., Mentzer, W., Davies, S., Ohene-Frempong, K., Bernaudin, F., Matthews, D., Storb, R., & Sullivan, K. (1996). Bone marrow transplantation for sickle cell disease. *New England Journal of Medicine, 335*(6), 369–376.

Walters, R., Cressy, J., & Adkins, R. (1996) Spinal cord injuries due to violence. *American Rehabilitation, 22*(3), 10–15.

Waxweiler, R., Thurman, D., Sniezek, J., Sosin, D., & O'Neill, J. (1995). Monitoring the impact of traumatic brain injury. *Journal of Neurotrauma, 2,* 509–516.

Wehman, P., Booth, M., Stallard, D., Mundy, A., Sherron, P., West, M., & Cifu, D. (1994). Return to work for persons with traumatic brain injury and spinal cord injury: Three case studies. *International Journal of Rehabilitation Research, 17,* 268–277.

Wehman, P., & Kregel, J. (Eds.). (1997). *Functional curriculum for elementary, middle, and secondary age students with special needs.* Austin, TX: PRO-ED.

Wehrmeyer, M. (1995). *The arc self-determination scale.* Arlington, TX: The Arc.

Weinberg, L. (1997). Problems in educating abused and neglected children with disabilities. *Child Abuse and Neglect, 21*(9), 889–905.

Welsh, M., & Smith, A. (1995). Cystic fibrosis. *Scientific American, 273*(6), 52–59.

Westat Corporation. (1993). *The incidence of maltreatment among children with disabilities.* Washington, DC: National Center on Child Abuse and Neglect.

Wheeler, D., Jacobson, J., Paglieri, R., & Schwartz, A. (1993). An experimental assessment of facilitated communication. *Mental Retardation, 31*(1), 49–60.

When your child has cerebral palsy. (1996). Interview with Steven Bachrach. KidsHealth.org.

White, J. (1997). *Weeding out the tears: A mother's story of love, loss and renewal.* New York: Avon Books.

White, J. (1997). Let's give landmine survivors a reason to live. *InMotion, 7*(5), 29–32, 36–39.

Wiese, D., & Daro, D. (1995). *Current trends in child abuse reporting and fatalities: The results of the 1994 annual fifty state survey.* Chicago: National Committee to Prevent Child Abuse.

Witte, R. (1998). Meet Bob—A student with traumatic brain injury. *Teaching Exceptional Children, 30*(3), 56–60.

Wolery, M., Bailey, D., & Sugai, G. (1988). *Effective teaching: Principles and procedures of applied behavior analysis with exceptional students.* Boston: Allyn & Bacon.

Woodside, M. (1988). Research on children of alcoholics: Past and future. *British Journal of Addiction, 83,* 785–792.

Woodward, B., & Bernstein, C. (1974). *All the president's men.* New York: Simon & Schuster.

Yancey, G. (1993). Importance of families in transition from school to adult life: A rehabilitation practitioner's perspective. *Journal of Vocational Rehabilitation, 3*(2), 5–8.

Young, W. (1996). Section Two Extension To Cure Paralysis Now's Web homepage (www.cureparalysis.org/faq).

Index